The Undeclared Bomb

The Undeclared Bomb

Leonard S. Spector

A Carnegie Endowment Book

BALLINGER PUBLISHING COMPANY
Cambridge, Massachusetts
A Subsidiary of Harper & Row, Publishers, Inc.

International Standard Book Number: 0-88730-303-X
0-88730-304-8 (pbk.)

Library of Congress Catalog Card Number: 88-28726

Printed in the United States of America

Library of Congress Cataloging-in-Publication Data

Spector, Leonard S.
    The undeclared bomb / Leonard S. Spector.
      p.   cm. — (The Spread of nuclear weapons)
    "A Carnegie Endowment book."
    Includes index.
    ISBN 0-88730-303-X.   ISBN 0-88730-304-8 (pbk.)
    1. Nuclear weapons. 2. World politics — 1985-1995.
    3. Nuclear nonproliferation. I. Title. II. Series.
U264.S636   1988
355.8'25119 — dc19   88-28726
                                          CIP

For Sybil and Allan

Contents

Foreword

This is the fourth in the Endowment's series on the spread of nuclear weapons. Through these reports, the Endowment seeks to increase public awareness of the fact and the danger of nuclear proliferation and to stimulate greater attention to this important issue by policymakers, the media, and the scholarly community.

The series was initiated with the publication of the *Nuclear Proliferation Today* (covering developments in 1984) and continued with the issuance of *The New Nuclear Nations* (covering 1985) and *Going Nuclear* (covering 1986). *The Undeclared Bomb* updates these prior volumes with an examination of trends in the field through the middle of 1988.

The events chronicled in this book are profoundly troubling. The persuasive evidence that Pakistan is now able to manufacture nuclear arms, taken together with India's proven ability to do so, means that for the first time in history two hostile regional powers appear to be in a position to wage nuclear war on one another. In the Middle East, Israel remains the only nuclear-capable state, but the rapid spread of ballistic missiles and chemical warfare capabilities to its potential adversaries could lead Israel to rely more heavily on nuclear arms than ever before, increasing the risk that it might feel compelled to use such weapons in a future conflict.

With Pakistan, India, Israel, and South Africa now able to manufacture nuclear arms, it may be necessary for the United States and other concerned nations to reexamine what objectives their "non-proliferation" policies are seeking to achieve. If the goal is to *prevent* additional states from acquiring nuclear arms, the policy has effectively failed in four important cases. In these instances, it appears, to be realistic non-proliferation efforts will have to give way to policies that seek *post-proliferation restraint*, *i.e.*, policies aimed at averting the testing and deployment of nuclear arms and the acquisition of advanced delivery systems. Traditional non-proliferation initiatives may still have utility where some nuclear-capable states are concerned—for example, in the efforts to encourage South Africa to join the Non-Proliferation Treaty—but they are rapidly slipping from center stage.

As tolerance for *de facto* proliferation in this setting grows and the focus of concerned policymakers shifts from acquisition to deployment and from prevention to restraint, the concept of non-proliferation more generally is becoming tarnished. This will make it increasingly difficult to mount the serious initiatives that will be necessary to restrain additional states from crossing the nuclear weapons threshold. Strong U.S. action in 1988 blocked Taiwan's apparent effort to take a first step toward nuclear arms. But such interventions have become the exception rather than the rule.

It remains to be seen how much longer a credible concept of non-proliferation can be sustained. During the next several years, Latin America— where both Argentina and Brazil are slowly advancing toward nuclear weapons capabilities despite their recent nuclear rappochement—is likely to present a key test of the international community's residual determination in this regard. The 1990 Non-Proliferation Treaty Review Conference will be the next formal occasion for assessing the international "commitment" to this principle. Unfortunately, the events of the recent past offer few grounds for optimism that effective action will be taken.

* * *

The Undeclared Bomb has been prepared by Leonard S. Spector, who also authored the previous volumes in this series. A Senior Associate at the Endowment, he has worked in the field of nuclear non-proliferation for more than ten years, first at the Nuclear Regulatory Commission, and then on the staff of the Senate Energy and Nuclear Proliferation Subcommittee, where he served as Chief Counsel from 1978 through 1980. While with the Subcommittee, Mr. Spector assisted in drafting the 1978 Nuclear Non-Proliferation Act, the basic law governing U.S. policy today. His writings on non-proliferation issues have appeared widely.

As always, Endowment sponsorship of this report implies a belief only in the importance of the subject and the credentials of the author. The views expressed are his. Comments or inquiries are welcome and may be addressed to the Carnegie Endowment for International Peace, 11 Dupont Circle, Washington, D.C. 20036.

Thomas L. Hughes
President
Carnegie Endowment
for International Peace

Preface

The Undeclared Bomb is my fourth review of the spread of nuclear arms, begun in 1984. Some reflections on the series as a whole will be useful for the reader.

Every volume after the first—*Nuclear Proliferation Today* (New York: Vintage Books, 1984)—has included an in-depth look at a particular facet of the non-proliferation problem, selected because of its timeliness and, usually, because it has received little attention elsewhere. In the second volume of the series, *The New Nuclear Nations* (New York: Vintage Books 1985), the thematic chapter described the many facets of clandestine nuclear trade under the title, "The Nuclear Netherworld." The lead chapter in the third volume in the series, *Going Nuclear* (Cambridge, MA: Ballinger Publishing Company, 1987), examined the risks of nuclear weapons or related nuclear assets being suddenly transferred from one regime to another as the result of war, revolution, or coup d'etat. It used the rubric "nuclear inheritance" to describe this phenomenon, and reviewed relevant historical episodes in French Algeria, China, Vietnam, and Iran. The thematic chapter of the current volume is devoted to the potential nuclear delivery systems of the emerging nuclear states.

The country-by-country studies have also evolved with the publication of subsequent volumes in the series. Over time, the analysis has been expanded to give greater emphasis to domestic political developments in the emerging nuclear states and to the security concerns that are prompting their nuclear ambitions. In addition, the list of countries surveyed has grown. In *Going Nuclear*, Iran was added to the list of emerging nuclear states after historical research (conducted in the course of preparing the chapter on nuclear inheritance) disclosed that both the Shah and elements of the Khomeini government had taken steps indicating an interest in acquiring nuclear arms. In the current volume, Taiwan's nuclear activities are examined in greater depth than in the past because of developments during 1987-1988 indicating that this country may continue to harbor nuclear ambitions. (See Introduction to Chapter III.)

Some revision of the historical analyses contained in earlier volumes has also been necessary, as relevant new evidence has surfaced. New details concerning the initial stages of Israel's and Pakistan's nuclear programs, for example, are discussed in the pages below. I have tried to alert the reader in the notes to instances in which new information has led me to alter conclusions reached in a prior volume.

A word concerning the methodology I have used in preparing these surveys is also in order. The nuclear capabilities and intentions of the emerging nuclear states are shrouded in considerable secrecy. To build up a picture of the nuclear status of many of the countries at issue has therefore required a considerable amount of intrepretation on my part. Through footnotes and explanations in the text, I have attempted to be as clear as possible about the basis for my conclusions, which, broadly speaking, rely on press reports, official statements and publications, and interviews—both on- and off-the-record—with U.S. and foreign officials.

In several cases, I have given particular weight to investigative reports by well-known journalists. Before doing so, however, I have attempted insofar as possible to confirm the substance of the report with knowledgeable official sources. When I have not been able to obtain such confirmation, I have treated the report as more speculative, suggested it represents a minority view, or, in some instances, chosen not to rely on it at all.

Finally, several corrections to previous volumes in the series are noted on page 491.

Leonard S. Spector

Acknowledgements

This book reflects the contributions of many individuals and institutions to whom I would like to express my thanks.

The Undeclared Bomb has been prepared under the auspices of the Carnegie Endowment for International Peace and is sustained by grants from the Carnegie Corporation of New York and the Rockefeller Brothers Fund. I greatly appreciate their generous support for this endeavor. I also wish to thank the Endowment's president, Thomas L. Hughes, for his continuing commitment to this project.

I am particularly indebted to Larry L. Fabian, the secretary of the Endowment, for his advice concerning the preparation and dissemination of this and previous annuals on the spread of nuclear weapons, and I am also especially grateful to Dr. Barry Blechman for his contributions as senior editorial advisor to the project.

In addition, I wish to thank Carnegie Endowment interns Jack Weiss, Joseph Jiampietro, and Kevin O'Prey, whose careful sifting and organizing of source materials provided the essential data for this book. Messrs. Jiampietro's and O'Prey's research on the proliferation of ballistic missiles in the Third World were also important contributions, and I would like to express appreciation, as well, to former intern Carol Kuntz for her work concerning the aircraft delivery systems of the emerging nuclear states. Mr. O'Prey and Endowment intern Adam Posen also provided invaluable editorial assistance during the production phase of the project.

I am also indebted to Endowment research associate Ms. Shelley Stahl for important work on the chapter concerning controls and safeguards, and I would also like especially to thank Ms. Betsy Hamilton for her substantial contribution in helping to manage the project and in preparing the numerous revisions of the manuscript.

The Undeclared Bomb has been greatly aided by an informal group of advisors that assisted in reviewing the manuscript for accuracy and completeness. In addition to Dr. Blechman, the group included Dr. Joseph Nye, who was a principal architect of U.S. non-proliferation policy during the Carter Administration, when he served as deputy to the under secretary of state for security assistance; Dr. Albert Carnesale, academic dean, John F. Kennedy School of Government; Mr. Charles Van Doren, former assistant director of the Arms Control and Disarmament Agency; and Mr. Myron Kratzer, former assistant secretary of state for oceans and international environmental and scientific affairs. I greatly appreciate their contributions in enhancing the text's balance and comprehensiveness. The views contained in this report, however, are my own and the participation of these individuals does not necessarily constitute an endorsement on their part of specific statements or conclusions.

In addition, a number of specialists provided important assistance that I would like to acknowledge, including David Albright, Pauline Baker, Rodney Jones, Selig Harrison, Geoffrey Kemp, Gary Milhollin, and Peter Zimmerman.

My thanks also to Simon Henderson and Egmont Koch. Without the investigative work and reporting of these and the numerous other journalists whose names appear in the notes to this volume, this book could not have been written.

I also want to express my appreciation to Mike O'Hare for his encouragement; to Endowment librarian Jane

Lowenthal and to John McHarris and Lynn Meininger for their excellent work in obtaining research materials.

Thanks also to Diane Bendahmane for her fine copy-editing work; to Steve Smith for his care in setting the manuscript into type; to Diana Reganthal for her preparation of the index; and to Brad Wye and Rick Clark, who prepared the maps used in the text.

Leonard S. Spector
Senior Associate
Carnegie Endowment
    for International Peace

Chapter I:
Overview

Since 1964, when the People's Republic of China joined the United States, the Soviet Union, Great Britain, and France, as the fifth declared nuclear-weapon state, no new country has announced that it possesses nuclear arms. Nonetheless, by the early 1980s, three additional countries had acquired the ability to manufacture these deadly weapons under circumstances indicating that they were prepared to deploy such armaments in a conflict or in response to other regional pressures: Israel, which apparently achieved this status in the late 1960s; India, which did so by the early 1970s; and South Africa, which crossed this threshold in 1980 or 1981. Between 1986 and 1988, after a decade of slow advances, Pakistan appears to have become the fourth country to join this group of unannounced, *de facto* nuclear powers.

The nuclear weapons capabilities of these four nations vary widely in terms of their size and their presumed stage of deployment. Only Israel, for example, is thought to have advanced beyond simple atomic weapons to devices employing the H-bomb principle or to have integrated nuclear weapons into its armed forces and military planning. And, only India is known to have conducted a nuclear test—a single nuclear detonation in May 1974, which it termed a "peaceful nuclear explosion." All of these countries, moreover, have routinely denied that they possess nuclear arms.*

Nonetheless, there is little question today that all could prepare and deploy such weapons at will, a fact well appreciated by their potential adversaries, despite the veil of secrecy that the four have drawn over key parts of their nuclear activities. Thus, though it remains undeclared, the nuclear weapons potential of each of these four nations is a military reality that could vastly increase the costs of future hostilities in some of the globe's most volatile regions. It has been estimated, for example, that a dozen nuclear weapons used against military, or "counter-force," targets in India or Pakistan could cause over a million casualties. Many believe, moreover, that a nuclear confrontation involving one of today's undeclared nuclear states is the most likely catalyst of a global nuclear holocaust.

The nuclear strategy that the four unannounced nuclear states have pursued—which might be termed the strategy of "the undeclared bomb"—has incurred surprisingly few diplomatic costs. This is partly because all of these states are perceived as strategically important by the United States or the Soviet Union, a factor that has led the superpowers to refrain from imposing tough non-proliferation measures that might injure underlying relations. In addition, the respective nuclear advances of the undeclared nuclear states have been largely hidden from view and have also proceeded incrementally, so that even when an isolated nuclear smuggling operation has been exposed or the opening of a sensitive new nuclear installation has been announced, the development has not appeared sufficiently grave, in itself, to warrant a strong response by the international community.

Thus, with the exception of South Africa, whose isolation is the product of its racial policies rather than its nuclear activities, all of the undeclared nuclear nations have continued to receive substantial economic and military aid from their

---

*See subsequent chapters for details and citations.

principal allies. The only sanction that the four have suffered for maintaining their nuclear weapons capabilities is that the advanced industrialized states have curtailed civilian nuclear transfers to them, and even this embargo has not been total, as the Soviet Union's recent decision to sell two nuclear power plants to India testifies. Judging from their actions, the four have perceived this penalty to be a small price to pay for the presumed security and prestige benefits of possessing a ready nuclear deterrent.

Other states have also seen undeclared proliferation as the preferred route to nuclear arming. Iraq pursued this strategy from the mid-1970s until 1981, when Israel destroyed the centerpiece of its nuclear program, the Osiraq research reactor. Similarly, in 1978, Argentina's military government secretly began work on a plant with the potential for providing an undeclared weapons capability, while the following year Brazil's military leaders launched a classified research program to develop a comparable capacity; publicly, both countries insisted their nuclear programs were entirely peaceful. (Both Latin American countries, now under civilian rule, have moved in recent years to ease their nuclear rivalry.) Iran, Libya, Taiwan, and South Korea, have also taken steps to acquire covert nuclear weapon capabilities, but for a variety of reasons, none has advanced significantly toward this goal.

Although relatively stable nuclear relationships have emerged among the five announced nuclear powers, the spread of nuclear arms to additional nations, even if unannounced, presents a host of unpredictable dangers. Most of the states that have acquired or pursued undeclared weapons capabilities, for example, have engaged in armed conflicts in recent years or have come dangerously close to doing so. The Iran-Iraq War, Israel's invasion of Lebanon, Argentina's conflict with Great Britain over the Falkland Islands, Libya's clashes with French-backed forces in Chad, South Africa's incursions into Angola, and a series of large-scale military deployments on both sides of the Indo-Pakistani border that nearly led to war in the winter of 1986-1987

are but some examples of the uncertainties of military decision-making in the emerging nuclear states that may some
day lead to nuclear confrontation.

Many of these emerging nuclear states are also racked by
internal strife or have faced the threat of coup d'état or revolution during the past decade. These instabilities raise the
risk that nuclear weapons or nuclear weapons materials,
whether or not declared, could fall into the hands of anti-
status quo groups that might seek to use them as bargaining
chips to advance their cause at home or internationally.
(This danger afflicted two of the declared nuclear powers,
France and China, during the early stages of their nuclear
weapons programs.)

The spread of nuclear weapons has also increased the
likelihood of conventional war, as governments have been
tempted to strike preemptively against the nuclear installations of potential adversaries. Israel, Iraq, and Iran have already carried out raids against foreign nuclear installations,
and there is evidence that Libya and India have contemplated similar action. That the target countries had kept their
nuclear intentions secret did little to allay their neighbors'
concerns.

For these reasons, the international community has taken
little solace from the fact that China was the last nation to
declare itself a nuclear power and has struggled to contain
the spread of nuclear arms, whether or not they are acknowledged. This book describes the progress and the setbacks during 1987 and the first half of 1988.

Slowing the Spread

Acquiring the capability to produce nuclear arms often
takes decades, starting with training programs and the establishment of nuclear research centers. The most difficult
obstacle is obtaining nuclear explosive material, either highly enriched uranium or plutonium. To obtain the former
material, natural uranium must be improved to weapons
grade in a highly complex enrichment plant. Plutonium is
produced in uranium fuel when this is used in a nuclear reac-

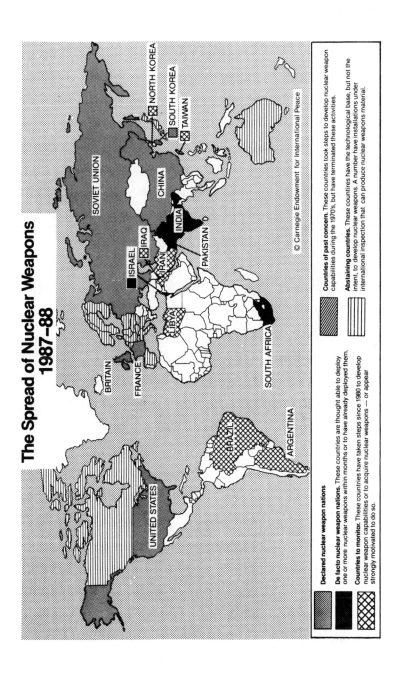

The Spread of Nuclear Weapons
1987-88

SOVIET UNION

NORTH KOREA

SOUTH KOREA

TAIWAN

CHINA

INDIA

PAKISTAN

IRAQ

ISRAEL

IRAN

BRITAIN

FRANCE

LIBYA

SOUTH AFRICA

UNITED STATES

BRAZIL

ARGENTINA

© Carnegie Endowment for International Peace

Declared nuclear weapon nations

De facto nuclear weapon nations. These countries are thought able to deploy one or more nuclear weapons within months or to have already deployed them.

Countries to monitor. These countries have taken steps since 1980 to develop nuclear weapon capabilities or to acquire nuclear weapons — or appear strongly motivated to do so.

Countries of past concern. These countries took steps to develop nuclear weapon capabilities during the 1970's, but have terminated these activities.

Abstaining countries. These countries have the technological base, but not the intent, to develop nuclear weapons. A number have installations under international inspection that can produce nuclear weapons material.

tor. The used fuel must then be transferred to a reprocessing plant where plutonium is extracted from other fuel constituents. For nuclear threshold countries, building the facilities for either process has proved a considerable technological challenge, requiring many years' effort even with active foreign assistance.

As noted above, with the exception of India's 1974 detonation, none of the emerging nuclear countries is known to have conducted a nuclear test and most, if not all, appear unlikely to do so for the foreseeable future. This has served as a valuable constraint on proliferation by reducing the risk of wide-open escalation of nuclear weaponry akin to that of the nuclear-weapon states. The absence of testing has also dampened pressures on neighboring states to develop their own nuclear capabilities.

Reliable early generation atomic weapons, however, can be developed without testing; indeed, the type of bomb dropped on Hiroshima had never been tested. Moreover, as discussed later in this book in greater detail, new evidence concerning the Israeli nuclear program suggests that advanced atomic weapons, employing some concepts of the hydrogen bomb, and nuclear weapons small enough to serve as ballistic missile warheads can be developed without testing, at least by scientifically advanced nations. Developing true hydrogen bombs, weapons hundreds of times as powerful as the atom bombs used in World War II, still apparently remains out of reach without nuclear weapons testing, however.

In addition to these technical constraints, the international non-proliferation regime imposes significant restrictions on the manufacture of nuclear arms. Its linchpin is the safeguards system of the International Atomic Energy Agency (IAEA), a Vienna-based international organization founded in 1957 and comprising more than 100 member states. The Agency's safeguards consist of reporting requirements, audits, and on-site inspections, which it applies to the vast majority of nuclear installations in non-nuclear-weapon countries to verify that these facilities are not used to support nuclear weapons programs. Despite certain shortcomings, these safeguards can probably detect most illegal uses of these plants and therefore pose a significant deterrent to proliferation. But safeguards are less effective against the misuse of highly enriched uranium or plutonium, both directly usable for nuclear weapons. If it had made the necessary preparations, a country possessing either substance could abrogate safeguards and build weapons before the international community could intervene.

The 1968 Treaty on the Non-Proliferation of Nuclear Weapons (NPT), now ratified by over 130 non-nuclear-weapon states, is a second key element of the regime. Three nuclear-weapon states, the United States, Great Britain, and the Soviet Union, are also parties to the pact. Non-weapon-state NPT signatories pledge not to manufacture nuclear arms and agree to accept IAEA safeguards on all of their nuclear installations, while all parties agree to require safeguards on all of their nuclear exports. Argentina, Brazil, India, Israel, Pakistan, and South Africa have not ratified the treaty, however, and each possesses unsafeguarded nuclear facilities. Moreover, although Iran, Iraq, and Libya are parties to the pact, their lack of respect for other norms of international behavior has called into question their commitment to the accord.

The Nuclear Suppliers Group, formed in 1974, at a time when several exporting states had not ratified the NPT, has also required IAEA safeguards on all of its participants' nuclear exports. Its most prominent members are Belgium, Canada, Czechoslovakia, East Germany, France (the only non-NPT participant today), Great Britain, Italy, Japan, the Netherlands, Poland, the Soviet Union, Sweden, Switzerland, the United States, and West Germany. Since the mid-1970s the nuclear suppliers, largely at U.S. urging, have also greatly restricted exports of enrichment and reprocessing technology. (The People's Republic of China is not a member of the Suppliers Group, but in 1984 it pledged that it would require safeguards on its future exports. Before it unilaterally adopted this policy, however, China, is believed to have helped Pakistan to develop its uranium enrichment capability—and to have given it the design of a nuclear device.)

Several individual supplier nations have adopted export policies that go beyond those adopted by the suppliers as a group. The 1978 U.S. Nuclear Non-Proliferation Act, for example, prohibits the sale of nuclear reactors and fuel to nations that have not placed *all* of their nuclear installations under IAEA safeguards. (More details on the technological requirements for nuclear weapons and related international institutions and treaties may be found in the appendices.)

More directly, the United States, the Soviet Union, and a number of advanced Western nations have from time to time applied strong diplomatic pressure to prevent individual states from pursuing their nuclear ambitions, and a number of U.S. laws provide for the termination of U.S. foreign aid to countries taking particular steps in this direction. (See Appendix G.) Despite the intensity of their own nuclear rivalry, the United States and the Soviet Union have cooperated actively to strengthen the non-proliferation regime. Unfortunately, U.S.-Soviet tensions in the Middle East, South Asia, and other troubled areas have all too often impeded respective efforts of the superpowers to arrest proliferation by their regional allies. Moreover, many fear that it will only be a matter of time until the unwillingness of the superpowers to restrain their own nuclear arsenals begins to undermine the non-proliferation system. The ratification of the Intermediate-Range Nuclear Forces Treaty in June 1988 was therefore an important first step toward alleviating these pressures on the regime.

In some respects, international efforts to curb proliferation are gaining strength. The renunciation of nuclear weapons by countries that do not now possess them has gradually become a norm of international conduct, as demonstrated by the increasing number of non-weapon-state parties to the Non-Proliferation Treaty and the slow rate at which new nations are crossing the nuclear weapons threshold. The recent decisions of China, Argentina, South Africa and, apparently, Brazil to require IAEA safeguards on their exports also indicate the vitality of this control. Moreover, the nuclear-supplier nations appear to be exercising greater care than ever before in restricting exports that could aid additional nations to develop nuclear capabilities, although their controls remain imperfect.

International pressure aside, self-interest has also played a significant role in retarding proliferation. The nuclear threshold nations have avoided overt nuclear arming, for example, partly for fear that this might stimulate rival powers to do the same or to enlarge pre-existing nuclear capabilities; concerns over possible preemptive action, noted above, have also been a restraining influence. In addition, military considerations dictate that along with nuclear weapons themselves, costly delivery systems must be acquired, customized, and maintained, all of which can impose a heavy burden on a developing economy. As suggested above, moreover, national leaders in states with deep ethnic or regional divisions must also consider domestic security, including whether the development of specialized nuclear forces will allow one or another group to gain unacceptable political leverage as the appointed guardian of the nation's nuclear arms and whether such arms might fall into the hands of the regime's domestic adversaries.

These various factors have not arrested the trend toward further proliferation, but they have reduced the attractiveness to emerging nuclear powers of overt development of nuclear weapons. Nonetheless, a world with a growing number of *de facto* nuclear-weapon states that could count on having such arms in any protracted conflict still poses serious dangers, as described above. Nor is there any guarantee that as more nations reach this level of nuclearization, they will remain at this plateau or that still others will not be encouraged to follow their example. For these reasons, international efforts continue to aim at preventing nations from reaching even this ambiguous stage of nuclear arming. As the events of the recent past indicate, these efforts have met with only limited success.

Nuclear Proliferation Today – Emerging Trends

The events of 1987 and the first half of 1988 described in this volume and summarized below suggest that the proliferation of nuclear weapons may be entering a new and increasingly dangerous phase.

Erosion of the norm against proliferation. First, global efforts to arrest proliferation have been dealt a series of damaging setbacks that will make limiting the spread of nuclear arms all the more difficult in the years ahead. Among the key developments that are eroding the norm against proliferation are:

● Pakistan's crossing the nuclear weapons threshold with seeming impunity and its ability to do so despite the repeated exposure of its progress toward this goal over the past decade—and despite considerable U.S. efforts to block it;

● The continued reluctance of the United States and its allies to object to Israel's nuclear arming notwithstanding the detailed revelations about Israel's capabilities published in late 1986; and

● The decision of the Soviet Union to transfer a nuclear-powered submarine to India—the first transfer of its kind in history—and to sell India two nuclear power reactors (under IAEA safeguards) at a time when India has been substantially expanding its nuclear weapons capabilities and openly declaring that it is prepared to build nuclear weapons if Pakistan does so.

These developments are creating the impression that, in some circumstances, at least, proliferation will be tolerated—a conclusion that is likely to encourage other would-be nuclear powers.

Iran and Iraq, for example, are already thought to be practiced in circumventing supplier-country controls on conventional arms sales and have previously demonstrated an interest in nuclear arming. As their war winds down and new financial resources become available, the two Middle East states could well calculate that, like Pakistan, they could readily develop nuclear weapon capabilities through clandestine nuclear purchases, while avoiding harsh non-proliferation sanctions because of their importance to the West.

The examples of Pakistan and Israel, moreover, may have already rekindled Taiwan's nuclear ambitions. Its attempt in 1987 to begin plutonium extraction experiments, summarized below and detailed in Chapter III, may well have been triggered by the belief—which proved to be mistaken—that since the United States had tolerated Pakistan's nuclearization and had remained silent about Israel's, it would wink at steps in this direction by another friendly state.

The norm against proliferation has also been damaged by the erosion of other arms control standards. The extensive use of chemical weapons in the Iran-Iraq War, the unprecedented sale by the People's Republic of China of conventionally armed intermediate-range ballistic missiles to Saudi Arabia, and the Soviet Union's nuclear submarine transfer to India, have tended to legitimize the unrestrained acquisition by regional powers of increasingly sophisticated and lethal weapons. In such an environment, nuclear arms may appear to be no more than the next rung on the ladder, making it increasingly difficult to sustain the taboo against their spread.

Constraining the undeclared nuclear powers. While these challenges will require renewed efforts to prevent proliferation through tough diplomacy and by sustaining such institutions as the NPT and the IAEA, strategies will also be needed to constrain the dangers posed by the growing capabilities of the undeclared nuclear powers, especially in South Asia and the Middle East, where volatile regional politics make the risk of nuclear confrontation particularly acute.

In South Asia, Pakistan's recent *de facto* nuclearization, together with India's pre-existing nuclear weapons capability, has created a form of crude, undeclared nuclear deterrence between two regional powers in which, so far, neither is thought to have integrated nuclear arms into its military operations or doctrine. Pressures to take such steps are likely to mount in both states, however, in part because each will fear that the other may be secretly proceeding down this path. Movement in this direction would inevitably increase the importance of nuclear weapons in a future Indo-Pakistani conflict and, with it, the risk that such weapons might actually be used.

This suggests that states concerned about the spread of nuclear arms will now need to focus increasingly on strategies for freezing the nuclear status quo in this region, to avert the further stockpiling of weapons-grade nuclear material and the further militarization of existing nuclear capabilities. Closer scrutiny of potential Indian and Pakistani nuclear delivery systems will also be needed to discourage the preparation of advanced Western and Soviet warplanes for nuclear missions and to delay the advent of missile-based delivery systems, as summarized below.

In the Middle East, strategies focused on freezing Israeli nuclear capabilities and constraining its delivery systems may also be appropriate, given recent Israeli advances, which reportedly include the development of weapons using the H-bomb principle and the testing of a missile able to reach the Soviet Union. Attention will also have to be paid, however, to the threat posed to Israel by its adversaries' missile and chemical warfare capabilities, since there is increasing evidence that Israel has begun to project its nuclear might as a deterrent to a massive attack against its cities using these non-nuclear armaments.

It must be acknowledged that opponents of nuclear proliferation may face a new risk as they expand their focus beyond measures at *preventing* proliferation to measures aimed at *containing* it after it has occurred on a *de facto* basis. This is the danger that they will be attracted to strategies drawn from the U.S.-Soviet arena that, in the name of nu-

clear stability, may tend to legitimize the possession of nuclear weapons by regional powers. It is one thing to seek to
prevent the militarization of the still inchoate nuclear weapon capabilities of India and Pakistan or to press both countries to renounce nuclear testing by treaty. But it is quite
another to begin counselling them to protect their nuclear
retaliatory forces in order to enhance deterrence or to urge
them to adopt supposedly stabilizing nuclear doctrines—
such as a ban on the first use of nuclear weapons—that treat
the deployment of nuclear armaments as a foregone
conclusion.

Unfortunately, the dividing line between urging restraint
and seeking stability may tend to blur in the years ahead,
creating confusion as to the meaning of "non-proliferation"
and making it more difficult to sustain traditional elements
of the non-proliferation regime, such as the NPT which are
aimed specifically at preventing the spread of nuclear arms.

Middle East-South Asian nuclear linkage. A third emerging trend of concern is that the Pakistan's acquisition of a
nuclear weapons capability has created a nuclear connection
between two of the globe's most troubled areas, the Middle
East and South Asia. Reports that Israel has approached India with a proposal to attack Pakistan's key enrichment plant
at Kahuta and that Pakistan has offered nuclear assistance to
Iran, together with speculation that Islamabad might someday assist Saudi Arabia to develop nuclear warheads for its
Chinese intermediate-range ballistic missiles, provide an indication of the new dangers that could result from the interaction of nuclear tensions in these two conflict-prone
regions.

Non-proliferation in Latin America. One ray of sunshine
in this gloomy picture has been the dramatic nuclear rapprochement between Argentina and Brazil. As explained
below, however, even in this case, prospects for halting the
spread of nuclear weapons remain highly uncertain. With
Latin America remaining one of the few regions of the world
where proliferation might actually be averted, encouraging

Buenos Aires and Brasilia to pursue their current program of mutual nuclear restraints will need to be a top non-proliferation priority in the coming year.

Nuclear Proliferation 1987-1988

The events of 1987 and the first half of 1988 described in this volume are summarized below. As noted in the preceding section, the trends they reflect are far from encouraging.

Delivery systems. During 1987 and the first half of 1988, the potential for emerging nuclear states to use ballistic missiles for the delivery of nuclear weapons grew substantially. India successfully test-fired its first short-range surface-to-surface missile, the Prithvi; Israel—thought to have deployed the 400-mile range, nuclear-capable Jericho II in the early 1980s—test-fired a longer range version of the missile, potentially capable of reaching the Soviet Union; Argentina and Brazil continued their development of medium-range nuclear-capable missiles; and Libya, Iran, and Iraq, already in possession of conventionally-armed Soviet- or North Korean-supplied Scud-Bs, showed interest in acquiring the new missiles from the two Latin American states when they become available in the next several years. China's unprecedented sale of conventionally armed intermediate-range CSS-2 missiles to Saudi Arabia and its plans to sell the medium-range M-9 and M-11 missiles internationally raised the possibility that Beijing might be prepared to transfer nuclear-capable rockets to Pakistan in the future. For now, however, only Israel among the emerging nuclear states is believed capable of mating a nuclear warhead to a ballistic missile.

Although the United States and six other leading Western nations announced a regime to control the spread of nuclear-capable missiles in April 1987, Soviet and Chinese missile transfers to the Middle East undermined the effectiveness of the new controls during its first year. It remains to be seen whether these powers can be persuaded to join the regime.

All of the emerging nuclear states already possess advanced fighter-bombers supplied by the United States, the Soviet Union, France, or Great Britain, which are likely to serve as their initial nuclear delivery systems. Despite the dangers involved, none of the aircraft-supplier countries is known to have prohibited the use of its aircraft for nuclear missions or to have obtained assurances from recipients that the warplanes would not be used in this capacity.

Asia. Amidst deteriorating Indo-Pakistani relations that many feared might lead to major hostilities in the winter of 1986-1987, Pakistan appears to have become the fourth undeclared nuclear-weapon state. By early 1988, it was thought to have acquired the essentials for a small number of nuclear weapons, although in December 1987, President Reagan was still able to certify that it did not "possess" a complete nuclear explosive device. Despite the revelations of new Pakistani smuggling operations in Europe and the United States and a report that Pakistan was beginning to construct a second uranium enrichment plant, the United States Congress in December 1987 voted to extend economic and military assistance to Pakistan for two and a half additional years because of concerns over the presence of Soviet forces in Afghanistan. As stressed above, Pakistan's *de facto* crossing of the nuclear weapons threshold has been a serious setback for global efforts to curb the spread of nuclear weapons and has significantly altered India's security environment.

India responded to this challenge by continuing the quiet expansion of its nuclear weapons capabilities—which far over-shadow Pakistan's—while maintaining an ambiguous public stance concerning its nuclear intentions. Most U.S. officials believe India has not begun to manufacture nuclear arms, however. In conjunction with these policies India also pursued a major build-up of its conventional forces that included the unprecedented lease of a Soviet nuclear-powered submarine, the deployment of a second aircraft carrier, and the successful flight-testing of the Prithvi surface-to-surface missile. By early 1988, though neither India nor Pakistan had deployed nuclear weapons or announced that it pos-

Emerging Nuclear Weapon Nations 1987-88

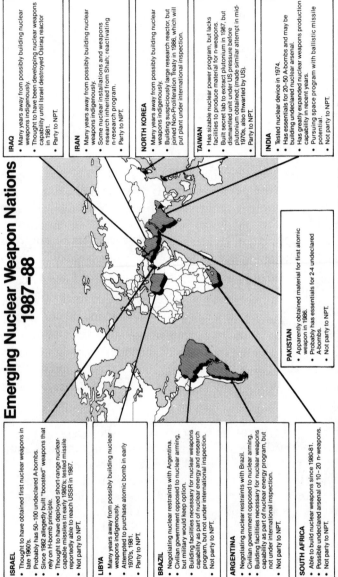

ISRAEL
- Thought to have obtained first nuclear weapons in late 1960's.
- Probably has 50–100 undeclared A-bombs.
- Since 1982 allegedly built "boosted" weapons that rely on H-bomb principle.
- Thought to have deployed short-range nuclear-capable missiles in early 1980's; tested missile reportedly able to reach USSR in 1987.
- Not party to NPT.

LIBYA
- Many years away from possibly building nuclear weapons indigenously.
- Attempted to purchase atomic bomb in early 1970's, 1981.
- Party to NPT.

BRAZIL
- Negotiating nuclear restraints with Argentina.
- Civilian government opposed to nuclear arming, but military would keep option.
- Building facilities necessary for nuclear weapons capability as part of nuclear energy and research program, but not under international inspection.
- Not party to NPT.

ARGENTINA
- Negotiating nuclear restraints with Brazil.
- Civilian government opposed to nuclear arming.
- Building facilities necessary for nuclear weapons capability as part of nuclear energy program, but not under international inspection.
- Not party to NPT.

SOUTH AFRICA
- Able to build nuclear weapons since 1980-81.
- Possible undeclared arsenal of 10–20 n-weapons.
- Not party to NPT.

PAKISTAN
- Apparently obtained material for first atomic weapon in 1986.
- Probably has essentials for 2-4 undeclared A-bombs.
- Not party to NPT.

IRAQ
- Many years away from possibly building nuclear weapons indigenously.
- Thought to have been developing nuclear weapons capability until Israel destroyed Osiraq reactor in 1981.
- Party to NPT.

IRAN
- Many years away from possibly building nuclear weapons indigenously.
- Some nuclear installations and weapons research inherited from Shah; reactivating n-research program.
- Party to NPT.

NORTH KOREA
- Many years away from possibly building nuclear weapons indigenously.
- Building suspiciously large research reactor, but joined Non-Proliferation Treaty in 1986, which will put plant under international inspection.

TAIWAN
- Has sizable nuclear power program, but lacks facilities to produce material for n-weapons.
- Built secret lab to extract plutonium in 1987, but dismantled unit under US pressure before plutonium obtained; (made similar attempt in mid-1970s, also thwarted by US).
- Party to NPT.

INDIA
- Tested nuclear device in 1974.
- Has essentials for 20-50 A-bombs and may be building undeclared nuclear arsenal.
- Has greatly expanded nuclear weapons production capability in recent years.
- Pursuing space program with ballistic missile potential.
- Not party to NPT.

NPT—The Nuclear Non-Proliferation Treaty. Requires all nuclear installations in a signatory country to be placed under International Atomic Energy Agency inspection.

sessed them, a rudimentary system of undeclared nuclear deterrence was emerging on the Indian subcontinent, based on the recognized capabilities of both states to deploy nuclear weapons during any future conflict.

During 1987, it also appeared that Taiwan secretly began construction of a small-scale plutonium extraction unit, in disregard of pledges given to the United States in the mid-1970s that it would not undertake research in this field. In March 1988, under U.S. pressure, Taiwan agreed to halt work on the unit and to dismantle a 40-megawatt research reactor supplied by Canada, the presumed source of spent fuel from which plutonium was to be extracted. Nonetheless, the episode was a troubling reminder that Taiwan continued to harbor an interest in acquiring the capability to produce nuclear arms.

The Middle East. In light of the revelations in the London *Sunday Times* by Israeli nuclear technician Mordechai Vanunu in the fall of 1986, it has become increasingly clear that Israel possesses a substantial, undeclared nuclear arsenal of at least fifty to sixty nuclear devices—and perhaps significantly more—some of which are of an advanced design that makes them many times more powerful than the atomic weapons used in World War II. Israel presumably continued to add to its nuclear armory during 1987 and the first half of 1988.

Since Vanunu's revelations, new information has emerged strongly suggesting that to achieve its nuclear status, Israel disregarded non-proliferation pledges covering a key nuclear commodity, heavy water, that it obtained from Norway in 1959.

On a separate front, as surface-to-surface missiles and chemical weapons capabilities proliferate among Israel's adversaries, Israel's nuclear arms are likely to play an increasingly important role as a deterrent to attacks with such advanced non-nuclear weapons on Israeli population centers—a factor that could heighten the risks of nuclear escalation in a future Arab-Israeli conflict. Indeed, in 1988, Israeli leaders began implicitly referring to this possibility by declaring that Israel would have the ability to retaliate against an anti-city missile or chemical attack "many times over." This stance appears to be an important new corollary to Israel's traditional pronouncements that it will "not be the first to introduce nuclear weapons" into the region.

Libya, Iraq, and Iran—all, unlike Israel, parties to the Non-Proliferation Treaty—are thought to harbor an interest in acquiring nuclear arms but all are far from possessing the necessary nuclear infrastructure to manufacture such weapons themselves. In 1987, Colonel Muammar Khadafi openly declared his desire for nuclear arms and for the first time engaged in "unconventional" warfare by using chemical weapons against Chadian forces. Iraq's nuclear program has been dormant since Israel's 1981 bombing raid destroyed the Osiraq reactor, but Iraq's extensive use of conventionally-armed surface-to-surface missiles and chemical weapons in the Iran-Iraq war could contribute to nuclear tensions in the future, as just noted. Iran continued its efforts to resuscitate its moribund nuclear program without success and suffered a serious setback when Iraq attacked its Bushehr nuclear-power plant construction site in November 1987. Iran has also employed conventionally armed surface-to-surface missiles in its war with Iraq, and in 1987 may have employed chemical weapons, as well.

Latin America. In September 1987, Brazil announced that it had mastered the process of enriching uranium and, in early 1988, inaugurated a pilot-scale enrichment facility at Ipero not subject to International Atomic Energy Agency safeguards. The advance matched a capability acquired by Argentina in the early 1980s and raised the possibility that both countries might soon be able to produce weapons-grade uranium free from non-proliferation controls. Both, however, have pledged not to enrich uranium to this level. During 1987 and early 1988, moreover, the two countries implemented a series of unprecedented confidence-building measures to ease their long-standing nuclear rivalry. These included a visit by Brazilian President José Sarney to Argentina's classified uranium enrichment plant at

Pilcaniyeu and a reciprocal visit by Argentine President Raul Alfonsín to Brazil's new Ipero plant.

These developments have raised the possibility that the spread of nuclear weapons in Latin America may be avoided. The bilateral confidence-building arrangements, however, have yet to be institutionalized and in their current form do not permit verification of the output of either country's unsafeguarded enrichment plants. These limitations could create dangerous ambiguities in the next several years as both states begin to enrich uranium above the extremely low levels achieved to date. The two nations will hold presidential elections by 1990, raising further questions about the permanence of their promising nuclear rapprochement.

Africa. South Africa has had the ability to produce weapons-grade enriched uranium not subject to international non-proliferation controls for a number of years. Given its past activities indicating an intent to develop nuclear arms, there is reason for concern that during 1987 and the first half of 1988 Pretoria used this capability either to add to its stocks of nuclear weapons material or, if it indeed has decided to build nuclear arms, to add several weapons to an undeclared nuclear arsenal of perhaps ten to twenty atomic weapons.

South Africa's announcement in September 1987 that it was prepared to begin negotiations on ratifying the Non-Proliferation Treaty has opened the theoretical possibility that its existing stocks of nuclear weapons material and all of its nuclear facilities might be placed under international inspection within several years. There is considerable doubt, however, as to whether Pretoria intends to ratify the pact, and through June 1988, it had not begun its promised negotiations on this matter.

Controls and Safeguards. The non-proliferation regime was strengthened in a number of important respects, as Spain ratified the Non-Proliferation Treaty, Saudi Arabia announced that it would join the pact, Pakistan and Argentina ratified the Partial Test Ban Treaty, and (in December 1986) the Treaty of Rarotonga, establishing a South Pacific nuclear weapon free zone, entered into force. Nuclear arms control norms were also reinforced by the ratification of the U.S.-Soviet Intermediate-Range Nuclear Forces Treaty. The April 1987 announcement by seven Western industrialized nations of new controls to curb the spread of missile technology was also an important, if limited, advance, and the exchange of visits by Argentina and Brazil to nuclear plants not under IAEA inspection—though intended as an alternative to traditional non-proliferation mechanisms— plainly contributed to the regime's longstanding objectives.

Nonetheless, the non-proliferation regime's limitations were also evident. Most importantly, the system of international nuclear restraints was unable to prevent Pakistan from effectively crossing the nuclear weapons threshold or to curb the continued enlargement of nuclear weapons capabilities in India, Israel, and South Africa. Similarly, disclosures of illicit transactions in nuclear equipment and heavy water (used to operate certain types of reactors) raised questions about the regime's ability to police international nuclear commerce. Finally, the Soviet Union's unprecedented lease of a nuclear-powered submarine to India and the U.S. decision to authorize Great Britain to sell Canada nuclear-powered submarines based on U.S. technology posed a serious new challenge for the regime by opening a door to legal transfers of nuclear equipment and materials outside the IAEA safeguards system.

*

The events of 1987-1988 are analyzed in detail in the chapters that follow, beginning with an in-depth look at the delivery systems of the emerging nuclear-weapon states. Subsequent chapters, organized by country, examine the steps that each of these states has taken toward acquiring or expanding nuclear weapon capabilities. Introductory sections of each chapter cover related regional developments.

Chapter II:
Delivering
The Bomb

As described in detail in subsequent chapters of this book, India, Israel, Pakistan, and South Africa are today each capable of building nuclear arms, and, if they have not done so already, each could well be prepared to deploy such weapons in any future war. Although attention has been focussed over the years on how these and other emerging nuclear nations have progressed toward the acquisition of nuclear weapons capabilities, it is now becoming increasingly important to understand how such capabilities, once acquired, are militarized, *i.e.*, transformed into "small nuclear forces."[1] An early and essential first step in this process is the mating of nuclear weapons with the means for delivering them to enemy targets.

Over the next decade, the delivery systems potentially available to the new nuclear states will fall into two principal categories: manned aircraft and ballistic missiles.[2] (Cruise missiles are a third possibility, but one that appears more remote at present.) Today, the emerging nuclear states possess some of the world's most advanced combat aircraft: U.S.-produced F-16s and F-15s, Soviet MiGs, French Mirages, and Franco-British Jaguars. Though transferred to enhance the recipients' conventional military capabilities, these warplanes could be readily adapted to deliver early-generation atomic bombs, a prospect that is generating concern in neighboring states.[3] Nuclear-capable missiles—in rough terms, those able to carry a half-ton payload two hundred miles or more and hit city-size targets—are also becoming increasingly available, and at least one of the emerging nuclear states, Israel, is believed to have already deployed medium-range missiles intended for use with nuclear warheads.[4]

The shroud of secrecy and ambiguity that these nations have drawn over sensitive aspects of their nuclear activities has also veiled their decision-making on possible delivery systems. This has hindered outside scrutiny and at least partially deflected attempts to slow proliferation by restricting the availability of advanced delivery capabilities.

For the past several years, a number of Western governments have attempted to slow the spread to additional states of nuclear-capable missiles, but even as these initiatives progressed, the problem was seriously worsening because of Soviet, Chinese, and North Korean transfers of nuclear-capable missile systems to Iran, Iraq, and Saudi Arabia. Where advanced aircraft are concerned, neither the West nor the Soviet Union has sought to prevent emerging nuclear countries from using these systems with nuclear arms, although they could readily be prepared for nuclear delivery at any time. As detailed below, moreover, in the Middle East, South Asia, and Southern Africa these aircraft could be used for many of the same missions as ballistic missiles and have already shown that they can penetrate regional air defenses and gravely threaten neighboring states, even when conventionally armed. To be sure, because of the distances involved, few of these aircraft delivery systems can threaten the major powers directly, as long-range missiles could, but the aircraft can jeopardize important major-power interests by threatening their regional allies.

In light of the heightened concerns over recent missile transfers to the Middle East, the analysis that follows begins with a review of the spread of nuclear-capable missiles to the emerging nuclear states and then examines the potential use of high-performance aircraft for nuclear missions by these nations.

Ballistic Missiles

Nuclear-armed missiles are coming to the Third World. Israel, thought to have nuclear arms since the late 1960s or early 1970s, is widely believed to have deployed a sophisticated medium-range missile system in the early 1980s intended to carry nuclear warheads some 400 miles.[5] Referred to by Western analysts as the Jericho II, it reportedly replaced the less accurate Jericho I, deployed some ten years earlier, and may be able to hit targets as small as airfields. In mid-1987, Israel drew a stern warning from Moscow for testing a longer-range version of the Jericho II, said by U.S. officials to be capable of striking the southern Soviet Union.[6] Other emerging nuclear states will be able to follow Israel's lead in the coming decade. (See chart at end of this chapter.)

India conducted a single nuclear test in 1974 but did not go on to deploy a nuclear force. It is now reconsidering that position as a response to neighboring Pakistan's progress toward nuclear arming. If New Delhi opts for a nuclear force, it will probably be able to deploy intermediate-range nuclear missiles during the 1990s accurate enough to hit cities, though probably not smaller military targets.[7] In 1980, India launched a 77-pound (35 kilogram) space satellite using a rocket, the SLV-3, that could be readily adapted to deliver a nuclear warhead over 1,000 miles, placing all of Pakistan, much of the Indian Ocean, and many Chinese cities in range.[8] A larger space launch vehicle, the ASLV, intended to loft a 330-pound (150 kilogram) satellite into low earth orbit, was launched for the first time in March 1987 but exploded early in its flight.[9] Adapted for military use, it could considerably extend India's reach, and more powerful rockets now in varying stages of development could give India an intercontinental missile capability early in the next century.[10] New Delhi has a parallel program to build military missiles, intended for now to carry conventional warheads, and is currently flight-testing the Prithvi, a short-to-medium-range surface-to-surface missile able to carry a 2,200-pound (1,000 kilogram) warhead in excess of 90 miles; longer-range versions are under development.[11]

Pakistan is believed to have obtained the essentials for its first nuclear device during 1986. Some years behind India, it hopes to launch its first satellite in 1988 and is also developing short-range military missiles. A nuclear-capable model—defined by U.S. missile-technology export regulations as a missile able to deliver a warhead weighing 1,100 pounds (500 kilograms) to a target the size of a small city 190 miles (300 kilometers) or more distant—is still probably at least five to ten years away.[12] South Africa, the fourth regional power able to manufacture nuclear weapons, has also announced a classified missile-development program.[13]

Though neither Pakistan nor South Africa is likely to be able to build nuclear-capable missiles until well into the 1990s, such weapons may be available to these states far sooner from friendly nations or on the international arms market. The Scud-B, originally produced by the Soviet Union, is one such missile, which Moscow has transferred to Iraq, Egypt, Libya, and Syria. During the first half of 1988, Iraq fired nearly 200 Scuds (with conventional warheads) at Tehran and other Iranian cities; the rockets had been modified to extend their range, in part by reducing their payload.[14] The rocket can normally deliver a 1,100-pound (500 kilogram) warhead 190 miles.

North Korea is said to have sold the missile to Iran and might offer it to Pakistan next. Similarly, Libya which is thought to have aided Pakistan's nuclear weapons program in the 1970s and which has sold Soviet-origin Scuds to Iran is another possible supplier.[15] (In addition, Libya is said to be financing Brazil's development of a 375-mile range nuclear-capable missile, to be available after 1990, which it could also sell to Islamabad.)[16] Egypt, which reportedly plans to manufacture the Scud-B (with North Korean assistance), could eventually become another supplier of the rocket.[17] (See chart at end of chapter.)

Two other rockets that may be available to Pakistan are the Chinese M-9, a missile with a 125- to 375-mile range that Beijing began marketing in 1986 for delivery after 1989 and the M-11, a second Chinese missile with a range of 190 miles by some reports, and a 1760-pound (800 kilogram) payload.[18] Even more disturbing, in 1988 China transferred CSS-2 "East Wind" intermediate-range missiles to Saudi Arabia. The missiles have a 2,200-mile range in the Chinese arsenal, where they carry nuclear warheads. The version sold to Saudi Arabia will carry a heavier conventional warhead, reducing the missile's range to about 1,600 to 1,860 miles.[19] Even so, the transfer of such a long-range rocket is unprecedented and represents a serious breach of the de facto restraints on transfers of large rockets that has prevailed for many years.

Saudi Arabia does not possess even a rudimentary nuclear infrastructure, so it will be unable to adapt the missile for nuclear use. But now that the precedent has been set, China might consider selling the missile to Pakistan in the future, where the rocket's nuclear potential would be far more troubling. (The possibility that Saudi Arabia and Pakistan might collaborate on developing a nuclear warhead for the missile must also be considered, particularly in light of rumors that the Saudis helped finance Pakistan's nuclear weapons program. Nevertheless, the likelihood of such collaboration appears small, because it is hard to imagine Pakistan providing any of its handful of nuclear devices to Saudi Arabia—and equally difficult to envision the latter offering any of its limited number of missiles to Pakistan.)

South Africa, similarly, might seek to purchase nuclear-capable missiles from Israel. Pretoria recently obtained Israeli assistance in upgrading its Mirage fighters and, although in mid-1987 Israel stated that it would not enter into new military contracts with South Africa, there have been reports that the two countries are building a joint facility for testing long-range missiles on Marion Island in the Antarctic.[20]

Brazil, still below the nuclear threshold, has been exporting small, conventionally armed missiles to such nuclear aspirants as Libya and Iraq. It will shortly be offering two more capable models for export: the Avibras SS-300, able to carry a 1,100-pound (500 kilogram) warhead 190 miles (comparable to the Scud-B), and a missile based on the Brazilian Sonda IV sounding rocket, to be produced by the firm Orbita, with a 375-mile range and a probable payload of 1,100 pounds. Either could be refitted with a nuclear warhead by a suitably advanced recipient. Longer-range Brazilian missiles are also under development, including one with a 625-mile capability.[21] Indeed, despite recent progress toward easing a potential nuclear arms competition with Argentina, the possible threat that Brazil could itself become a nuclear power in the next decade and incorporate these missiles into its nuclear forces cannot be ruled out. In September 1987, Brazil announced that it had mastered the uranium enrichment process, a critical step in the production of nuclear weapons material and in April 1988, it inaugurated a small enrichment plant near the town of Ipero.[22]

Argentina is also an arms exporter with nuclear-capable surface-to-surface missiles under development, though its program is a number of years behind Brazil's.[23] Like its northern neighbor, it could become a nuclear power in the 1990s, if regional and domestic political circumstances were to change. In 1983 Argentina began producing low-enriched uranium not subject to any non-proliferation controls.

Iran, Iraq, and Libya are many years away from producing nuclear weapons indigenously. Given their growing access to Scuds and comparable Brazilian and Argentinian systems, however, should they ever cross the nuclear threshold, there can be little question that they would seek to adapt these and subsequently acquired missiles for nuclear delivery. Iraq flight-tested a medium-range (375-mile) rocket in August 1987, which it claimed to have developed indigenously, but which was probably a modified Scud-B of the type used in the subsequent attacks on Iran; in May 1988, it tested a 560-mile version of the missile, said to carry a 250-pound (113-kilogram) payload. Iraq has also received the Soviet SS-12, a still more potent missile with a range of 500 miles and a payload of 2,750 pounds (1250 kilograms).[24]

In short, nuclear-capable missiles are already being deployed by regional powers—in one case with nuclear warheads available—and the further spread of these advanced weapons appears to be accelerating.

*

For today's six most advanced emerging nuclear weapon states, nuclear missiles offer two important benefits: assured delivery capability and prestige. As mentioned earlier, each of these countries already possesses sophisticated Western or Soviet warplanes capable of delivering early generation nuclear weapons. However, at times aircraft delivery is unsatisfactory because essential targets are beyond the range of available warplanes or are so heavily defended that the ability of aircraft to reach them is in doubt. In such instances, ballistic missiles can make a militarily significant contribution to the delivery capabilities of these countries. In addition, missiles can strengthen a national nuclear deterrent by diversifying delivery capabilities, helping to ensure survivability and certainty of retaliation.[25] In terms of prestige, longer-range ballistic missiles, like nuclear weapons themselves, symbolize technological prowess and are indicators of major power status.

Although Israel has never acknowledged the existence of the Jericho II, the missile is undoubtedly seen as a means for strengthening the country's undeclared nuclear force. Said to be deployed in hardened bunkers and on mobile launchers, the missile would be less vulnerable to a pre-emptive attack than Israeli aircraft.[26] The threat of a sudden knockout strike against Israel's airfields has been a matter of concern ever since the Soviet Union supplied Syria with advanced, conventionally armed surface-to-surface missiles several years ago.[27] In addition, the Jericho II guarantees penetration of enemy air defenses, which, especially in Syria, have been strengthened in recent years. The missile also provides Israel an autonomous nuclear delivery system, independent of imported spare parts and unencumbered by political linkages to a particular supplier state.

More disturbing is Israel's apparent rationale for building a longer-range version of the missile, which seemingly is directed not only at Baghdad, Benghazi, and Riyadh (500, 800, and 770 miles, respectively from Israel), but also at least in part at the Soviet Union. Presumably, Israel's objective in this regard is to deter significant Soviet military intervention in any future Middle East conflict by threatening retaliation against Soviet targets. Such a scenario, which could all too easily involve the United States and raise the risk of a superpower nuclear confrontation, graphically demonstrates the dangers that the proliferation of nuclear-armed missiles may pose in the years ahead.

If India decided to build a nuclear arsenal, it would have a number of incentives for adapting its various large-scale rockets into nuclear delivery systems. Most important, with many key Chinese industrial and population centers located 1,500 to 2,000 miles from India, intermediate-range missiles would be essential for New Delhi to develop a nuclear deterrent against Beijing. Though long concerned about the potential nuclear threat from this quarter, India has so far refrained from building a nuclear force to counter this challenge, but its calculations could change if tensions with China, which some feared might lead to a border war in early 1987, were to increase.

If the current stirrings of a Sino-Soviet rapprochement bear fruit, moreover, New Delhi could see its defense ties to Moscow weakened and could well look to nuclear arms as a substitute for checking possible Chinese aggression. On another front, New Delhi must also worry that if it deployed even a limited nuclear force against Pakistan, as it is now considering, China could feel threatened and make clear that it was directing part of its own nuclear might against India; such a step would undoubtedly be seen as calling for an Indian counter-China deterrent in response. Even if China did not feel directly threatened by a small Pakistan-oriented Indian nuclear force, New Delhi would have to be concerned that, as Pakistan's ally, China might threaten nuclear retaliation against India if this force were ever used. This, too, might make a deterrent against China seem attractive.

In more political terms, India considers itself an equal of China in the global arena, but perceives that it is rarely treated this way. Indian hawks argue that only through nuclear arming—presumably including nuclear missiles as befits a modern major power—will India be able to attain its rightful place in world affairs. Indian officials have also complained that the presence of U.S. nuclear forces in the Indian Ocean is inimical to Indian security, and they sometimes describe India as surrounded by three nuclear powers—the United States, the Soviet Union, and China. Intermediate-range Indian nuclear missiles, which would nominally extend India's reach from Beijing to the Persian Gulf, could serve as a political counter to these pressures and unambiguously establish India's credentials as a regional superpower.

Pakistan would have less complex reasons to pursue nuclear missiles, either through its indigenous program or by adapting imported launchers from such potential suppliers as China or Brazil. Since Pakistan can produce only one or two nuclear weapons per year, its potential nuclear arsenal will remain quite small for some time to come, making it an attractive target for Indian pre-emptive attack. India's numerical superiority in warplanes would make a Pakistani aircraft-based nuclear force particularly vulnerable. In principle, missiles would be easier to harden against surprise bombing than aircraft or could be made mobile, making it more difficult for India to find and destroy them. Missiles would also offer Pakistan diversity of delivery systems—another protection against successful pre-emptive attack—and would permit Pakistan to devote a larger proportion of its air force to non-nuclear combat operations.

For South Africa, the foremost conventional power in its region and one which appears to view nuclear arms more as potent political symbols than as instruments of military force, the need for a missile delivery system is less obvious. South Africa's conventional edge will likely erode in the years ahead, however, if the Soviet Union continues to supply sophisticated weaponry to South Africa's neighbors, especially Angola, and if Pretoria's access to advanced Western weaponry remains closed by the 1977 arms embargo mandated by the United Nations. Were South Africa to deploy a nuclear force in the future, missile delivery might be useful for threatening more distant targets, such as Luanda, which might then be protected against Pretoria's aging long-range bombers by modern air defenses. The missile option would look all the more attractive if, in the interim, Pretoria had already obtained a conventionally armed rocket that could be adapted to nuclear delivery.

Brazil and Argentina, if they develop nuclear arms at all, will likely do so more for reasons of prestige than security. Nonetheless, given their progress in building conventionally armed rockets, the missile-delivery option will be available to both countries, its costs partly underwritten by export sales.

*

The potential dangers to global security from the further spread of nuclear missiles to regional powers are profound. At the most rudimentary level, the extended range that some of these weapons will likely possess will create new arenas for nuclear tension. Israeli missiles, it appears, will soon be able to threaten parts of the Soviet Union with nuclear arms, increasing the risk of a superpower nuclear confrontation in the event of a future Arab-Israeli conflict, as noted earlier. Similarly, intermediate-range Indian missiles would pose a serious nuclear threat to China that barely exists today. An escalating crisis between the two could lead to Soviet intervention on India's behalf and, in turn, to American involvement in support of China, a situation not unlike that during the 1971 Indo-Pakistani War, when President Richard M. Nixon feared that the U.S. might have to use nuclear arms to defend China against Soviet nuclear attack.[28]

Nuclear missiles in the hands of regional powers can also stimulate further proliferation of these capabilities. The fear that Israel may be able to target Baghdad with missiles may have contributed to Iraq's decision to modify its Scud-Bs, which flew over 500 miles in a recent test and which have been characterized by Israel as a direct strategic threat.[29] Iraq's nuclear weapons program was derailed in 1981, when the Israelis destroyed its principal nuclear reactor in a surprise air raid. Although Iraqi nuclear weapons are at least a decade away, Iraq has a significant arsenal of chemical weapons and might deploy its missiles with chemical warheads as a partial deterrent against Israeli nuclear attack.

If Pakistan eventually develops missiles capable of striking deeply into India or acquires them from China, Iran could also perceive them as threatening, especially if tensions between the two Islamic states grow. Although this remains a more distant scenario, it could stimulate Tehran's nuclear ambitions.

Inasmuch as nuclear missiles could increase the survivability of nuclear retaliatory forces in Israel, India, and Pakistan, some might argue that such weapons would enhance stability in the Middle East and South Asia, much as U.S. and Soviet strategic missiles have contributed to stability at the superpower level. Although the point may be valid in a bipolar nuclear relationship, such as that between the United States and the Soviet Union, the security equations of these volatile regions are far more complex, and, as suggested above, the introduction of nuclear missiles could be expected to give rise to serious new dangers and uncertainties.

*

With the risks of such advanced proliferation in mind, in 1982, the United States secretly began discussions with Canada, France, Italy, Japan, the United Kingdom, and West Germany to establish a regime for controlling transfers of equipment and technology that might contribute substantially to the development of unmanned nuclear delivery systems. After more than four years of negotiations, the regime was announced on April 16, 1987, in the form of a set of parallel export controls adopted by the seven participating states. The seven had been informally enforcing the new rules for about two years prior to the announcement of the new regime.[30]

The assumption underlying the new export regulations is that Third World missile and space programs, though often officially termed "indigenous," remain critically dependent on assistance from the industrialized states. Hence restricting such aid is expected to slow the development of nuclear-capable missiles significantly. All of the items covered by the new regulations were already subject to export controls in the seven participating countries aimed at restricting their transfer to the Soviet bloc. Under the new controls, transfers to non-aligned and friendly states will also be restricted.

The new export regulations are targeted on slowing the development of missiles that are capable of hitting a target the size of a small city from a distance of 190 miles (300 kilometers) or further and which are able to carry a warhead weighing 1,100 pounds (500 kilograms) or more. This relatively short distance was set as the criterion to ensure that missiles usable in the Middle East theater would be covered. The payload standard is based on the assumption that emerging nuclear states will be unable to build nuclear warheads weighing less than 1,100 pounds. The rules cover transfers relevant to both ballistic missiles and cruise missiles, the latter comprising a more distant threat not discussed here.

The new regime attempts to place restrictions on the range of mechanisms by which the emerging nuclear states can take advantage of imported rocket equipment and technology to develop nuclear-capable missiles. First, the controls virtually prohibit the transfer of conventional missiles and space-launch vehicles above the payload and range standards just noted, *i.e.*, of a size and range that would make them directly adaptable for the delivery of Third World nuclear warheads. Requests for licenses to export key sub-systems for such large rockets—including individual rocket stages, rocket motors, sophisticated guidance systems, and warhead components—and the export of facilities and equipment to manufacture the rockets or sub-systems are also to be barred in virtually all instances.

An exception is made for transfers authorized by treaty, in order to permit U.S. sales of Trident submarine-launched ballistic missiles to the United Kingdom and transfers of major space-launcher components to the European Space Agency by member countries. (Israeli participation in the U.S. Strategic Defense Initiative research and development program apparently will not be affected on the theory that U.S.-Israeli cooperation will involve only work on anti-tactical-ballistic-missile defenses and will not contribute to Israeli offensive ballistic missile capabilities.)

The new regulations plainly reflect the worry that prior transfers of missiles and missile technology had gone too far. As the regulations were announced, however, officials were silent about such transactions. Nonetheless, some details can be gleaned from published sources.

Except for transfers to its North Atlantic Treaty Organization (NATO) allies and Japan, the United States has generally refrained from exporting military missiles that would be categorized as nuclear-capable under the new export controls. In the mid-1970s, for example, Washington rejected Israel's request for conventionally armed, intermediate range Pershing 1a missiles, fearing that Israel might adapt them for nuclear use. In the 1960s and 1970s, however, the

United States transferred the Nike-Hercules surface-to-air missile to South Korea and Taiwan; both countries were considered nuclear aspirants at the time. The Nike-Hercules can be converted to a surface-to-surface missile able to carry a 1,100-pound (500-kilogram) payload 250 miles, and indeed, by 1978 Korea is believed to have modified or replicated a number of the U.S. missiles to build a surface-to-surface, conventionally armed missile, albeit with a range of only 150 miles.[31] At this point, Seoul had ratified the Non-Proliferation Treaty, but may have been continuing some activities related to the development of nuclear arms. (See the discussion of South Korea in the introduction to Chapter III.)

The only other reported transfer of military missiles in this category by a Western supplier to a Third World country is believed to have taken place in the 1960s, when the French armorer Dassault is said to have built the Jericho I for Israel. The missile reportedly had a range of 250 to 300 miles and a payload of 1,000 to 1,500 pounds (450 to 680 kilograms). Supposedly fourteen Jerichos were delivered to Israel before the French suspended military assistance following the 1967 Arab-Israeli War, and thereafter Israel began to produce them indigenously.[32] There have been reports that Israel readied the missiles for use with nuclear warheads during the 1973 Arab-Israeli War.[33]

With regard to large *non*-military rockets, U.S. policy since 1972 has been to deny exports of space-launch vehicles.[34] In 1969, Washington had agreed to transfer Thor-Delta launcher technology to Japan, the only known sale of U.S. orbital launch vehicle know-how.[35] Questions remain, however, concerning America's contribution to the SLV-3, the rocket which lofted India's first space satellite in 1980 and which embodies its near-term intermediate-range missile capability. The rocket is said by some to have been modeled on the U.S. Scout, also a four-stage, solid-fuel space-launch vehicle, which the United States developed in the 1950s. In 1965, India inquired about obtaining the U.S. system, which was then, in principle, available for sale.[36]

Washington never transferred the rocket or the technology for its production to New Delhi, but India may have advanced the SLV-3 project by taking advantage of the design, which is unclassified.[37] What steps Washington may take under the new export control system to prevent others from following suit remains to be seen.

Prior to the advent of the new control regime, certain French, Italian, and Japanese rocket propulsion systems with a nuclear-missile potential were also, in principle, available to foreign purchasers.[38] The only transfers that have come to light, however, involve France. During the 1970s, for example, Paris licensed both India and Pakistan to produce a rocket engine similar to France's Mammoth propulsion system. According to one analysis, the system could be readily configured as a two-stage rocket, using one Mammoth engine for each stage; the rocket would be able to carry a 1,100-pound (500 kilogram) payload over 500 miles.[39] France has also licensed India to produce the powerful liquid-fuel Viking rocket engine, used on the European Space Agency's Ariane launcher. The Indian version will serve as the second stage of India's Polar Space Launch Vehicle.[40] The Indian rocket, intended to loft a 7,700-pound (3,500-kilogram) payload into low earth orbit sometime in the coming decade, will also provide India with an intercontinental ballistic missile capability. In 1985, a prototype of the Indian-produced version was tested in France.[41] France has not announced whether, in view of the new missile-technology control regime, it intends to reduce its participation in this project.

In addition to limiting transfers of entire rockets and major sub-systems, the new export controls also attempt to restrict more indirect aid to space-launcher and missile programs by limiting the transfer of smaller, but important components, including on-board computers, inertial navigation systems, liquid and solid rocket fuel, testing equipment, flight controls, and the advanced composite materials used to construct rocket-body and engine parts. Related know-how and hardware for the manufacture of these items are also to be restricted. U.S. officials believe that most rocket development programs of emerging nuclear states are heavily dependent on imports in these high-technology fields.

Most of the items at issue, however, are also used for other purposes, such as in the manufacture or maintenance of civilian or military aircraft. Exports for these purposes, expected to comprise the bulk of export license requests, will still be permitted under the new system, necessitating a case-by-case review for each proposed transfer to assess its precise characteristics and intended use. Where the transfer could potentially contribute to an unmanned nuclear-weapons delivery system, the recipient government will have to provide assurances that the transferred item will be used only for a permitted purpose and that it will not be modified, replicated, or retransferred without the permission of the exporting country. As discussed below, the enforcement of these restrictions may be difficult once the exported item is in the hands of the recipient country.

Some details have come to light on past transfers of this type by Western governments in support of emerging-nuclear-state missile and space-launcher programs. In the early 1970s, for example, France helped India set up a rocket propellant production plant, a key step in India's development of the solid fuel rocket engines of the SLV-3.[42] In 1974 and 1975, West Germany's Aeronautical Research and Testing Laboratory ("DFVLR") tested models of the rocket in special wind tunnels to replicate supersonic flight outside the Earth's atmosphere, and the institute subsequently helped Indian technicians design and build an indigenous test facility that opened in 1980.[43] Through the early 1980s, German experts also provided "on-the-job" skills in working with the composites used for key rocket structures, such as engine nozzles, and supplied computer software and know-how for advanced rocket guidance systems.[44] The DFVLR also plans to aid in testing the Indian version of the Viking rocket.[45]

West Germany also appears to have provided important assistance to Brazil in building the Sonda IV rocket, the space probe expected to become the basis for one of Brazil's first nuclear-capable missiles. Messerschmidt-Boelkow-Blohm, for example, assisted in the basic development of the steering mechanism ("secondary injection system") for the Sonda IV rocket and between 1976 and 1981, the DFVLR and associated West German research institutes provided instruction in such fields as the design and production of components from composite materials, rocket guidance techniques, the determination of payload trajectories, and the flight dynamics of the Sonda IV.[46] In 1980, West Germany also reportedly held discussions with Brazil on supplying the high-strength steel structures needed for the body of the Sonda IV, but it is not clear from published sources whether these talks bore fruit.[47] Brazil has also sought an advanced guidance system from Sweden for the rocket, based on Japanese technology.[48]

The United States also appears to have contributed at least indirectly to the Brazilian rocket program. In 1983, a Sonda III was launched from the U.S. Wallops Island launch site and at least one Sonda IV flight in 1984 carried a package of experiments for the U.S. Air Force Geophysics Laboratory.[49] In effect, U.S. funds were helping to underwrite the Sonda program, even as U.S. diplomats were trying to establish an international export control regime to slow it. Similarly, the simplified inertial guidance system of the Avibras SS-300, a Brazilian surface-to-surface missile now under development with a 190-mile range, is said to use American technology.[50]

During the mid-1970s, the United States assisted South Korea to establish a facility for maintaining the Nike-Hercules, transferring know-how that is said to have aided Seoul in converting some of these anti-aircraft missiles into surface-to-surface rockets.[51] And, as recently as 1986, Washington authorized AT&T Technology, Inc., to provide engineering services for the U.S. missile, although the content of these services has not been made public.[52] The United States is also transferring special radars for India's new military missile test site in Orissa. The capabilities of the transferred equipment will be limited, according to Pentagon spokesmen, to conform to the new missile-technology transfer rules.[53]

Finally, Italian and West German experts are reported to be working with Argentina to develop the Condor II (Alacran) missile. Supposedly, the rocket will be capable of reaching the Falklands from the Argentine mainland.[54]

The foregoing examples of Western equipment and technology transfers in support of actual or potential nuclear missile programs are drawn from public sources. They undoubtedly represent only a small sample of the actual transfers over the past decade, and they do not include the extensive technical assistance given by the United States, France, and West Germany during the 1960s, which was essential for creating the basic infrastructure needed to support emerging-nuclear-state rocket programs. The new missile-technology control regime can be expected to curtail such transfers significantly in the future, despite the exceptions that may be made for pre-existing space cooperation and military agreements and despite the fact that smuggling and other abuses of the system will pose a continuing risk to its integrity.

As stressed below, however, the significance of these transfers pales in comparison to continuing Soviet and Chinese tranfers of complete nuclear-capable missile systems to various Middle East states.

Indeed, for the moment, the greatest weakness of the missile-technology regime is the lack of participation by key supplier countries. Soviet participation would give the system considerably greater political stature. More to the point, it would avert possible future exports of nuclear-capable Soviet missiles, such as the Scud-B, which Moscow has reportedly transferred to Iraq in recent years, permitting the latter's extensive missile attacks against Tehran, noted earlier.

The Soviet Union was an original member of the 1975 Nuclear Suppliers Group, which established guidelines for the transfer of nuclear equipment and technology. Close U.S.-Soviet cooperation in that forum helped legitimize the new export controls as norms for international nuclear trade and underscored the resolve of the superpowers and their industrialized partners to curb further proliferation. In contrast, lack of Soviet participation gives the new missile-technology control system a more provisional appearance. At Washington's invitation, the Soviet Union in mid-1987 agreed to consider whether to join the regime. If reports are true that Moscow subsequently transferred hundreds of Scuds to Iraq, Soviet participation appears to be unlikely for some time. On June 1, 1988, in the final communiqué of the Moscow summit, President Reagan and Soviet General Secretary Mikhail Gorbachev stated that they had agreed to "bilateral discussions at the level of experts on the problem of proliferation of ballistic missile technology." This raises the possibility that Moscow may yet be willing to join the new missile export control system.

Participation by the People's Republic of China is also essential to the effectiveness of the new controls. As noted earlier, Beijing disregarded pre-existing international norms in 1988 by transferring the 1,600- to 1,860-mile range CSS-2 to Saudi Arabia. China could offer this missile, the soon to be available 375-mile range M-9, or the 190-mile range M-11 to Pakistan in the future. In 1986, moreover, China agreed to provide technology to Brazil on liquid rocket fuels and rocket guidance systems in return for Brazil's know-how on solid rocket fuels—conduct that also deviates from the new export standards.[55]

Several important Western suppliers and "middleman" states, such as Sweden, Switzerland, and Belgium, also need to be brought into the regime to ensure its effectiveness. As if to emphasize the importance of closing this gap, in early 1988 a Brazilian newspaper stated in reporting on the Brazilian rocket program that Brazil had had difficulty in obtaining some rocket components because of the U.S. embargo, "but it found other suppliers." The report went on to note that, "should it become necessary, the Aeronautics Ministry will seek the technology for altitude guidance and control of rockets in the PRC [People's Republic of China] or Soviet Union."[56]

A second important weakness in the new controls is the difficulty of verifying that recipients are using exported equipment and technology exclusively for authorized purposes. For example, recipients will be permitted to stock various inertial navigation system components and other electronics as replacement parts for manned aircraft, providing opportunities for their replication or diversion to use in missiles. According to a 1981 study for the U.S. Arms Control and Disarmament Agency, at least twenty widely available, Western-produced inertial navigation systems could be readily adapted for use in ballistic missiles.[57] The falsification of end-use certificates, a common ploy in the arms transfer field, similarly cannot be ruled out.

In the case of transfers of nuclear equipment and materials, recipients must accept International Atomic Energy Agency audits and inspections to confirm that transferred items are not being diverted for unauthorized uses. The new missile regulations, however, do not provide a comparable post-export verification system, leaving suppliers to rely on *ad hoc* measures, whose rigorousness may vary from exporter to exporter.

As suggested earlier, diversions in this field are not unknown. In addition to South Korea's reported modification of the Nike-Hercules into a surface-to-surface missile, Israel is believed to have adapted the guidance system of the U.S.-supplied Lance, a 75-mile range surface-to-surface missile, for use in its 400-mile range Jericho II.[58] Israel is also reported to have transferred Lance technology to Taiwan, where it was used in developing the Green Bee missile, with capabilities comparable to the Lance.[59] At a more general level, it is also widely assumed that Brazil's Sonda series rockets, developed as part of Brazil's peaceful space program with extensive external assistance, subsequently became prototypes for Brazil's widely exported military missiles.[60] The same civilian-to-military transference may be taking place in India, despite official insistence that India's space and missile programs do not overlap.

*

Restrictions on missile technology transfers, standing alone, will not prevent the proliferation of nuclear-capable missiles, even if questions of wider participation, verification, and implementation are successfully addressed. Israel, India, and possibly Brazil, for example, can already produce nuclear-capable missiles, and the first two can manufacture the nuclear weapons to arm them. To ensure that this potential does not contribute further to regional and international instability, direct diplomatic intervention by the United States, the Soviet Union, and other interested states will be required.

Washington has vocally, and successfully, opposed Israel's development of the advanced Lavi fighter, albeit on economic grounds. The Reagan Administration, however, did not discourage Jerusalem from deploying the Jericho II in the early 1980s, apparently because it considered the weapon, when conventionally armed, to be an appropriate addition to Israel's arsenal.[61] Nor is Washington known to have actively objected to the testing of the longer-range version of the missile, which recently drew Moscow's ire. If the United States does not persuade Jerusalem to abandon this new system, the U.S. initiative to curb nuclear missile proliferation could be perceived as having failed an important test. Moreover, if Washington is not seen to be working to halt the Israeli program, its efforts to gain wider acceptance of missile-technology export controls and to build an international consensus on curbing the spread of these weapons could well be undermined. On the other hand, the recent proliferation of missiles in the Middle East has demonstrated that the Soviet Union and China are not prepared to participate in a missile control regime at this time and has provided added justification for Israel to pursue the development of longer-range missiles.

Whether or not the Soviet Union adopts the new Western export controls, as India's patron, it could play an important role in discouraging New Delhi from building nuclear-capable missiles that might threaten China. A nuclear competition between the two Asian states would not be in Soviet interests. Given the fact that India has not yet converted its rocket potential into powerful missiles, time still remains to avert this outcome.

On a separate front, a U.S. effort, possibly in conjunction with West Germany, to discourage Brazil from exporting nuclear-capable missiles, at least to states currently able to manufacture nuclear arms, would also be a valuable adjunct to current export control efforts.

Finally, Washington must address the risk that China might transfer nuclear-capable missiles to Pakistan. In the course of negotiations on the U.S.-China nuclear trade pact in 1984 and 1985, Beijing assured the Reagan Administration that it would not assist Pakistan in developing nuclear weapons. At that time, Washington believed that China was helping Pakistan operate a plant able to manufacture nuclear-weapons material, and published reports stated that several years earlier, China had given Pakistan a nuclear weapon design. Washington could seek Beijing's assurances that its pledge to end nuclear assistance to Pakistan would rule out the transfer of nuclear-capable missiles to Islamabad, even if conventionally armed.

*

Advances in Third World space launcher and missile capabilities pose a proliferation danger of increasing gravity. Indeed the advent of the missile-technology control regime is itself a reflection of the growing risks in this field. For some nuclear threshold states, missile-based nuclear delivery systems will remain unattainable until well into the next decade, offering hope that the spread of these systems can be contained. In other instances, however, advanced nuclear delivery systems are a more immediate concern. Especially in these cases, tough diplomacy, in addition to export controls and international consensus building, are urgently needed if the further deployment of these dangerous new arms is to be checked.

Aircraft Delivery Systems[62]

If ballistic missiles represent the nuclear delivery system of the future for most of the emerging nuclear weapon states, advanced combat aircraft—almost always supplied by the West or the Soviet Union—are the delivery system of today. Mated with nuclear weapons, these aircraft can transform the inchoate nuclear capabilities of India, Pakistan, and South Africa into concrete military threats, probably within a matter of months. Given the advanced state of Israel's nuclear weapons program, it is highly probable that Israel has already prepared aircraft for delivering nuclear weapons. The suppliers of these warplanes are not known to have taken any measures to prevent the use of their aircraft for nuclear missions.

It is generally assumed that the undeclared nuclear-weapon states will choose their most advanced combat aircraft as their initial nuclear-weapon delivery systems.[63] In theory, these nations might select less sophisticated aircraft, and might even use commercial jets, if, for example, subterfuge were essential in a particular scenario. However, these countries presumably have only a limited number of nuclear weapons, and the few they have comprise their most potent and costly armaments, ones which would likely be used only in the most dire circumstances. Therefore, it seems far more probable that the undeclared nuclear states would rely on those aircraft with the greatest certainty of penetrating enemy air defenses and reaching their targets.[64]

The essential requirement for these aircraft is that, in addition to having a range sufficient to reach potential targets, they have sufficient payload capacity to be able to carry an early-generation nuclear weapon. Using the standard adopted by the missile technology control regime described above, it must be assumed that emerging nuclear states can build weapons weighing as little as 1,100 pounds (500 kilograms). This would be well within the payload capacity of most advanced ground-attack aircraft in the arsenals of the undeclared nuclear states. Indeed, many of these warplanes are equipped to carry several 2,000-pound conventional bombs or drop-tanks of comparable weight.

In selecting among its available combat aircraft, a new nuclear-weapon state will seek to optimize a number of factors, especially those which enable an aircraft to penetrate enemy defenses—electronic warfare avionics (target acquisition radar, electronic counter-measures against enemy radar, and navigation systems) and combat characteristics (speed, maneuverability, and armaments).[65] The aircraft's range will also be a key factor.

No attempt will be made here to make fine judgments as to which of the high-performance warplanes in the arsenals of each of the four *de facto* nuclear states would be the most likely to be assigned the mission of nuclear weapons delivery. What is significant here is that each of these countries has obtained from one or more of the major industrialized aircraft-supplier states numerous top-flight fighters well suited to this role.

All of the aircraft now in the Israeli arsenal have been supplied by the United States or depend critically on U.S.-supplied components. Israel's most capable warplanes for ground attack missions are the U.S. F-16, the U.S. F-15, the U.S. F-4E (now being upgraded with advanced avionics), and the Israeli-built Kfir, which uses the U.S.-supplied General Electric J79 engine.[66] All can carry a 1,100-pound bomb easily. Israel demonstrated the strategic bombing potential of its F-16s and F-15s—and its ability to extend their range through aerial refuelling—when it destroyed Iraq's principal nuclear reactor outside Baghdad in 1981 and the Palestine Liberation Organization's headquarters in Tunis in 1985, targets that were approximately 600 miles and 1,500 miles respectively from Israel.

The top rank of fighter-bombers in India's air force includes the British-French Jaguar, the Soviet MiG-29 and MiG-23, and the French Mirage 2000. (The highly capable Soviet MiG-27 is on order.)[67] Any of these could readily carry a 1,100-pound nuclear device to targets throughout Pakistan.

Pakistan's top strike aircraft, in turn, are its U.S. F-16s, the French Mirage V, and the somewhat older Mirage III/EP.[68] These aircraft could reach key cities and military targets throughout northwest India.

South Africa, subject to a U.N.-mandated arms embargo since 1977, would have to rely on somewhat less capable aircraft. Its foremost potential nuclear delivery systems are its Mirage F-1AZ's and its older British-supplied Buccaneer bombers.[69] South Africa recently unveiled a new addition to its air force, the Cheetah, a warplane which, like the Israeli Kfir, is apparently based on the Mirage III, and whose upgraded airframe and avionics are based on Israeli technology.[70]

If nuclear arms spread to Iran, Iraq, or Libya, all would have available for use as delivery systems the first-rank aircraft they have already received from the West or the Soviet Union. Iran, however, has been unable to obtain replacements for planes in this category that it has lost in its conflict with Iraq. It is now purchasing the less capable Q-5 from China. Argentina and Brazil, which are considerably closer to possessing a nuclear weapons capability than these Middle East states (though they are less likely to exercise this option once it is in hand), have also purchased relatively modern, though not top-of-the-line, U.S. and French aircraft.

*

Modifying any of these aircraft for the delivery of nuclear ordnance would be relatively simple. In principle any advanced aircraft with a location either on its wings or fuselage (a hardpoint) able to carry a 1,100-pound (500 kilogram) conventional bomb or a 1,100-pound releasable fuel tank is capable of carrying a nuclear weapon of the same weight. In terms of hardware on the aircraft, all that is needed is a release mechanism permitting the weapon to be dropped. In the forces of the nuclear-weapon states, aircraft that are intended for nuclear use also contain special circuits, which permit nuclear weapons to be armed in flight, and combination locks, known in the United States as "permissive action links" or "PALs", that prevent such arming from taking place until the pilot receives the correct combination from the proper authority.[71]

These mechanisms serve both as safety precautions to avoid accidental detonations and as a means of protecting against the unauthorized use of nuclear arms. Western suppliers do not sell aircraft with these nuclear circuits, however, and the Soviet Union presumably follows suit.[72] Whether an emerging nuclear state would want to install such circuits on its own is uncertain, but Sweden's 1958 bomb design contained an arming mechanism, suggesting that in-air arming was probably contemplated.[73] An emerging nuclear state could provide for in-air arming today by slightly modifying circuits used for conventional munitions— circuits which are included on American and possibly other aircraft. As for PALs, states with only a handful of nuclear weapons, which presumably would be under the close control of top civilian leaders, might be prepared to forego this safeguard, which is important to the U.S. arsenal in part because of the great number of U.S. weapons deployed around the world.

While standard hardpoints and circuits could thus be readily adapted for nuclear delivery, this conversion would nonetheless require careful analysis and probably on-the-ground testing to ensure the system's reliability. A more serious reliability problem relates to the aerodynamics of the nuclear weapon to be used, which can have a significant impact on the performance of the aircraft carrying it. The weapon's location on the aircraft, the weapon's shape, its internal weight distribution, and its other characteristics would be critical factors. A measure of the importance of these characteristics can be seen in the extensive computer analyses and flight tests required by the United States before new conventional weapons are certified for use on U.S. advanced combat aircraft. Similar testing would be needed before a near-nuclear country could have confidence in its own aircraft delivery system.

The ballistic characteristics of the weapon after its release from an aircraft would also have to be determined and could well require flight-testing with mock-ups. To permit an aircraft to escape the blast of a nuclear bomb it has released, moreover, nuclear weapons are often equipped with mechanisms for delaying their detonation, such as a parachute or time-delay fuse, and pilots sometimes use a special bombing technique known as "toss bombing." If a near-nuclear country elected to follow either approach, further testing and training to ensure reliability would be required.[74]

Finally, readying aircraft for nuclear delivery would almost certainly require the designation of special crews (for political reliability, if for no other reason), the implementation of strict security procedures, increased protection for the particular aircraft intended for this mission, and similar measures. These steps, like the adaptation of the aircraft themselves and the testing and training noted above, would all be signs that foreign-supplied aircraft were being prepared for nuclear use.

*

In the regional military theaters of the Middle East, South Asia, and Southern Africa the nuclear potential of high-performance warplanes adds significantly to the dangers posed from the spread of nuclear arms themselves. If readied in advance to receive such arms, these warplanes could be rapidly launched on nuclear missions and could reach key targets in an hour or less, permitting surprise or preemptive attacks and heightening tensions in any conflict. Indeed, this speed and the ability of the planes to penetrate the often rudimentary air defenses of today's regional powers would make them virtually as effective as missile-delivery systems in many cases (although this situation is likely to change in the years ahead as air defenses improve).

Additional risks are posed by the fact that small nuclear forces are, themselves, potential targets of pre-emptive attack by conventional or nuclear means. Many analysts believe that an emerging nuclear power that feared such an attack would be tempted to use its limited number of nuclear weapons early in a conflict rather than risk their destruction. To protect its nuclear option, such a nation would likely keep its aircraft in a state of alert from the outset of hostilities, with nuclear arms deployed or ready to be deployed on a moment's notice. In effect, its nuclear forces would be on a "hair trigger."

The fact that in these countries imported high-performance aircraft are both top-of-the-line conventional weapons and potential nuclear delivery systems greatly magnifies the danger of tragedy. A decision by an emerging nuclear state to use its nuclear arms early in a conflict could be triggered not only by fear of an attack against its key nuclear installations, but also by fear of an attack against its aircraft, since the loss of its delivery system would greatly reduce the military value of its nuclear weapons. Unfortunately, the risk of such an attack would be considerable since the very aircraft designated for nuclear use would, by virtue of their superior conventional capabilities, represent highly attractive targets to an enemy hoping to gain conventional air-superiority. Indeed, pre-emptive destruction of enemy air forces is a standard element of modern military tactics, with ample historical precedent.[75]

Even in the absence of a pre-emptive strike, once hostilities began, the dual function of these advanced military aircraft would contribute to uncertainty over whether or not a near-nuclear nation was moving toward the use of nuclear arms, and thus would increase the risk of escalation through miscalculation. In all likelihood, these aircraft—conventionally armed—would see continuous action from the beginning of any conflict. This fact, together with the secrecy that inevitably surrounds undeclared nuclear weapons programs, the small number of weapons actually involved, and the limited real-time intelligence collection capabilities of potential adversaries, means that there would be few warning signs of an emerging nuclear state's decision to escalate from conventional to nuclear warfare. In essence, the carefully modulated nuclear deployments and phased alerts observable to the other side that have served as firebreaks restraining escalation in U.S.-Soviet nuclear confrontations would be totally lacking.

The sale of potential nuclear-weapons delivery systems to the emerging nuclear states could also unexpectedly entangle the supplier country's interests. First and most obviously, the practice undercuts the longstanding efforts of the United States, the Soviet Union, France, and Great Britain to curb the spread of nuclear arms by withholding material and equipment needed to develop a nuclear force. Supplier countries often justify the transfer of advanced aircraft to the quasi-nuclear-weapon states by arguing that these transfers will ease pressures on the recipient countries to develop nuclear arms by providing them with an alternative means of enhancing their national security. The approach appears not to have worked in the case of Israel, however, and the jury is still out on its effectiveness in blunting Indian and Pakistani nuclear ambitions. Where it proves ineffective, the policy can aggravate the impact of the emerging nuclear state's decision to go nuclear by removing the country's need to develop an indigenous high-quality delivery system. Thus, sales of nuclear-capable aircraft could not only set back the suppliers' efforts to halt proliferation, but also incrementally increase the long-term risk of a regional nuclear war into which the supplier nations might ultimately be drawn.

Second, the sales undercut the principal sanction that nuclear suppliers have exercised to discourage the threshold nations from nuclear arming. Led by the United States, the advanced industrial states of East and West, organized as the Nuclear Suppliers Group, have imposed a *de facto* moratorium on new nuclear power reactors and new nuclear fuel sales to Israel, India, Pakistan, and several other near-nuclear states.[76] Since these sales would in any event be subject to the inspection regime of the Vienna-based International

Atomic Energy Agency and thus would be unlikely to contribute directly to any recipient's nuclear weapons program, the moratorium is largely a symbolically important economic sanction. The value of the embargo as an expression of disapproval, however, is at least partially undercut by the readiness of the three principal nuclear suppliers—the United States, the Soviet Union and France—to sell to threshold nations aircraft that are of direct value to their nuclear-weapons programs.

Third, suppliers could suffer direct political costs from their sales of potential nuclear delivery systems. Both seller and purchaser could be embarrassed if it became known that an emerging nuclear nation had taken steps to prepare imported aircraft for wartime nuclear strikes. Exposure of such steps, discussed further below, is by no means unlikely, given current superpower intelligence-gathering capabilities.

Graver, perhaps, are the potential political repercussions the United States and the Soviet Union would experience if one of their clients actually delivered a nuclear weapon with an aircraft supplied by a superpower. To be sure, the use of such a weapon by a regional party would, in itself, trigger a serious international crisis. Within the wider crisis, however, the issue of whose aircraft served as the delivery system could prove a volatile question.

If Israel or Pakistan ever resorted to nuclear arms, the United States would inevitably be accused of complicity with or at least acquiescence in the deed because of its close political ties to these clients. To a lesser extent, the Soviet Union—though not Britain or France—might face similar charges if India took such a step. The use of U.S. or Soviet aircraft in a nuclear attack would lend concreteness to the link many critics would draw between client and patron—particularly if the advanced aircraft in question had been essential to the client's ability to reach its target because of the aircraft's range, electronic-warfare equipment, or other unique capabilities. The controversy triggered by Israel's use of U.S. F-15s and F-16s to destroy Iraq's large research reactor in 1981 gives some indication of the potential discomfort for aircraft suppliers caused by client-state actions.[77] In the context of a nuclear attack by a client government using superpower-supplied aircraft, the added appearance of superpower involvement could magnify the diplomatic repercussions for the supplier state involved and increase the danger of superpower confrontation.

There can be little question that the suppliers of advanced nuclear-capable warplanes are well aware of their nuclear potential. In 1968, for example, when Israel was negotiating to purchase fifty F-4s from the United States, it reportedly requested that specialized nuclear systems not be removed from the aircraft. The request was denied, although the Johnson Administration approved the sale of non-nuclearized versions of the aircraft.[78] In 1976 an American intelligence official reported in a classified briefing to the Nuclear Regulatory Commission that Israeli pilots had been observed using U.S.-supplied A-4s to practice bombing runs of a type used often for dropping nuclear weapons.[79] Similarly, at hearings on the sale of U.S. F-16s to Pakistan in 1981, Senator S. I. Hayakawa (R-Calif.) specifically asked if the planes would provide Pakistan with a delivery system for nuclear devices. Under Secretary of State James L. Buckley conceded: "Yes, they would. But by the same token that is not the only aircraft that would have that capability."[80]

In principle, many of the foregoing risks could be mitigated if emerging nuclear-weapon states could be effectively prohibited from using their top-of-the-line Western and Soviet warplanes for nuclear missions. Plainly, such a step would not preclude the development of small nuclear forces, but in most cases it would significantly constrain their capabilities, limiting options for military planners and, possibly, reducing the chance that nuclear arms would actually be used in regional conflicts.

Israel's aircraft-based nuclear delivery capability would be eliminated if it were unable to use U.S. warplanes for this purpose, assuming that the Kfir, because of its U.S.-supplied engine, were placed under the same restrictions as U.S.-built aircraft. Pakistan, deprived of the use of its

American F-16s and French Mirages, would have to rely on its increasingly obsolete, short-range Chinese Q-5s and J-6s. This would greatly reduce the capabilities of its potential nuclear forces. India, similarly, would have to rely on its subsonic Ajeets, if its British Canberras and its advanced MiGs, Mirages, and Jaguars were not available for nuclear missions.

South Africa's nuclear capabilities would probably be less affected, however, if it were forced to rely on its Cheetahs, rather than on its Buccaneers, Canberras, and Mirage F1-AZs.[81]

Despite its potential benefits, the supplier governments are not known to have pursued a ban on the use of advanced Western and Soviet warplanes as nuclear delivery systems, even though at least some of these governments have sought to arrest the spread of ballistic-missile delivery capabilities. One reason for this inaction, no doubt, is that imposing nuclear controls over dual-capable combat aircraft would be a difficult challenge.

Among other obstacles, it seems evident that for reasons of *realpolitik* and profit, sales of advanced aircraft to Israel, India, and Pakistan are likely to continue for the foreseeable future. Any comprehensive solution, moreover, must address not only new transfers but also those high performance aircraft already supplied and those that may be produced in recipient states through existing co-production or licensing arrangements. In addition, to ensure that no near-nuclear state gains an advantage over another in its region—and that no vendor gains a competitive advantage over any other—it would appear essential to ensure that any limits on the use of advanced Western and Soviet aircraft be adopted uniformly by all relevant suppliers. Given the willingness of these same suppliers to cooperate with each other and with other advanced states in implementing uniform standards on sales of nuclear equipment and material, and given the new accord restricting missile technology transfers and the hope that the Soviet Union may eventually join it on non-proliferation grounds, the possibility of common no-nuclear-use restrictions on advanced military aircraft should not be ruled out.

Taking a cue from the nuclear supply regime, the principal warplane suppliers could require the emerging nuclear states to provide explicit pledges not to use new and previously supplied foreign aircraft for nuclear weapons delivery. Supplier countries could specify that any violation of the pledge would trigger the suspension of new aircraft transfers, shipments of spare parts for previously supplied aircraft, and existing co-production agreements. Or, the sanction could be left more ambiguous. The key point is that an explicit no-nuclear-use pledge would be given and that recipient states would recognize that violating this pledge would, at the least, carry substantial political costs. As in the case of nuclear transfers, to ensure the effectiveness of the no-nuclear-use pledge for combat aircraft, suppliers could make clear that actions well before actual use of these planes to drop a nuclear bomb—that is, steps taken to prepare the aircraft, crews, etc., for nuclear delivery—would be viewed as a breach of recipient country commitments.[82]

At the very least, to require such a pledge would focus international attention on the potential nuclear dangers posed by foreign-supplied advanced aircraft, make clear the strong opposition of the supplier states to the use of their aircraft for such purposes, and raise the stakes for any recipient that sought to rely on such aircraft for nuclear delivery. Even if the pledges proved completely unverifiable—though, as discussed below, some level of verification would be possible—this incremental addition to the political restraints against nuclear arming would be worthwhile. On the other hand, if verification did prove to be feasible and if suppliers therefore were able to convince recipients that the risk of detection and subsequent sanctions were high, recipients might well be deterred from taking the preparatory steps needed to deploy a highly capable nuclear force using their top-of-the-line aircraft.[83]

Could the no-nuclear-use pledges be verified? As noted earlier, there would be many telltale signs that a near-nuclear nation was preparing to use imported combat aircraft for nuclear purposes. Given the extensive human and electronic intelligence-gathering capabilities of the superpowers and the ongoing spare-parts and training relationship between suppliers and users—a relationship which often requires nationals of the supplier to visit air bases of the recipient—near-nuclear states would have considerable reason to fear that attempts to ready imported aircraft for nuclear missions would be discovered.

Indeed, suppliers could consider more formalized verification mechanisms, such as periodic on-site inspections. While uncommon today, on-site inspections have been implemented by the United States in certain advanced-weapons transfer cases to protect against the misuse or diversion of U.S. equipment. The United States insisted on the right to make on-site inspections of the sophisticated Airborne Warning and Control System (AWACS) planes sold to Saudi Arabia in 1981, for example, and apparently at one time inspected Stinger ground-to-air anti-aircraft missiles sold to certain other nations.[84] While the request for such intrusive verification procedures would undoubtedly meet with objections from the recipient states, the interest of the supplier states in controlling the use of their aircraft and in retarding proliferation should provide strong incentives for them to press for the adoption of such safeguards.

*

With the march of events, missile- and aircraft-based delivery systems are becoming an increasingly important dimension of nuclear proliferation. Despite the growing availability of nuclear-capable missiles on the international market, in a sense these systems are spreading slowly, in that it will be a number of years before these missiles might be deployed with nuclear warheads by any emerging nuclear state other than Israel. The 1987 missile-technology control regime, if it is embraced by additional suppliers beyond the original seven Western governments and if it is accompanied by focussed diplomatic pressure, may go far toward further retarding this trend. A critical first step will be to persuade the Soviet Union and China to halt further missile transfers in the Middle East.

A more immediate nuclear threat, however, is posed by the high-performance Western and Soviet aircraft, weapon systems that are already in the arsenals of the emerging nuclear states and that could be adapted for nuclear service far more quickly than conventionally armed missiles. Effectively discouraging the use of these warplanes for nuclear missions will be particularly difficult. Given the critical importance of these aircraft in permitting nuclear threshold states to militarize their nuclear weapon capabilities, new efforts are needed to address this growing danger.

NUCLEAR-CAPABLE MISSILES AND SPACE LAUNCH VEHICLES (SLVs) IN THE THIRD WORLD
(Payload>1100 lbs., Range>190 mi., per "Missile Technology Control Regime")[1]

Missile	Producer(s)	Owner(s)	Range	Payload	Status
Scud-B (SS-1C)	USSR N. Korea (?)[3]	Iran Iraq Libya Syria S. Yemen Egypt[4]	190 miles	1,100 lb.[2]	Deployed
SS-12	USSR	Iraq	500 miles	2,750 lb.[5]	Deployed
CSS-2 "East Wind" (DF-3A)	PRC	Saudi Arabia	1,600-1,860 miles	1,650 lb.[6]	Deployed
M-9	PRC	(Syria?)[7] (Iran?)	125-375 miles	—	Testing[8]
M-11	PRC	—	90-190 miles	1,760 lb.	Available[9]
Jericho II	Israel	Israel	400 miles	180-220 lb.[10]	Deployed
Jericho "IIB"	Israel	Israel	900 miles[11]	?	Testing

			Range	Payload	Status
Avibras SS-300	Brazil	Brazil (Iraq?)	190 miles[12]	1,100 lb.[13]	Testing
Orbita MB/EE-600	Brazil	Brazil (Libya?)[15]	375 miles	1,100 lb.[14]	Under developm't[16]
VLS*	Brazil	Brazil	1,860 miles**[17]	2,000 lb.**	SLV (1st test, 1989)[18]
Alacran (Condor II)	Argentina	Argentina (Egypt?)(Iraq?)	500 miles**[19]	?	Under developm't
Prithvi	India	India	93+ miles	2,200 lb.[20]	Testing
SLV-3*	India	India	1,000-1,550 miles**[21]	880 lb.**[22]	In use as SLV[23]
ASLV*	India	India	greater than SLV-3**	greater than SLV-3**	Testing as SLV[24]
PSLV*	India	India	intercontinental**	2,200+ lb.	Under developm't as SLV[25]

*Space launch vehicle   **If adapted as a ballistic missile

Sources
Nuclear-Capable Missiles and Space Launch Vehicles (SLVs) in the Third World

1. The Missile Technology Control Regime was established by seven Western states (Canada, France, Great Britain, Italy, Japan, the United States, and West Germany) in April 1987 to slow the spread of nuclear-capable missiles to the Third World. The Regime defines a "nuclear-capable" missile as one with a payload capacity in excess of 1,100 lbs. (500 kg.) and a range in excess of 190 miles (300 km.). Although some U.S. and Soviet missile systems deployed in the Third World are nuclear armed in the superpowers' arsenals (e.g. the U.S. Lance, supplied to Israel, and the Soviet SS-21, supplied to Syria), these are not considered "nuclear-capable" missiles in this context because their range is well below the threshold used by the Regime.

2. Since late February 1988, Iraq has attacked Iranian cities with some 200 modified Scud-B missiles. Apparently with foreign assistance, the Iraqis have extended the range of the Scuds, probably by reducing the weight of their warheads. See, "600 km. Surface-to-Surface Missile Tested 3 August," *Baghdad Voice of the Masses*, 0855 GMT, August 4, 1987, translated in *FBIS/NES*, August 4, 1987, p. K-1; George C. Wilson, "Air Attacks, Recruiting Woes Said to Have Weakened Iran," *Washington Post*, April 15, 1988, p. 26. In May 1988, Iraq tested a version of the missile with a 250-pound payload and a 560-mile range. See Bernard E. Trainor, "Iraqi Missile With Extended Range Is New Peril to Iran's Cities and Oil," *New York Times*, May 1, 1988.

3. *Military Balance 1987-1988,* (London: International Institute of Strategic Studies: 1987). It has been reported that the PRC also manufactures the Scud-B and has transferred the missile to Third World states. (See, for example, Dilip Hiro, "Iran: Up in Arms with a Big Hand From the Chinese," *Wall Street Journal,* June 5, 1987; "Iran's Chinese HY-2 missiles and Iraq's French Exocets," *International Defense Review,* June 1987.) However, authoritative Reagan Administration sources state that China has not been a producer of the missile.

4. There has been one report that Egypt, with North Korean assistance, may be developing an improved version of the Scud-B, with twice the normal payload. See Tony Walker, Andrew Gowers, and David Buchan, "Argentina, Egypt, and Long-Range Missile Project," *Financial Times*, December 21, 1987.

   Also, there has been one report that Iraq has based some of its Scud-Bs (unmodified) in Jordan. See, Hirsh Goodman, *Israel's Strategic Reality: The Impact of the Arms Race,* (Washington, D.C.: Washington Institute for Near East Policy, 1985); "Surrounded by Enemies: The Battlefield Equation," *U.S. News and World Report,* April 4, 1988, pp. 42-43 (which uses Goodman as a source). Reagan Administration officials, however, state that this claim is incorrect, and it has not been substaniated by other sources.

5. *Jane's Weapons Systems: 1984-1985,* (London: Jane's Publishing Co., Ltd. London, 1985), p. 851; Christopher Chant, *A Compendium of Armaments and Military Hardware,* (New York: Routledge and Kegan Paul, Ltd., 1987), p. 500. The Soviets have stated that they retain "political control" over Iraq's SS-12s, and that they have not authorized the use of those weapons against Iranian cities. See Patrick Tyler, "Iraq Targets Bigger Missile on Tehran," *Washington Post,* March 28, 1988.

6. The 1,650 lb. payload assumes that the Saudis have equipped their missile with a conventional warhead, which is heavier than the nuclear warhead in the Chinese version. While the nuclear armed, Chinese missile is said to have a 2,200 mile range, the range of the Saudi missile, due to its heavier payload, is considerably shorter (probably 1,600 miles). See Doug Rabnif, "Fallout from Saudi Missiles," *Christian Science Monitor,* March 30, 1988; David Ottaway, "U.S. Asks Soviets, Chinese to Cease Ballistic Missile Sales in Middle East," *Washington Post,* May 26, 1988.

   In congressional testimony, Assistant Secretary of State Richard Murphy stated that the United States has "ascertained" that the Saudi CSS-2s are equipped with conventional warheads and are capable of a range of "up to" 1,860 miles. "Testimony of Richard Murphy, Assistant Secretary of State for Near Eastern and South Asian Affairs," before the Subcommittee on Arms Control, International Security, and Science, and the Subcommittee on Europe and the Middle East of the House Committee on Foreign Affairs, May 10, 1988.

7. Reportedly, Syria and Iran have held talks with the PRC on acquiring the missile. See Michael Gordon, "Syria is Studying New Missile Deal," *New York Times,* June 22, 1988.

8. *IISS Military Balance 1987-1988* (London: International Institute for Strategic Studies, 1987), p. 146.

9. "China's M-11 Is Revealed," *Jane's Defense Weekly,* April 9, 1988, p. 655.

10. Payload based on description of nuclear warhead said to be carried by missile. Total payload capability is greater. The missile is believed to have been developed during the late 1970s and to have been deployed on mobile launchers and in concrete bunkers by 1985. See "Israel's Jericho IRBM Completes Long Range Test," *International Defense Review,* July 1987; "Behind the Walls of Jericho I," and "Much Ado About Jericho II," *Defense and Foreign*

Affairs Weekly, August 3, 1987; Aaron Karp, "Ballistic Missile Development," *Journal of Defense and Diplomacy*, December 1987, p. 16 (stating that the missile has 1,650-lb. payload and a range of 310 to 465 miles). "Jericho II" is the designation given to the missile by Western analysts; the Israeli name for the missile is said to be different.

11. See references in previous note. Apparently derived from the Jericho II, the Jericho IIB was flight-tested to a distance of 500 miles in May 1987. A report quoting U.S. government sources states that the missile will eventually have a range of 900 miles, making it capable of striking Riyadh, Baghdad, Benghazi, and the southern Soviet Union. Several months after the test, Moscow Radio issued a warning to Israel against developing the missile. See Thomas L. Friedman, "Soviet Cautions Israel Against a New Missile," *New York Times*, July 29, 1987.

12. "First Tests Over on Brazil's SS-300," *Jane's Defense Weekly*, December 29, 1986; "Avibras, Engesa Missile Projects Described," *Folha de Sao Paulo*, January 11, 1987, p. A8. The missile's range and payload are comparable to the Scud-B.

13. Aaron Karp, "Ballistic Missile Development," *Journal of Defense and Diplomacy*, December 1987.

14. "Libya/Brazil," *Current News* (U.S. Department of Defense), February 4, 1988, (citing *Jane's Defense Weekly*), p. 3; "Tactical Missile Development Reported," *O Globo*, January 3, 1988 (report states that rocket has a 435-mile range). The missile is derived from the Sonda IV sounding rocket.

15. In January 1988 Libya was reported to have entered into an agreement with the Brazilian firm, Orbita, under which the Libyans would provide $2 billion in financing for the development and procurement of the MB/EE-600 and MB/EE-1,000 missiles, both derived from the Sonda IV sounding rocket. (The MB/EE-1,000 is a version that will have a longer range, but a smaller payload, below the 1,100-lb. threshold of the Missile Technology Control Regime.) The agreement is said to provide an option for the Libyans to purchase some of the missiles in return for their investment. See John Barham, "Brazil Ignores US Protest Over Arms for Libya," *The Sunday Times*, January 31, 1988; Mac Margolis, "Brazil Plans to Resume Weapons Sales to Libya," *Washington Post*, January 28, 1988, p. 22; "Missiles to Libya," *Washington Times*, February 22, 1988, p. 10.

16. The missile is to be deployable in 5 years.

17. Four launches of the VLS are planned for 1989. Although it is currently under development as a space booster, the VLS is said to have a potential surface-to-surface payload capability of 2,000 lb. and a range of 1,860 miles. See Eustaquio de Freitas, "Tactical

Missile Development Reported," *O Globo*, January 3, 1988; Pierre Condom, "Brazil Aims for Self-Sufficiency in Space," *Interavia*, January, 1986, p. 99; "Satellite Launcher Directory," *Flight International*, January 11, 1986, p. 30; "Prototype of Brazilian Launch Vehicle Fails," *Defense Daily*, January 8, 1986, p. 30.

18. See previous note.

19. The Alacran, referred to as the Condor II in some sources, is a two stage, multi-purpose (space launch/tactical) missile. The Alacran is said to have an eventual capability of lifting a payload of nearly 2,000 lb. 125 miles into space. The first stage of the rocket, itself a separate system known as the Condor C1-A3, has been flight-tested and reportedly can carry a 2,500 lb. warhead 62 miles into space. See Tony Walker, Andrew Gowers, and David Buchan, "Argentina, Egypt in Long-Range Missile Project," *Financial Times*, December 21, 1987; "Flight of the Condor," *International Defense Review*, vol. 18, no. 8, 1985; "Argentina: Pre-satellite Launching Rocket Tested by the Air Force," *La Rioja*, October 14, 1986; "Argentina Develops Condor Solid-Propellant Rocket," *Aviation Week and Space Technology*, June 17, 1985.

20. The missile was successfully tested in February 1988. See Shekhar Gupta, "Shooting Ahead," *India Today*, March 31, 1988, p. 96; "Earthshaker," *The Economist*, March 26, 1988, p. 31. Although the range of the Prithvi in its present configuration is less than the amount stipulated by the Missile Technology Control Regime, its large payload capability affords the possibility of reducing warhead weight, thereby extending the missile's range.

21. Tyler Marshall, "India Launches Its First Space Satellite," *Los Angeles Times*, July 19, 1980 (950 miles); "India Becomes Sixth Country to Put Satellite in Orbit," *Washington Post*, July 18, 1980 (950 miles); "India's Rocket Meets Military Ambitions," *New Scientist*, August 26, 1982 (1550 miles); Noel Robbins, "Experts Say Satellite Could Be Turned Into Nuclear Missile," UPI, PM Cycle, April 18, 1983 (1550 miles).

22. "Satellite Know-How Has Military Potential," *Asian Defense Journal*, July 1983, p. 92. It is usually assumed that the third and fourth stages of the rocket could be made into a warhead, permitting a payload in excess of the 1,100 lbs. pounds specified by the Missile Technology Control Regime.

23. The SLV-3 has successfully launched a 75 lb. satellite (1980) and a 180 lb. satellite (1983) into near-earth orbits. See Jerrold F. Elkin and Brian Fredericks, "Military Applications of India's Space Program," *Air University Review*, May-June 1983; "Satellite Launcher Directory," *Flight International*, January 11, 1986, p. 32; "India's Launch Vehicle Program Moves Ahead," *Space World*, December 1983.

24. The Augmented Satellite Launch Vehicle (ASLV) will reportedly have the capability to put a 330-lb. satellite into low-earth orbit. Its first test flight in March 1987 was a failure. A second launch, scheduled for June 1988, is to carry a Rohini satellite with a remote sensing system. See "Rocket Set for 2d Development Test Flight," Dehli Domestic Service, 0630 GMT, 22 May 1988, in *FBIS/NES*, May 24 1988; "Heavy Indian Rocket Fails First Test," *International Herald Tribune*, March 25, 1987; "ASLV-2 Set for 1988," *Flight International*, May 16, 1987, p. 44. Payload figures for the ASLV assume the rocket has been modified to carry a missile payload in a non-orbital trajectory.

25. The Polar Satellite Launch Vehicle (PSLV) is currently under development and is to be ready for use in the late 1990s. Reportedly it will be capable of lifting a 2,200-lb. satellite into a 560-mile polar orbit. See Jerrold F. Elkin and Brian Fredericks, "Military Applications of India's Space Program," *Air University Review* (May-June 1983); "Satellite Launcher Directory," *Flight International*, January 11, 1986, p. 32; "India's Launch Vehicle Program Moves Ahead," *Space World*, December 1983.

There is a report that India is also developing a Geo-Synchronous Satellite Launch Vehicle (GSLV) with a capability to place a 2.5-ton satellite in a geostationary orbit. This rocket is in an early development stage. See "India Goes For Hi-Tech Launcher" *News India*, February 19, 1988.

Chapter III:
Asia

Developments in Asia related to the proliferation of nuclear weapons during 1987 and early 1988 were particularly disturbing. The nuclear competition between India and Pakistan intensified, evidence emerged of Taiwan's renewed interest in moving towards a nuclear weapons capability, and a new study revealed that South Korea had engaged in nuclear weapons-related activities until 1978, several years after it supposedly abandoned its nuclear weapons program under U.S. pressure.

India and Pakistan. Between late 1986 and mid-1988, Pakistan almost certainly crossed the nuclear weapons threshold in the limited sense that it acquired the essentials for a small number of nuclear weapons, while India, which conducted its first and only nuclear test in 1974, declared that it was reconsidering the stance it has taken since that date against building nuclear arms.

For the moment, both remain in the early stages of nuclearization, with India's program by far the more extensive. Neither nation has deployed a nuclear force, and, indeed, neither may possess a completely fabricated nuclear device. It appears, however, that both have all of the essentials needed to manufacture atomic bombs and to deliver them by aircraft during any crisis lasting more than several weeks.

Momentum is building, moreover, toward further nuclearization. A critical factor is that both nations appear to be striving to accumulate nuclear weapons material free from non-proliferation controls. Thus, even if their nuclear weapons programs remain undeclared, the number of weapons available to each side will steadily increase in the months and years ahead. By 1991, Pakistan could have as many as 15 Hiroshima-sized devices, while India could have produced more than 100.

If current trends persist—including the on-going tensions between the two states, which some observers feared might lead to war in early 1987—it is likely that these capabilities will continue to grow, and there is reasonable cause for concern that momentum will build for integrating nuclear armaments into the armed forces of both nations and for conducting tests. Indeed, it is possible that an open-ended nuclear arms race could ensue unless Indo-Pakistani relations improve and the threats posed by their respective nuclear programs are reduced through the adoption of mutual confidence-building measures or related strategies. In the first half of 1988, as tensions between the two states remained high, prospects for such a rapprochement in the near term were not promising. (India and Pakistan are discussed in detail in subsequent sections of this chapter.)

The Koreas. Nuclear developments on the Korean Peninsula will also bear watching, although for now there is no publicly available evidence suggesting that either South Korea, which ratified the Non-Proliferation Treaty in 1975, or North Korea, which joined the pact in 1985, is pursuing the development of nuclear weapons. In the early 1970s, however, South Korea is known to have initiated a nuclear weapons program.[1] While it has been widely believed that Seoul ended this effort after acceding to the pact, a detailed new study of South Korean nuclear activities, based on interviews with former U.S. officials, states that Seoul continued weapons-related activities through 1978, raising questions about its commitment to the treaty, at least during the tenure of President Park Chung Hee.[2] Some senior civilian South Korean officials, according to the study, still harbor an interest in acquiring a nuclear weapons option.[3]

In 1984-1985, South Korea and Canada held discussions on Canada's extracting plutonium from spent South Korean reactor fuel, apparently for the purpose of recycling the plutonium as a fuel in a new power reactor Canada was to supply to Seoul. According to one account, South Korea was in fact seeking to obtain detailed technical data on plutonium extraction. Intervention by the United States, however, led Canada to end the talks.[4]

North Korea's decision to ratify the NPT in 1985 is believed to be the result of Soviet pressure initiated at U.S. urging.[5] Apparently in late 1984, Washington became concerned that a large unsafeguarded research reactor that North Korea was building at Yong Byon might be the first stage of a nuclear-weapons development program. The reactor was unusually large, given the early stage of North Korea's nuclear energy and research program, apparently in the thirty-megawatt range, and was a natural-uranium/graphite unit, an out-of-date design, but one well suited to a clandestine nuclear-weapons development effort. In early 1985, U.S. non-proliferation aides quietly raised the matter with their Soviet counterparts, but received no response until the announcement of North Korea's ratification of the non-proliferation pact.

If either of the Koreas were to acquire the capability to extract plutonium from spent reactor fuel, nuclear tensions would intensify significantly. Any separated plutonium would have to be placed under (International Atomic Energy Agency) safeguards (since this would be required by the NPT), but the possibility would remain that the country accumulating the plutonium might abrogate its NPT commitments or withdraw from the treaty and rapidly manufacture nuclear weapons with the material, a scenario the other regional party would have to take seriously.[6] Relations between the two Koreas have been tense in recent years, but appear to be undergoing a modest improvement.[7]

Japan. While Japan unquestionably has the capacity to produce nuclear weapons and is developing sizable reprocessing and enrichment capabilities, the strong domestic opposition to nuclear weapons, resulting from Japan's history as the first victim of nuclear attack, excludes it as a proliferation threat at least for the present. It is conceivable, however, that were North or South Korea or Taiwan to acquire such weapons, Japanese attitudes might change. (A new U.S.-Japan agreement for nuclear cooperation, which triggered controversy in the U.S. Congress, is discussed briefly in Chapter VII.)

The People's Republic of China. The activities of the People's Republic of China are also critically important to the risk of further proliferation in Asia. China has been a nuclear-weapon state since 1964, when it tested its first nuclear device. Through the 1970s, its policy was not to oppose the spread of such weapons to additional countries, which it saw as a means of diminishing the power of the United States and the Soviet Union. Indeed, during the early 1980s, there were repeated reports that China had disregarded international norms by making sales of nuclear materials to such countries as South Africa, India, and Argentina, without requiring them to place the imports under IAEA inspection.[8] From 1982 to 1984, several press accounts, usually quoting anonymous U.S. government sources, reported that China was aiding Pakistan's efforts to acquire nuclear arms by providing it with nuclear-weapons design information and technical assistance in completing an unsafeguarded uranium-enrichment plant, potentially capable of producing weapons-grade material.[9] Against this background, the Reagan Administration suspended the talks it had initiated with Beijing in mid-1981 on an agreement for cooperation in the field of nuclear energy.

In mid-1983, China began a dramatic shift in its posture, and the U.S.-China talks were renewed. In January 1984, China joined the IAEA and subsequently advised the United States that in the future it would require IAEA safe-guards on its nuclear exports to non-nuclear-weapon states. In a series of statements beginning that month, top Chinese leaders declared China's firm commitment to non-proliferation. Premier Zhao Ziyang stated in an address to the Sixth National People's Congress in May 1984, for example, that China does "not engage in nuclear proliferation by helping other countries to develop nuclear weapons."[10] Based on these developments, a nuclear trade agreement was initialed in Beijing during President Ronald Reagan's April 1984 visit.

The administration did not submit the accord for the required review by Congress until July 1985, over a year later, reportedly because of concerns that Chinese nuclear aid to Pakistan was continuing.[11] After further talks, however, China agreed to implement its non-proliferation policy, according to U.S.officials, "in a manner consistent with basic non-proliferation practices common to the United States and other suppliers," an official U.S. circumlocution apparently intended to signify that any Chinese assistance to Pakistan had been halted.[12] China has repeatedly denied that anything beyond normal scientific exchanges ever took place.[13] In the fall of 1985, China also announced it would voluntarily place some of its civilian nuclear installations under IAEA safeguards, matching a step previously taken by all other nuclear-weapon states.

The U.S.-China agreement, the first U.S. nuclear accord with a nuclear-weapon state that is not an ally, went into effect in December 1985 after a lengthy congressional review.[14] Through a joint resolution, Congress required that before a license could be issued for any nuclear exports to China under the agreement, the President—after further negotiations with Beijing—would have to certify to Congress that the provisions of the accord would be "effective" in ensuring that U.S. nuclear exports were used exclusively for peaceful purposes.[15]

The pact itself provided only for "visits" and "exchanges of information" with respect to U.S. nuclear exports, but

not for the full range of accounting and surveillance procedures akin to those used by the IAEA. The Reagan Administration made clear that it considered the agreement sufficient and would not demand such iron-clad procedures from
Beijing in any further negotiations. Congress, fearing that
China would back away from the accord, rejected a legislative proposal that would have made U.S. exports condition-
al on China's accepting verification procedures equivalent to
those of the IAEA.[16]

U.S. and Chinese negotiators reached an agreement on
the details of the visitation procedures under the agreement
in June 1987, but these details were not revealed, and the
understanding had not been submitted to Congress as of
June 1988.[17]

In April 1986, China announced a drastic cutback in its
nuclear power program, apparently because of a shortage of
foreign exchange.[18] This has effectively precluded any major
U.S. nuclear sales to China for the time being, rendering the
verification question moot, at least temporarily. In the
meantime, under its offer to accept safeguards voluntarily
on some of its civilian nuclear plants, China has announced
that its largest nuclear power project, at Daya Bay near
Hong Kong, will be placed under the IAEA system.

In mid-September 1986, China signed a nuclear cooperation accord with Pakistan. The agreement provides that all
equipment and materials supplied by China will be covered
by IAEA safeguards, but the accord does not require as a
condition of supply that Pakistan place all of its nuclear installations under the IAEA system. (The United States and,
at least for the moment, all other Western nuclear supplier
countries have made such comprehensive coverage a condition for major new nuclear transfers.) It remains possible
that China will use the accord as a cover so that it can offer
technical assistance—for which safeguards are not apparently required—for more sensitive aspects of Pakistan's nuclear program.[19]

A new development of concern is the possibility that
Beijing might transfer nuclear-capable missiles to Pakistan.

China has transferred the conventionally armed inter-mediate-range CSS-2 missile to Saudi Arabia and has plans to offer a conventionally armed medium-range missile, known as the M-9, on the international market. (See Chapter II.) Whether China's pledge not to assist Pakistan in developing nuclear weapons extends to the withholding of such advanced delivery systems is not known. With its still limited nuclear weapons capabilities, Pakistan, in any event, will probably not be able to equip any missile it might possess with a nuclear warhead for many years, unless it receives outside assistance.

*

Although in previous volumes of this series Taiwan was not considered to have an ongoing interest in developing a nuclear weapons capability, events during 1987-1988 suggested that it may still harbor nuclear ambitions. These developments are discussed below.

Taiwan. During 1987, according to U.S. officials quoted in the press, Taiwan secretly began construction of a small-scale plutonium extraction unit. In March 1988, under U.S. pressure, it agreed to halt work on the facility—probably a laboratory with a number of radiologically shielded "hot cells"—and to dismantle a 40-megawatt research reactor supplied by Canada, which was delivered in 1969. U.S. officials suspected that Taiwan intended to extract plutonium from the reactor's spent fuel clandestinely, apparently as part of an effort either to develop nuclear weapons—if, indeed, a final decision to pursue this course had been taken by Taiwan's leaders—or at least to create the option to build such arms at a later time.[20]

Given the small size of the plutonium separation unit, Taiwan would probably have needed several years to acquire sufficient plutonium for a nuclear device (usually assumed to require 11 to 17.6 pounds—5 to 8 kilograms—of the material). Assuming that Taiwan expected to obtain the plutonium secretly, it would also have had to circumvent

IAEA safeguards covering the Canadian reactor's spent fuel.[21] U.S. officials stated that Taiwan had not violated IAEA safeguards covering the spent fuel, however, indicating that no plutonium extraction had taken place.[22]

Taiwan formally advised the IAEA that it was closing the Canadian-supplied reactor, located at the Institute for Nuclear Energy Research at Lung Tan, for "economic" reasons and denied that it had deviated from its commitments under the NPT, which it had ratified in 1970, or from its policy of pursuing nuclear energy exclusively for peaceful purposes.[23]

U.S. officials, however, viewed the clandestine construction of a plutonium separation, or "reprocessing," laboratory as a violation of Taiwan's assurances that it would not pursue research in this field, which it had given Washington in 1976. The assurances had been offered after an almost identical episode that year, when the United States had discovered that work on a secret plutonium extraction unit was under way—an episode that itself had been preceded by numerous attempts by Taiwan dating back to 1969 to obtain a reprocessing capability.[24] In a diplomatic note dated September 17, 1976, Taiwan had declared at U.S. insistence that "the government of the Republic of China has no intention whatsoever to develop nuclear weapons or a nuclear explosive device, or to engage in any activities related to reprocessing purposes."[25]

As late as 1977, however, Washington remained concerned that Taipei was continuing to engage in activities relevant to nuclear arms, although no details have been publicly revealed.[26] In addition to its diplomatic initiatives, from 1975 to 1978, the United States reportedly sought to thwart Taiwan's nuclear ambitions by mounting a covert operation that led to the theft of its weapons plans and files and by attempting to choke off its efforts to purchase sensitive items.[27]

Although Taipei had agreed to dismantle the plutonium laboratory involved in the 1976 episode, it continued to operate the Canadian-supplied reactor. By 1988, it had apparently accumulated 93.5 tons (85 metric tons) of spent fuel from the unit, containing roughly 190 pounds (85 kilograms) of plutonium, enough (if it were separated) for between ten and seventeen weapons using the standard assumption that 11 to 17.6 pounds (5 to 8 kilograms) of the material are needed per device.[28] While this fuel is subject to periodic inspection by the IAEA, as an added precaution, Washington has sought since the Carter Administration to work out arrangements for bringing the spent fuel to the United States for permanent storage.[29] After lengthy discussions with Taipei on financing and other issues, Washington announced in December 1985 that it was beginning the process of transferring 27.5 tons (25 metric tons) to the United States. The program was slowed during 1986 by a U.S. lawsuit challenging the spent fuel shipments on environmental grounds. Arrangements to bring an additional 66 tons (60 metric tons)— apparently the remainder of the spent fuel from the reactor—to the United States were announced in November 1987.

It is not clear why Taiwan decided in 1987 to reactivate a clandestine plutonium extraction program. The decision was made amidst growing concerns about the country's future security, fueled by Washington's increasing ties, even under the conservative Reagan Administration, to the People's Republic of China and the concomitant weakening of American commitment to Taiwan's independence.[30] On the other hand, the decision to build the clandestine plutonium laboratory was taken at a time when Taiwan's president, Chiang Ching-kuo, was successfully pursuing a policy of rapprochement with the mainland. In principle, this relaxation of tensions should have lessened Taiwan's security concerns vis-à-vis the Beijing government, which has pledged to seek reunification only through peaceful means, reducing the possible need for a Taiwanese nuclear deterrent.

Chiang may have reasoned, however, that as Beijing pursued its on-going liberalization of its economy and political structures, the rationale for an independent non-communist Taiwan might erode, leading to a still further reduction of U.S. support for Taiwanese autonomy. Not wishing to see

Taiwan absorbed into the People's Republic as Hong Kong will be in 1997—albeit under special arrangements that will protect its democratic institutions and free-market economic system—Chiang may have viewed nuclear arms, not as a military deterrent, but as a symbol of Taiwan's permanence as an independent entity. Nuclear weapons might serve as a token of nationhood that would make the absorption of Taiwan "unthinkable," much as the mainland's absorption of a country that enjoyed widespread diplomatic recognition would be unacceptable in today's international climate.

It is also possible that the decision to conduct limited plutonium extraction was triggered, ironically, by the U.S. spent-fuel take-back plan. For a variety of technical reasons, it is far easier to extract plutonium from the Lung Tan reactor's spent fuel than from the spent fuel of Taiwan's power reactors.[31] Moreover, because it is far less irradiated than power-reactor spent fuel, the research reactor's spent fuel contains weapons-grade plutonium (i.e., plutonium that consists mostly of the isotope plutonium-239), whereas the plutonium contained in power-reactor spent fuel, though usable for nuclear weapons, is less desirable (since it contains more than 10 percent of the isotope plutonium-240). If Taiwan's underlying objective in building the secret reprocessing unit was to gain experience in plutonium extraction in order to support a possible future nuclear weapons program, Taiwanese nuclear aides may have reasoned that they would soon lose access to the spent fuel that was best suited to this purpose. Accordingly, when the last obstacles to the spent-fuel take-back program were removed at the end of 1986 with a settlement of the U.S. environmental lawsuit, Taiwan may have launched construction of the clandestine reprocessing unit on the theory that it was about to forfeit its last chance to conduct hands-on experiments with weapons-quality material.

Chiang died on January 13, 1988, but the reprocessing initiative continued under his immediate successor, Lee Teng-hui—possibly because of bureaucratic momentum—until blocked by U.S. intervention in March. Whether Taiwan's

new leadership will retain Chiang's apparently strong interest in acquiring plutonium and whether it will seek to obtain
the material by other means are issues that will bear close
monitoring.

India

Deteriorating relations with Pakistan, which some feared might lead to the outbreak of hostilities in the winter of 1986-1987, formed the backdrop for Indian nuclear activities in succeeding months. As Pakistan apparently crossed the nuclear weapons threshold by acquiring the essentials for its first nuclear weapons during 1987 and early 1988, the government of Prime Minister Rajiv Gandhi responded by continuing its strategy of recent years, quietly expanding India's nuclear weapons capabilities, while maintaining an ambiguous public stance on the country's nuclear intentions. By mid-1988, though neither India nor Pakistan had deployed nuclear weapons or announced that it possessed them, a system of undeclared nuclear deterrence, based on the recognized capabilities of both states, was emerging on the Indian Subcontinent.

Background

The dynamics of the incipient Indo-Pakistani nuclear-arms race are complex. As in the case of U.S.-Soviet nuclear relations, Indian and Pakistani decision-making on this issue takes place against a backdrop of intense mutual suspicion and domestic political considerations, as well as in relation to specific developments in the nuclear programs of the two countries. Centuries old Hindu-Muslim antagonisms, for example, remain a factor in this ultra-modern realm, even among the governing elites in both countries, and the three wars fought between the two states since independence from the British in 1947 have left a legacy of deep distrust.[1]

Pakistan's dismemberment in the 1971 Indo-Pakistani War, in which the independent country of Bangladesh was created out of territory that had formerly been East Pakistan, left India by far the dominant power in the region. India's modernization and expansion of its conventional forces in the past fifteen years have heightened its military supremacy—it is generally thought to have a several fold advantage in military equipment and man-power over Pakistan—while its size and its economic development during this period have led inevitably to its political dominance in regional affairs.

Post-1971 Pakistani foreign policy, including new links with other Islamic countries (especially the oil rich members of the Organization of Petroleum Exporting Countries—OPEC) and growing ties to the United States in the aftermath of the 1979 Soviet invasion of Afghanistan, has sought to counterbalance India's regional pre-eminence. But initiatives seen by Pakistan as essential to avoid becoming a mere satellite of its eastern neighbor have been perceived in New Delhi as unfriendly challenges to India's natural leadership role in the Subcontinent. Even domestic political unrest in both nations is seen partly through the prism of these mutual antagonisms, as each accuses the other of being the unseen hand behind anti-government agitation.

While some policymakers in both countries, seemingly including Pakistani President Mohammad Zia ul-Haq and Indian Prime Minister Gandhi, favor improved relations, other factions remain intensely nationalistic and hostile to rapprochement. This lack of consensus has restricted the maneuvering room of both leaders, leading them to be cautious in their efforts to improve bilateral ties and making accommodation in the nuclear sphere particularly difficult.

The histories of both nations' nuclear programs also critically affect the current state of their nuclear relations. In retrospect, it appears that the groundwork for an Indian nuclear weapons program was laid in the 1950s.[2] Nonetheless, until the mid-1960s, India's public nuclear stance was one of unequivocally rejecting the development of nuclear arms. In late 1964, however, shortly after China's first nuclear test and at a time when India's defeat in its 1962 border war with China was still vivid, Prime Minister Lal Bahadur Shastri indicated that India might develop nuclear explosives—ostensibly for peaceful purposes, such as civil excavation. Despite further advances in the Chinese nuclear weapons program, Indira Gandhi, who took over as Prime Minister in 1966, downplayed the nuclear weapons issue until late 1969, when the development of "peaceful nuclear explosives" was again openly declared to be an objective of India's nuclear program. (In 1968, India declined to sign the Nuclear Non-Proliferation Treaty, which would have required it to renounce nuclear explosives and to place all of its nuclear installations under international inspection. The decision allowed India to retain the option of developing nuclear arms.)

In May 1974, while Mrs. Gandhi was still prime minister, India conducted its first—and only—nuclear test, which it referred to as a peaceful nuclear explosion. The failure of India to respond directly to the Chinese nuclear weapons program for a decade and the fact that after the 1974 test Mrs. Gandhi did not proceed to build a nuclear arsenal suggest that the test was intended as a political gesture, aimed at enhancing India's international stature, rather than as a military response to a perceived nuclear threat from China. Only since the late 1970s, when confronted with Pakistan's growing nuclear weapons program, have Indian leaders openly considered exercising the nation's nuclear weapons option.[3]

In 1972, following Pakistan's defeat in the 1971 Indo-Pakistani War, Prime Minister Zulfikar Ali Bhutto is believed to have launched Pakistan on the path to nuclear arms.[4] At this point, two years prior to India's test (though after India had reiterated its interest in peaceful nuclear explosives), Pakistan may have been seeking to offset its conventional military inferiority, as well as to counter India's emerging nuclear weapons potential.

Pakistan has consistently denied that it is building nuclear weapons and has repeatedly asserted that its nuclear program is entirely peaceful. The program, parts of which have been shrouded in secrecy, has relied heavily on technology, equipment, and materials imported from the West, often illegally.[5] The cornerstone of the program is a uranium enrichment plant (a facility theoretically capable of upgrading natural uranium to weapons-grade) located at Kahuta. The plant was discovered by the United States in the late 1970s, when the facility was still under construction, and was subsequently acknowledged by the Pakistani government.[6] Pakistan claimed that it was building the costly facility to supply low-enriched uranium fuel for future nuclear power stations. But construction of the enrichment plant was so premature by normal civilian nuclear energy standards that the facility is presumed by India, the United States, and other observers to be intended for the development of nuclear arms.[7] Since disclosure of the plant, Indian concerns over Pakistani nuclear activities have been exacerbated by repeated revelations of Pakistani nuclear smuggling operations, reports of Pakistani efforts to design nuclear arms and test their components, and the early 1984 announcement that the Kahuta plant had begun producing enriched uranium—though not weapons-grade material.[8]

Indira Gandhi, who, after being ousted as prime minister in India's 1977 general elections, returned to power in 1980, tended to minimize the Pakistani nuclear threat in her public utterances. In early 1980, however, she declared that she would "not hesitate from carrying out nuclear explosions

. . . or whatever is necessary in the national interest," and in 1981 and again in 1983 it was reported that India was maintaining a nuclear test site in a state of readiness.[9] In addition, several reports suggested that Mrs. Gandhi had authorized work on improved nuclear weapon designs and, possibly, the fabrication of nuclear weapon components.[10]

Moreover, until her assassination in October 1984, Mrs. Gandhi quietly enlarged India's actual capability to produce nuclear arms and, despite strong pressure from the United States, refused to place the key installations involved under International Atomic Energy Agency (IAEA) safeguards—in effect, keeping them free of legal constraints that might limit their use for nuclear weapons. The facilities, some of which were completed after Rajiv Gandhi became prime minister following his mother's death, now form the backbone of India's nuclear weapons potential and remain outside the IAEA system. They include two nuclear power reactors (Madras I and II, commissioned in 1983 and 1985, respectively), the Dhruva research reactor (commissioned in 1985), the refurbished Trombay reprocessing plant (reopened in late 1983 or early 1984) and the Tarapur reprocessing plant (which began operating at full capacity in 1982).[11] Together, these facilities provide India with the theoretical capability to manufacture nearly thirty nuclear weapons annually. Although actual production is likely to be considerably lower, India's nuclear potential has greatly increased in comparison to the country's 1974 nuclear capability of one bomb per year.[12]

In the months preceding Mrs. Gandhi's death, nuclear tensions with Pakistan increased, spurred by new revelations of Pakistani nuclear smuggling and of reports that China had given it nuclear-weapon-design information.[13] These anxieties were heightened by press accounts stating that Mrs. Gandhi was being urged to launch a pre-emptive attack against Pakistan's Kahuta enrichment plant.[14] Overall Indo-Pakistani relations also deteriorated seriously, as India accused Pakistan of fomenting unrest by Sikh nationalist groups in the Punjab region and of making incursions into

Kashmir, which led to a series of border clashes. Against this background, in mid-October 1984, Mrs. Gandhi departed from her earlier muted statements, and in an address to a group of army commanders, declared that the Pakistani nuclear program was "a qualitatively new phenomenon in our security environment," which must add a "new dimension" to India's defense planning.[15]

On October 31, Indira Gandhi was assassinated by Sikh members of her bodyguard, and Rajiv Gandhi was appointed prime minister. He was confirmed in the post after a landslide victory in the December 28, 1984, general election. By April 1985, he had taken his mother's expressions of concern about the Pakistani nuclear program a step further. In a series of interviews and statements that continued for the next eight months, he openly accused Pakistan of seeking to build nuclear weapons and declared that this development was causing India to reconsider its position against nuclear arming.[16] Indeed, in a June 5 interview in Paris, he hinted that India had already made the components for nuclear arms and, if it chose to, could assemble such weapons rapidly:

In principle we are opposed to the idea of becoming a nuclear power. We could have done so for the past 10 or 11 years, but we have not. *If we decided to become a nuclear power, it would take a few weeks or a few months.*
Q. Are you contemplating this?
A. Not yet . . .
Q. . . . Will you or will you not take the decision to produce nuclear weapons?
A. We have not yet reached a decision, but we have already worked on it.[17]

India's verbal attacks against the Pakistani nuclear program took a more ominous turn in early August 1985, following the report on American television that Pakistan had recently detonated the non-nuclear portion of a nuclear device, a significant milestone toward nuclear arming.[18] On August 8, following a series of parliamentary calls for action, Indian Atomic Energy Commission Chairman Raja

Ramanna announced the start-up of the Dhruva research reactor. Rather than merely extolling India's achievement in commissioning one of the world's largest civilian non-power reactors, the announcement carefully underscored the fact that the plant would give India the ability to produce plutonium from domestic technology and fuel—a none-too-subtle declaration that India had a new source of nuclear weapons material free from all non-proliferation controls.[19] The announcement, which was widely publicized in Pakistan, appeared to be a clear warning that India's considerable nuclear capabilities would guarantee it superiority in any regional nuclear arms race.[20] (As described below, the plant has been plagued with technical problems and only began to operate at full capacity in 1988.)

Despite these growing tensions on nuclear issues, a slow thaw in overall Indo-Pakistani relations was evident throughout much of 1985. The warming trend reached its peak on December 17, when President Zia visited New Delhi and reached agreement with Prime Minister Gandhi on a step-by-step process for normalizing relations, including new discussions to end border clashes over the disputed Siachen Glacier region in Kashmir, the expansion of trade links, and the resumption of talks on draft peace treaties.[21] On the nuclear front, the two leaders announced that they had reached an agreement not to attack each other's nuclear installations. In late September 1985, rumors had surfaced in Pakistan that India was about to attack the Kahuta enrichment plant, a plan supposedly conceived by Indira Gandhi but postponed after her death.[22] The no-attack understanding, which was to be formalized at a later date, did not restrict Indian or Pakistani nuclear activities as such. Nonetheless, it appeared to be a cautious first step in this direction, raising hopes that more comprehensive measures might follow.

The early months of 1986 were notable for a virtual absence of Indian verbal attacks against the Pakistani nuclear program. Such attacks had been prominent throughout 1985. The anticipated process of overall normalization, however, soon bogged down, largely, it seems, because of domestic political difficulties on both sides. Most prominent were the resurgence of Sikh unrest in India's Punjab state and the tumultuous return to Pakistan in April 1986 of Benazir Bhutto, daughter of Pakistan's former prime minister, which led to a series of anti-government disturbances throughout the spring and summer. With each country accusing the other of being the unseen hand behind these and other domestic challenges, the efforts to normalize relations stalled.

New plutonium source. Against this background, India significantly advanced its nuclear weapons capabilities by obtaining for the first time separated plutonium that was totally free from any external non-proliferation restrictions. The plutonium had been produced in the spent fuel of the Madras I nuclear power reactor, which was inaugurated in July 1983, and beginning in the second half of 1985 was separated at the Tarapur reprocessing plant, nearly 1,000 miles away.[23] (Ironically, the Dhruva reactor, whose plutonium production capabilities had been highlighted at its inauguration, had experienced severe operating problems that would not be corrected for many months.)

At the time, India appeared to possess ample stocks of plutonium for its energy research and development needs, but this material was subject to non-proliferation restrictions of one type or another.[24] Thus it is difficult to comprehend why New Delhi would have gone to the considerable cost of obtaining unrestricted plutonium unless it intended to use the material for the one purpose to which India's other plutonium could not be put—the manufacture of nuclear arms. While the extraction of the Madras I plutonium does not necessarily mean that the Gandhi government had decided to build nuclear weapons, it does provide strong evidence that, at a minimum, Gandhi was taking steps to ensure that India would have the option to do so rapidly if circumstances warranted. For some years to come, the twin Madras I and Madras II power reactors are likely to remain the most important potential sources of plutonium for an Indian nuclear weapons program.[25]

Developments: Increasing Tensions and Growing Capabilities

It appears that between late 1986 and mid-1988, a change of historic proportions in India's security environment took place, as Pakistan acquired the essentials for a rudimentary nuclear deterrent of perhaps three to six nuclear devices. During this period, India responded to Pakistan's nuclear advances by continuing the strategies that, except for the brief thaw in relations with Pakistan in late 1985 and early 1986, had been staples of Indian policy since early in Rajiv's tenure.

First, India continued to strengthen its own nuclear weapons capabilities, while keeping its nuclear posture ambiguous.[26] Second, though it avoided major hostilities with Pakistan and pursued talks on a range of bilateral issues—whose promise waxed and waned over the months—India tended to deal with its western neighbor confrontationally, a stance that stemmed in large part from New Delhi's belief that Islamabad was actively aiding Sikh separatists in India's Punjab state. Third, in keeping with this hard-line stance, New Delhi rejected Pakistani overtures on possible nuclear arms control measures. At the same time, it denounced each Pakistani nuclear advance and pressed the United States, as Pakistan's principal patron, to check the latter's nuclear ambitions.

In conjunction with these policies, India also pursued a major build-up of its conventional forces. This has confirmed India as the pre-eminent military power in the region, but has undoubtedly added to the security concerns that have prompted Pakistan's quest for nuclear arms.

New capabilities. In November 1986, a U.S. press report quoted American intelligence sources as stating that Pakistan had produced weapons-grade uranium for the first time at its Kahuta uranium enrichment plant.[27] In effect, Pakistan was on the verge of obtaining the essentials for its first nuclear device.

In less than twenty-four hours, the chairman of the Indian Atomic Energy Commission, Raja Ramanna, responded to the new report by declaring that India had also mastered the uranium enrichment process and could enrich the material to "any level."[28] Subsequent reports indicated that India had built an experimental enrichment facility not subject to IAEA safeguards at the Bhabha Atomic Research Center. The facility used the gas centrifuge method of enrichment—the same technology as Pakistan used in the Kahuta facility—and had achieved a relatively modest 2 percent-enrichment level, far short of the 93 percent-enrichment level used in nuclear weapons.[29] (Indian officials denied reports that a large-scale enrichment facility was under construction in southern India.)[30] In addition to demonstrating India's considerable technical capabilities, Ramanna's announcement revealed New Delhi's acute sensitivity to nuclear developments next door.

How important the new capability may be to India's nuclear weapons potential is not clear. India, as noted earlier, is able to produce large quantities of plutonium for nuclear weapons and does not require highly enriched uranium for this purpose. Nor does it require enriched uranium to fuel its power reactors, most of which use unenriched, natural uranium fuel; only the twin Tarapur reactors use low-enriched uranium, but India has a contract with France to supply fuel for those units.[31]

Ramanna did not offer an explanation as to why India had decided to pursue this technology, but it is possible that domestic politics played a role. Uranium enrichment has long been considered one of the most challenging—and therefore one of the most prestigious—parts of the nuclear "fuel cycle." Some Indian politicians have accused the Gandhi government of falling behind Pakistan by not mastering this technology, although in reality, there is no question that even in the absence of an enrichment capability, India's nuclear infrastructure is far more extensive and advanced than its neighbor's. Gandhi and Ramanna may thus have been seeking to silence these critics by developing the experimental enrichment unit.

In addition, it is known that highly enriched uranium is used in U.S. thermonuclear (hydrogen) weapons and may be preferred over plutonium for this purpose. India is said to be doing research on these advanced weapons and may have wanted an enrichment capability for this reason.[32] Enriched uranium is also used to fuel nuclear-powered submarines. As discussed below, India is known to be interested in these, as well, although for the time being it will apparently rely on the Soviet Union to supply fuel for this purpose.[33]

From late 1986 through mid-1988, India also appeared to be working actively to add to its stocks of unsafeguarded plutonium. In a March 1987 interview, an unnamed nuclear official at the Bhabha Atomic Research Center made clear that the weapons potential of the material was well understood. "We have the plutonium to manufacture as many bombs as the country needs," he stated. "What is required is the political will to do so."[34]

During this period, Indian nuclear aides labored to bring the Dhruva reactor up to its full 100-megawatt capacity. The unit was shut down for ten months after its commissioning in August 1985, restarted briefly in October 1986, and in December of that year was operating at one-fourth its rated capacity.[35] By May of 1988, however, it was fully operational.[36] The unsafeguarded reactor can produce 55 pounds (25 kilograms) of plutonium annually, enough (after it is separated) for three to five weapons using the standard assumption that 11 to 17.6 pounds (5 to 8 kilograms) of the material are needed per device.[37] According to the 1986-1987 annual report of India's Department of Atomic Energy (which uses the nuclear industry term "reprocessing" to refer to the plutonium extraction process), "plans for reprocessing spent fuel from the new reactor, Dhruva, are being prepared."[38]

India's plutonium stocks will continue to grow at a substantial rate in the years ahead. Indeed, in a May 1988 interview, M. R. Srinivasan, the head of the Department of

Atomic Energy and chairman of the Indian Atomic Energy Commission, declared that India will acquire tons of the material over the next decade.[39] This would be enough for hundreds of nuclear weapons, although he and other Indian nuclear aides have stated that the material is intended for India's nuclear power and research program. See Tables 1 and 2 for a detailed estimate of India's plutonium production and nuclear weapons potential.[40]

Bilateral Antagonisms. As India pursued these various expansions of its nuclear capabilities, New Delhi's relations with Islamabad continued to deteriorate. Bilateral tensions seriously increased in December 1986 and January 1987, when major Indian military exercises near the Pakistani border, known as Operation Brass Tacks, led to a series of mobilizations and counter-mobilizations that some feared might lead to the outbreak of major hostilities. The episode was resolved after talks, hastily initiated by President Zia and Prime Minister Gandhi, led to an agreement on a series of mutual troop withdrawals.[41] Nonetheless, the confrontation once again demonstrated the volatility of Indo-Pakistani relations, which form the backdrop for the nuclear competition between the two states and significantly increase its dangers.

In ensuing months, relations between the two countries continued to be strained. Skirmishing between Indian and Pakistani troops continued in the Siachen Glacier region of Kashmir; unrest in Punjab state forced Prime Minister Gandhi to reimpose central government control, amidst accusations that Pakistan was aiding and providing sanctuary for Sikh extremist elements; and Pakistan, in turn, accused India of contributing to sporadic rioting and terror bombings throughout the country.[42]

A. Q. Khan and Zia interviews. In March 1987, nuclear frictions were seriously exacerbated by a series of provocative statements on Pakistan's nuclear advances attributed to top Pakistani nuclear scientist A. Q. Khan and President Zia. In a controversial interview with Indian journalist Kuldip Nayar published on March 1, Khan, the head of Pa-

Table 1
Potential Annual Plutonium (Pu) Production in India

Facility (1st yr. on line)	Max. Pu Output/yr. Max. No. of Weapons*	Restrictions on Use of Pu	Pu Available for Weapons 1/1/87
Madras I (1983)	60 kgs 12 wpns	None	15–20 kgs??? <5 wpns??
Madras II (1985)	60 kgs 12 wpns	None	0
Dhruva (1985)	25 kgs 5 wpns	None	0
Total	145 kgs 29 wpns		
Cirus (1966)	9 kgs 1 wpn	May be used only for peaceful purposes under agreement with Canada (not under IAEA safeguards)	(50–100 kgs) (10–20 wpns)
Total with Cirus	154 kgs 30 wpns		65–120 kgs. 15–20 wpns.
Fast Breeder Test Reactor (1985)	Will consume more Pu than it will produce thru 1992	Same as Cirus, since fueled with Pu from Cirus.	0
Tarapur I (1969)	50 kgs	IAEA safeguards at least until 1993**	0
Tarapur II (1969)	50 kgs 10 wpns	Same as Tarapur I	0
Rajasthan I (1973	60 kgs 12 wpns	IAEA safeguards	0
Rajasthan II (1976)	60 kgs 12 wpns	IAEA safeguards	0

* Assumes maximum possible plutonium output; actual numbers likely to be considerably lower. Also assumes 5 kilograms of plutonium needed per device. For range of estimates, see Table 2.

** India has pledged to use the plutonium produced in the reactor only for fueling the reactor in the future (a fueling option known as "plutonium recycle") and has agreed to permit periodic audits and inspections by the International Atomic Energy Agency to verify that the material is not being used for military purposes. India has sometimes asserted that it is legally bound to permit IAEA safeguards to be applied to the Tarapur reactors only as long as the Indo–U.S. agreement covering the supply of the reactor is in force. The pact is due to expire in 1993. The U.S. position is that IAEA safeguards apply in perpetuity.

Table 2
Speculative Estimate of Indian Nuclear Weapons Potential Through 1992

(Cumulative Amount of Pu Available for Weapons and
Cumulative Number of Weapons*)

	1/1/1986 Lo	Hi	1987 L	H	1988 L	H	1989 L	H	1990 L	H	1991 L	H	1992 L	H	
Madras I															
	10	20?	40	80	70	140	100	200	130	260	160	320	190	380	kgs
	1	4	5	16	8	28	12	40	16	52	20	64	23	76	wpns
Madras II															
	0		30	60	60	120	90	180	120	240	150	300	180	360	kgs
	0		3	12	7	24	11	36	15	48	18	60	22	72	wpns
Dhruva															
	0		0		12	25	25	50	37	75	50	100	62	125	kgs
	0		0		1	5	3	10	4	15	6	20	7	25	wpns
Total															
	10	20	70	140	142	285	215	430	287	575	360	720	432	865	kgs
	1	4	8	28	17	57	26	86	35	115	45	144	54	173	wpns
Cirus**															
	50	100	54	109	59	118	63	127	67	136	71	145	75	154	kgs
	6	20	6	21	7	23	7	25	8	27	8	29	9	30	wpns
Total with Cirus**															
	60	120	124	249	201	403	278	557	355	711	432	865	508	1019	kgs
	7	24	15	49	25	80	34	111	44	142	54	173	63	203	wpns

* "High" assumes that maximum possible plutonium production is realized and that five kilograms of the material are used for each weapon; "low" assumes (1) that somewhat lower amounts of plutonium are produced in the reactors and that reprocessing plants operate below capacity, resulting in only 50% of the maximum possible plutonium production, and (2) that eight kilograms of material are used for each weapon. (All fractions are rounded down.)

** Plutonium from the Cirus reactor may be used only for peaceful purposes under the Indo–Canadian agreement covering the reactor; this would preclude the use of such material for nuclear weapons. There is some question as to whether India accepts this restriction today.

kistan's classified uranium enrichment program, was quoted as declaring that Pakistan had built nuclear arms. "They told us that Pakistan could never produce the bomb and they doubted my capabilities," Khan was reported as saying, "but now they know we have done it."[43]

Khan immediately denied making these statements after the interview appeared, and there is considerable uncertainty as to whether he was correctly quoted.[44] The ambiguity created by Khan's disclaimer blunted the impact of the interview somewhat, but it nonetheless caused a furor in India. Although it appears most likely that the statements attributed to the Pakistani scientist were an acute embarrassment to the Pakistani government, which has consistently denied that it is developing nuclear weapons and which at the time was seeking a renewal of economic and military assistance from the United States, Indian officials saw Khan's statements as having been specifically approved by higher Pakistani authorities, in a deliberate attempt to establish Pakistan's nuclear credentials.[45] The Indian public also appeared to take Khan's statements seriously. An opinion poll conducted shortly after the Khan interview showed that 69 percent of those interviewed believed Pakistan indeed possessed nuclear weapons and 68 percent believed India should follow suit.[46]

The impact of the Khan interview was compounded at the end of March, when President Zia, in an interview with *Time* magazine, stated that "Pakistan has the capability of building the Bomb whenever it wishes." He continued, "Once you have acquired the technology, which Pakistan has, you can do whatever you like." Zia stressed, however, that Pakistan did not intend to manufacture nuclear arms and asserted that it had not yet enriched uranium to weapons grade.[47] Zia later declared that he had been speaking only of Pakistan's broad technological capabilities, and had not meant to imply that it was pursuing an on-going nuclear weapons program.

Cautious Response. However provoked Indian policymakers may have been by the Khan and Zia interviews, in their public statements they reacted cautiously, reiterating past pronouncements that India was prepared to develop a nuclear deterrent in response to Pakistan, if necessary, but never openly declaring that this step was being taken. On March 27, 1987, Gandhi was quoted as stating, "We intend meeting President Zia's threat. We will give an adequate response." When asked what options India was considering, however, he added, "We'll keep them open at the moment. We would still like an option where we would not go nuclear. We do not want to go nuclear."[48] A month later, Indian Defense Minister K. C. Pant spoke in similarly vague terms to the lower house of India's parliament stating that "the emerging nuclear threat to us from Pakistan is forcing us to review our options," while Indian external affairs minister N. D. Tiwari declared before the upper house the same day that India would "take all necessary measures for our security" without offering any specifics.[49] Indeed, there have been no indications that the Pakistani statements resulted in a decision by India to build and deploy nuclear arms, although, as discussed below, there have been a handful of reports alleging that India has pursued this path for a number of years. Indian officials would restate this ambiguous formula frequently in subsequent months.[50]

Pressure on the U.S. New Delhi did, however, use the A. Q. Khan and Zia statements as part of a continuing campaign to press the United States to halt Pakistan's nuclear advances. In February 1987, the U.S. Congress had begun deliberations on whether to authorize a six-year $4.02 billion renewal of aid to Islamabad; Washington had initiated a massive aid program to Pakistan in 1981 after the Soviet occupation of Afghanistan. A central question in the congressional debate, which was to continue until mid-December, was whether the United States should suspend a key nonproliferation restriction, the Symington Amendment, that would otherwise prohibit aid to Islamabad because of its nuclear activities. (This issue is discussed in detail later in this chapter in the section on Pakistan. See also, Appendix G, which reviews U.S. non-proliferation restrictions on aid to Pakistan.) The Gandhi government, by publicizing throughout the year how Pakistan was progressing toward nuclear arms in defiance of U.S. policy, sought to have Washington enforce the aid cut-off so that Islamabad would be obliged either to curtail its nuclear program or lose American assistance, which would also have been to India's advantage.[51]

This overall approach had been a staple of Gandhi's nuclear policy since June 1985, when he made it a centerpiece of his visit to Washington.[52] The United States had refused to take a tough line with Islamabad in the interim, however, and in mid-April 1987, a consensus appeared to be growing in Congress in favor of a proposal by Congressman Stephen Solarz to grant Pakistan two more years of aid despite the Khan and Zia interviews. Nonetheless, India's strategy helped to keep U.S. attention focused on the Pakistani nuclear program, while deflecting possible criticism of India's own nuclear advances.

Moreover, after mid-July it appeared that Congress, in a sudden turnabout, might indeed cut off American aid to Pakistan. The apparent reversal was triggered by the July 11 arrest in Philadelphia of Arshad Pervez, a Pakistani-born Canadian, for attempting to smuggle nuclear commodities to Pakistan. Pervez's activities appeared to violate a 1985 U.S. law prohibiting aid to non-nuclear-weapon states that engage in nuclear smuggling in the United States. The sponsor of the proposal, Congressman Stephen Solarz, had been the architect of the two-year aid extension compromise of March and April, but he now declared that in light of the Pervez affair, U.S. aid to Islamabad should be suspended unless Pakistan stopped producing weapons-grade uranium, a position that appeared to have growing support on Capitol Hill. India cited Pervez's arrest as further proof of Islamabad's quest for the bomb, emphasizing that in contrast, India's own nuclear program was entirely in the open and above-board.[53] (As discussed below, however, new evidence emerged in 1987 indicating that India, too, in recent years had advanced its unsafeguarded nuclear activities through illicit nuclear purchases.)

Pakistani test ban offer. In late September, as the tide in Congress seemed to be turning against further assistance, Pakistani Prime Minister Mohammad Khan Junejo in a speech to the United Nations General Assembly proposed that India and Pakistan agree to a ban on nuclear tests.[54]

The proposal, which he had first broached with Gandhi when the two had met in June at a meeting of the South Asian Association for Regional Cooperation, appeared to be more realistic than earlier Pakistani regional nuclear arms control proposals in that it did not require the comprehensive restrictions on India's nuclear activities that New Delhi was known to find objectionable. Pakistan had previously proposed a number of comprehensive bilateral nuclear arms control options, including mutual ratification of the Nuclear Non-Proliferation Treaty (NPT), a bilateral acceptance of IAEA safeguards on all nuclear facilities, the establishment of a South Asian nuclear-weapon-free zone, comprehensive bilateral nuclear inspections, and a joint declaration renouncing nuclear weapons.[55]

India had rejected these proposals for a variety of reasons. It has long opposed the NPT and comprehensive IAEA safeguards on the grounds that they are discriminatory instruments of the nuclear weapon powers designed to legitimize the latter's nuclear status while freezing others in permanent inferiority. Citing the potential threat from China's nuclear weapons, India has also opposed the establishment of a South Asian nuclear-weapon-free zone unless China is included in the arrangement, a condition China is certain to reject.[56] New Delhi has also turned down comprehensive bilateral nuclear inspections with Pakistan, arguing that this (like ratification of the NPT and acceptance of comprehensive IAEA safeguards) would foreclose its nuclear option while leaving a nuclear-armed China on its border.

A further Indian objection applicable to all of these measures is that they treat India and Pakistan as relative equals, elevating Pakistan's importance despite India's far greater size and economic and military power. Indian analysts have also complained that even if some form of comprehensive inspections were adopted, India could never be confident that Pakistan had not previously hidden away some nuclear weapons material, thereby retaining a secret nuclear weapons option. (India has said little about a possible joint declaration renouncing nuclear arms.)

Since many of India's objections to these proposals have a long history, India has questioned whether Pakistan has advanced them in good faith. India, however, has refused to put Pakistan to the test by agreeing to discuss any of these initiatives, despite the possibility that some of New Delhi's concerns might be resolvable through negotiation.[57]

Junejo's test ban offer, in addition to avoiding the comprehensive controls that would constrain India's nuclear option, also appeared more practical than prior proposals because it is apparently consistent with the actual nuclear testing policies of both countries. Most observers believe that neither is likely to test a nuclear device because of fears that this might trigger a test or a series of tests by the other and because a test would likely result in the imposition of sanctions by the United States and, possibly, additional nations.[58] Since India has already conducted a test, while Pakistan has not, and since both would be prohibited from conducting tests during the period of the ban, the proposal, it may be noted, would appear to be highly advantageous for New Delhi; in effect, it would perpetuate India's current lead in this area. (Pakistan is thought to have obtained a validated design for a nuclear weapon from the People's Republic of China and to have tested the non-nuclear parts of the weapon. Accordingly, it is generally believed that Pakistan could have confidence in its first generation nuclear weapons without the need for a full-scale test.)[59]

India's response to Junejo's initiative, however, was to reject it immediately, labeling it "not serious," and New Delhi has previously stated that a regional test ban should await the adoption of a comprehensive test ban by the superpowers.[60] Undoubtedly, one factor contributing to Gandhi's dismissal of the test ban proposal was the desire to avoid yet another controversy at home where he had suffered a series of major political setbacks during the course of the year.[61] Even if the moment been more auspicious from the standpoint of domestic politics, however, there is little to suggest that Gandhi would have been prepared to pursue the Junejo initiative.

Unfulfilled hopes for U.S. pressure on Pakistan. In light of events over the summer of 1987, Gandhi may also have maintained the hope that the United States would apply sufficient pressure on Pakistan to slow its nuclear program so that India would not be obliged to make parallel concessions through bilateral negotiations with Islamabad. Gandhi pressed this point during his visit to Washington in October 1987, rejecting President Ronald Reagan's appeal that India enter into a dialogue with Pakistan on the nuclear question.[62]

The Indian gambit proved unsuccessful, however, and, indeed, after a countermove by the supporters of Pakistan, India's nuclear program itself briefly became the target of U.S. sanctions legislation.[63] In the end, in late December, Congress adopted legislation authorizing $480 million in economic and military aid to Pakistan and waiving the Symington Amendment's aid cut-off for two and a half years.[64] Despite their concerns over Pakistan's growing nuclear capabilities and U.S.-based nuclear smuggling activities—Arshad Pervez was convicted even as Congress acted—U.S. lawmakers were unwilling to risk a breach with Pakistan at a time when negotiations over the withdrawal of Soviet troops from Afghanistan were reaching a critical point.

Pakistani deterrent. In late December 1987 and mid-January 1988, the Reagan Administration removed the last remaining obstacles to providing American aid to Islamabad by certifying that Pakistan did not "possess" a nuclear explosive device and by waiving the non-proliferation restriction prohibiting assistance to non-nuclear countries that engage in nuclear smuggling in the United States.[65] In testimony on the latter decision, however, the administration for the first time publicly acknowledged that Pakistan was developing nuclear weapons and that the country's enrichment program was being pursued for this purpose.[66]

On March 6, the *New York Times Magazine* published a detailed report by Hedrick Smith on the Pakistani nuclear program based on information from U.S. government sources. The account stated that Pakistan had accumulated enough highly enriched uranium for four to six nuclear weapons and that its devices, based on a Chinese design, weighed only 400 pounds (180 kilograms), indicating that they were considerably more advanced than the first U.S. weapons, which weighed approximately 10,000 pounds (4,545 kilograms).[67] The article, which went on to state that Pakistan had fabricated virtually all of the components for these devices, made it clear that Pakistan could rapidly deploy nuclear weapons in any future conflict, even if, technically speaking, it did not yet "possess" a fully assembled nuclear device, as President Reagan had certified in December. Administration sources subsequently suggested in off-the-record interviews that not all of the details in the Smith article were correct, but confirmed that its overall characterization of the status of the Pakistani program was accurate.[68] New Delhi responded, as it had to prior revelations of Pakistani nuclear advances, by reiterating that Pakistan's nuclear activities would force India to reconsider its policy against nuclear arming, and by claiming that it was still not manufacturing nuclear weapons itself.[69]

New Indian weapon systems. These events have significantly—and perhaps permanently—worsened India's security environment. Nonetheless, the country's expansion of its conventional military capabilities in recent years—which has included the acquisition of the Soviet Union's most advanced fighter, the MiG-29, and the deployment of a second aircraft carrier—has confirmed it as by far the region's foremost military power.[70] Two advances in India's conventional capabilities during 1988, each having a nuclear dimension, are particularly noteworthy: India's lease of a nuclear-powered submarine from the Soviet Union in January and its successful flight-testing of a short-range nuclear-capable surface-to-surface missile the following month.[71]

Nuclear submarine. The lease of the Soviet sub is the first ever transfer of such a system and makes India the only non-nuclear-weapon state to possess such a vessel. The submarine is said to be a 1960s vintage "Charlie I" class model, which in the Soviet navy is capable of firing conventional or nuclear-armed cruise missiles while submerged.[72] India does not possess such missiles, and it appears highly unlikely that the ship will ever serve as a platform for launching nuclear weapons. Indeed, Indian spokesmen have asserted that the vessel, christened the *Chakra*, will be used only for training purposes, which means, according to Western sources quoted in the press, that it will not be fitted with weapons or deployed in combat.[73]

Nonetheless, the ship, with its long-range cruising capabilities, appears to symbolize India's intent to extend its reach throughout the Indian Ocean, and for this reason, its advent set off alarms in Pakistan.[74] India is to receive three additional Soviet nuclear subs in the future, according to some reports.[75]

Nuclear submarines are usually fueled with weapons-usable highly enriched uranium. Thus a central issue raised by the transfer of the Soviet vessel is whether it will provide India access to additional amounts of nuclear weapons material free from non-proliferation restrictions. Apparently in the case of the *Chakra*, the Soviet Union has imposed strict controls over the sub's fuel, which it supplied, including periodic inspections; Moscow will also apparently retain custody over spent fuel from the vessel's twin forty-megawatt reactors.[76] Although the NPT—to which the Soviet Union, but not India, is party—prohibits exports by parties of nuclear materials for peaceful purposes unless they are covered by IAEA safeguards in the recipient state, it does permit unsafeguarded transfers for military purposes other than the manufacture of nuclear explosives, such as submarine propulsion.

Soviet motives for leasing the sub are unclear, but Moscow may have have been seeking to reinforce its status as India's principal arms supplier at a time when New Delhi was building additional ties to the United States that envisaged expanded purchases of U.S. military technology.[77] Washington condemned the Soviet transfer on the grounds that it introduced a new weapons technology into the region and hurt global non-proliferation efforts by breaking a *de facto* supplier-country embargo on new reactor and fuel transfers to countries that refuse to place all of their nuclear facilities under IAEA safeguards.[78] (Several months later, Moscow broke this embargo more directly by signing an agreement with India to sell it two new nuclear power plants. The new reactors will be subject to IAEA safeguards, however, and the Soviet Union will take back the plutonium-bearing spent fuel they produce; thus the facilities will not contribute to India's nuclear weapons potential.)[79]

New missile tested. On February 18, 1988, India successfully test-fired its first surface-to-surface missile, the Prithvi. The missile, discussed in detail in Chapter II, is said to have a range of roughly 100 miles and can carry a payload of 2,200 pounds (1,000 kilograms). With modifications, it could probably carry a 1,100 pound (500 kilograms) payload 200 miles (300 kilometers), making it a "nuclear capable" missile under the standards of the missile technology control regime implemented by seven Western nations in April 1987.[80]

Reports in the Indian press state that the missile, when fully developed, will be highly accurate.[81] Indian officials note that this will make the missile effective as a conventionally armed system and that India would have no need to equip it with a nuclear warhead.[82] Not surprisingly, Pakistan has expressed concern at the new development, which in the words of one Indian press account, "could change the very doctrine of defense along the Indo-Pakistan border."[83] (As discussed in Chapter II, India's space program will provide it with the capability to deploy longer-range missiles in the years ahead.)

Heavy water smuggling. As noted earlier, India has sought to portray its own nuclear program as entirely open and legitimate—and therefore presumptively peaceful—while casting Pakistan as a nuclear outlaw bent on obtaining nuclear arms by hook or by crook. There is increasing evidence, however, that India, too, has expanded its nuclear weapons capabilities by circumventing international controls to obtain a key nuclear commodity, heavy water. (See Glossary). However, India's resort to clandestine nuclear trade has not been established in a formal legal proceeding or through a governmental determination, as has Pakistan's.[84]

The four unsafeguarded nuclear reactors that form the backbone of India's nuclear weapons capability—the Madras I and II nuclear power plants and the Cirus and Dhruva research reactors—all require heavy water to operate. To keep these facilities free from IAEA oversight, India has attempted to produce this material domestically, since countries exporting it (with one important exception noted below) have long required that recipients operating any unsafeguarded nuclear installations place transferred heavy water under the IAEA system and that IAEA coverage extend to any plutonium produced in a reactor using heavy water.

India has experienced serious shortfalls in heavy water production, however, and it is known, for example, that in the early 1980s, the Madras I reactor stood idle for well over a year because India lacked sufficient domestically produced material to start it and was not prepared to purchase the needed heavy water through legitimate channels because of the safeguards that would have been applied.[85]

In 1986, a major study of India's heavy water production capabilities by Gary Milhollin, an American law professor and government consultant, concluded that in the early 1980s, India had been forced to import over 110 tons (100 metric tons) of heavy water clandestinely in order to start up the Madras I and II plants and the Dhruva reactor, all of which commenced operating between 1983 and 1985.[86] The study surmised that the material had come from the People's Republic of China, since all other suppliers of heavy water—the United States, the Soviet Union, Canada, and Norway—required safeguards on their heavy water exports. China, on the other hand, is believed to have made a number of undeclared (and unsafeguarded) exports of nuclear materials during the early 1980s, a practice that would have been consistent with an unannounced sale to India. Except for citing China's urgent need for foreign exchange, however, the study did not explain why China would have provided India with a commodity essential for the latter's expansion of its nuclear weapons capabilities, especially at a time of increasing tensions between India and China's regional ally, Pakistan.

Indian nuclear officials, while dismissing the study's charges, have never offered a detailed explanation of how India was able to fill the reactors with unsafeguarded heavy water, but new evidence has since emerged that supports the clandestine import hypothesis and may explain how Chinese heavy water could have wound up in India.

On the basis of this evidence, it appears that a West German company, Rohstoff Einfuhr, obtained multi-ton quantities of heavy water from Norway in 1983 and the Soviet Union in 1985 and arranged for the material to be shipped to a destination unknown to the selling country. Norwegian and Soviet officials have confirmed the diversion of the material, and American officials believe that it was ultimately sent to India.

The first diversion took place in 1983 and involved 17.4 tons (15.8 metric tons) of heavy water. According to a spokesman for the Norwegian Foreign Ministry, Norway sold the material to Rohstoff Einfuhr, which prepared proper export license documents indicating the material was to be flown to Frankfurt, West Germany, by West African Airlines. At the last minute, the pilot filed a revised flight plan and flew instead to Basel, Switzerland; from there the material was shipped to an unknown destination.[87] The Oslo daily *VG*, asserted that the material was trans-shipped to India via Dubai in a Liberian-registered aircraft.[88] Norway did not realize that the material had been diverted until press stories on the subject appeared in 1988. Rohstoff Einfuhr denied that the change of destination had been secret or illegal.[89] India also denied it had received the material.

The second episode, which involved 6.8 tons (6.2 metric tons) of Soviet heavy water, was strikingly similar. According to a 1986 West German television documentary, an Aeroflot jet brought the material to a bonded warehouse at the Zurich, Switzerland, airport, where it was supposed to be distributed by Rohstoff Einfuhr to eight European countries. Instead it was transferred to the airport at Basel, for shipment to Sharjah in the United Arab Emirates by Trans Mediterranean Airlines.[90] According to a Trans Mediterranean spokesman quoted in the documentary, "The understanding was that the material would be kept in transit there to be transported to Bombay via a booked charter flight of Air India."[91]

Trans-Mediterranean subsequently refused to handle the shipment, however, but according to sources interviewed by the documentary team, the material was subsequently shipped to Dubai. As noted above, U.S. officials believe it was then sent to India. At a 1987 conference on clandestine nuclear trade at Columbia University, a Soviet official confirmed that the Soviet material had been diverted, but declined to name the West European company involved or the ultimate recipient.[92] A spokesman for Rohstoff Einfuhr interviewed on the West German documentary denied any wrongdoing.

Neither of these episodes sheds light directly on the allegation that India obtained Chinese heavy water. However, they do demonstrate that Norwegian and Soviet controls were so lax that multi-ton quantities of the material could be obtained from these countries and shipped to unknown destinations. Chinese controls may have been no better. If they were not, Rohstoff Einfuhr—which is rumored to have been involved in the Chinese transaction—or some other intermediary might have been able to defeat them and ship Chinese material to India contrary to Beijing's wishes.[93]

Prospects

The precise status of India's nuclear program remains uncertain. India is known to be stockpiling unsafeguarded plutonium, as described earlier, and most observers assume that it has continued to work on the design of nuclear weapons. A U.S. State Department official testified to Congress in February 1988, however, that India has not "actually taken the final step to acquire nuclear weapons" and in off-the-record interviews other administration and congressional sources have stated that they believe that India is not developing an undeclared stockpile of nuclear devices or their components.[94]

On the other hand, an April 1988 press report, citing U.S. intelligence sources, stated that New Delhi has moved far down this road. The report, citing two unnamed Reagan Administration officials, stated that India began producing nuclear weapons at a rate of twenty weapons a year beginning in late 1986.[95] It also quoted a State Department aide as stating that India had manufactured a number of nuclear devices between 1974 and 1977 (when Moraji Desai became prime minister and halted the process), but that the State Department did not believe that India had an on-going program to manufacture nuclear weapons.

Whether or not India in fact possesses a number of nuclear weapons at this time, it clearly has the capability to manufacture them quickly and, as noted above, Pakistani strategists would have to assume that Pakistan would confront a nuclear-armed adversary in any future conflict.

Since late 1986, as Pakistan approached and apparently crossed the nuclear weapons threshold, Indian nuclear policy has remained relatively constant. Its main strands were evident through numerous governmental decisions and official statements: the expansion of a nuclear weapons capability within the framework of a peaceful nuclear energy and research program; an ambiguous public posture that hints at a nuclear deterrent capability without embracing one; the rejection of substantive bilateral nuclear negotiations with Pakistan; the encouragement of U.S. non-proliferation pressure on Islamabad; and a concomitant build-up of conventional forces.

As a counter to the growing nuclear threat from Pakistan, this strategy has many advantages over the open development of a nuclear arsenal. First, it is likely to be sufficient to deter a nuclear attack by Pakistan, since in any future crisis, as just noted, Pakistani military planners, using conservative assumptions, would have to assume that India possessed a nuclear retaliatory capability. At the same time, it avoids the further exacerbation of bilateral nuclear tensions, which could provoke an unrestrained regional nuclear race. In addition, it avoids the high economic costs of building a militarized nuclear force.

If India were to conduct another test or declare it possessed nuclear weapons, moreover, it would likely suffer serious diplomatic costs, as well. These could include a chilling of relations with the Soviet Union, the undermining of improving ties with the United States, possible economic sanctions (which would be activated under U.S. law in the event of an Indian test and might well be imposed by other Western governments), and the loss of stature in the Non-Aligned Movement, which is strongly committed to disarmament. Finally, as long as India desists from these overt steps and maintains its current nuclear posture, China is unlikely to consider India's nuclear capabilities a direct threat, and New Delhi will be able to forego the costs of developing a deterrent against nuclear pressure from this quarter. India's conventional military advances, it may be added, appear to be bringing it many of the prestige and power-projection benefits associated with the open possession of nuclear arms.

India's nuclear policies have not, however, achieved one important goal, that of averting the emergence of a second, unfriendly nuclear-capable state on its borders. It is possible that a more conciliatory stance toward Pakistan and a greater willingness to enter into bilateral nuclear talks might have accomplished more for New Delhi in this regard, but this is by no means certain, given Pakistan's apparent determination to acquire a nuclear weapons capability. It will be for historians to ponder whether India's leaders might have prevented this outcome by more adept statecraft during the mid-1980s.

For the near term, it is likely that India will adhere to the policies that it has pursued for the past several years and which appear to be firmly entrenched. As Pakistan's nuclear capabilities grow, however, pressures within India are likely to mount for it to militarize its own nuclear potential—by building nuclear arms (if it has not done so), matching them with delivery systems, training specialized military units to use them, and integrating them into the country's military doctrines. The costs of regional nuclearization are also likely to become more apparent, including the vulnerability inherent in a defense based on a "balance of terror" and the genuine risk that in the volatile climate of the Subcontinent nuclear weapons might be used, risking a vast increase in the costs of future conflict. Possibly these realities will lead New Delhi to look more favorably on negotiated nuclear restraints with Pakistan as a means for enhancing India's security—much as the United States and the Soviet Union have.[96]

One glimmer of hope is that both India and Pakistan are apparently prepared to formalize the December 1985 understanding against attacking each other's nuclear plants, a step which could open the door to additional confidence-building measures. Unfortunately, India postponed a planned signing of a written accord on the issue in the spring of 1988 after obtaining new information that it said demonstrated direct Pakistani support for the Sikh separatist movement. Until tensions on the Sikh question—now Gandhi's most difficult challenge—can be reduced, even limited progress on the nuclear front is unlikely.

In mid-May, 1988, the Soviet Union began withdrawing its forces from Afghanistan, a step that many hope will ease tensions in the region. It appears, however, that the Soviet exodus is likely to add a yet another controversy to the agenda of bilateral Indo-Pakistani differences, as India extends increasing political support to the Soviet-backed Najibullah government—apparently in a bid to project its influence in this part of the region—while Pakistan continues to assist Afghan rebel forces, in the hope that pro-Pakistani elements will succeed to power in Kabul.[97]

Against this background, absent a major diplomatic effort by outside powers to encourage nuclear restraint in the region or some unexpected breakthrough in Indo-Pakistani relations, the prospects for slowing the open-ended expansion of the undeclared nuclear weapons capabilities of the two regional antagonists are not encouraging.

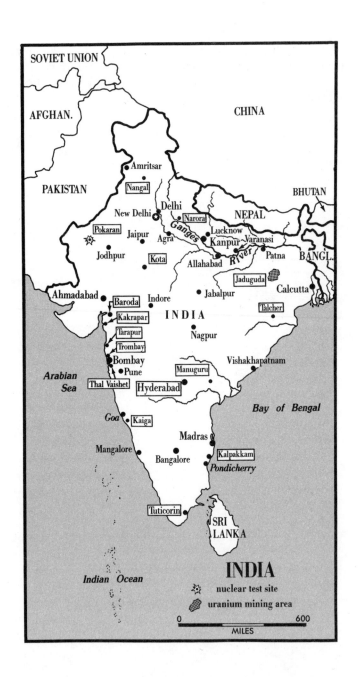

SOVIET UNION

AFGHAN.

CHINA

PAKISTAN

● Amritsar

Nangal

New Delhi Delhi

BHUTAN

NEPAL

Pokaran Jaipur

Narora

Lucknow
Kanpur Varanasi

Ganges

● Jodhpur

Agra

Kota

Allahabad

River

Patna

BANGL.

Ahmadabad

Baroda

Indore

INDIA

Jabalpur

Jaduguda

Calcutta

Kakrapar

Talcher

Tarapur

Trombay

Nagpur

Bombay

Vishakhapatnam

● Pune

Manuguru

Arabian
Sea

Thal Vaishet

Hyderabad

Bay of Bengal

Goa ● Kaiga

Madras

Mangalore

Bangalore

Kalpakkam

Pondicherry

Tuticorin

SRI
LANKA

Indian Ocean

INDIA

☼ nuclear test site

▨ uranium mining area

0   600

MILES

India

Power Reactors/Operating or Under Construction

Tarapur I (light-water/low-enriched uranium, 160[b] MWe)
* supplier: General Electric (U.S.)
* start up: 1969
* fuel source: U.S.; France after 1982
* safeguards: yes

Tarapur II (light-water/low-enriched uranium, 160[b] MWe)
* supplier: General Electric (U.S.)
* start up: 1969
* fuel source: U.S.; France after 1982
* safeguards: yes

Rajasthan I, Kota (heavy-water/natural-uranium, 200 MWe)
* supplier: Canadian General Electric (Canada)
* start up: 1972[g]
* fuel source: Initial load, half Canadian Westinghouse, half Indian; subsequently all Indian.[a]
* heavy water: 130 metric tons from Canada and U.S.; 80 metric tons from USSR in 1973.[a]
* safeguards: yes

Rajasthan II, Kota (heavy-water/natural-uranium, 200 MWe)
* supplier: Larsen and Toubro (India), following termination of Canadian assistance in 1976.
* start up: 1980[g]
* fuel source: India
* heavy water: USSR,[a] India
* safeguards: yes

Madras I, Kalpakkam (heavy-water/natural-uranium, 220 MWe)
* supplier: Larsen and Toubro (India)
* start up: 1983[b]
* fuel source: India
* heavy water: India (?)[c,j]
* safeguards: no

Madras II, Kalpakkam (heavy-water/natural-uranium, 220 MWe)
* supplier: Larsen and Toubro (India)
* start up: 1985[e]
* fuel source: India
* heavy water: India (?)[c,j]
* safeguards: no

Narora I (heavy-water/natural-uranium, 220 MWe)
* supplier: Larsen and Toubro/Walchandnagar Industries, Ltd. (India)
* start up: 1988[e] (est.)
* fuel source: India
* heavy water: India
* safeguards: no

Narora II (heavy-water/natural-uranium, 220 MWe)
- supplier: Larsen and Toubro/Walchandnagar Industries Ltd.
                    (India)
- start up: 1989[e]
- fuel source: India
- heavy water: India
- safeguards: no

Kakrapar I (heavy-water/natural-uranium, 220 MWe)
- supplier: Larsen and Toubro/Walchandnagar Industries, Ltd.
                    (India)
- start up: 1991[g]
- fuel source: India
- heavy water: India
- safeguards: no

Kakrapar II (heavy-water/natural-uranium, 220 MWe)
- supplier: Larsen and Toubro/Walchandnagar Industries, Ltd.
                    (India)
- start up: 1992[g]
- fuel source: India
- heavy water: India
- safeguards: no

Kaiga I, Karnataka (heavy-water/natural-uranium, 220 MWe)
- supplier: Larsen and Toubro/Walchandnagar Industries, Ltd.
                    (India)
- start up: mid-1990s[g]
- fuel source: India
- heavy water: India
- safeguards: no

Kaiga II, Karnataka (heavy-water/natural-uranium, 220 MWe)
- supplier: Larsen and Toubro/Walchandnagar Industries, Ltd.
                    (India)
- start up: mid-1990s[g]
- fuel source: India
- heavy water: India
- safeguards: no

Uranium Resources/Active Mining Sites/Uranium Mills
- reasonably assured
  reserves: 46,090 metric tons[f]
- currently active site: Jaduguda[f,g]
- mills in operation: Jaduguda[f,g]

Uranium Purification (UO$_2$)[e]
Hyderabad
- capacity: ?
- supplier: India
- start up: ?
- safeguards: partial (?)

112

Uranium Conversion (UF$_6$)
Trombay/Bhabha Atomic Research Center (B.A.R.C.) (?)
- capacity: sufficient for experimental enrichment program at B.A.R.C., presumed
- supplier: India, presumed
- start up: 1984?
- safeguards: no

Enrichment
Trombay/B.A.R.C.
- type: ultracentrifuge
- capacity: pilot scale, 100 (?) centrifuges, uranium reportedly enriched to "less than two percent"[x]
- supplier: India
- start up: 1984?
- safeguards: no

Heavy Water
Nangal
- capacity: 14 metric tons per year[a]
- supplier: Linde Gmbolt (West Germany)[a]
- start up: 1962[a]
- safeguards: no

Baroda
- capacity: 45 metric tons per year[a,j]
- supplier: GELPRA (Swiss-French)[a]
- start up: 1977 (closed 1977-80; intermittent operation thereafter)[k]
- safeguards: no

Tuticorin
- capacity: 49 metric tons per year[a,j]
- supplier: GELPRA (Swiss-French)[a]
- start up: 1978
- safeguards: no

Talcher
- capacity: very little production[a,j]
- supplier: Friedrich Unde Gmbolt (West Germany)[a]
- start up: 1979, but has operated at less than 10% capacity[k]
- safeguards: no

Kota
- capacity: 85 metric tons per year[a,j]
- supplier: India, Canada (Canadian aid terminated 1974)[l]
- start up: 1984[m]
- safeguards: no

Thal-Vaishet
- capacity: 110 metric tons per year[m]
- supplier: Rashtriya Chemicals and Fertilizers (India)[j]
- start up: 1987[e]
- safeguards: no

Manuguru
- capacity: 185 metric tons[e]
- supplier: India
- start up: after 1988[e]
- safeguards: no

Hazira
- capacity: 110 metric tons per year[e]
- supplier: KRIBHCO and Projects Development India Ltd. (India)
- start up: 1990 (est.)
- safeguards: no

Fuel Fabrication
Hyderabad
- capacity: 90 metric tons/yr. for Rajasthan, Madras, Tarapur, Narora, and FTBR blanket assemblies; being expanded to 180 metric tons/yr.[e,h]
- supplier: India
- start up: 1971[z]
- safeguards: partial[z]

Trombay/B.A.R.C.
- capacity: sufficient for Cirus, Dhruva, FBTR fuel pins[e]
- supplier: India
- start up: late 1960s (Cirus), 1981-1982 (Dhruva), 1983-1984 (FTBR)
- safeguards: no

Reprocessing
Trombay/B.A.R.C.
- capacity: 30 metric tons of spent fuel per year (CIRUS, Dhruva fuel)[r]; has been enlarged[a]
- supplier: India[s]
- start up: 1966; shut down, 1974; restarted late 1983 or early 1984[w]
- safeguards: no

Tarapur
- capacity: 100 metric tons of spent fuel per year; 135-150 kg. plutonium per year when at full capacity[n]
- supplier: India
- start up: trial runs, 1979;[a] full scale operations, 1982[n]
- safeguards: partial (only when plant is processing spent fuel from safeguarded reactors)

Kalpakkam
- capacity: laboratory scale
- supplier: India
- start up: 1985
- safeguards: no

Kalpakkam
- capacity: 125 metric tons per year (for Madras I, II, and FTBR)[e,o]
- supplier: India
- start up: 1991 (est.)
- safeguards: no

Research Reactors

Apsara, Trombay/B.A.R.C. (light-water/medium-enriched-uranium, 1 MWt)[p]
- supplier: India
- start up: 1956
- fuel source: United Kingdom
- safeguards: no

Cirus, Trombay/B.A.R.C. (heavy-water/natural-uranium, 40 MWt)[p]
- supplier: Canada
- start up: 1963[q]
- fuel source: Canada, then India
- heavy water: United States
- safeguards: no

Zerlina, Trombay/B.A.R.C. (heavy-water/variable-fuel, 400 Wt)[p]
- supplier: India
- start up: 1961; decommissioned 1983[d]
- fuel source: India?
- safeguards: no

Purnima II, Trombay/B.A.R.C. (uranium-233)[d]
- supplier: India
- start up: 1984, dismantled 1986? 1987?[e]
- fuel source: India
- safeguards: no

Purnima III, Trombay/B.A.R.C. (uranium-233)
- supplier: India
- start up: 1988 (est.)[t]
- fuel source: India
- safeguards: no

Kamini, Kalpakkam (uranium-233, 30 KWt)[e]
- supplier: India
- start up: 1988 (est.)
- fuel source: India[v]
- safeguards: no

Dhruva (formerly R-5) Trombay/B.A.R.C. (heavy-water/natural-uranium, 100 MWt)[d]
- supplier: India
- start up: 1985[d]
- fuel source: India
- heavy water: India (?)[j]
- safeguards: no

FBTR, Kalpakkam (fast breeder/plutonium & natural uranium, 42 MWt, 15MWe)
- supplier: India, with French assistance[a]
- start up: 1985
- fuel source: India
- safeguards: no

Sources and Notes

a. David Hart, *Nuclear Power in India, A Comparative Analysis* (London: George Allen and Unwin, 1983), pp. 45-54. GELPRA is a consortium of Sulzer Brothers,

Cie de Construction Mecaniques (a French licensee of Sulzer Brothers) and Société Air Liquide (France). See "India and France," *Nucleonics Week,* July 4, 1985.

b. "Sethna Present as Kalpakkam Reactor Goes Critical," *The Hindu,* reprinted in *Joint Publication Research Service (JPRS)/Nuclear Development and Proliferation (NDP),* August 3, 1983, p. 30.

c. Judith Miller, "U.S. Is Holding Up Peking Atom Talks," *New York Times,* September 19, 1982. Gary Milhollin, "Dateline New Delhi: India's Nuclear Cover-Up," *Foreign Policy* (Fall 1986): 161. (Both suggest China supplied heavy water that may have been used in these plants.)

d. *The Annual Report of the Department of Atomic Energy, 1986-1987,* (New Dehli: 1987), p. 37. The Dhruva reactor was shut down shortly after commissioning. Its operations resumed in November 1986, after it was loaded with modified fuel assemblies. In early 1987 the reactor was said to be operating at a level of 40 MWt, and it reached 100 MWt by May 1988. See, Sheila Tefft, "Dhruva Reached Full Power, But High Costs and Delays are Criticized," *Nucleonics Week,* May 12, 1988, p. 13.

e. *The Annual Report of the Department of Atomic Energy, 1986-1987,* (New Delhi, 1987.)

f. Reasonably Assured Reserves at less than $130 per kilogram. OECD Nuclear Energy Agency and the International Atomic Energy Agency, *Uranium, Resources, Production and Demand* (Paris: OECD, 1986), pp. 223-225. Reference in note g. states that reasonably assured reserves amount to only 29,000 metric tons. India also has two plants for recovering uranium from copper tailings at Surda and Kakha. See note g.

g. "Datafile: INDIA," *Nuclear Engineering International,* May 1987.

h. David Hart, *Nuclear Power in India,* p. 43. The Indian fifteen year plan calls for an eventual expansion of the uranium fuel fabrication capacity to 1,500 metric tons/year. See note g.

i. "DAE Chief Denies Industrial HEU Production at BARC," *Nuclear Fuel,* June 29, 1987, p. 6.

j. "DAE Official Writes on Heavy Water Production," *The Hindu Survey of Indian Industry,* reprinted in *JPRS/NDP,* April 9, 1984, pp. 18-20. "Commissioning of Vitrification Facility," *Nuclear Fuel,* June 3, 1985, p. 9. In 1983, the capacities of Baroda, Tuticorin, Talcher, and Kota plants were derated from 67, 71, 65, and 100 metric tons per year respectively. Actual production has been below derated capacities. Dpt. Atomic Energy testimony before Consultative Committee of Parliament, May 1986. It has been widely reported that during the mid-1980s, India made a series of clandestine imports of heavy water to meet its needs. See *e.g.,* Gary Milhollin, "Dateline New Delhi: India's Nuclear Cover-Up," *Foreign Policy* (Fall 1986): 161; Michael R. Gordon, "Norway is Missing Atom Arms Water," *New York Times,* May 4, 1988; Mark Hibbs, "Norway Investigating Reports of Heavy Water Diversions," *Nuclear Fuel,* May 30, 1988, p. 9. "Wanted: Bombs for Business: Nuclear Aid for Pakistan and India," ARD (West German TV), 2115, November 3, 1986. India has denied these charges.

k. Pearl Marshall, "India's Desperate Push for Enough Indigenous Heavy Water to Commission," *Nucleonics Week,* May 27, 1982, p. 12.

l. "Problems in Production of Heavy Water Discussed," Jairam Ramesh, *The Times of India,* reprinted in *JPRS/NDP,* August 18, 1982, p. 11.

m. *The Annual Report of the Department of Atomic Energy, 1984-1985,* (New Dehli: 1984), p. 23.

n. Milton Benjamin, "India Storing Arms Grade Plutonium," *Washington Post,* February 20, 1983. Plant is currently reprocessing fuel from the safeguarded Rajasthan I

116

reactor and from the unsafeguarded Madras I reactor. India is barred by the United States from reprocessing spent fuel from the Tarapur reactors until at least 1993 under the 1963 Indo-U.S. agreement for nuclear cooperation and a follow-up agreement with France. India disputes this view, however.

o. "ISI Gives Details on Nuclear Reprocessing Plant," *ISI Diplomatic Information Service,* reprinted in *FBIS/South Asia,* December 16, 1982, p. E-1.

p. Albert Wohlstetter, ed., *Swords From Plowshares* (Chicago: University of Chicago Press, 1979), p. 206.

q. Fully operational in 1963; started up in 1960.

r. David Hart, *Nuclear Power in India,* p. 54; but see, sixty metric tons per year, "ERDA: Fuel Reprocessing Capabilities, 1977," *Nuclear Proliferation Factbook,* Subcomm. on Int'l. Trade and Policy of the House Int'l. Relations Comm. and Subcomm. on Energy, Nuclear Proliferation and Federal Services, Senate Comm. on Governmental Affairs (Washington: Gov't. Print'g. Off., 1977), p. 200; one hundred metric tons per year, Wohlstetter, *Swords From Plowshares,* p. 214. Thirty metric ton figure selected because it is the most conservative and may best reflect actual operating experience.

s. India received engineering assistance from Vitro International (U.S.) and from French engineering consultants, Roberta Wohlstetter, *"The Buddha Smiles": Absent-minded Peaceful Aid and the Indian Bomb,* Monograph 3, Energy Research and Development Administration, Contract No. (49-1)-3747, April 30, 1977, p. 63.

t. *Annual Report of the Department of Atomic Energy, 1986-1987,* p. 25. Purnima III is a full-scale zero-power mock up of the Kamini reactor. The Purnima II reactor system was dismantled to make way for the Purnima III experiments.

u. "Indian Nuclear Industry," *Nucleonics Week,* May 23, 1985, p. 14.

v. *Annual Report of the Department of Atomic Energy, 1986-1987,* p. 34. Fuel for the Kamini reactor will be provided partially from reprocessed and fabricated fuel from the Purnima II reactor.

w. "Trombay Is Ready for Work," *Nuclear Engineering Int'l,* June 1983, p. 6; "Interview, Nuclear Energy," *India Int'l Center Quarterly,* Vol. 10, No. 4, 1983, p. 379. Some sources state plant was shut down in 1972, not 1974.

x. According to one report, the pilot scale enrichment facility consists of one hundred centrifuges and had "achieved enrichment of less than 2%." See Ivan Fera and Kannan Srinivasan, "Keeping the Nuclear Option Open: What It Really Means," *Economic and Political Weekly,* December 6, 1986, p. 2119. See also "DAE Chief Denies Industrial HEU Production at BARC," *Nuclear Fuel,* June 29, 1987.

y. Both of the Tarapur reactors were derated from 200 to 160 MWe in April 1985. See Shri K.P. Rao, "Nuclear Plants Described," *The Times of India,* October 16, 1987, in *JPRS/Nuclear Developments (TND),* January 28, 1988.

z. *Annual Report of the Department of Atomic Energy, 1982-1983.* Line for fabricating enriched uranium fuel for Tarapur reactors is safeguarded; line for fabricating natural uranium fuel for the Rajasthan, Madras, and Narora reactors and rods for FTBR blanket is not safeguarded.

Photo 3.1 shows the Dhruva (left) and Cirus (right) research reactors at the Bhabha Atomic Research Center, near Bombay. *Courtesy of the Indian Atomic Energy Commission.*

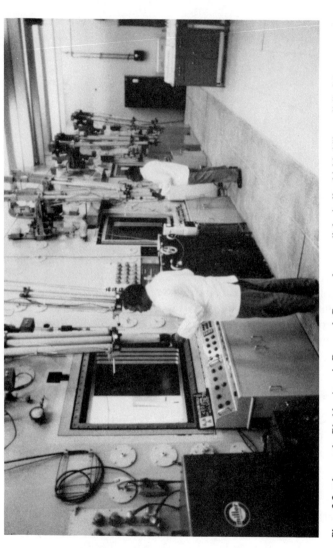

Photo 3.2, taken at the Bhabha Atomic Research Center, shows radiologically shielded "hot cells" of the type used to handle plutonium metal.

© *Jehangir Gazdar – Woodfin Camp & Assoc.*

Pakistan

Between late 1986 and mid-1988, convincing evidence emerged that Pakistan had crossed the nuclear weapons threshold and had acquired the essentials for its first nuclear weapons. Amidst revelations of its on-going clandestine nuclear procurement activities, the government of President Mohammad Zia ul-Haq nonetheless managed to maintain its close ties to the United States.

Background

Pakistani leaders have repeatedly denied that their nation is developing nuclear arms. Nevertheless, the available evidence leaves little doubt that Pakistan is indeed pursuing this course, a conclusion shared by the United States, the Soviet Union, India, and other nations.

Although Pakistan, like India, refused to join the Non-Proliferation Treaty (NPT) in 1968, thereby leaving itself free to develop nuclear arms, Pakistan's nuclear weapons program was not initiated until shortly after the country's devastating defeat in the 1971 Indo-Pakistani War. The following year, according to eye-witnesses, then-Prime Minister Zulfikar Ali Bhutto announced his plan to develop nuclear arms at a secret meeting of Pakistan's top scientists and nuclear aides in Multan.[1] The program appears to have been aimed at countering India's substantial conventional military superiority and its significant, but then still undemonstrated, nuclear capability. India's nuclear test in May 1974 would give added impetus to the Pakistani program.[2]

Plutonium route. Initially, it appears that Bhutto intended to pursue nuclear weapons by acquiring a large reprocessing plant from France for extracting plutonium from spent power-reactor fuel. Although France insisted that the facility and any others based on its technology be placed under International Atomic Energy Agency (IAEA) safeguards, the installation would have nonetheless permitted Pakistan to accumulate weapons-usable plutonium. Pakistan had no apparent need for this material in its civilian nuclear power program, which then, as now, has only one small, natural-uranium-fueled nuclear power reactor.[3]

By 1976, American concerns over Pakistan's possible misuse of the plant had intensified to the point that President Gerald Ford dispatched Secretary of State Henry Kissinger to Islamabad and then to Paris in an unsuccessful bid to head off the reprocessing plant sale. In August 1977, however, France suspended deliveries for the plant after U.S. nuclear aides showed their French counterparts intelligence data revealing Pakistan's intentions. The following month, to underscore its concern, Washington cut off economic and military aid to Islamabad. It was restored in August 1978, however, after France stopped all performance under the plutonium plant contracts.[4]

Indeed, Bhutto himself ultimately acknowledged the veiled purpose behind the French deal, after he was ousted by Pakistan's military in July 1977. In a testament written in 1978 shortly before his execution at the hands of his successor, General Zia ul-Haq, he declared that Pakistan was "on the threshold of a full nuclear capability." "All we needed," he wrote, "was the nuclear reprocessing plant."[5] (Pakistan would subsequently complete a smaller, pilot-scale plutonium extraction plant, known as the New Labs, using equipment clandestinely obtained from a number of Western firms, but the installation is not thought to be operating.)[6]

Enrichment route. Reprocessing, however, was not the only route Pakistan was pursuing to obtain nuclear arms. In 1975, according to a subsequent Dutch government investigation, Pakistan began acquiring hardware and technology for a uranium enrichment plant using ultra-high-speed centrifuges, a plant potentially capable of producing highly enriched uranium, the alternative nuclear weapons material to plutonium.[7] (See Glossary.)

A key figure in the effort was Dr. Abdul Qadeer Khan, a German-trained metallurgist, who worked intermittently at a classified centrifuge enrichment plant at Almelo, the Netherlands, where he is believed to have gained access to key plans and listings of component suppliers. In 1975, Dr. Khan suddenly returned to Pakistan. The Dutch government investigation concluded, "It is reasonable to assume that through Dr. Khan, Pakistan has been able to obtain possession of essential gas centrifuge know-how."[8]

In 1986 a number of additional details concerning the early stages of Pakistan's uranium enrichment program were disclosed in an article in a prominent Pakistani defense publication, apparently based on authoritative Pakistani sources. According to the article,

Dr. A.Q. Kahn used to visit Pakistan quite regularly during his sojourn in Holland. When he came at the end of 1974 [in the aftermath of India's test], he contacted some top influentials in the establishment and advised them that Pakistan should endeavour for uranium enrichment. He also told them about the kind of facilities that would be needed. The following year in December, when he again visited Pakistan, the government asked him to assess the progress made. It was a great disappointment to him to see that instead of making any headway on the project, people were engaged in empire-building. Dr. Qadeer informed the government accordingly and stated that he would be returning to Holland in the second week of January. He was asked to stay on and to resign from his post in Holland. Dr. Qadeer agreed on condition that he would be given complete independence to carry on his work. Assurances given, he took up the assignment.

It did not take him long to find out that it was not possible for him to carry on as the work was not progressing at all. Frustrated, he wrote to the prime minister [Zulfikar Ali Bhutto] . . . .

He was called by the Prime Minister who sought his advice on the reorganization of the outfit. Dr. Khan suggested that the project be made autonomous. In July 1976, the project was separated from the Pakistan Atomic Energy Commission and put under Dr. Qadeer Khan. Dr. Khan began collecting committed and qualified personnel whenever he could locate them. The Government of Pakistan gave him its whole hearted support in assembling the team he wanted. Pakistani scientists working overseas too were approached and brought home to contribute their expertise and know-how to the project.

The manner the Kahuta project was organized was unconventional to begin with. It may even be termed revolutionary. Instead of the conventional step by step sequential approach that is the norm, all the steps were taken simultaneously for the Kahuta project. While preliminary work was being undertaken at Rawalpindi and procurement was being done for the most essential and sophisticated equipment and materials, they were manufacturing the first prototypes of centrifuges, as well as setting up a pilot plant at Sihala and preparing blue prints for the construction of the main facility at Kahuta . . . .

Search for a suitable site had begun a couple of months before the enrichment project was separated from the Atomic Energy Commission, [*i.e.*, in the spring of 1976] and given an autonomous status. Kahuta was eventualy selected, as Dr. A. Q. Kahn has said, "it was the most suitable site because (i) being out of normal traffic it could fully meet security requirements and (ii) it was close enough to the capital to enable him to have "full support and quick decisions . . . . "

Kahuta would therefore seem to have been selected because of its proximity to the seat of the federal government. It was necessary for the completion of a plant of such a critical and strategic nature, to be close to the top decision-makers of the country. It helped greatly not only in the flow of funds but also in the avail-ability of water and electricity. Located between hills, Kahuta was just the right site from the point of view of air defence . . . .

The chief of the army staff, General Mohammad Zia-ul-Haq reportedly entrusted the responsibility to a competent and efficient engineer, *Brigadier Zahid Ali Akbar Kan* [sic] (who is now a lt. general and a corps commander). Brig. Zahid was young and full of enthusiasm and vigour . . . .

After about a year [*i.e.*, around July 1977] Brigadier Zahid was transferred to some other post and his place was taken by Brig. (now Major-General) *Anees Ali Syed*. This was a very crucial peri-od indeed. Drawings of the plant were finalized. The land was pur-chased. It was the beginning of the construction work . . . .

The project reached a crucial stage about the year 1978. The principle of uranium enrichment was successfully tested. A small pilot plant was now needed. A site at Sihala was selected while the construction of Kahuta was being done. The work was undertaken expeditiously and within a year a small plant was operative at Sihala. It was now evident that Pakistan has made a distinct achievement. A detailed programme was then chalked out jointly by Dr. Abdul Qadeer Khan and Brig. Anees, which buildings were to be built first and which offices be moved from Rawalpindi . . . .[9]

To support the enrichment project, Pakistan launched a clandestine effort to obtain hardware for the Kahuta plant and several related installations from a number of Western nations, often in violation of their export control laws—a pattern which has become a hallmark of Pakistan's nuclear program and has continued to this day, as discussed below. The effort, which has involved the use of dummy corpora-tions and trans-shipments through third countries, has by now been well-documented in the press and has been offi-cially recognized by West Germany, Canada, Britain, the Netherlands, and the United States either in the course of prosecutions or in published government reports.[10]

Perhaps the most egregious case involved the smuggling from West Germany between 1977 and 1980 of an entire plant for converting uranium powder into uranium hexafluoride, the easily gasified material that is the feedstock for the Kahuta enrichment facility. In March 1985 a West German court convicted Albrecht Migule for the deed.[11] The plant, located in the town of Dera Ghazi Khan, is continuing to operate, producing material that is essential for the Pakistani nuclear weapons effort. Pakistan, it may be noted, has refused to place the Kahuta facility and the Dera Ghazi Khan plant under IAEA inspections.

U.S. response. In May 1979, Washington made public its own concerns over the Pakistani enrichment program by terminating aid to Islamabad for a second time. In announcing the decision, Assistant Secretary of State Thomas Pickering declared in congressional testimony that Pakistan's enrichment program was not justified by its nuclear energy needs. "We are concerned, therefore," he concluded, "that the Pakistani program is not peaceful but related to an effort to develop a nuclear-explosive capability."[12]

On December 25, 1979, barely six months after Washington had reimposed sanctions on Islamabad, Soviet forces began their occupation of Afghanistan, leading Washington to reverse course and to offer economic and military aid to Islamabad at increased levels. Although Pakistani president General Zia ul-Haq rejected the $400 million in assistance initially offered by the Carter Administration, he ultimately accepted a six-year $3.2 billion aid package subsequently proffered by President Ronald Reagan. The package included an agreement to sell Pakistan forty advanced F-16 fighter-bombers. In approving the aid in 1981, Congress granted Pakistan a six-year exemption from a U.S. non-proliferation law, familiarly known as the "Symington Amendment," that had previously prohibited such assistance because of Pakistan's importation of enrichment equipment, and had triggered the April 1979 cutoff. However, Congress also strengthened a portion of the law prohibiting U.S. aid to any non-nuclear-weapon state that subsequently detonated a nuclear explosive device.[13] (See Appendix G.)

The Reagan Administration argued that the aid package would help slow the Pakistani nuclear weapons program by providing an alternate means for Pakistan to protect its national security. So far, however, as detailed below, the aid has failed to halt the program, although the risk of losing American assistance may forestall a Pakistani nuclear test. India, it may be noted, whose concerns over the Pakistani nuclear weapons effort began to mount in 1979, saw the six-year exemption from the Symington Amendment as a sign that the United States was easing its efforts to retard Islam-abad's progress towards nuclear arming.[14]

1984: Progress toward weapons capability; krytron affair; Chinese assistance. In early 1984, Dr.A.Q.Khan announced that the Kahuta plant had succeeded in producing enriched uranium.[15] President Zia subsequently confirmed the point but stressed that only low-enriched, non-weapons-grade material had been produced.[16] A June 1984 speech by Senator Alan Cranston, meanwhile, declared that the Pakistani nuclear weapons program was continuing, and Reagan Administration officials at the time privately confirmed that this effort included nuclear-weapon design work and the acquisition of hardware from abroad.[17]

Also in June, still further evidence of Islamabad's pursuit of nuclear arms surfaced when three Pakistani nationals were indicted for attempting to smuggle fifty krytrons—high-speed electronic switches used in nuclear weapons—out of the United States. Two of the three were released after turning state's evidence and the third, Nazir Vaid, ultimately pleaded guilty to a lesser charge, serving a total of three months in jail before being deported to Pakistan.[18] Official Pakistani denials that the defendants were linked to the Pakistani government only made matters look worse when cables, taken from the defendants at the time of their arrest, revealed that the parts were ordered by S.A.Butt, a director of supply and procurement for the Pakistani Atomic Energy Commission.[19] The episode left little doubt about Islamabad's nuclear intentions.

The krytron affair was soon followed by press accounts that quoted Reagan Administration officials as saying that the People's Republic of China was assisting Pakistan, its long-time ally, in operating the Kahuta plant and had given

Pakistan the design of a nuclear weapon.[20] Such data might allow Pakistan to manufacture reliable nuclear arms without the need for a nuclear test. Although China denied the reports that it was aiding Pakistan, the Reagan Administration took the extraordinary step of halting for nearly a year the formal approval of a highly publicized nuclear trade pact with China, suggesting that the evidence available to the government was persuasive.[21]

The Reagan September 1984 letter. Apparently in response to Khan's enrichment breakthrough, the krytron affair, and China's nuclear assistance, in September 1984 President Reagan sent a letter to President Zia expressing strong U.S. concern over Pakistan's continuing nuclear activities and threatening "grave consequences"—but not explicitly threatening the termination of U.S.aid—if Zia used the Kahuta enrichment plant to produce uranium enriched to more than the relatively innocuous 5 percent level.[22] (Ninety-three percent-enriched uranium is used for nuclear weapons.) Such a limitation on the Pakistani nuclear program would keep it an important step short of nuclear arms. In this respect the Reagan letter went considerably further than U.S.legislation at the time, which made the detonation of a nuclear device the trigger for U.S. sanctions, but which would not have penalized Pakistan's acquisition of an untested (though potentially reliable) nuclear arsenal.[23]

According to unnamed Reagan Administration officials quoted in the press, Pakistan subsequently gave Washington written assurances that the 5 percent level would not be exceeded, and Pakistani Prime Minister Muhammad Khan Junejo confirmed in a 1986 interview that Pakistan had given such pledges.[24] In 1988, however, Pakistan's ambassador to the United States, Jamsheed K. A. Marker, denied that Pakistan had ever given assurances on the precise level of enrichment that it would undertake at Kahuta.[25]

1985: Non-nuclear tests, new U.S. laws. Pakistan's seeming acquiescence in the American restriction came at a time of its increasing dependence on the United States. In the fall of 1984, some 40,000 additional Soviet troops were deployed in Afghanistan, many close to the Pakistani border, bringing the total to 120,000. At the same time, Soviet planes began repeatedly violating Pakistani air space to bomb Afghan refugee camps in Pakistan. As these incursions continued, in March of 1985, the Reagan Administration agreed to supply Pakistan with sophisticated air-to-air missiles, and key congressional committees demonstrated their support by approving another installment of the $3.2 billion in U.S. aid begun in 1981.[26]

Congress authorized this assistance in late July, barely three weeks after a report that Pakistan had passed yet another major milestone on its quest for nuclear arms: the successful test of the non-nuclear triggering package for a nuclear weapon.[27] In approving continued U.S. assistance, however, Congress tightened existing U.S. non-proliferation restrictions by requiring, before aid to Pakistan could be disbursed in any subsequent year, that the President certify that Pakistan did not "possess a nuclear explosive device."[28] In addition, as a result of the Vaid affair (and a similar episode disclosed in 1985, involving the smuggling of krytrons to Israel in the early 1980s) Congress included a stipulation prohibiting aid to any non-nuclear-state found to have smuggled items from the United States for use in a nuclear explosive device.[29]

Turning Point. It now appears that late 1985 was a crucial turning point in U.S. efforts to slow Pakistan's nuclear weapons program. Sometime prior to October of that year—despite what American officials claim were explicit pledges given to Washington—Pakistan crossed the "red line" that had been set out in the September 1984 Reagan letter and produced uranium enriched to more than 5 percent. Whether this was widely understood by members of Congress when they authorized aid to Islamabad in July, is not known, but according to a detailed news story that appeared in March 1988, the Reagan Administration was aware of the development by October. When President Reagan met with General Zia that month at the United Nations, however, he did not challenge the Pakistani leader about the violation, undoubtedly in order to avoid a rift with a key ally assisting U.S. efforts to oust the Soviet Union from Afghanistan.[30] (Administration officials have subsequently confirmed this account in off-the-record interviews.) Thus, the United States, at the highest political level, had decided to acquiesce in Pakistan's decision to move toward production of weapons-grade uranium, the final step in its development of a *de facto* nuclear weapons capability. The Zia government had taken a gamble in crossing the 5 percent "red line", but, fully aware of administration and congressional actions since 1981, had correctly read American priorities.

In March 1986, as the first published report was about to appear that Pakistan had produced uranium enriched to 30 percent, the Reagan Administration announced that it would provide Pakistan a second six-year aid package, to begin in October 1987, in the amount of $4.02 billion.[31] From this point onward, there could be no doubt in Islamabad that the Reagan Administration was aware of its advances at Kahuta and was prepared to look the other way.[32]

Threshold Crossed. A series of press stories in July 1986, citing Reagan Administration sources, stated that Pakistan was considered to have the capacity to build nuclear arms or to be on the verge of having that capability, with one account stating that all that remained was for Pakistan to assemble the components.[33] By the fall of 1986, a "Special National Intelligence Estimate," circulated to senior U.S. officials, had concluded that Pakistan had produced weapons-grade material.[34] According to the report, Pakistan had also conducted two additional tests during the year of the non-nuclear portions of the device.[35] U.S. aid remained unaffected, however, and on October 27, President Reagan certified—as he had late in 1985—that Pakistan did not "possess" a nuclear explosive device, a finding necessary under the 1985 legislation noted earlier, to permit the disbursement of funds for Islamabad.[36] According to administration sources, the 1986 non-possession finding was based on the view that despite Pakistan's advances in enrichment, it had still not fabricated certain key weapon components.

Nonetheless, India and other observers would henceforth have to assume that Pakistan could rapidly assemble at least one such device in the event of a future war. Thus Pakistan, it appears, had become a *de facto* nuclear weapons state, albeit at this juncture only in a very limited sense.

Relations with India. There is little question that Pakistan has sought nuclear weapons principally to meet the threat from India's conventional military superiority and substantial nuclear potential, as well as to counter more subtle forms of Indian dominance in regional affairs.[37] The ups and downs in Indo-Pakistani relations in recent years, however, seem to have had relatively little impact on the pace or direction of Pakistan's nuclear weapons activities, which appear to have been aimed at acquiring a weapons capability at the earliest possible time. (In contrast, U.S.-led efforts to thwart Pakistan's clandestine nuclear purchasing activities and the threat of U.S. sanctions appear to have had a more direct impact on the day-to-day conduct of Pakistani nuclear affairs and for this reason have been emphasized in this account.)

Nonetheless, the ebb and flow of relations with India remains a factor of considerable importance. Broadly speaking, the normalization of Indo-Pakistani relations would advance the prospects for mutual nuclear restraints, an approach that Pakistan has pursued as a second track of its nuclear policy for more than a decade.[38] At the other extreme, the outbreak of bilateral hostilities could lead to increasingly serious consequences as the nuclear capabilities of both countries grow.

After the 1971 conflict, the two countries experienced a period of "cold peace," marked by non-interference in each other's internal affairs. This era—which nonetheless saw Pakistan initiate its nuclear-weapons development program—came to an end in 1983, when bilateral relations turned increasingly hostile. An uprising of separatists in Pakistan's Sind Province in August 1983 sparked accusations by Islamabad that India was aiding and encouraging the rebels. Over the following year, New Delhi, in turn, accused Islamabad of fomenting unrest by Sikh nationalists in India's Punjab region and of making incursions into Kashmir, which had led to a series of border clashes. As described in detail in the section on India earlier in this chapter, these issues have troubled relations repeatedly in subsequent years and, despite periods of harmony, mutual antagonisms became so intense in the early fall of 1984 that general war was considered a distinct possiblity.

After the assassination of Indian Prime Minister Indira Gandhi in late October 1984, President Zia launched a "peace offensive" aimed at improving ties between the two countries. Though a brief warming trend ensued, by mid-1985 a decline was again evident. On the nuclear front, in June and July Zia and his top aides accused India of provoking a nuclear arms race by building up its nuclear capabilties and by refusing Pakistan's repeated offers of mutual inspections and bilateral non-proliferation pledges. The effectiveness of this campaign was severely undercut, however, by the July 1985 report, noted earlier, that Pakistan had tested the non-nuclear triggering package for a nuclear device.

Despite this development, other well publicized Pakistani nuclear advances, and India's commissioning of the Dhruva research reactor in early August 1985 with a provocative announcement highlighting its plutonium-producing capabilities, overall relations with New Delhi managed to improve in the latter half of 1985, leading to the watershed Zia-Gandhi meeting in New Delhi in December 1985 at which the two leaders agreed not to attack each other's nuclear installations and took steps toward normalizing relations in a number of areas.[39] (Ironically, late 1985 was the time when Washington had learned of Pakistan's crossing the 5 percent enrichment "red line" at Kahuta. Either India was unaware of this development or chose to ignore it.)

The warming trend was short-lived, however, in part because of domestic political difficulties on both sides, including serious anti-government disturbances in the two countries, which each accused the other of secretly abetting.[40]

The first published report that Pakistan had enriched uranium to 30 percent, it may be added, appeared in March 1986; possibly this contributed to increased tensions between the two countries.[41]

Developments

From the end of 1986 through the first half of 1988, as relations with India remained tense, evidence that Pakistan possessed the essentials for a small number of nuclear weapons continued to mount. Equally disturbing were a series of separate revelations, including the exposure of several major nuclear smuggling attempts, indicating that Pakistan intended to expand its weapons capabilities substantially in future years. While the Zia government pursued these clandestine efforts to enhance its nuclear potential, it also successfully maneuvered to retain U.S. military and economic assistance, as the U.S. Congress, from February to December 1987, deliberated whether to renew Pakistan's six-year exemption from the Symington Amendment. Simultaneously, Pakistan pursued the arms control track of its nuclear policy, by proposing a regional nuclear test ban with India and ratifying the Partial Test Ban Treaty, apparently to demonstrate its seriousness in pursuing nuclear restraints—and possibly to help deflect criticism of its other nuclear activities.

Indo-Pakistani tensions. As described in the preceding section of this chapter on India, at the end of 1986—by which point Pakistan had apparently acquired its first stocks of weapons-grade uranium—Indo-Pakistani relations deteriorated seriously, and major Indian military exercises near the Pakistani border, known as Operation Brass Tacks, led to a series of mobilizations and counter-mobilizations that some feared might lead to war. The crisis eased after agreement was reached on a mutual pull-back of forces, but bilateral frictions continued, with accusations by each country that the other was interfering in its internal affairs and skirmishing on the disputed Siachen Glacier in Kashmir dominating the bilateral agenda. In this uncomfortable security environment—made all the more stressful by the continued Soviet presence in Afghanistan—Pakistan continued to advance its nuclear capabilities, and indeed, by early 1987, it appeared Pakistan had decided to declare itself a nuclear power.

A. Q. Khan interview. On March 1, 1987, a controversial interview with the head of Pakistan's classified uranium enrichment program, A. Q. Khan, was simultaneously published in Islamabad, New Delhi, and London.[42] In the interview—written by the well-known Indian journalist Kuldip Nayar—Khan was quoted as declaring that Pakistan had built nuclear arms. "They told us that Pakistan could never produce the bomb and they doubted my capabilities," Khan was reported as saying, "but now they know we have done it . . . America knows it. What the CIA has been saying about our possessing the bomb is correct and so is the speculation in some foreign newspapers." Khan was also reported to have explicitly stated that Pakistan had produced weapons-grade uranium, declaring, "We have upgraded it to ninety percent to achieve the desired result."

Immediately after the interview appeared, the Pakistani government issued a release containing a denial by Khan in which he claimed that the piece had attributed to him "false and concocted statements" and insisted that Pakistan's enrichment program was entirely peaceful.[43] Khan also declared that he had never given an interview to Nayar, claiming that the Indian journalist had arrived at his home unannounced in the company of a friend of Khan's who was delivering a wedding invitation.[44] The picture became further confused when a Pakistani editor, Mushahid Hussein, who had been present at the meeting, told a British reporter that it was, indeed, a prearranged interview that lasted an hour. Hussein's statement forced Khan to acknowledge that the meeting had been set up in advance, though he still claimed it was only a "chat" during a brief social call. Hussein then wrote an editorial that confirmed the substance of what Nayar had reported by strongly endorsing the message of the Khan interview.[45] Days later, apparently under pressure from the Pakistani government, Hussein resigned from his paper—and declared that Khan had been misquoted.

Despite the furor that the interview caused, Khan's denial and the ensuing confusion over Hussein's confirmation blunted the article's political impact—particularly in the United States, where congressional consideration of continued U.S. aid to Pakistan was getting under way—and prevented it from being used as an authorative acknowledgement of Pakistan's nuclear ambitions. Nonetheless, the interview was generally taken seriously, and in India it sparked an outcry, as described earlier.[46]

On close examination it appears that much of the interview, though not its most provocative passages, was an unattributed, nearly verbatim repetition of an article Khan had written six months earlier in the Karachi English language newspaper, *Dawn*. Nayar's presentation, however, made it appear that the passages from the earlier article were actually said by Khan in the face-to-face meeting with the Indian reporter, a manipulation that raises serious questions about the authenticity of other statements attributed to Khan.[47] (When asked by the author in July 1988 why he had repeated the material from Khan's earlier article, Nayar stated that Khan, in responding to certain questions during the interview, had told him to consult the previously published piece; Nayar also insisted that the key statements in the Khan interview on Pakistan's possession of nuclear arms were accurate.)

Zia interview. At the end of March, President Zia appeared to amplify the remarks attributed to Khan, when, in an interview with *Time* magazine, he stated that "Pakistan has the capability of building the Bomb whenever it wishes." "Once you have acquired the technology," he continued, "which Pakistan has, you can do whatever you like." Zia's remarks, however, also contained ambiguities, as he stressed that Pakistan did not intend to manufacture nuclear arms and asserted that it had not yet enriched uranium to weapons-grade.[48] Zia later declared that he had been speaking only of Pakistan's broad technological capabilities, and had not meant to imply that his country was pursuing an ongoing nuclear weapons program.[49]

Congressional response. In early March 1987, U.S. lawmakers and officials began to acknowledge publicly Pakistan's growing nuclear capabilities. In an open letter to President Reagan of March 5, Senator John Glenn declared that evidence available to him "points to the conclusion that all the components and the means for assembling a working nuclear explosive device are in Pakistan's possession."[50] The statement was echoed several days later by an unnamed State Department official, who told a reporter, "We think they have the capability of producing one [nuclear bomb] now, but we're convinced they don't have one yet."[51] Glenn demanded that new U.S. aid be withheld until the President had received "reliable reassurances" that Pakistan was not seeking to manufacture nuclear weapons. In hearings before a House Subcommittee on March 5, however, Deputy Assistant Secretary of State Robert Peck, when asked if the President could obtain such assurances stated, "I doubt the President could, certainly not under the present circumstances."[52]

The mounting evidence that Pakistan, in violation of pledges given the United States, was marginally across the nuclear weapons threshold and was continuing to build up its nuclear capabilities appeared to have little impact on Congress, however. In March and April 1987, respectively, key commitees of the House and Senate, spurred by their concerns over Afghanistan, voted in favor of a proposal crafted by Congressman Stephen Solarz to continue aid to Islamabad, albeit only for two years rather than the six sought by the Reagan Administration. The vote in the Senate Foreign Relations Committee on April 23 was particularly noteworthy because the committee rejected even the partial cut in aid proposed by Senator Alan Cranston as a means for demonstrating displeasure over Pakistan's nuclear activities without rupturing relations.[53]

European smuggling operation. Within days of the Senate committee vote, the West German weekly, *Stern*, published a lengthy article detailing a West German and Swiss investigation of an extraordinary Pakistani nuclear smuggling operation. The operation involved the custom-manufacture in Switzerland of major pieces of equipment designed specifically for the production of highly enriched uranium and the secret transfer of closely-held blueprints of parts of West Germany's own uranium enrichment facility at Gronau.[54]

The first step in the operation unearthed by *Stern* took place in June 1983, when two executives from the Cologne-based materials processing and electronics firm, Leybold-Hereaus, Gmbh, contracted with a Swiss industrial equipment manufacturer, Metallwerke Buchs, to build a number of pieces of specialized enrichment-plant equipment according to Leybold's detailed blueprints. Leybold had apparently obtained the plans legally from West Germany's quasi-governmental uranium enrichment corporation, Uranit, when it had unsuccessfully bid on a contract to supply vacuum equipment for Uranit's facility in Gronau.[55]

The specific items that Metallwerke was to fabricate included: a number of large autoclaves—electronically controlled, air-tight, precision furnaces, fifteen feet long and six feet in diameter—for heating uranium hexafluoride at the "front-end" of the enrichment process, so as to transform it from a solid into a gas; special 48-X steel containers, to hold the highly corrosive hexafluoride during the heating process; and type "CD-AB-1" de-sublimers—cooling traps to take the uranium hexafluoride gas after enrichment and return it to a solid state.[56] All of the items require export licenses in Switzerland and West Germany.

Swiss authorities opened an investigation in 1984, when they learned that plans from the West German facility were being used by a Swiss firm, but made little headway until January 1986, when they raided Metallwerke's workshops, seizing additional equipment and the Uranit blueprints. Apparently a number of autoclaves had already been transferred to Pakistan via France. A joint investigation with West German authorities subsequently connected Leybold-Hereaus to the affair.

West German enrichment specialists interviewed by the press stated that it was certain that the equipment was to be used to produce highly enriched uranium because the desublimers were far narrower than those used in plants, like Gronau, which produce only low-enriched uranium; the narrower size is required to avoid criticality accidents, *i.e.*, unintended, potentially explosive chain reactions, triggered when sufficiently large quantities of highly enriched uranium (or plutonium) are permitted to accumulate. This detail thus leaves little doubt as to Pakistan's ultimate objective in acquiring this hardware.[57]

Although fewer details have been published concerning the blueprints that Leybold obtained and allegedly passed on to Pakistan, it appears that they covered elements of the Gronau facility designed for handling the uranium hexafluoride gas as it moved through the enrichment process. Details of the centrifuges themselves were apparently not involved. According to the 1979 Dutch government investigation noted earlier, however, Pakistan is thought to have already obtained information on centrifuges as a result of A. Q. Khan's work at the Dutch enrichment plant at Almelo. Both this facility and the Gronau plant are operated as part of the British-Dutch-West German uranium enrichment consortium, Urenco. The Leybold-Hereaus affair would thus represent the second time that the consortium's information security system had been breached.

Significantly, according to Western officials quoted by the press, the sizable Leybold-Hereaus operation appeared to be part of a Pakistani effort to acquire the hardware for a second uranium enrichment plant, suggesting that a major expansion of Pakistan's nuclear weapons program was under way.[58] Pakistani officials denied Pakistan was involved in the affair, calling it a "smear."[59]

Smuggling in U.S.; Congressional response. The Leybold-Hereaus affair received little attention in the United States, and it appeared that a strong congressional consensus had been achieved in favor of the Solarz proposal for two years of further aid to Islamabad. This consensus was shattered on July 11, 1987 when Arshad Pervez, a Pakistani-born Canadian, was arrested in Philadelphia for attempting to export illegally to Pakistan twenty-five tons of "maraging" steel, an especially strong form of the metal used in uranium enrichment centrifuges, and beryllium, used in nuclear weapons themselves to increase their yield.

Pervez's activities appeared to violate a 1985 law prohibiting U.S. assistance to non-nuclear-weapon states that illegally attempt to export nuclear commodities from the United States to develop nuclear weapons. The law had been sponsored by Congressman Solarz and, in a startling reversal of his position during the spring, in mid-July Solarz called for the termination of further U.S. assistance to Pakistan unless Islamabad accepted verifiable restraints on the production of weapons-grade uranium. Within a week, leading House and Senate moderates echoed Solarz's call for tough measures, and it appeared that a major change in congressional attitudes was under way.[60] Seeming to recognize the new climate, administration aides declared that during his upcoming visit to Islamabad, Assistant Secretary of State for Political Affairs Michael H. Armacost would press Pakistan to provide "concrete" evidence that it was restraining its nuclear program.[61]

Before Armacost departed, both the House and the Senate had passed unanimous non-binding resolutions declaring that future U.S. military aid would be jeopardized unless Pakistan provided verifiable assurances that it would cease producing weapons-grade uranium at Kahuta. Nonetheless, congressional commitment to this new get-tough policy remained uncertain. On July 29, the House subcommittee responsible for appropriating foreign-aid funds voted the full measure of assistance for Pakistan sought by the administration for fiscal year 1988. The only non-proliferation condition it attached was to delay the availability of the funds until January 15, 1988.[62]

With congressional thinking thus uncertain and with the Reagan Administration plainly hoping to avoid a rupture with Islamabad, on August 4, Pakistan's President Zia ul-

Haq not unexpectedly rebuffed Armacost's request for clear-cut limits on Pakistan's nuclear activities.[63] Members of Pakistan's parliament, both in the ruling Pakistani Muslim League Party and in the opposition, forcefully echoed Zia's stance in early September.[64] In Washington, the impasse led to a *de facto* suspension of congressional action on the aid issue, while lawmakers debated other portions of the omnibus "continuing resolution" spending bill to which it would be attached.

Test ban offer. In mid-September, with the aid question still unresolved, Pakistani Prime Minister Junejo announced in a speech to the United Nations General Assembly that in June he had proposed a bilateral ban on nuclear testing to Indian Prime Minister Gandhi. Although Junejo's public disclosure of the initiative appeared timed to placate American critics of Pakistan's nuclear program, the fact that the ban had been proposed privately in June suggests that it was aimed more at India and represented a new element in Pakistan's long-standing efforts to engage New Delhi in bilateral nuclear-arms-control arrangements. These efforts appear to represent a second track of Pakistani nuclear policy aimed at placing limits on India's nuclear potential, even as Pakistan has sought to achieve a nuclear weapons capability of its own.

As described in detail in the the section on India in this chapter, Pakistan has over the years offered to enter into a wide range of comprehensive bilateral nuclear arrangements with India, including reciprocal ratification of the NPT, mutual acceptance of IAEA safeguards on all nuclear installations, comprehensive bilateral nuclear inspections, the establishment of a nuclear-weapon-free zone in South Asia, and formal mutual pledges not to manufacture nuclear arms. India has rejected these proposals in large part because all but the last would restrict India's right to develop nuclear arms at some future time in reponse to China, a nuclear-weapon state since 1964.

Junejo's test ban offer, in addition to avoiding the comprehensive controls that would constrain India's nuclear options, also appeared more practical than prior proposals because it was apparently consistent with the actual nuclear testing policies of both countries. Most observers believe that neither is likely to test a nuclear device because of fears that this might trigger a test or a series of tests by the other and because a test would likely result in the imposition of sanctions by the United States and, possibly, additional nations.[65] Since India has already conducted a test, while Pakistan has not, and since both would be prohibited from conducting tests during the period of the ban, the proposal, it may be noted, would appear to be highly advantageous for New Delhi; in effect, it would perpetuate India's current lead in this area. (Pakistan is thought to have obtained a validated nuclear weapon design from the People's Republic of China and to have tested the non-nuclear parts of the device. Accordingly, it is generally believed that it could have confidence in its nuclear weapons without the need for a full-scale test.)[66]

For these reasons, the Junejo proposal appears to have been a serious attempt to engage India in substantive nuclear talks that might eventually place a cap on the region's emerging nuclear arms race, a race that otherwise could lead to an Indian nuclear arsenal that vastly overshadowed Pakistan's. (See discussion in the section on "Prospects," below.) It also provided Islamabad the short-term political advantage of casting itself as the champion of nuclear restraint in the region, particularly after India's rejection of the test ban proposal as "not serious."[67]

Aid suspended. On September 30, the end of fiscal year 1987, Congress remained deadlocked over spending priorities and, unable to pass a government-wide appropriation for fiscal year 1988, enacted a short-term continuation of existing appropriations in order to keep the U.S. government functioning. In so doing, however, Congress declined to include an extension of Pakistan's six-year waiver from the Symington Amendment, which had expired with the end of the fiscal year. With the Symington provision now applicable, Pakistan's importation of uranium enrichment equipment, together with its failure to place all of its nuclear facilities under IAEA safeguards, made it ineligible for further U.S. assistance.[68]

As a practical matter, this had little impact on Pakistan's economy or on its military capabilities, since the considerable quantities of aid previously authorized and in the process of being transferred to Pakistan were unaffected. Nonetheless, the failure to renew the Symington Amendment waiver inevitably sowed additional doubt as to whether U.S. aid would be renewed, despite the Reagan Administration's pains to assure Islamabad that it had nothing to fear in this regard. Pakistan responded defiantly to the aid suspension, as it had to congressional non-proliferation pressure throughout the summer, declaring that it would not accept new nuclear restraints as a condition for renewed U.S. assistance.[69]

As the war of nerves continued, U.S. Ambassador-at-Large for Non-Proliferation Richard T. Kennedy was forced to acknowledge at a hearing before Congressman Solarz in late October that Pakistan had enriched uranium to more than the 5 percent level specified in President Reagan's September 1984 letter—the administration's first public admission that Pakistan had taken this step.[70] India, meanwhile, intensified its long-standing campaign of urging the United States to intervene more forcefully with Pakistan, an issue that Rajiv Gandhi made a central theme of his visit to Washington in late October.[71]

Thirty-month extension. Behind the scenes, however, the key development that would govern congressional thinking was unfolding, as negotiations on the withdrawal of Soviet troops made unexpected progress and brought the prospect of a Soviet pull-out within reach. On December 17, 1987, only hours before Arshad Pervez was convicted in Philadelphia for nuclear smuggling[72]—and barely a week after a startling report that Pakistan had begun construction of a second uranium enrichment plant, in the town of Golra, some six miles west of Islamabad[73]—a House-Senate conference committee approved a compromise authorizing $480 million in economic and military aid to Pakistan and waiving the Symington Amendment's aid cut for two and a half years.[74] Both houses ratified the measure on December 22.[75] Despite its repeated disregard of U.S. non-proliferation laws and policies, Pakistan had continued to advance its nuclear capabilities—and had managed to retain U.S. economic and military support.

U.S. acknowledgement. In late December 1987 and mid-January 1988, respectively, the Reagan Administration removed the last remaining obstacles to providing American aid to Islamabad by certifying that Pakistan did not "possess" a nuclear explosive device and by waiving the non-proliferation restriction prohibiting assistance to non-nuclear countries that engage in nuclear smuggling in the United States.[76] In testimony on the latter decision—a decision which amounted to a finding that the Pakistani government had been behind the Pervez operation and which then excused the offense—the administration for the first time publicly acknowledged that Pakistan was developing nuclear weapons and that the country's enrichment program was being pursued for this purpose.[77] The administration also stated that there was "a substantial international network of nuclear procurement agents working on Pakistan's behalf that must be closely monitored" and that even in the United States, some Pakistani smuggling activities were continuing.[78] (One on-going overseas operation appears to have involved the procurement of electronic controllers, known as "inverters," from Turkey.)[79]

Prospects

On March 6, 1988, the *New York Times Magazine* published a detailed report by Hedrick Smith on the Pakistani nuclear program based on information from U.S. government sources. The account stated that Pakistan had accumulated enough highly enriched uranium for four to six nuclear weapons; Smith said in a subsequent interview that he had been told that Pakistan had accumulated 220 pounds (100 kilograms) of the material. Sources quoted in the piece also confirmed earlier accounts that Pakistan's weapons are based on a Chinese design and provided the new information that the weapons weighed only 400 pounds (180 kilograms),[80] indicating that they were considerably more advanced than the first U.S. weapons, which weighed approximately 10,000 pounds (4,500 kilograms). The article went on to state that Pakistan had fabricated virtually all of the components for these devices and made it clear that Pakistan could rapidly deploy nuclear weapons in any future conflict, even if technically speaking, it did not yet "possess" a fully assembled nuclear device, as President Reagan had certified in December.[81] Reagan Administration sources subsequently suggested in off-the-record interviews that not all of the details in the piece were correct but confirmed that its overall characterization of the status of the Pakistani nuclear program was accurate.[82]

As noted above, U.S. officials believe that Pakistan began to produce weapons-grade uranium sometime in 1986. This would mean, in rough terms, that it had produced 220 pounds (100 kilograms) over about two years, giving it an annual production capacity of about 110 pounds (50 kilograms), enough for two to three weapons, using the standard estimates that between 33 and 55 pounds (15 to 25 kilograms) of the material are required per device. This is consistent with previously published estimates of Pakistan's nuclear capabilities. See Tables 3 and 4.

Judging from Pakistan's attempts to acquire large quantities of maraging steel in the United States through the Pervez operation, its attempted purchase of a number of custom-made autoclaves and related equipment in Switzerland via Leybold-Hereaus, and the report that it had begun construction of a second enrichment facility in the town of Golra, it appears that Pakistan has been seeking to expand its uranium enrichment capabilities substantially. Successful law enforcement efforts in the United States and Switzerland may have set back this expansion for some time.

Nonetheless, even if Pakistan's expansion plans have been temporarily stymied, its ability to prepare at least a

Table 3

Potential Annual Production of Weapons Grade Uranium (WGU) By Pakistan Through 1992

Facility (1st yr. WGU made)	Annual WGU Output/ No. of Weapons*	Restrictions on Use of WGU	WGU On Hand for Weapons 1/1/87
Kahuta (1986)	21-63 kgs <1-4 wpns	None**	25-50 kgs 1- 3 weapons

* The number of centrifuges operating at Kahuta is not known, but estimates vary from 1000 to 14,000 (for higher estimate, see, "Inside Kahuta," *Foreign Report*, May 1, 1986). Pakistan is reported to have had considerable difficulty operating these units, however. Therefore, to be conservative, the low estimate here assumes that 1000 centrifuges are operating, and the high estimate assumes that 3000 are operating.

The units are said to be based on a type used at the Dutch enrichment facilty at Almelo, the Netherlands, assumed to have a capacity of five kilograms of "separative work units" (the measure of enrichment capability) per year. It is also assumed that uraniun-235 is culled from the uranium initially fed into the plant (which contains .7 percent U-235) at a rate that leaves only .2 percent of these atoms in the residue, or "tails," of the process. WGU is assumed to be uranium enriched to 93 percent.

Finally, for low estimates it is assumed that 25 kilograms of WGU are needed for a nuclear device; for high estimates, it is assumed that only 15 kilograms are required. This analysis is based on David Albright, "Pakistan's Bomb-Making Capability," *Bulletin of the Atomic Scientists*, June 1981: p.30.

** The Kahuta facility is widely believed to employ various pieces of equipment obtained in violation of Western export laws. In part because of difficulties of proof, no Western government has demanded that the facility be placed under IAEA safeguards, a condition that would have been imposed had such equipment been exported through normal channels.

---

small number of nuclear devices quickly places it in roughly the same position as India, with neither state having deployed nuclear weapons or, it appears, having taken steps to integrate such weapons into its armed forces and military doctrine. Although the number of weapons India could manufacture would presumably far surpass the number potentially available to Pakistan for the foreseeable future,[83] at present some form of rough-hewn mutual nuclear deterrence must be assumed to exist on the Indian Subcontinent.[84] Indeed, in a July 1988 interview with a member

Table 4
Speculative Estimate of Pakistani Nuclear Weapons Potential Through 1992
(Cumulative Amount of Weapons Grade Uranium (WGU) and Cumulative Number of Weapons*)

1/1/1986		1987		1988		1989		1990		1991		1992	
Lo	Hi	L	H	L	H	L	H	L	H	L	H	L	H
0		25	50	46	113	67	176	88	239	109	302	130	365 kgs
0		1	3	1	7	2	11	3	15	4	20	5	24 wpns

* For low estimates it is assumed that 25 kilograms of WGU are needed for a nuclear device; for high estimates, it is assumed that only 15 kilograms are required. This analysis is based on David Albright, "Pakistan's Bomb-Making Capability," *Bulletin of the Atomic Scientists*, June 1981: p.30.

of a delegation, sponsored by the Carnegie Endowment for International Peace, which was examining nuclear proliferation in South Asia, President Zia declared:

With respect to their [India's] nuclear capabilities, if they create ambiguity, that ambiguity is the essence of deterrence. The present programs of India and Pakistan have a lot of ambiguities, and therefore in the eyes of each other, they have reached a particular level, and that level is good enough to create an impression of deterrence.

With its tacit acknowledgement that Pakistan may possess a de facto nuclear weapons capability, the statement, it may be added, marks a major departure from Zia's past insistence that Pakistan's nuclear program is devoted exclusively to peaceful purposes.

The principal factor that has prompted Pakistan to pursue the acquisition of nuclear arms—the fear of Indian hegemony by virtue of its conventional military superiority and its nuclear capabilities—remains a central concern. Although Pakistan has sought to modernize its own conventional forces in recent years, India's military build-up has at the very least maintained New Delhi's pre-existing advantage, and its steps to acquire new high-visibility systems, including its lease of a Soviet nuclear-powered submarine, the test-firing of the Prithvi surface-to-surface missile, and its deployment of a second aircraft carrier, have undoubtedly increased Pakistani anxieties. The generally antagonistic relations between the two countries, to which both are thought to contribute, show few signs of abating, despite occasional improvements in bilateral links. Thus there is good reason to believe that Pakistan will continue the course it has pursued for over a decade of acquiring a nuclear deterrent capability. Indeed, given the evidence of Pakistan's plans to expand its enriched uranium production capacity and its apparently continuing clandestine nuclear purchasing activities, it appears that Pakistan is firmly committed to enlarging its *de facto* nuclear weapon stockpile.

At the same time, because of the threat of U.S. sanctions and the fear of stimulating India to pursue its own nuclear capabilities more aggressively, Pakistan appears unlikely to alter its ambiguous nuclear status by conducting a test or declaring it possesses nuclear arms. As the appreciation of the *de facto* bilateral nuclear deterrence relationship grows, however, pressures are likely to mount in Pakistan to move toward militarizing the country's nuclear potential, to begin testing, to acquire additional delivery capabilities, and to expand the country's nuclear stockpile in order to increase targeting options and ensure the survivability of a Pakistani retaliatory force in the event of an Indian attack. Indeed movement to enlarge Pakistan's weapons production capabilities is already evident, as suggested above.[85]

In this regard, entering into nuclear arms limitations with India would appear to be a desirable alternative to open-ended nuclearization and one that Pakistan has been pursuing. Pakistan's proposal for a bilateral test ban, discussed above, is a more practical initiative than Islamabad's past bids to engage India in this process. In December 1987, Pakistan ratified the Partial Test Ban Treaty, prohibiting nuclear tests in the atmosphere, in outer space, or under water. Pakistan had signed the accord in 1963. The action brings Pakistan in line with India, which has also ratified the pact, and could counter Indian charges that Pakistan's offer of a comprehensive regional test ban is not serious.

On May 29, 1988, President Zia suddenly dissolved Pakistan's parliament, as permitted under the country's constitution. Zia, who also serves as Army Chief of Staff, declared that he would announce new elections within ninety days—meaning, it subsequently appeared, that within this period he would announce the date when elections would eventually be held. The move was perceived as a reassertion of power by Pakistan's military, whose authority was being challenged by Prime Minister Junejo. The development is unlikely to affect Pakistan's nuclear weapons program directly, since the program appeared to have both civilian and military backing. The development, however, highlights the risk of political instability in Pakistan, which could lead to nuclear weapons (or highly enriched uranium) becoming bargaining chips in a struggle for domestic power. Episodes of this kind appear to have occurred during periods of internal unrest in France and China during the 1960s and are not as far-fetched as they may first appear.[86]

The presence of Soviet troops in Afghanistan since 1979 has seriously exacerbated Pakistani security concerns and has probably contributed indirectly to its quest for nuclear arms. Moscow began withdrawing its forces from Afghanistan in May 1988. How this will affect nuclear developments in Pakistan remains uncertain.

The Soviet withdrawal will leave a political vacuum in Afghanistan that could contribute to internal instability in Pakistan, if internecine fighting among Pakistan-based anti-Soviet Afghan guerrilla forces spills over there. More directly, the Soviet exodus is likely to add yet another controversy to the agenda of bilateral Indo-Pakistani differences, as India extends increasing political support to the Soviet-backed Najibullah government in Afghanistan—apparently in a bid to project its influence in this part of the region—while Pakistan continues to assist Afghan rebel forces, in the hope that pro-Pakistani elements will succeed to power in Kabul. This suggests that the security concerns that have prompted Pakistan to pursue nuclear arming may be little changed by the Soviet move.

As the threat of Soviet expansionism in the region eases, however, it is possible that the United States will begin applying greater pressure on Islamabad to halt its nuclear advances. On the other hand, Washington will have strong reasons for maintaining close ties with Islamabad, given the prospect of continued turmoil in Afghanistan and broader U.S. interests in maintaining Pakistan as a strategic partner in the Persian Gulf region, where the destabilizing influence of Iran will continue to pose a threat. Changes in Pakistan's nuclear status will also limit American options. By 1991, if estimates of Pakistan's existing capabilities are correct, Pakistan could possess the essentials for as many as fifteen nuclear devices. It is hard to imagine U.S. pressure eliminating this *de facto* nuclear deterrent. U.S. diplomacy may be able to achieve a freeze on Pakistan's further production of weapons-grade uranium (possibly in conjunction with the adoption of similar restraints by India); the elimination of a two-party undeclared nuclear deterrence system in South Asia, however, may well be beyond reach.

Barring significant changes in Indo-Pakistani relations or a major diplomatic initiative by extra-regional states that succeeds in encouraging added nuclear restraints by both parties, an open-ended, if relatively slow-paced and still unannounced, nuclear arms race appears likely to remain a troubling new element of the South Asian security environment.[88]

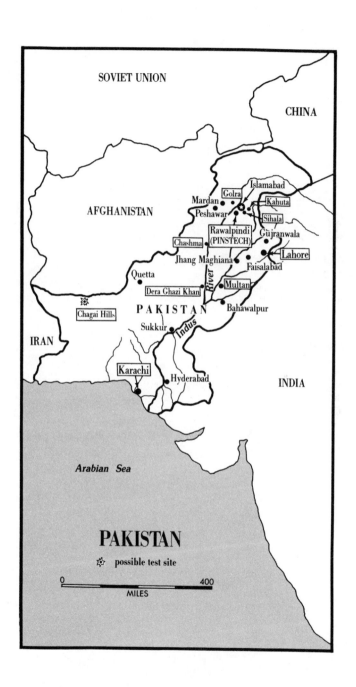

SOVIET UNION

CHINA

AFGHANISTAN

Mardan
Golra
Islamabad
Kahuta
Peshawar
Sihala
Chashma
Rawalpindi
(PINSTECH)
Gujranwala
Jhang Maghiana
Lahore
Faisalabad
Quetta
Multan
Dera Ghazi Khan
PAKISTAN
Bahawalpur
Chagai Hills
Sukkur
Indus
River

IRAN

Karachi
Hyderabad

INDIA

Arabian Sea

PAKISTAN

✿ possible test site

0   400

MILES

Pakistan

Power Reactors/Operating or Under Construction
KANUPP, Karachi (heavy-water/natural-uranium,125 MWe[a])
- supplier: Canadian General Electric (Canada)
- start up: 1972
- fuel source: Canada[b], also Pakistan after 1980
- heavy water: United States and Canada[c]
- safeguards: yes[d]

Uranium Resources/Active Mining Sites/Uranium Mills
- reasonably assured   sufficient for Kahuta
  reserves: enrichment plant[e]
- currently active site: Dera Ghazi Khan
- mills in operation: Lahore[f]

Uranium Conversion (UF$_6$)
Dera Ghazi Khan
- capacity: max. 198 metric tons of hexafluoride per year[g]
- supplier: CES Kalthof G.m.b.H. of Freiburg (West Germany)[h]
- start up: 1980[h]
- safeguards: no

Heavy Water
Multan
- capacity: 13 metric tons[c]
- supplier: Belgonucléaire (Belgium)[f](?)
- start up: 1980 (?)[f]
- safeguards: no

Karachi
- capacity: upgradation unit to serve KANUPP, quantity unknown[f]
- supplier: Canada (?)
- start up: 1976
- safeguards: (?)

Enrichment
Kahuta
- type: ultracentrifuge
- capacity: Currently 1,000-14,000 (?) centrifuges[i]; 100 kilograms of highly enriched uranium reportedly produced as of early 1988[p]
- supplier: Pakistan, with extensive use of equipment and technology clandestinely acquired from various Western countries.[r]
- start up: 1984 (partial); highly enriched uranium first produced in 1986[j]
- safeguards: no

Sihala
- type: ultracentrifuge[f]
- capacity: experimental scale

• supplier:	same as Kahuta (presumed)
• start up:	1979[t]
• safeguards:	no

Golra (reported)[s]

• type:	ultracentrifuge
• capacity:	?
• supplier:	Pakistan with equipment clandestinely aquired from various Western countries
• start up:	?
• safeguards:	no

Fuel Fabrication
Chashma/Kundian

• capacity:	sufficient fuel for KANUPP[c]
• supplier:	Pakistan, plans from Canada[k]
• start up:	1980[l]
• safeguards:	no

Reprocessing
Chashma

• capacity:	100 metric tons of spent fuel; 100 to 200 kg of plutonium per year[g]
• supplier:	SGN (France)
• start up:	France terminated this project in 1978; construction may be continuing.
• safeguards:	uncertain; agreement between Pakistan, France, and IAEA provides for safeguards, but these provisions not yet in force.

New Labs, Rawalpindi

• capacity:	capable of extracting 10 to 20 kg of plutonium per year[q]
• supplier:	SGN (France), Belgonucléaire (Belgium)[g,m]
• start up:	cold tests 1982; plant believed not to be operating.[n]
• safeguards:	no (but might be subject to safeguards as a "replicated" plant under Pakistan-France-IAEA agreement covering Chashma plant, if safeguards under this agreement are implemented).

PINSTECH, Rawalpindi

• capacity:	experimental scale[o]
• supplier:	Pakistan (?); plans from Great Britain[o]
• start up:	?
• safeguards:	no

Research Reactor
PARR, Rawalpindi (light-water/highly enriched uranium, 5 MWt)[a]

• supplier:	United States[a] (through the IAEA)
• start up:	1965[a]
• fuel source:	United States
• safeguards:	yes[a]

Sources and Notes

a. International Atomic Energy Agency, *The Annual Report for 1981* (IAEA, 1982), pp. 73-76. An enlargement of the research reactor to 10MWt is planned. "LWR's for Pakistan," *Nuclear Engineering Int'l*, April 1986, p.5.

b. Canada terminated fuel supplies in 1976 because of Pakistan's unwillingness to sign the Non-Proliferation Treaty; since 1980, plant has run partly on Pakistani-produced fuel and on remaining Canadian-supplied material.

c. David Hart, *Nuclear Power in India: A Comparative Analysis* (London: George Allen and Unwin), p. 133; "Pakistan AEC Journal Says Nation Has Mastered Front End of Fuel Cycle," *Nuclear Fuel*, March 25, 1985, p.10.

d. From September 1980 until March 1983, IAEA was unable to certify that no diversion of spent fuel occurred. Milton Benjamin, "Pakistan Backs Atomic Safeguards," *Washington Post* , November 17, 1982.

e. "Scientist Affirms Pakistan Capable of Uranium Enrichment, Weapons Production," *Nawa-I-Waqt* (Lahore). February 10, 1984, translated in *Joint Publication Research Service/Nuclear Proliferation and Development*, March 5, 1984, p. 36; "Pakistan AEC Journal . . .," *Nuclear Fuel* (see note c).

   According to press reports in November 1979, Pakistan had obtained as much as 100 metric tons of uranium concentrate, or "yellowcake," not subject to International Atomic Energy Agency monitoring from Libya. The material had originally been purchased by Libya from Niger and then re-exported to Pakistan, possibly along with material that Pakistan had itself purchased from Niger through normal, above-board channels. John J. Fialka, "West Concerned by Signs of Libyan-Pakistan A-Effort," *Washington Star,* November 25, 1979.

f. P. B. Sinha and R. R. Subramanian, *Nuclear Pakistan* (New Delhi: Vision Books 1980), pp. 35, 121.

g. Weissman and Krosney, *The Islamic Bomb* (New York: Times Books, 1981), p. 219, (UF_6); pp. 80-84 (New Labs); p. 81, (experimental reprocessing unit); "Germans Fostered Climate for Bombs," *Der Stern,* July 2, 1981, pp. 96-99.

h. Weissman and Krosney, *The Islamic Bomb,* p. 219. John M. Geddes, "Bonn Says Firm Illegally Sent Pakistan Gear That Can Be Used for Atomic Bombs," *Wall Street Journal,* July 16, 1981.

i. Senator Alan Cranston, "Nuclear Proliferation and U.S. National Security Interests," *Congressional Record,* June 21, 1984, p. S 7901; "Inside Kahuta," *Foreign Report,* May 1, 1986.

j. "Scientist Affirms," *Nawa-I-Waqt,* pp. 43-44 (see note e); Hedrick Smith, "A Bomb Ticks in Pakistan," *New York Times Magazine,* March 6, 1988, p. 38.

k. "Nuclear Facilities in the Middle East," Department of State, submitted in *Hearings on the Israeli Air Strike,* June 18, 19, and 25, 1981, 97th Congress, 1st Session (Washington, D.C.: Government Printing Office, 1981), p. 40.

l. James Katz and Onkar Marwah, *Nuclear Power in Developing Countries* (Lexington, MA: Lexington Books, 1982), p. 268.

m. According to Weissman and Krosney, *The Islamic Bomb,* France may not have been aware of SGN participation.

n. Cranston, "Nuclear Proliferation and U.S. National Security Interests." Cranston states facility has operated with radioactive material, but U.S. officials deny this. (Personal communication). Seymour M. Hersh, "Pakistani In U.S. Sought to Ship A-Bomb Trigger," *New York Times,* February 25, 1985.

o. Thomas W. Graham, "South Asian Nuclear Proliferation and National Security Chronology," Center for International Affairs, Massachusetts Institute of Technology, 1984, citing Weissman and Krosney, *The Islamic Bomb,* p. 81.

p. Hedrick Smith, "A Bomb Ticks in Pakistan," *New York Times Magazine,* March 6, 1988, p. 38.

q. Milton R. Benjamin, "Pakistan Building Secret Nuclear Plant," *Washington Post,* September 23, 1980.

r. See Leonard S. Spector, *The New Nuclear Nations* (New York: Vintage Books, 1985) Chapter II, "The Nuclear Netherworld," and accompanying notes, especially note 31. See also discussion in text above.

s. Simon Henderson, "Pakistan Builds Second Plant to Enrich Uranium," *Financial Times,* December 11, 1987. But see, "Reports of Pakistan Uranium Plant Weighed," *New York Times,* January 10, 1988; "Pakistan Denies New Enrichment Plant," *Nuclear Engineering International* (February 1988): 7.

t. Hafiz R. Khan, "The Kahuta Story," *Defence Journal,* (August 1986): 11-13.

Photo 3.3 shows Pakistan's classified Kahuta enrichment plant (see arrow) taken by the French SPOT earth observation satellite. *Courtesy, Space Media Network/SPOT CNES.*

Photo 3.4 shows Pakistan's research reactor at the Pakistan Institute of Nuclear Science and Technology, near Rawalpindi. The reactor is covered by International Atomic Energy Agency inspections. (Note anti-aircraft guns in foreground.)
© *Sandro Tucci – Gamma/Liason.*

Photo 3.5 shows the Karachi Nuclear Power Plant. This unit (known as the KANUPP reactor) is covered by International Atomic Energy Agency inspections.
© *Sandro Tucci – Gamma/Liason.*

Chapter IV:
The Middle East

Israel remains the only Middle Eastern nation thought to possess nuclear weapons or the ability to manufacture them. On the basis of revelations by Israeli nuclear technician Mordechai Vanunu published in October 1986 and other recent reports and analyses, there is increasing evidence, which many find compelling, that Israel possesses a nuclear arsenal of at least fifty to sixty nuclear weapons, and perhaps considerably more, as well as delivery systems which include medium-range ballistic missiles. Some of Israel's nuclear weapons are thought to be of a type that would make them many times more powerful than the Hiroshima and Nagasaki bombs. Israel is not a party to the Non-Proliferation Treaty (NPT).

Three other states in the region—Libya, Iraq, and Iran—are thought to harbor an interest in acquiring nuclear arms and at one time or another have taken steps toward this goal, despite their status as parties to the NPT. All, however, are far from possessing the necessary nuclear infrastructure to manufacture such weapons themselves. Libya and, it appears, Iraq have made unsuccessful attempts to purchase nuclear weapons or nuclear weapons material from other nations or on the international black market; fortunately such commodities do not appear to be available from either source.

Syria, despite its minuscule nuclear infrastructure, must also be factored into the Middle East nuclear equation. In two interviews, one in September 1984 and the second in October 1985, Syrian Defense Minister Mustafa Tlas declared that the Soviet Union had "guaranteed" it would give Damascus nuclear weapons if Israel employed nuclear arms against Syria.[1] A Soviet spokesman claimed Tlas's statement was untrue, but other Soviet officials have reportedly told Western visitors that if Israel were to attack Syria itself—even if only with conventional armaments—Moscow would assist its ally with military force, including tactical nuclear weapons if necessary.[2] It seems most unlikely that Moscow would place nuclear arms under Syrian control; nevertheless, these reports, together with the presence of several thousand Soviet military advisers in Syria, leave little question that Israeli planners have to weigh seriously the risk of a Soviet response.

Israel recently tested a nuclear-capable missile that could reach the southern Soviet Union.[3] Israeli officials have indicated in off-the-record interviews that the missile is intended in part to deter massive Soviet intervention on behalf of Syria in any future conflict—a scenario that could all too easily escalate into a high-stakes U.S.-Soviet confrontation.

In the late 1970s, Egypt announced a major nuclear-power program but has yet to start construction of its first nuclear power plant. It is believed to have sought Chinese aid in developing nuclear arms during the 1960s[4] and is known to have used chemical weapons—mustard gas and possibly other chemical agents—in 1967 when its troops were fighting in North Yemen.[5] Since concluding its peace treaty with Israel in 1979 and ratifying the NPT in 1981, however, Egypt's nuclear intentions have appeared entirely peaceful.

Farther afield, Pakistan is believed to have manufactured the components for several nuclear weapons in 1987-1988.

While it is unlikely that the Pakistani nuclear program would pose a direct threat to Israel or that Pakistan would share its nuclear weapons with other states, given the country's strong Islamic orientation and its ties to Arab states in the Persian Gulf, Pakistan's growing nuclear capabilities could serve at least as a symbolic counterweight to Israel's. How concerned Israel may be about the so-called "Islamic bomb" is not clear. In recent years there have been occasional rumors, however, of Israeli discussions with India concerning a possible joint attack on Pakistan's key uranium enrichment plant at Kahuta.[6]

A new dimension to the problem is the possibility that Saudi Arabia, which recently purchased conventionally armed intermediate-range (1,800 mile) missiles from China in an unprecedented transfer, might collaborate with Pakistan to develop a nuclear warhead for the rocket. Saudi Arabia is thought to have provided financing for Pakistan's nuclear weapons development program and might hope to capitalize on this tie. In late April 1988, however, Saudi Arabia announced it would accede to the NPT, a step that will reaffirm and formalize its pledges not to develop or acquire nuclear arms.[7]

The spread of chemical warfare capabilities in the Middle East, the repeated use of chemical weapons in the Iran-Iraq war, and the spread of intermediate-range missiles that might be mounted with chemical warheads are adding new dangers to the regional security environment that Israel may hope to mitigate through nuclear deterrence. These issues and Iraq's renewed attacked on Iran's unfinished nuclear power plants at Bushehr are discussed in subsequent sections of this chapter.

Israel

In light of the revelations made to the London *Sunday Times* by Israeli nuclear technician Mordechai Vanunu in the fall of 1986, it has become increasingly clear that Israel possesses a substantial, undeclared nuclear arsenal of at least fifty to sixty nuclear devices—perhaps, significantly more—some of which are of an advanced design that makes them many times more powerful than the atomic weapons used in World War II.[1] During 1987 and the first half of 1988, Israel presumably continued to add to its nuclear armory.

Israel is also known to possess medium-range (400-mile) surface-to-surface ballistic missiles intended for use with nuclear warheads, and in May 1987, it tested a nuclear-capable missile with a 900-mile range, potentially able to reach targets in the southern Soviet Union.[2] Although Israel has not acknowledged that it possesses nuclear weapons and is not known to have conducted a nuclear test, there is increasing—some would say compelling—evidence that it should be thought of as the world's sixth nuclear power. Indeed, even among Israeli officials, veiled references to Israel's nuclear might are becoming more common, a distinct shift from the near total silence on the issue that has prevailed for decades.

Since Vanunu's revelations, new information has emerged strongly suggesting that to achieve its nuclear status, Israel has disregarded non-proliferation pledges covering a key nuclear commodity, heavy water, that it obtained from Norway in 1959. On a separate front, as surface-to-surface missiles and chemical weapons capabilities proliferate among Israel's adversaries, Israel's nuclear arms are likely to play an increasingly important role as a potential counter to attacks with such advanced non-nuclear weapons—a factor that could heighten the risks of nuclear escalation in a future Arab-Israeli conflict. These and other developments are discussed below.

Background: Vanunu's Disclosures and the Historical Record

In October 1986, the London *Sunday Times* published a lengthy story disclosing many new details about Israel's undeclared nuclear weapons program. The exposé was based on information and photographs supplied by Mordechai Vanunu, who, from August 1977 to November 1985, worked as a nuclear technician at Israel's classified Dimona nuclear complex in the Negev.

Vanunu told the *Sunday Times* in great detail how Israel produced plutonium for nuclear weapons at an underground plutonium extraction plant where he worked and where, he stated, the material was fabricated into components for nuclear weapons. Thus he unambiguously confirmed the existence of an Israeli nuclear weapons program.[3]

He also stated that Israel produced 88 pounds (40 kilograms) of plutonium annually, several times more than previously imagined. Vanunu's photos included pictures of a model of the interior components of an Israeli atomic device and of an actual weapon component. This led Dr. Theodore Taylor, a former U.S. nuclear weapons designer who was consulted by the *Sunday Times*, to conclude that Israel could build a nuclear weapon using only 8.8 pounds (4 kilograms) of plutonium—half the usually posited amount—and perhaps even less. On the basis of this information, Taylor, and Dr. Frank Barnaby, a nuclear physicist who had worked in the British nuclear weapons program, estimated that Israel's nuclear arsenal might comprise as many as 100 to 200 weapons, not the 20 to 25 usually estimated.[4] (U.S. officials accept the authenticity of Vanunu's technical data, but in off-the-record interviews, they have challenged the conclusion that Israel has more than 100 nuclear weapons because it is inconsistent with other relevant information in their possession suggesting that Israel has no more than 50 to 60 plutonium-using nuclear devices. See the discussion below in the section on developments.)

Despite the lack of evidence that Israel has conducted nuclear tests, which are usually deemed essential for the development of advanced nuclear weapons, Vanunu also stated that Israel had produced weapons that use nuclear fusion, the principle of the H-bomb.[5] Vanunu backed up his claim with a photo of a weapon component said to be made of lithium deuteride, a fusion material. On the basis of this evidence, Taylor and Barnaby concluded that Israel had indeed produced such advanced weapons. No new information has emerged to dispute their conclusions in this regard.[6]

Abduction. Vanunu disappeared from his London hotel several days before the *Sunday Times* story was published. Apparently a female Israeli intelligence operative lured him to Rome, where he was abducted by other Israeli agents and taken to Israel.[7] He was subsequently tried by a secret tribunal and convicted of espionage and treason on March 24, 1988, receiving an eighteen-year prison term.[8]

Israel's decision to detain and prosecute Vanunu indicates that his revelations were considered a major security leak and tends to confirm the authenticity of his disclosures. Indeed, since the *Sunday Times* story appeared, the authenticity of Vanunu's data and photographs has not been seriously challenged.[9]

Filling in the historical gaps. Vanunu's revelations and other newly available information, including details concerning Norway's early role in Israel's nuclear program, help to fill some of the gaps in what is known about the history of Israeli nuclear affairs. Still, a number of important questions remain unanswered.

In 1982, a detailed study by French journalist Pierre Péan, traced the early stages of the Israeli nuclear weapons program, relying on extensive documentation and interviews with the former French officials and industrialists who had assisted the Israeli effort.[10] Péan states (as do a number of prior studies) that the Israeli program was launched in the fall of 1956, when France secretly agreed to supply Israel with a sizable plutonium-producing reactor to be built at Dimona, in the Negev, some forty miles from Beersheba. The initial agreement for the construction of the reactor between the atomic energy commissions of the two countries was signed on September 17, 1956, with further details set forth in a classified accord entered into on October 10 of that year. France's secret pledge to help Israel develop nuclear arms would be made in November.

Mollet's commitment to Israel. At the time, France's Socialist government, led by Guy Mollet, was deeply committed to Israel's survival, and the two states confronted threats stemming from Arab nationalism—Israel because of its isolated position in the Middle East and France because of growing unrest in French Algeria.[11] Indeed, the secret agreement for cooperation in the field of nuclear weapons was cemented in the midst of the 1956 Suez crisis, when French and British forces mounted a joint military campaign to gain control of the Suez Canal, and Israeli troops simultaneously launched an invasion of the Sinai Peninsula.[12] In July, Egyptian President Gamal Abdul Nasser, the Soviet-backed leader of the Pan-Arab movement, had nationalized the waterway.

Under American pressure, Israel's two allies in the campaign were forced to accept a U.N.-backed ceasefire on November 6, while still short of their goal. According to Péan, that very night, while Israeli leaders debated whether to halt hostilities in the Sinai, Israeli Prime Minister David Ben Gurion sent Shimon Peres and Golda Meir to Paris to seek guarantees that France would help Israel develop the atomic bomb. Mollet agreed the following morning, states Péan, quoting eye-witnesses: the Suez debacle had persuaded the French leader both to accelerate France's own efforts to acquire nuclear arms—a program Mollet had previously opposed—and to provide Israel with a nuclear capability. (Mollet is said to have viewed the Israeli capability not only as a means to ensure its security but also as a way to provide France with a counter-balance to Egypt in the Middle East.[13]) On November 9, under increasing political and economic pressure from the Eisenhower Administration, Israel announced that it, too, would accept the U.N. ceasefire.

The Mollet government fell in the spring of 1957, but thereafter, a number of Mollet's top aides who had been among Israel's strongest sympathizers served as a caretaker government. According to Péan, they made good on Mollet's commitment in mid-1957, when, with French Atomic Energy Commission approval, Israel signed an agreement with the French firm of St. Gobain Techniques Nouvelles for the construction of several additional facilities at the Dimona site, including the key installation—where Vanunu would subsequently work—for extracting plutonium from the Dimona reactor's spent reactor fuel.[14] St. Gobain was the architect-engineering firm that had built France's plutonium extraction plant at Marcoule. (During this period, France and Israel also collaborated on the development of a short-range nuclear-capable missile, which Israel deployed in the late 1960s.)[15]

Dimona reactor enlarged. Excavation work for the Dimona reactor and for the plutonium extraction plant began early in 1958.[16] Officially, Israel was to receive a research reactor, nominally based on France's EL-3 experimental reactor, built at Saclay between 1954 and 1957.[17] In reality, Péan writes, the reactor was considerably more powerful than the EL-3 plant, a clear indication to the French technicians charged with building it that it was intended for plutonium production. Péan states that the Dimona reactor's cooling circuits were two to three times more capable than needed for the 24-megawatt reactor that was specified in the formal French-Israeli agreement covering the unit.[18]

This, he concludes, would have increased its annual plutonium production capability from about 17 pounds (8 kilograms), a production rate of roughly one and a half devices per year using standard estimates, to between 22 and 33 pounds (10 to 15 kilograms), possibly enough for about two or three weapons per year. The larger output would have been approximately the output of France's 42-megawatt G-1 reactor at Marcoule, he states, a plutonium production reactor that would supply France's nuclear weapons program. (Here Péan is a bit conservative, since increasing the cooling capacity of the reactor by a factor of two to three could be expected to increase its power to between 48 and 72 megawatts, with a proportional increase in plutonium production.) As explained below, in light of Vanunu's revelations, the actual size of the reactor has become the key variable in assessing Israel's current nuclear weapon capabilities.

De Gaulle. When Charles De Gaulle took power in France in June 1958, he authorized continued work on the reactor but sought to slow further construction of the sensitive plutonium extraction unit. According to Péan, however, his instructions on the extraction unit were thwarted, and major construction proceeded through 1959 and much of 1960. Initially, it appears, this was at the direction of Jacques Soustelle, an ardent supporter of Israel, who became De Gaulle's minister for atomic research, overseeing the French Atomic Energy Commission, in January 1959 and remained in the key post until early 1960.

During this period, Israel also received important information from France on the design and manufacture of nuclear weapons per se.[19] Israel may also have obtained data from France's first nuclear test, which took place in February of 1960.[20]

Péan's account confirmed. Francis Perrin, the scientific head of the French Atomic Energy Commission from 1951 to

1970, was intimately involved with the French-Israeli nuclear program. He has confirmed several key points of Péan's account in a 1986 on-the-record interview with the *Sunday Times*, acknowledging that France supplied the Dimona reactor and the plutonium extraction plant and that for at least two years during the late 1950s, France and Israel collaborated on the design and development of nuclear weapons.[21]

Enter the United States. After Soustelle's departure as minister for atomic research De Gaulle reiterated his instructions that work should cease on the Israeli plutonium facility, but, according to French participants interviewed by Péan, work continued until late in the year.[22] It was suspended only when a political storm erupted in December after the United States discovered—supposedly by means of a U-2 reconnaissance plane—that Israel was building a reactor in the Negev. Until then, Israel had kept Washington in the dark about the facility and apparently replied to initial U.S. inquiries about its French-assisted construction activities by stating that it was building a textile plant.[23]

Under U.S. pressure, on December 21, Israeli Prime Minister David Ben Gurion publicly acknowledged that Israel was building the reactor, which he said was rated at 24 megawatts, and declared that the facility would be used exclusively for peaceful research and training.[24] Israel claimed that it had kept the facility secret not because it intended to produce nuclear arms there, but because it feared attacks on the installation by Arab commandos and was worried that Arab states, through the threat of a boycott, might try to interfere with the French and other suppliers of equipment for the project.[25] To allay American concerns, on December 23, Israel agreed to permit scientists from friendly countries to visit the reactor,[26] and in May of the following year, the arrangement was formalized when Ben Gurion agreed to permit American specialists to visit the reactor and verify how it was being used.[27]

Plutonium plant secrecy maintained. When the story about the Dimona reactor broke, there was no indication that the

United States knew of the existence of the plutonium processing plant. Had Washington known about the installation, Israel would have found it difficult to deny that it had built the reactor as part of a nuclear weapons program. Indeed, the secrecy surrounding the reactor project and the size of the reactor had already triggered considerable suspicions on this score: even with a declared power rating of 24 megawatts, the reactor was unusually large for research and training and could produce about 18 pounds (8 kilograms) of plutonium a year, enough for one nuclear device, by the usual standards.[28]

Vanunu's disclosures may explain why the plutonium plant went apparently unremarked. According to him, the facility was built largely underground. All of the plutonium processing equipment was housed in six below-ground stories, which were topped with two stories of innocuous changing rooms and offices. The unit (which was not completed until at least 1966) would have required an eighty-foot deep excavation, but if this had been dug in 1958, as Péan suggests, before American suspicions were fully aroused, it is possible that this part of the Dimona complex could have remained undiscovered.

Uranium. As construction proceeded on the reactor and plutonium plant in the late 1950s, Israel was still missing two key items, uranium fuel for the reactor and heavy water, a commodity needed to permit the fissioning of the uranium within the reactor—the process by which some uranium atoms are transmuted into plutonium.[29] According to Bertrand Goldschmidt, one of France's top senior nuclear scientists who played a key role in France's nuclear weapons program, Israel obtained uranium on the world market from a number of sources, mainly Western and African.[30] The latter probably included French-controlled mines in what are today Gabon, the Central African Republic, and Niger; South Africa may have been another source.[31] Argentina also supplied 15 tons (13.6 metric tons) of uranium, and Israel may have produced some of the material itself as a byproduct of phosphates processing.[32]

It is not clear precisely when these various purchases may have taken place. If they predated the public disclosure of the reactor, the supplier country must have understood that it was selling uranium for a clandestine plant, although Israel might have justified the secrecy surrounding the reactor on the grounds that it was concerned about Arab reactions; indeed some suppliers might have preferred such a confidential arrangement for the same reason.[33]

Heavy water. As for heavy water, Israel is known to have obtained 22 tons (20 metric tons) of the material from Norway in 1959.[34] In 1986, Norway revealed that it had imposed what were at the time unusually strict controls over the material, obtaining Israel's pledge to use it exclusively for peaceful purposes and obtaining the right to inspect it to verify that Israel was adhering to its pledge.[35] Norway conducted only one such inspection, however, in 1961, before the Dimona reactor was completed, when the heavy water was still in storage.[36]

Israel would have needed at least 20 tons (18 metric tons) of heavy water to operate even a 24-megawatt reactor. Since Israel is not known to have ever obtained substantial quantities of heavy water from any other source, it appears that Israel must have continued to use the Norwegian material in the Dimona reactor in subsequent years, when the unit was apparently being employed to produce plutonium for nuclear arms. This would have violated its pledge to Norway.[37] In the wake of the Vanunu revelations, this possibility led Norway in late 1986 to attempt to exercise its inspection rights, triggering a major controversy with Israel, discussed below in the section on developments. Israel has since acknowledged that the Norwegian material was used in the Dimona unit but claimed that it did not violate the agreement covering the material.[38]

Norway, it may be noted, shipped the heavy water to Israel at a time when the existence of the Dimona reactor was still secret and when, accordingly, there would have been grounds for suspecting that Israel intended to use it for nuclear arms.[39] Either Oslo was satisfied by the safeguards it had required and by Israel's assurances that the heavy water transfer would not be used in the manufacture of nuclear weapons—or, like France under Mollet, Norway hoped to aid a friendly, endangered country to acquire such arms. If such were the case, it would have to be assumed that Norway never intended to enforce its inspection rights, but sought them only so that it could deflect criticism if the deal ever became public.[40]

Péan states that Israel also received a number of tons of heavy water from France in a single shipment in 1960. If that transfer actually had occurred, it would have violated re-transfer restrictions in France's nuclear supply agreements with the United States and Norway, which up until then had provided France with all of its heavy water.[41] The United States also supplied 4.3 tons (3.9 metric tons) of U.S. heavy water to Israel, but according to a former senior U.S. nuclear aide, the material was not used in Dimona; the material was covered initially by bilateral U.S. safeguards, and is now under International Atomic Energy inspection.[42] Israel may also have been able to produce small quantities of heavy water on its own.[43]

The plutonium plant: work continues. Following the public disclosure of the Dimona reactor in late 1960, De Gaulle's order to halt construction on the plutonium extraction facility was apparently enforced, but work was allowed to continue on the reactor itself and, after a delay, on three less sensitive units: a fuel fabrication workshop, a "hot cell" laboratory for examining radioactive samples, and a waste storage facility.[44]

By this stage, however, Israel had acquired the plans for the plutonium facility, and, although the principal French architect-engineer, St. Gobain, was forced by Paris to withdraw from the project, Péan states that Israel was able to take over its management. Israel then recruited the key French subcontractors that had worked on France's own plutonium plant at Marcoule to complete the job.[45] With a French and Israeli construction crew that numbered in the thousands working on various parts of the Dimona site through 1964, Israel was apparently able to maintain a considerable degree of secrecy about the plutonium unit.

U.S. visits. Péan states that the Dimona reactor was operating at full capacity at the end of 1962 and that the first plutonium extraction tests took place at the plutonium unit in 1965; by 1966 or 1967, he writes, Israel had apparently acquired enough plutonium for its first weapon.[46] From 1965 to 1969, however, U.S. nuclear specialists were making annual visits to the Dimona reactor, attempting to detect whether Israel was taking steps to produce plutonium for weapons; among other indicators, the US. aides were specifically looking for signs that Israel might be building a plutonium extraction plant.[47] As late as 1970—some two years after Washington had concluded that Israel did possess nuclear arms or their components—U.S. analysts reportedly had not found evidence of such an installation.[48] This raises questions as to how Israel could have completed the facility and begun operating it without detection.

Part of the answer may lie in the fact that, from the outset, the visits—which never amounted to rigorous "inspections"—were so infrequent and limited in scope that the U.S. officials could not, in fact, be completely confident about what was occurring at the site.[49] In 1968, the United States became suspicious that spent fuel was being diverted so that its plutonium could be extracted. (U.S. aides reportedly thought that Israel might be shipping the material to France for this purpose.) But the U.S. specialists visiting Dimona were unable to resolve the matter. In 1969 the U.S. site-visit team complained in writing about Israel's restrictions on its activities,[50] but Israel refused to alter them. The Nixon Administration, for reasons that are still unclear, dropped the matter, and the visits ceased.[51]

Not only did Israel place tight restrictions on the U.S. visitors, it also reportedly engaged in deliberate deception. Vanunu, relying on stories he heard from more senior coworkers, states that the door to the stairs leading down to the subterranean plutonium plant where he later worked was bricked up for the annual U.S. visits, so that all the U.S.

specialists saw were the innocuous two upper stories of the building. And Péan claims that even the operations of the reactor were disguised. The inspectors were taken, not to the unit's actual control room, but to a mock-up, whose meters were connected to simulators that showed the reactor was operating at a very low power level.

Whatever the details, by virtue of Vanunu's disclosures the existence of the plutonium plant is known today; the U.S. site visits are known to have been seriously limited; Péan's account of the construction arrangements is persuasively documented; and his and Vanunu's independent reports of deception have a similar ring that gives them an air of credibility. While questions remain—the United States, for example, never detected krypton emissions at the site, the telltale sign of an operating plutonium extraction plant—for now the evidence in the public record most strongly supports the view that the plutonium plant was completed in the mid-1960s without detection by the U.S. site visit teams.[52]

Possible diversion of U.S. weapons-grade uranium. It is also widely believed that during the mid-1960s, Israel was able to obtain 220 pounds (100 kilograms) of U.S.-owned highly enriched uranium—material that, like plutonium, can be used as the core of a nuclear weapon. The material is thought to have been stolen from a uranium fabrication plant in Apollo, Pennsylvania, owned by the Nuclear Materials and Equipment Corporation (NUMEC). The material would be sufficient for four to six weapons, using the standard measure of 33 to 55 pounds (15 to 25 kilograms) of material per weapon.[53] The plant was to have processed the material, received between 1962 and 1965, for the U.S. Atomic Energy Commission, which discovered the inventory discrepancy in 1966.

According to former senior U.S. Central Intelligence Agency official, Carl Duckett, by 1968 the agency had concluded that "the most likely case," was that the "NUMEC material had been diverted and had been used by the Israelis in fabricating weapons."[54] The episode has remained controversial, however, and conclusive evidence that Israel obtained the material is still lacking.[55] Vanunu's disclosures have not shed any additional light on the matter.

The 1967 Arab-Israeli war and its aftermath. If Péan is correct that Israel obtained plutonium for its first nuclear weapons in 1966, or if Israel was able successfully to divert highly enriched uranium from NUMEC in the mid-1960s, this would suggest that Israel possessed at least a handful of nuclear weapons at the time of the June 1967 Six-Day War. If so, these weapons are not known to have figured in that conflict, perhaps because Israel's lightning victory made it unnecessary for Israel's leaders to consider threatening to use them.

Following the 1967 conflict, Israel's adversaries refused to negotiate a permanent peace settlement, and military tensions continued, eventually leading to the so-called "War of Attrition" in March 1969. Against this background, Israel is widely believed to have undertaken a secret mission in November 1968 to acquire large amounts of processed uranium ore, or "yellowcake". Using intermediaries, Israeli agents are believed to have arranged to have 200 tons of yellowcake shipped from Antwerp to Genoa and then to have orchestrated its "disappearance" while it was in transit on the Mediterranean Sea in a vessel that had been secretly purchased by an Israeli front company.[56] Converted to uranium metal, the yellowcake could make 168 tons of fuel for the Dimona reactor, enough for perhaps five to seven years' operation of a 40-megawatt unit (the size Péan estimated), assuming it was operating to produce plutonium and was therefore being refueled several times a year.[57]

In addition, by 1972, Israel had built three phosphoric acid plants from which it was able to extract uranium as a by-product, using an indigenously developed technique. The plants theoretically could produce about 100 tons (90 metric tons) of uranium annually.[58] (As noted earlier, Israel also sought to obtain additional heavy water from Norway in 1970, but received only 1.1 tons of the 5.5 it requested.)[59]

The 1973 Arab-Israeli War. By time of the 1973 Arab-Israeli conflict, it appears that Israel did indeed possess nuclear arms, and in 1976 *Time* magazine, in a widely cited article, reported that in the early days of that war, when Israel was being threatened on two fronts, Prime Minister Golda Meir took steps to deploy nuclear warheads on some of its short-range (260 miles) Jericho missiles.[60] (The missiles had been developed with French assistance in the 1960s.[61]) Use of these weapons proved unnecessary, however, once the tide of battle turned. Former and current U.S. officials have confirmed that Israel secretly readied nuclear weapons for possible use at this time, although not necessarily in conjunction with the missiles.[62]

In the aftermath of the 1973 war, a series of hints by senior Israeli officials and statements by authoritative sources in the United States lent further credence to the view that Israel possessed nuclear arms.[63] Virtually all of these sources, if they described Israel's nuclear capabilities, indicated that the country was probably able to produce only one or two weapons per year using the Dimona reactor and associated installations.[64] If these estimates were correct, and if Israel had continued to produce weapons at this rate, today it would have an arsenal of no more than forty to fifty weapons (roughly two devices a year from 1963 to 1988). It was not until the 1980s that reports began to suggest that Israel's arsenal might be considerably larger.[65] Until Vanunu's disclosures, however, there seemed to be little basis for such larger estimates. (This discrepancy is analyzed below in the section on developments.)

South Africa. It has been alleged for many years that Israel and South Africa have collaborated in the development of nuclear arms and may have conducted a joint nuclear test in the South Atlantic in September 1979. Although this relationship has not been conclusively established, circumstantial evidence of it has slowly accumulated over time. The detailed discussion of this matter in the South Africa section of this book concludes that allegations of an Israeli-South African nuclear connection deserve to be taken seriously, even if the precise contours of the connection remain unknown.

Iraqi reactor. In 1981, Israel destroyed Iraq's large "Osiraq" research reactor outside Baghdad. This plant and other installations at the site appear to have been the first elements of an Iraqi nuclear weapons program. The evidence supporting this analysis is detailed in the section on Iraq, later in this chapter, which also highlights how Israel planned for the raid, including its use of U.S. reconnaissance satellite photos, and describes the essential role of U.S.-supplied F-16 aircraft.

In 1982, a group of Arab states succeeded in an effort to have the General Conference of the International Atomic Energy Agency (IAEA) reject Israel's credentials as a response to its attack on Osiraq and, it appeared, as an expression of disapproval for Israel's alleged complicity in the then-recent massacres of Palestinians living in refugee camps in Beirut.[66] This led the United States to withdraw from the IAEA for a number of months, until the diplomatic groundwork had been laid for Israel's participation in the Agency's subsequent annual meetings. Efforts to impose sanctions against Israel were narrowly averted at the 1983 and 1984 general conferences, but after Israel issued a clarifying statement of its policy concerning attacks on nuclear installations at the 1985 General Conference, the issue appeared to be laid to rest, and subsequent Arab-sponsored efforts to condemn it have failed to attract broad support.[67] It is possible that the upsurge of violence in the Israeli-occupied West Bank and Gaza Strip during late 1987 and 1988 will be used to rally support for anti-Israel measures at the 1988 General Conference, which could once again plunge the Agency into crisis.

Further smuggling. During the 1980s, Israel is known to have engaged in at least one additional clandestine transaction that may have contributed to its nuclear capabilities. On May 16, 1985, federal prosecutors in Los Angeles indicted Richard K. Smyth for illegally exporting 810 high-speed electronic switches to Israel between 1980 and 1983. The switches, known as krytrons, are used in the triggering mechanisms of U.S. atomic weapons.[68]

The Israeli Defense Ministry at first denied but subsequently acknowledged being in possession of the switches, which, it claimed, had been employed exclusively for research and development on conventional weapons, such as laser range-finders.[69] Israel later returned the krytrons that had not been used.[70] Smyth disappeared shortly before his trial and is still a fugitive.

Smyth's smuggling activities on behalf of Israel may have involved far more than krytrons. According to two separate reports, in 1972 he illegally obtained special butyl rubber compounds, used as a binder in solid rocket fuel, for Israel's Jericho II missile, and later he smuggled specially hardened aluminum extrusions to be used as the rocket's body, as well as inertial gyroscopes for its advanced guidance system.[71]

Developments: An Undeclared Nuclear Power

In the aftermath of Vanunu's revelations, Israeli leaders continued to deny that Israel possessed nuclear arms and reiterated the longstanding position that Israel "will not be the first country to introduce nuclear weapons into the Middle East."[72] It is becoming increasingly difficult, however, to disregard the evidence that Israel in fact possesses a substantial nuclear arsenal. Indeed, despite the stance of their superiors, a number of second-echelon Israeli officials have begun openly alluding to it.

Shortly after the *Sunday Times* ran the Vanunu story, for example, Israeli radio carried a report of a lecture given by Major General Amnon Shalhaq, chief of Israeli Defense Force Intelligence, at Hebrew University in Jerusalem. The news report states, " . . . Shalhaq says it is obvious to the Arabs that because of Israel's military strength and the backing it enjoys from the United States they will not be able to annihilate Israel in a military strike. The Arabs believe Israel also has nonconventional power."[73]

Less than a month later, Gideon Raphael, the former director general of the Israeli Foreign Ministry and Israel's ambassador to the United Nations in the late 1960s, made a comparable allusion to Israel's nuclear might. In a *Washing-*

ton Post op-ed piece, he stated that Syria's chemical warfare capabilities " . . . could mean that the next war between Syria and Israel will degenerate into a contest between chemical and radiation weapons—with global implications."[74] In a similar vein, several days later, Amos Rubin, then recently installed as an economic advisor to Israeli Prime Minister Yitzhak Shamir, gave an interview to the *Christian Science Monitor* in which he pressed for increased U.S. aid by stating that, "If left to its own [Israel] will have no choice but to fall on a riskier defense which will endanger itself and the world at large . . . . To enable Israel to abstain from dependence on nuclear arms calls for $2 to $3 billion in U.S. aid."[75]

Differing estimates. As suggested above, estimates as to the size of the Israeli nuclear arsenal vary significantly, depending on the interpretation given to the technical data Vanunu disclosed. The *Sunday Times* projected that Israel might have as many as 100 to 200 devices. The consensus among U.S. officials who have attempted to harmonize Vanunu's testimony with other relevant information, however, is that Israel's nuclear armory probably contains no more than 50 or 60 weapons. This would still be sufficient, it should be stressed, to permit Israel to use a number of its nuclear weapons tactically, *i.e.*, against military targets, during any conflict with its neighbors, while keeping a number of weapons in reserve to threaten enemy cities and thereby deter actions that might imperil Israel's existence.

Vanunu's most specific data concerned the chemical processes and flow rates at the plutonium extraction plant where he worked. The key piece of information was that the unit produced 2.6 pounds (1.17 kilograms) of plutonium per week, for thirty-four weeks per year, the remaining weeks being used for plant clean out and maintenance. This meant that the plutonium plant produced a total of about 88 pounds (40 kilograms) of plutonium per year, enough for possibly ten weapons, if former U.S. weapons designer Theodore Taylor is correct that Israel has the sophistication to build weapons using only 8.8 pounds (4 kilograms) of plutonium per device. Since Vanunu worked at the plant for eight years, this would mean that during that time Israel could have produced 80 weapons, and if it is assumed that the facility operated at the same rate for some time prior to his employment and after he left, reaching a total of considerably more than 100 weapons would be fairly easy.

As the *Sunday Times* recognized, however, if the Dimona reactor was only 24 megawatts, as announced by Israel in 1960, it could not irradiate enough spent fuel each year to create the 88 pounds (40 kilograms) of plutonium; probably it could produce only about 18 pounds (8 kilograms) of the material. This led the *Sunday Times* to hypothesize that the reactor had been substantially enlarged—nearly six-fold—possibly to 150 megawatts. Some British reactor specialists that the *Sunday Times* consulted stated that it might be possible to increase the reactor's power to this level without rebuilding the unit, although substantial additional cooling would be required. Without offering any details, the *Sunday Times* suggested that the reactor had "an ingenious cooling system" that disguised its output. On this basis, the *Sunday Times* developed an internally consistent argument that Israel had manufactured 100 to 200 nuclear weapons.

U.S. view. In a series of off-the-record interviews, however, U.S. government specialists have challenged the key assumption that the Dimona reactor has been dramatically enlarged to approximately six times its original capacity. A scale-up of this magnitude of the reactor's cooling system would have required a significant number of additional external cooling units, but, they claim, there is no evidence to suggest that such units have been built.[76]

They speculate that the original 24-megawatt reactor was not changed substantially but may have operated at about a 40-megawatt level, because of cooling efficiencies permitted by the desert climate. This would have permitted the production of about 22 pounds (10 kilograms) of plutonium annually in the unit's uranium fuel from the time the reactor began operating in 1962 or 1963, or around 440 pounds (200 kilograms) of plutonium altogether, assuming that production was intermittent through the mid-1960s, when U.S. specialists were making their annual visits. Assuming 8.8 pounds (4 kilograms) of plutonium per device, this would mean Israel could have an arsenal of about fifty weapons. Even if the reactor had been upgraded to 70 megawatts in 1980, as one published report assumes,[77] this would have permitted the production of only 38 pounds (17 kilograms) of plutonium annually after that date. Israel then might have a total of about 550 pounds (250 kilograms) of plutonium, resulting in a possible arsenal of perhaps sixty or so devices at the most. (The four to six devices possibly made with highly enriched uranium supposedly diverted from the NUMEC plant would, in theory, be added to this total.)

To explain why the throughput of the plutonium plant was so high during Vanunu's tenure, U.S. analysts speculate that there might have been a large backlog of spent fuel from the Dimona reactor to work off, possibly because Israel had trouble running the plutonium plant for a number of years.[78] It appears that Vanunu was hired as part of a large group of technicians in 1977 and was part of a 1985 lay-off that involved 180 workers at the Dimona site. The enlargement and sudden reduction in staff would be consistent with the hypothesis that extra manpower was needed for a number of years while a backlog was being worked off.

Adding to the confusion, however, is that when Vanunu was debriefed by nuclear physicist Frank Barnaby, he insisted that the plutonium plant was operating at a high level of production for the entire time he worked there and had been working at that rate even before his arrival. This would mean that the total amount of plutonium-bearing spent fuel being processed at the plutonium plant has indeed been greater than could have been produced at the Dimona reactor unless it had been substantially enlarged—which American analysts seem to have ruled out.

For now, the matter cannot be resolved. Possibly, the reactor, as Péan indicates, has always been larger than publicly described, and the American visitors were deceived on that point. When the cooling efficiencies of the desert climate are added in, perhaps Israel was able to operate the reactor at 70 megawatts from the outset, a figure favored by Barnaby and other British analysts. And, perhaps operating difficulties in the plutonium plant led to a backlog, which was larger than supposed by the U.S. specialists and which necessitated the long periods of high throughput described by Vanunu. This would all add up to an Israeli nuclear armory larger than U.S. estimates, but still short of the highest alternative projections.

In sum, the *Sunday Times* estimate that Israel has 100 to 200 nuclear weapons may ultimately prove correct, but it has been challenged by knowledgeable analysts who doubt that Israel has more than 50 or 60 such devices. Even an arsenal of this size, however, would be considerably larger than most past estimates, which numbered it at 20 to 25 devices and, significantly, would provide Israel considerable flexibility in its nuclear strategy.

Norwegian heavy water inspections. As discussed above, in 1959, Norway provided Israel with 22 tons (20 metric tons) of heavy water, essential for running the Dimona reactor. Israel had pledged to use the material only for peaceful purposes and had granted Norway the right to inspect the material to verify this pledge. Norway supplied an additional 1.1 tons (1 metric ton) of the material in 1970.

When inspection rights of this type are fully implemented—either by the seller country or by the IAEA, which Israel and Norway had contemplated would take over the job—inspectors check periodically to determine that plutonium-bearing spent fuel from a reactor using the heavy water at issue has not been diverted into a nuclear weapons program; steps are also taken, by using seals or surveillance cameras, to ensure that spent fuel is not diverted between inspections.

Norway inspected its heavy water only once, however, in 1961, before the Dimona reactor began operating and took no steps to check further about how Dimona's spent fuel was being used. Why Norway did not implement its verification rights is not known, but given published accounts of American suspicions about Israel's nuclear weapons program dating back to at least 1970, there is reason to suspect that Norway, like France in the 1950s, was sympathetic to Israel's desire for a nuclear deterrent and deliberately chose not to pursue its inspection rights.[79]

Although Norway acknowledged in 1979 that it had provided the heavy water to Israel, it was not until November 1986 that its right to inspect the material was publicly revealed as the result of an investigation by University of Wisconsin law professor Gary Milhollin.[80] Coming on the heels of Vanunu's revelations a month earlier, the disclosure that Norway had apparently turned a blind eye to Israel's nuclear advances by not exercising its rights created considerable political pressure on the Norwegian government to determine the status of its past nuclear exports and ensure that they were not being used to support a nuclear weapons program.

In mid-February 1987, Norway announced it would ask Israel to submit the material to IAEA inspection,[81] and formally presented the request on March 4. In early April, however, Israel rejected the Norwegian initiative. Israel claimed that it had received numerous shipments of heavy water over the years and that it would be "impossible" to determine what had happened to specific shipments.[82] Israel also charged that the IAEA had traditionally been "unobjective" in dealing with Israel, a somewhat surprising stance, since the Agency had been inspecting a U.S.-supplied research reactor and some four tons of U.S. heavy water at Nahal Soreq for many years.[83]

By July, Norwegian displeasure with Israel's response was evident, and, according to press stories, Norwegian government sources stated that Israel's refusal to permit inspections would be a violation of its agreement with Norway and might lead Oslo to insist that its heavy water be returned.[84] In October, Norway sent a technical team to Israel to pursue the issue.[85] During the visit, Israel acknowledged that the heavy water had in fact been used in the Dimona reactor, but it insisted that it had not violated its agreement with Norway.[86] In December, Israel agreed to "investigate" whether the Norwegian material had been misused, but it continued to reject the possibility of a Norwegian inspection.[87]

In principle, to account for the heavy water, Israel would need to show how it had been used since 1961. Since Israel has acknowledged that the material has been in the Dimona reactor for at least part of this time, the next steps would be to determine how much plutonium had been produced in the reactor during this period (by reconstructing operating records) and to verify that the plutonium was being used for peaceful purposes, as promised. Since Israel has sought to maintain secrecy about its nuclear activities and since most observers assume that the plutonium at issue has, in fact, been used for nuclear weapons, the reasons for Israel's reluctance to permit rigorous inspections are obvious.

In mid-June 1988, the two countries announced that they had reached a tentative compromise: Israel would permit the IAEA to inspect periodically all the Norwegian heavy water that remained in its possession, amounting to about ten tons (nine metric tons). Israel claimed the remainder had been lost in the normal course of operating a reactor.[88] The arrangement will permit Norway to ensure that in the future the heavy water still in Israel's hands does not contribute to the manufacture of nuclear weapons, but the compromise does not provide an account of how this material (and the rest of what was originally transferred) was used over the years. Thus the understanding represents only a partial vindication of Norway's rights.

The ten tons of heavy water will apparently be made available for inspection at a location outside the Dimona complex, so that Israel will not have to open the site to outsiders. Although the new arrangement will mean that the material will, in practice, be unavailable for use in the Dimona reactor, there have been no indications that this will force Israel to shut down the unit, and it appears that Israel's nuclear capability will be unaffected.

Growing missile, chemical threat. In recent years, Israel has become increasingly concerned about the growing chemical warfare and ballistic missile capabilities of its potential adversaries in the Middle East.[89] The repeated use of chemical weapons in the Iran-Iraq war, discussed in the sections of this chapter covering those countries, could well lower the threshold for their use in a future Israeli-Syrian conflict, a theater of more immediate concern to Israeli strategists.

One scenario that is repeatedly cited in the Israeli literature, for example, is the possibility that Syria will arm its highly accurate Soviet SS-21 missiles with chemical warheads and launch a sudden attack on Israeli airfields, incapacitating them for perhaps twenty-four hours. With Israel denied air superiority, Syrian troops could then theoretically seize the Golan Heights, leaving Israeli forces the difficult task of retaking them, while Israel's leaders fended off the inevitable calls by outside parties for a ceasefire in place aimed at avoiding an escalation of the conflict.[90]

As discussed in Chapter II, Libya, Iraq, Iran, Saudi Arabia, and Egypt all possess or are all acquiring ballistic missiles capable of hitting Israel, and all but Saudi Arabia are believed to possess chemical warfare capabilities. None of these missiles is likely to have the accuracy needed to hit military targets, but they—and Syria's less accurate Scud-B missiles—might be used as weapons of terror against civilians, much as they are being used, so far without chemical warheads, in the Iran-Iraq War. Without predicting which of these countries might participate in a future conflict with Israel, the dangers for Israel are obvious.

Israel is also believed to possess chemical arms[91] and a number of ways to deliver them, including missiles. These could well deter a wholesale chemical attack, but more obviously, Israel's adversaries would also have to fear that Israel might retaliate with nuclear arms, including those placed on the Jericho II missile. Indeed, in the wake of Saudi Arabia's acquisition of intermediate-range ballistic missiles from China in early 1988, top Israeli officials hinted at this possibility: Defense Minister Yitzhak Rabin, stated, for example,

Israel not only has the deterrent power to face down the missiles held by Syria, Iraq, and now also Saudi Arabia, and the temptation to attack our populated areas; we also have the ability to attack their populated areas to a degree that outstrips theirs many times over.[92]

Similarly, Israeli Defense Force Chief of Staff General Dan Shomron, noting that the missiles of other Middle East states are generally too inaccurate to have a significant impact on the military course of a conflict, acknowledged in an interview shortly afterwards that they and chemical weapons could cause serious harm to civilians. He went on to note, however, that

A: Every country that uses [chemical] weapons calculates the advantages and the disadvantages. Look, when Egypt fought Yemen before 1967, it used chemical weapons. When it fought us in 1967, it had chemical weapons, and when it fought us in 1973, it certainly had chemical weapons. Syria also had chemical weapons in 1973. These two armies were in a difficult situation in 1973 . . . .

The Egyptians fired Scud missiles, but neither of them used chemical weapons. Why not?

Q: Are you hinting that they knew we could have retaliated with the same weapons?

A: I am sure they know that our ability to hit them is greater, much greater than their ability to hit us.[93]

Simply stated, as the chemical and missile capabilities of Israel's enemies grow and its cities become more vulnerable to attack, the importance of Israel's nuclear deterrent will increase. If, as a result of the Iran-Iraq conflict, inhibitions against the use of chemical weapons and missiles against civilians are overcome, the risk that nuclear weapons might be used in the Middle East could be commensurately heightened.

Prospects: Vanunu's Legacy

Vanunu did more than reveal the technical details of Israel's nuclear activities: he also appears to have opened the door to an official acknowledgement, however veiled, of a potent Israeli military deterrent. Israel has not declared that it has nuclear weapons, but, as just described, it has invoked the concept of deterrence to assuage public concerns over new military threats in the region and, it seems, to warn potential adversaries against using these new capabilities. This appears to be a subtle, but important, shift in the Israeli nuclear posture.

There is increasing evidence that in the past eight years, Israel has deployed nuclear-armed Jericho II missiles in hardened bunkers or silos, thereby acquiring a secure retaliatory capability against virtually all regional threats. If so, this increased military strength may have contributed to a new willingness to introduce deterrence into the public debate on the nation's security.

The growing visibility of Israel's nuclear might—visibility that has also been increased in part by the dispute with Norway—is also likely to play a growing role in the current debate over the central political issues facing the country: making peace with its Arab neighbors and charting the future for the occupied West Bank and Gaza Strip. Ironically, Israeli doves, who might be expected to oppose Israel's nuclear weapons program, are citing it to show that Israeli security will not be jeopardized even if the country were to give up the occupied territories in a "land for peace" swap. In contrast, Israeli hawks, who might be expected to favor an open nuclear deterrent, are seeking to maintain the secrecy of the program and keep it out of the public debate, both to deprive their opponents of an argument for giving up the occupied territories and to avoid stimulating Israel's adversaries to seek nuclear arms of their own.[94] The trend toward more open discussion of Israel's nuclear capabilities, however, seems irreversible.

If Vanunu is to be believed, during the past eight years, Israel advanced from fission to fusion weapons and, according to other reports, during the same period, Israel deployed the nuclear-capable Jericho II. The United States during this time concentrated its efforts on building closer ties with Israel, bonds that can be seen in massive foreign aid disbursements, the establishment of a joint free trade area, Israeli participation in the Strategic Defense Initiative, and, most recently, the signing of a formal accord codifying the U.S.-Israeli strategic relationship. Efforts to curb Israel's nuclear advances, according to Reagan Administration sources, have been essentially dropped from the U.S. agenda of significant issues to be addressed in bilateral negotiations with Israel. In this respect, Vanunu's revelations appear to have had little impact.

It remains to be seen whether public disclosure that Israel is apparently developing a missile that can reach the Soviet Union will induce Washington to make a major effort to restrain this new element of Israel's strategic potential; the advent of long-range missiles in other Middle Eastern states may be seen as justification for Israel's program, whatever its potential for increasing the long-term risks of U.S.-Soviet nuclear confrontation.

Israel's decades-long commitment to acquiring nuclear arms, the vital role nuclear deterrence appears to play in Israeli strategic thinking, and the recent advances Israel appears to have made in its nuclear capabilities—no doubt at great economic cost—leave little doubt that its nuclear forces will remain a major feature of the Middle East security landscape for the foreseeable future. In this context, hopes for non-proliferation gains are probably best focused on limited initiatives, perhaps aimed at emerging elements of Israel's program, that seek to reduce the risks of nuclear weapons use, enhance stability, and limit the damage of Israel's example to non-proliferation efforts elsewhere.

LEBANON

SYRIA

Sea of
Galilee

Haifa

Mediterranean Sea

WEST
BANK

Tel Aviv

Rehovot

Amman

Nahal Soreq

Jerusalem

Dead
Sea

Gaza
Strip *I S R A E L*

Beersheba

Dimona

JORDAN

Negev Desert

EGYPT

ISRAEL

phosphate/uranium
mining area

0   50

MILES

Gulf of
Aqaba

Israel

Research Reactors

IRR I Nahal Soreq (light-water/highly enriched uranium, 5MWt)[a]
- supplier: United States
- start up: 1960
- fuel source: United States, through 1977 (expiration of U.S. agreement).
- safeguards: yes

IRR 2, Dimona (heavy-water/natural-uranium, 40? 70? 150? MWt)[b,c]
- supplier: France
- start up: 1963
- fuel source: Israel, Argentina, South Africa(?), Belgium(?), France(?), Niger(?), Central African Republic(?), Gabon(?)[d]
- heavy water: Norway[a,m], Israel(?)[a], France [f]
- safeguards: no

Uranium Resources/Active Mining Sites/Uranium Mills
- reasonably assured reserves: 30-60,000 tons is available from processing phosphate ores.[a]
- currently active site: phosphate deposits in the Negev near Beersheba.[e]
- mills in operation: phosphoric acid plants producing yellowcake as by-product, two in Haifa, one in southern Israel. Combined output, 100 tons.[a]

Uranium Purification (UO_2)
- capacity: sufficient to supply Dimona reactor (presumed)
- supplier: Israel(?)
- start up: ?
- safeguards: no

Heavy Water Production
Rehovot
- capacity: pilot scale[a]; sufficient to replace Dimona reactor losses (presumed).
- supplier: Israel
- start up: 1954(?)[a]
- safeguards: no

Fuel Fabrication
Dimona(?)[i]
- capacity: sufficient to supply Dimona reactor (presumed)
- supplier: France[f]
- start up: mid-1960s(?)
- safeguards: no

Reprocessing (Plutonium Extraction)

Dimona[c,f,l]
- capacity: Probably 15[f] - 40[c] kilograms of plutonium per year
- supplier: Israel and France[c,f,h]
- start up: probably 1966, full operation sometime later[c,f]
- safeguards: no

Nahal Soreq
- capacity: laboratory-scale[j]
- supplier: Great Britain; some U.S. equipment(?).[j]
- start up: 1960(?)
- safeguards: no[k]

Enrichment(?)
- type: laser(?)[g]
- capacity: 2-3 kilograms highly enriched uranium per year(?)[g]
- supplier: Israel
- start up: 1974(?)
- safeguards: no

Uranium Conversion (UF$_6$)
- capacity: Small capacity to permit enrichment activities, if any, presumed.
- supplier: Israel (?)
- start up: 1974(?)
- safeguards: no

Sources and Notes

a. *Israeli Nuclear Armament,* Report of the Secretary General, United Nations General Assembly A/36/431, September 18, 1981, pp. 8-11, 15-18.

b. Pierre Péan, *Les Deux Bombes* (Paris: Fayard, 1982), p. 96 (75 megawatts); "The Middle East's Nuclear Arms Race," *Foreign Report,* August 13, 1980 (reactor upgraded from 26 megawatts to 70 megawatts in 1980). Traditional estimate of size is 24-26 megawatts; see reference a. Estimate of 150 megawatts given in reference c. U.S. officials believe the facility has operated at 40-70 megawatts (see discussion in text).

c. "Revealed: The Secrets of Israel's Nuclear Arsenal," *Sunday Times* (London), October 5, 1986.

d. John R. Redick, *The Military Potential of Latin American Nuclear Energy Programs* (Beverly Hills, CA: Sage Publications, 1972) p. 13 (Argentina); personal communication with informed former U.S. official (Argentina); Richard Kessler, "Argentine Officials Deny Rumors of Trade With Israel," *Nucleonics Week,* May 29, 1986, p. 6. Bertrand Goldschmidt, *Le Défi Atomique* (Paris: Fayard, 1980) pp. 205-206 (initially, uranium bought on world market from a number of sources, mainly Western and African); Fuad Jabber, *Israel and Nuclear Weapons* (London: Chatto and Windus, 1971) p. 89 (first load of Dimona reportedly comprised of 10 tons from South Africa, 10 tons from Dead Sea phosphates, 4 tons from French sources); Christopher Raj, "Israel and Nuclear Weapons," in K. Subrahmanyam, ed. *Nuclear Myths and Realities* (ABC: New Delhi, 1981) p. 105 (South Africa, France, French-controlled uranium mines in Gabon, Central African Republic, and Niger); William Drozdiak "Uranium Loss is Admitted," *Washington Post,* May 3,

1977 (200 tons of yellowcake diverted on Mediterranean Sea from Belgium thought to wind up in Israel.)

e. "Yellowcake from Phosphates," *Business Review and Economic News from Israel* (Tel Aviv), reprinted in *Joint Publication Research Service/Nuclear Development and Proliferation,* March 14, 1983, p. 28.

f. Péan, *Les Deux Bombes* (see reference b).

g. Robert Gillette, "Uranium Enrichment: Rumors of Israeli Progress with Lasers", *Science,* No. 183, March 22, 1974, p. 1172; U.N., *Israeli Nuclear Armament,* p. 15. It is not certain whether Israel possesses an operating enrichment facility.

   CIA officials were convinced that Israel diverted approximately 100 kilograms of highly enriched uranium from the NUMEC plant in Apollo, Pennsylvania, between 1964 and 1966. Transcript of "Near Armageddon: The Spread of Nuclear Weapons in the Middle East," ABC News Close-Up, April 27, 1981, pp. 13-14 (Statement by former CIA official Carl Duckett). No conclusive evidence that the material was diverted has come to light, however.

h. Weissmann and Krosney, *The Islamic Bomb,* (New York: Times Books, 1981) p. 113, citing Charles de Gaulle, *Memoirs of Hope: Renewal and Endeavor* (New York: Simon and Schuster, 1971), p. 266.

i. Fuad Jabber, *Israel and Nuclear Weapons* (London: Chatto and Windus, 1971), p. 45.

j. Ibid. p. 43.

k. Not listed in 1985 IAEA Annual Report among safeguarded installations.

l. IAEA Bulletin, Vol. 19, No. 5, p. 2; Weissman and Krosney, *The Islamic Bomb,* p. 110.

m. Charles R. Babcock, "Norway Eyes Israel's Use of Nuclear Ingredient," *Washington Post,* November 10, 1986.

Photo 4.1, taken by former Israeli nuclear technician Mordechai Vanunu, is said to be a cutaway model of an Israeli atomic bomb. Dark metal sphere (front left) represents the plutonium core of the bomb. This would be enclosed by the silvery metal pieces (rear left), which screw together, making a second larger sphere. The silvery metal pieces are thought to represent a beryllium reflector/tamper, intended to compress the smaller sphere of plutonium during detonation and enhance yield. The silvery sphere would then be surrounded by high explosives, represented by the dark hemisphere (rear right).
© *London Sunday Times*.

Libya

The image of a nuclear-armed Libya has become a symbol of the dangers posed by unrestrained proliferation. Although Libya has made little progress toward this goal, as an international embargo of nuclear transfers to Tripoli has gained strength over the years, events during 1987 and the first half of 1988 have been cause for concern. During this period, Colonel Muammar Khadafi openly declared his interest in acquiring nuclear arms and for the first time engaged in "unconventional" warfare by using chemical weapons against Chadian forces.

Background: Nuclear Ambitions Constrained

During the 1970s, after its attempt to purchase nuclear arms from China was rebuffed,[1] Libya established a network of nuclear trade relations through which it hoped to gain rapid access to nuclear-weapons related technologies and assistance in developing an indigenous nuclear infrastructure. By the mid-1980s, however, virtually all of these links had been severely curtailed or terminated.

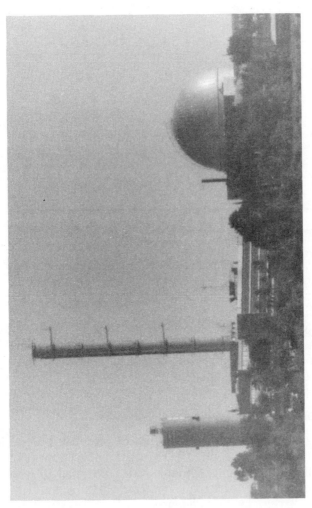

Photo 4.2, taken from the perimeter of Israel's classified Dimona nuclear complex with a telephoto lens, shows the Dimona reactor (dome at right), waste treatment building (center left, with tall tower), and above-ground portion of plutonium extraction facility (between reactor and waste treatment building). © *Norsk Telegrambyra.*

Libya seems to have received few if any benefits from its reported 1973 accord with Pakistan, under which Tripoli is said to have agreed to finance Pakistan's nuclear weapons effort in return for access to technology for producing nuclear weapons material or possibly nuclear weapons themselves.[2] Between 1978 and 1980, Libya is believed to have supplied Pakistan with significant quantities of uranium concentrate, or yellowcake, not subject to International Atomic Energy Agency (IAEA) monitoring. The material, originally purchased from Niger, was apparently intended for use in Pakistan's clandestine uranium-enrichment program. (See Chapter III, Pakistan.) Although Libya ratified the Non-Proliferation Treaty (NPT) in 1975, it did not enter into a formal safeguards agreement with the Agency until 1980 and thus was able to import and export uranium concentrate without having to list the transactions on an IAEA-monitored inventory.[3] Since 1980, however, all Libyan yellowcake purchases have been covered by the IAEA, depriving Tripoli of additional unrestricted material that it might barter for the bomb. Presumably all of Libya's previous stocks of yellowcake were disclosed to the Agency when it established its initial inventory, although it is possible that Libya has secretly set aside some of the material.[4]

Similarly, Libya appears to have garnered little from its open nuclear cooperation agreement with India. When he was in New Delhi in July 1978 to sign the accord, Libyan Prime Minister Abdul Salam Jalloud is said to have pressed Indian nuclear officials for a commitment to assist Libya in obtaining an "independent nuclear capability"—a veiled reference to plutonium extraction and nuclear explosives technology.[5] India, over the course of the following year, limited nuclear cooperation to strictly innocuous areas, and Libya abruptly terminated its oil shipments to New Delhi—expected to amount to one million tons per year—in an attempt to force India to share more sensitive nuclear technology. India refused and recalled its ambassador from Tripoli for consultation.[6]

In August 1984, then Indian Prime Minister Indira Gandhi, in response to a parliamentary question, revealed that she had had "some reservations" about the Indo-Libyan accord, which had been negotiated by former Prime Minister Moraji Desai without consulting senior Indian nuclear aides. Accordingly, she stated, she had confined activities to the exchange of scientists before allowing the agreement to lapse. This foreclosed further Indo-Libyan cooperation of any kind.[7]

Tripoli's gains from its nuclear dealings with Moscow have also been modest. In 1975, the two signed a nuclear trade pact under which the Soviets agreed to provide a small research reactor and help Libya build an associated atomic research center.[8] The reactor, located at Tajoura, is believed to have begun operating in 1981.[9] In 1977 Tripoli and Moscow signed a second accord for the construction of two 440-megawatt nuclear-power reactors.[10] In early 1986, after years of inconclusive negotiations, however, the deal appeared to have been shelved indefinitely, only to be rekindled in May of that year. Nonetheless, it seems that the Soviet Union, like India, is wary of extensive nuclear trade with Colonel Khadafi, and no further progress on the nuclear power plant sale has been reported.[11]

The United States has not made any sales to Libya of nuclear equipment or materials. In 1983 Washington prohibited the training of Libyan nationals in nuclear sciences at U.S. universities and placed Libya on a list of states subject to especially strict nuclear export controls.[12]

During the early 1980s two Belgian firms, Belgatom and Belgonucléaire, provided Libya with extensive technical assistance on the Tajoura Research Center, the then pending Soviet nuclear-power reactor sale, and the development of a number of Libyan uranium deposits.[13] In 1982, Libya began negotiations with Belgonucléaire for the purchase of a plant for producing uranium tetrafluoride. The material itself is not usable for nuclear weapons or as nuclear fuel; however, both uranium metal, which can be irradiated to produce plutonium, and uranium hexafluoride, which can be enriched to produce highly enriched uranium, are made from uranium tetrafluoride.[14]

In 1984, Belgian nuclear officials announced that the two countries would shortly sign an agreement for nuclear cooperation. This would have provided the legal framework for the sale not only of the uranium tetrafluoride plant but also for a $1 billion contract under which Belgium was to sell Libya non-nuclear equipment and architect-engineering services for the twin Soviet nuclear power plants.[15] Concerned that there appeared to be no logical use for the tetrafluoride plant's output within Libya's nuclear energy and research program, Washington pressed Brussels to cancel the pending accord.[16] Belgium ultimately rejected the Libyan nuclear trade pact in early 1985.[17]

Argentina and Libya have also had a long-standing nuclear relationship, which Tripoli may have hoped to strengthen by its reported sale of $100 million worth of arms to Buenos Aires during the 1982 Falklands/Malvinas War.[18] In mid-1983 an Argentine nuclear trade delegation reportedly visited Tripoli, and at approximately the same time Libya tried unsuccessfully to purchase an Argentine research reactor.[19] There have been no reports of continuing Libyan-Argentine nuclear trade, however, since the civilian government of Raul Alfonsín took power in late 1983.

Nuclear relations with Brazil may run counter to this overall trend. In late 1984, Brazil began negotiations to supply Libya, a major purchaser of Brazilian armaments, with uranium prospecting and development services.[20] No further nuclear commerce between the two countries has been reported, but in early 1988 Libya agreed to purchase $2 billion worth of arms from Brazil, including intermediate-range ballistic missiles, now under development.[21] No nuclear commodities are apparently involved. Libya could, however, use such lucrative arms contracts as inducements to obtain such items in the future. Given Libya's long-standing interest in acquiring sensitive enrichment and reprocessing technology and Brazil's emerging capabilities in these fields, nuclear cooperation between the two could pose significant proliferation dangers in the years ahead.

In addition to these dealings with the various nuclear-supplier countries noted above, in 1981 Libya sought to obtain nuclear weapons on the black market from former CIA employee Edwin Wilson. Wilson's offer was plainly a hoax; nevertheless, the seriousness with which Libya approached the negotiations is testimony to Khadafi's desire to acquire such arms.[22]

The lurid history of Wilson's dealings with Libya throughout the mid- and late-1970s is extensively discussed elsewhere.[23] By the time of the 1981 nuclear negotiations, Wilson had supplied Khadafi with more than 20 tons of C-4 plastique explosive, notorious for its use in terrorist bombings; a thousand miniature timer/detonators for use with the C-4; training by former Green Berets in producing and disarming explosives; and, reportedly, embargoed spare parts for Libya's C-130 air transports. Wilson had also signed a multi-million dollar contract for the complete arming of a 3,500-man Libyan infantry strike force.[24]

The nuclear scam was reportedly initiated in February or March 1981, when Wilson was contacted by a Belgian associate, Armand Donnay, who claimed to have access to enough "fissionable material" to build a nuclear weapon.[25] It was decided that a formal proposal would be made to Wilson's contacts in Libya, and soon afterwards, Donnay went there with a stack of documents containing the details of the deal.[26]

John Heath, an associate of Wilson's, was present at the first of the meetings with the Libyans at which Wilson and Donnay discussed the sale of nuclear weapons. According to Heath's testimony at Wilson's 1983 trial for illegally exporting the C-4 explosive, the meeting was held with top Libyan nuclear officials—the "Libyan nuclear committee," in Heath's words—and Wilson and the others were introduced to the group by a senior military aide.[27] The Libyans quickly rejected Donnay's presentation as incomplete. One account—apparently based on Heath's recollections—states that the Libyans wanted to know the quality of the fissionable material Donnay had to offer. When he told them it was "twenty percent"—presumably twenty-percent enriched uranium, unsuitable for weapons—the group's chairman stated, "That's no good for us. We need eighty percent. If you can't do better than this, we have no business."[28]

Donnay then offered to rework and expand his offer and one or more additional meetings were held with the Libyans to discuss the nuclear weapons deal.[29] The Libyans rejected the revised proposal, however, because of its incompleteness and technical defects. Though the deal did not go through, the episode provides strong evidence—the seniority of the Libyan officials involved, the explicit request for weapons material, and the willingness to extend negotiations over two or more meetings—that the Libyans were seriously interested in acquiring nuclear arms by clandestine means.

Political and Technical Developments

Libya's negligible nuclear infrastructure—limited to the small Soviet-supplied research reactor and associated facilities at the Tajoura Research Center, noted above—remained unchanged through the first half of 1988. The reactor is subject to IAEA safeguards and is too small to pose a potential proliferation risk.

Nuclear goals described. These limitations notwithstanding, Colonel Khadafi, in two major statements in 1987, strongly called for the Arab states to acquire nuclear arms—presumably under Libyan leadership. In a televised address to Libyan university students in June, he declared:

. . .They make bombs daily; why should we not do likewise. The Arabs must possess the atomic bomb to defend themselves until their numbers reach one billion, until they learn to desalinate seawater, and until they liberate Palestine. We undertake not to drop the atomic bomb on any state around us, but we must possess it.

***

If there is going to be a game using atomic bombs, then it should not be played against the Arab nation. The Arabs should have it, but we undertake not to drop it on anyone. However, if someone is going to drop one on us, or if someone is going to threaten our existence and independence even without the use of an atomic weapon, then we should drop it on them. This is an essential defensive weapon.

***

We should be like the Chinese—poor and riding donkeys, but respected and possessing an atom bomb. Then they will not be able to fool anyone with this weapon.[30]

Khadafi reiterated his stand at a press conference in November, at which he declared that he intended to boycott an Arab summit meeting to be held later that month in Amman, Jordan. Challenging the proposed agenda for that meeting, he stated:

. . .I will work for attendance at an Arab summit, one whose agenda will include the fight against the United States; the boycott of the United States; the fight against France; the boycott of France; the liberation of Palestine; the creation of an Arab federation according to a charter I will present to them; and the manufacture of an Arab atomic bomb, since the Israelis, with the assistance of the United States, France, Western nations, and Britain possess it and target it against every Arab country. They are now working day and night to manufacture missiles with a range of 4,000 km that can strike every Arab city from the ocean to the Gulf. The Arabs thus have the right to manufacture nuclear weapons and to acquire the atomic bomb to defend their existence. After all, their enemy possesses this weapon, and atomic bombs are now found in the Middle East.[31]

Given Libya's prickly relations with other Arab countries—triggered by Khadafi's efforts to destabilize neighboring states and his past support for Iran in the Gulf War—they appear unlikely to join in a common effort with Libya to develop atomic arms. Moreover, the other Arab states, like Libya itself, lack the necessary nuclear infrastructure for such an endeavor. Nonetheless, as expressions of Libya's intentions, Khadafi's open calls for nuclear arms remain disturbing and belie Libya's renunciation of nuclear weapons under the NPT.

Related capabilities growing. Libya's mounting capabilities in the field of chemical weapons are another disturbing trend. Libya is believed to have used such weapons against Chadian forces in late 1986 and again in the summer of 1987.[32] Libya apparently used chemical agents obtained from Iran, reportedly in exchange for Soviet-made mines, or possibly, for Soviet-made Scud-B missiles.[33] By early 1988, however, Libya was thought to have acquired its own chemical weapons manufacturing capability.[34]

As in the case of Iraqi and Iranian use of chemical arms, Libya's resort to these weapons violates the 1925 Geneva Protocol, which Libya ratified in 1971. Its readiness to disregard this arms control pact raises further questions about its commitment to the NPT.

The spread of chemical weapons capabilities to Libya and its readiness to use chemical arms is likely to contribute to Israeli security anxieties. In early 1988, Libya entered into a $2 billion contract with Brazil to purchase 600-mile range ballistic missiles, which could be equipped with chemical warheads and would be capable of reaching Israel from eastern Libya.[35] Such developments are likely to increase the attractiveness of nuclear deterrence for Israel and to make possible restraints on Israel's nuclear program all the more difficult to obtain.

Prospects

For the foreseeable future, nuclear weapons are likely to remain beyond Libya's grasp. Its indigenous capabilities are too rudimentary to permit the production of weapons-grade nuclear materials, and the global embargo on nuclear transfers to Libya is likely to prevent it from making further advances. In short, although Colonel Khadafi's nuclear ambitions are obviously strong, there is little reason to believe they will soon be realized. Nonetheless, his outspoken advocacy of nuclear arming and his growing military capabilities are disturbing trends that are likely to increase nuclear tensions in the region.

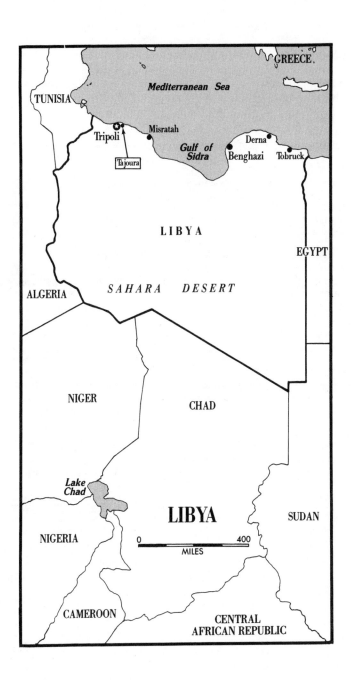

Libya

Research Reactor

Tajoura (light-water/highly-enriched uranium, 10 MWt)[a]
- supplier: Soviet Union[a]
- fuel source: Soviet Union[a]
- start up   1981[b]
- safeguards: yes[c]

Power Reactor Planned

Gulf of Sidra (light-water/low-enriched uranium, 440 MWe)[d]
- supplier: Atomenergoexport (USSR)[e]
- fuel source: Soviet Union?
- start up: (?)
- safeguards: yes

Uranium Resources/Active Mining Sites/Uranium Mills

- reasonably assured
  reserves: none assessed, some known past exploration.[f]
- currently active sites: none
- mills in operation: none

Sources and Notes

a. Senate Foreign Relations committee, *Hearings on the Israeli Air Strike,* June 18, 19, and 25, 1981, 97th Congress, 1st Session (Washington, D.C.: Government Printing Office, 1981) p. 40.

b. Claudia Wright, "Libya's Nuclear Program," *The Middle East,* February 1982, p. 47; *Hearings on the Israeli Air Strike,* p. 50.

c. International Atomic Energy Agency, *The Annual Report, 1985,* (Vienna, Austria: International Atomic Energy Agency, 1986), p. 81.

d. Claudia Wright, "Libya's Nuclear Program," p. 50; "Envoy Says Soviets May Build Nuclear Plant in Libya," Associated Press, May 10, 1986, AM cycle.

e. Robin Miller, "Nuclear Power Plans Outlined," *Jamahiriyah Review, Joint Publication Research Service/Nuclear Development and Proliferation,* March 22, 1982, p. 17.

f. OECD Nuclear Energy Agency and the International Atomic Energy Agency, *Uranium Resources, Production, and Demand* (Paris: OECD, 1983), p. 208. Libya reportedly purchased several hundred tons of uranium concentrate from Niger between 1978 and 1980. Steve Weissman and Herbert Krosney, *The Islamic Bomb,* (New York: Times Books, 1981), p. 210.

Iraq

Iraq's nuclear program has been dormant since Israel's 1981 bombing raid destroyed its centerpiece, the large French-supplied Osiraq research reactor outside Baghdad. Although France agreed in principle to help rebuild the facility under strict non-proliferation controls, no steps toward implementing this commitment are known to have been taken.[1] Similarly, implementation of the Soviet Union's offer to build a nuclear power plant in Iraq appears not to have progressed beyond the site-selection stage.[2]

Iraq's continued possession of 27.5 pounds (12.5 kilograms) of French-supplied highly enriched uranium fuel, possibly enough for one carefully designed nuclear weapon, however, presents a proliferation threat whose danger could increase if Iran were to make significant advances in the eight-year Iran-Iraq War.[3] Indeed, Iraq appears to have remained interested in acquiring nuclear arms. In 1982, according to evidence obtained in an ongoing Italian prosecution, it expressed interest in purchasing plutonium from an Italian arms smuggling ring.[4] Iraq is a party to the Non-Proliferation Treaty (NPT), but its continuing violations of the 1925 Geneva Protocol against using lethal chemical weapons, to which it had agreed, raise fundamental questions as to the strength of its other arms-control commitments.[5]

Background

There is a growing consensus, based on strong circumstantial evidence, that the hidden objective behind Iraq's expansion of its nuclear sector in the mid-1970s was the gradual acquisition of a nuclear weapons capability—a capability intended to serve as a deterrent against Israel's presumed nuclear arms and to advance Iraq's claim to Arab leadership.[6] First, the Osiraq research reactor, purchased from France in 1976, was unusually large and capable of irradiating uranium specimens to produce significant quantities of plutonium. Iraq had simultaneously acquired from Italy three radiologically shielded "hot cells," in which at least small quantities of plutonium could be extracted from irradiated uranium specimens—possibly enough over a period of years for a single weapon—and a model of a larger reprocessing unit that might have permitted a subsequent expansion. In 1981 Baghdad was also negotiating with Italian vendors to buy a larger heavy-water power reactor (an efficient plutonium producer) and a sizable plutonium extraction, or "reprocessing" facility, which would have been a highly premature addition to Baghdad's nascent nuclear energy program, but an essential part of a nuclear weapons effort. All of these negotiations were conducted in secret, or at least outside of public view.[7]

In 1980 and 1981, Iraq also bought inexplicably large amounts of natural uranium from Brazil, Portugal, Niger, and Italy, suggesting a secret intention to irradiate the material in Osiraq to produce plutonium. (The natural uranium could not be used to fuel Osiraq because the reactor required enriched uranium fuel.) And a number of statements by Iraqi officials strongly suggested that Baghdad had a deep interest in acquiring nuclear arms.[8]

Perhaps most revealing of Iraq's intentions to use Osiraq to produce plutonium was that in early 1980 Baghdad placed an order with a West German firm, NUKEM, for 25,000 pounds (11,364 kilograms) of depleted-uranium-metal fuel pins.[9] The pins were sized to fit into Osiraq, where they could be irradiated to produce plutonium, and were unsuited to any other nuclear purpose—including use in a lab-scale "subcritical assembly," which was the stated end-use for the NUKEM pins. The deal, which could have netted Iraq one or two bombs' worth of plutonium, was ultimately aborted when NUKEM's subcontractors in the United States and Canada were told by regulatory officials that they could not get export licenses for the material.

Whatever its covert intentions, Iraq, as a party to the NPT, had to place all of its nuclear installations under International Atomic Energy Agency (IAEA) inspection, and as Osiraq neared completion, the Agency was preparing plans to apply stringent controls to the facility.[10] In 1978, Iraq had also agreed to permit French technicians to remain at the Osiraq plant until 1989; so it seems almost impossible that by the time of the Israeli raid in 1981 Osiraq could have secretly produced plutonium in the quantities needed for a clandestine nuclear weapons program. It is more likely that Iraq intended to pursue a plan, similar to Sweden's in the 1960s, of mastering plutonium-production technology in the open and building a nuclear infrastructure, perhaps with a stockpile of plutonium, which could later be turned into nuclear armaments, if such a decision were taken.[11] (The NPT allows parties to withdraw from the pact on ninety days' notice if their "supreme interests" are threatened.)

When it appeared that the Osiraq reactor would shortly go into operation, despite a series of temporary setbacks to the Iraqi nuclear program and extensive Israeli lobbying for the imposition of additional controls by Iraq's European suppliers, Israel mounted its highly controversial June 7, 1981, air attack.[12] Caught up in its deadly war with Iran, Iraq was unable to respond militarily to the Israeli raid, but Baghdad subsequently mounted an aggressive campaign against Israel at the United Nations and the IAEA, seeking to impose sanctions against Jerusalem for its refusal to rule out future military action against nuclear installations in the Middle East. When the 1982 IAEA General Conference, at Iraqi instigation, refused to accept Israel's credentials, the United States temporarily withdrew from the Agency. This precipitated a crisis that was not finally resolved until the 1985 General Conference, when Israel's assurance that it would not "attack or threaten to attack any nuclear facilities devoted to peaceful purposes either in the Middle East or anywhere else" was accepted as a basis for its continued participation.[13]

After Osiraq was destroyed, it is possible that Baghdad pursued a separate track for obtaining a nuclear weapons capability. According to evidence obtained in a 1984 Italian prosecution, senior Iraqi military figures expressed interest in obtaining 74.6 pounds (33.9 kilograms) of plutonium— enough for several weapons—from an Italian arms smuggling ring purporting to have such material for sale.[14] One member of the ring, interviewed in 1985, claimed that he met first in Baghdad and then in Rome with members of the Iraqi military to discuss the sale; 1982 telexes between members of the smuggling ring contained in the prosecution file are consistent with this claim.[15] The deal fell through when, after a third meeting in Baghdad, the smugglers were unable to produce samples of the nuclear material. Although it is virtually certain that the plutonium offer was a hoax, possibly intended as a come-on to pave the way for sales of conventional arms, the episode suggests that through mid-1982, when negotiations on the matter ended, at least some in the Iraqi government remained interested in nuclear arming.

Political and Technical Developments

Iraq's nuclear program is now at a virtual standstill, both because of the Osiraq raid and because of a lack of funds resulting from Iraq's declining oil revenues and the demands of its war with Iran. This situation appears unlikely to change any time soon. In August 1987, it was reported that two months earlier French Prime Minister Jacques Chirac had promised Iraqi President Saddam Hussein to rebuild the

Osiraq plant, but French officials immediately denied the claims. As of mid-1988, the project appeared to be dormant.[16]

Israeli raid. Additional details about the Israeli raid on the Osiraq facility have recently come to light, however. In a book published in 1987, Israeli journalist Shlomo Nakdimon, who served as a press attaché to former Israeli Prime Minister Menacham Begin, states that Begin initiated military planning for the attack in December 1979, some eighteen months before the raid.[17] Nakdimon also indicates that Israel's long-range American F-16s were particularly important in ensuring the success of the strike and states that Begin postponed the raid until Israel had received two squadrons of the warplanes so that they could be used in the attack.[18] Israel also appears to have used detailed U.S. reconnaissance-satellite photos of the Osiraq site in planning the raid.[19]

Chemical weapons and medium-range missiles. Of more immediate concern to the question of nuclear proliferation in the Middle East, however, is Iraq's continued resort to another unconventional weapon—lethal chemical agents. In March 1986, a team of U.N.-appointed experts found that Iraq had used chemical weapons "on many occasions" against Iranian forces. The agent most commonly used was mustard gas, but nerve gas was also deployed on "some occasions." The investigation also found that "the use of chemical weapons appear[ed] to be more extensive than in 1984," when the organization had last conducted an inquiry into the matter.[20] Especially disturbing was the U.N. team's finding that Iraq had used chemical weapons against a major civilian target, the city of Abadan, in southern Iran. In May 1987, another U.N. inspection team found that Iraq had stepped up its use of chemical arms against Iran and was continuing to use them against civilian targets.[21]

On March 20, 1988, however, a still more shocking episode occurred when Iraq was accused of using cyanide and mustard gas against Halabja, an Iraqi border city 150 miles northeast of Baghdad that had recently been overrun by Iranian forces. Western reporters brought to the city by the Iranian government saw streets strewn with hundreds of corpses of unwounded civilians, leaving no question that they had been slain in a gas attack. Iran reported that 5,000 had perished and another 4,000 had been wounded in the attacks.[22]

As long the use of these weapons remains confined to the Iran-Iraq theater, the direct threat of escalation from this level of unconventional warfare to the nuclear level remains quite small, given the negligible nuclear capabilities of both states.[23] Indeed, it appears that to meet the Iraqi threat Iran has acquired chemical weapons of its own.[24]

Unfortunately, as chemical weapons are used more and more routinely in this context and as chemical weapons capabilities spread in the region—Libya and Syria, for example, are also thought to possess them[25]—the threat that chemical weapons will be used against Israel in any future Arab-Israeli conflict is growing dramatically.

As discussed in greater detail in the section on Israel earlier in this chapter, this threat is being compounded by the fact that Iraq, along with Iran, Libya, and Syria, are acquiring conventionally armed ballistic missiles that could be adapted to carry chemical warheads. (Saudi Arabia has also acquired intermediate-range missiles from China, but is not known to have a chemical weapons capability.)

In February and March 1988, Iraq fired nearly 200 conventionally armed missiles at cities in Iran—many of them 300 to 400 miles distant—as part of a terror campaign.[26] Iran has responded with shorter range missile attacks of its own. It may only be a matter of time before one of these countries combines its missile and chemical warfare capabilities, launching rockets with chemical warheads against its adversary's cities in an unprecedented campaign of terror.[27]

When Iraq test-fired its new medium-range missile in August 1987, Israel declared that it considered the rocket to pose a strategic threat, and Israeli military analysts specifically pointed to its chemical weapons potential.[28] Israel has also expressed fears over Syria's more accurate Soviet-supplied SS-21s, which if mated with chemical warheads, could be used to knock out air bases and similar military targets in Israel in a surprise attack.

Israel has reportedly produced chemical weapons of its own, and these may deter others from using such arms against it.[29] Israel's nuclear capability also serves as an important deterrent in this context, however, since Israel's adversaries would have to be concerned that it might retaliate with nuclear weapons, at least to more egregious chemical attacks.[30]

In sum, the Iraqi-led escalation to the use of chemical weapons and longer-range missiles in the Gulf War is indirectly increasing the threat that such weapons may someday be used against Israel. As a result, the overall importance of Israel's nuclear deterrent in the eyes of its security planners is likely to grow, and with it, the long-term risk that nuclear arms might be used in a future Arab-Israeli conflict.

(Iraq conducted three air strikes against Iran's unfinished Bushehr nuclear power reactors in November 1987. The raids are discussed in the next section of this chapter, covering Iran.)

Prospects

In the near term, there is little risk that Iraq's now dormant nuclear program could lead to the production of nuclear arms or that Iraq could obtain nuclear weapons material clandestinely, because such material does not appear to be available for sale. Baghdad's continued possession of 27.5 pounds (12.5 kilograms) of highly enriched uranium, which is subject to periodic IAEA inspections, however, must remain a source of concern.

Iraq has been threatened repeatedly with defeat at the hands of Iran; it has shown itself ready to disregard international arms control agreements and norms by its repeated use of chemical weapons; and it may have seriously considered trying to obtain plutonium by clandestine means in 1982. Although it would be an extraordinary step for Iraq to terminate IAEA inspections and appropriate the French-supplied uranium, the action would be an effective way of signaling to Iran that Baghdad was readying a nuclear device as a last resort deterrent against an overwhelming Iranian offensive. If faced with an all-out Iranian invasion, the Baghdad regime might believe it had few other options for ensuring its survival.[31]

In the longer term, Iraq's increasing alignment with moderate Arab states and its reestablishment of full diplomatic relations with Washington in 1984 may be harbingers of an increasing willingness on the part of President Saddam Hussein to adopt a more conciliatory stance vis-à-vis Israel in the years ahead.[32] If hostilities with Iran could be ended, this could ultimately reduce Iraqi motivations for developing nuclear arms. With Iran's Ayatollah Khomeini declaring until recently that Hussein's ouster is one of his nation's principal war goals, however, predictions about future Iraqi nuclear policy can be little more than speculation until the denouement of that conflict or a change in the complexion of the Iranian regime.

SOVIET UNION

TURKEY

Mosul

Arbela

SYRIA

Kirkuk

Sulaymaniyah

IRAN

Tigris River

Euphrates

Baghdad
(Tuwaitha)

IRAQ

Karbala

Hillah

Najaf

River

JORDAN

Basra

Persian
Gulf

SAUDI ARABIA

IRAQ

0   300

MILES

Photo 4.3 shows the Osiraq reactor outside Baghdad before (inset) and after the Israeli air strike of June 7, 1981.
Courtesy of the Iraqi Atomic Energy Commission.

Iraq

Research Reactors
Osiraq, Tammuz I (light-water/highly enriched uranium, 40 MWt)
- supplier: France
- start up: Destroyed by Israel June 1981, prior to start up; future status uncertain.
- fuel source: France
- safeguards: yes

Isis, Tammuz II (light-water/highly enriched uranium, 800 KWt)[a]
- supplier: France
- start up: 1980 (?)
- fuel source: France
- safeguards: yes

IRT-2000 (light-water/highly enriched uranium, 5 MWt)[b]
- supplier: Soviet Union
- start up: 1968
- fuel source: Soviet Union[b]
- safeguards: yes

Uranium Resources/Active Mining Sites/Uranium Mills
- reasonably assured reserves: none
- currently active site: none
- mills in operation: none[c]

Uranium Purification (UO_2)
Tuwaitha (laboratory scale)
- capacity: ?
- supplier: Italy
- start up: not operating (?)
- safeguards: yes

Fuel Fabrication
Tuwaitha
- capacity: ?
- supplier: Italy
- start up: not operating (?)
- safeguards: yes

Reprocessing (Plutonium extraction)
- capacity: 8 kg plutonium per year(?)[d]
- supplier: Italy
- start up: not operating
- safeguards: yes

Sources and Notes

a. Steve Weissman and Herbert Krosney, *The Islamic Bomb* (New York: Times Books, 1981), pp. 94, 100, 266. See also, Congressional Research Service, *Analysis of Six Issues About Nuclear Capabilities of India, Iraq, Libya, and Pakistan,* prepared for the Subcommittee of Arms Control, Oceans, and International Operations and Environment of the Senate Foreign Relations Committee (1982).

b. Jed C. Snyder, "The Road to Osiraq: Baghdad's Quest for the Bomb," *The Middle East Journal,* (Autumn 1983), p. 1.

c. Yellowcake supplied from Portugal, Brazil, Niger, and Italy. *Congressional Research Service, Six Issues,* p. 46; see notes 6 and 8 of this section.

d. Richard Burt, "U.S. Says Italy Sells Iraq Atomic Bomb Technology," *New York Times,* March 18, 1980, p. 1. Five to ten kg of plutonium per year. Weissman and Krosney, *The Islamic Bomb,* p. 268; Italian and U.S. officials state only hot cells, not reprocessing equipment, supplied.

Iran

Given its radical foreign policy, its bitter eight-year war with Iraq, and its efforts to enlarge its nascent nuclear infrastructure, Iran is a nation that poses a future proliferation threat. Thus, despite its adherence to the Non-Proliferation Treaty (NPT), Iran's nuclear activities deserve to be monitored closely.

Background

When it took power in late 1979, the government of Ayatollah Ruhollah Khomeini inherited extensive nuclear hardware, materials, and technology that had been built up during the Shah's reign, although some of the former regime's accomplishments were dissipated during the turmoil of the revolution. Construction of two partially completed, West German-supplied nuclear power plants at Bushehr was halted by the end of 1979, as was a French project to build another pair of reactors at Darkhouin.[1] In addition, many of the Iranian technicians involved in the projects fled the country. Although Tehran has sought to restart work on the Bushehr plants since 1984, West Germany has stated it will not renew construction activities until hostilities in the Iran-Iraq War have ended.[2]

The nuclear research activities inherited from the Shah, however, suffered less upheaval, and work at the Tehran Research Center has apparently continued without major interruption since Khomeini took power.[3] This means that Iran has been able to train specialists and perform experiments using a small U.S.-supplied research reactor, which remains under International Atomic Energy Agency (IAEA) safeguards.

In addition, researchers at the center have presumably had access to the know-how obtained during the years of work under the Shah, which included investigations concerning plutonium extraction and, according to several current and former U.S. officials, nuclear weapons design.[4] The Khomeini regime has apparently pursued the research side of its nuclear program with some vigor, and in 1984, opened a new research center at Isfahan, for which ground had been broken under the Shah.[5] For now, however, there is little to suggest that Iran has or will soon have the capability to produce nuclear weapons material.

Similarly, although in 1979 some elements of Iran's revolutionary government expressed an interest in acquiring nuclear arms, there have been no reports in recent years of Khomeini regime officials manifesting a similar interest. Nonetheless, Iran might be motivated to move in this direction in the future.

Should the war with Iraq drag on, for example, nuclear weapons could give Iran a means for achieving victory, although it would have to consider the possible responses of the United States and the Soviet Union to any nuclear threat it might make against Iraq. Nuclear arms would also make Iran indisputably the dominant power in the Persian Gulf, increasing its ability to intimidate neighboring states and to advance its brand of messianic Muslim fundamentalism. In addition, such weapons would enable Tehran to challenge the superpowers' political and military involvement in the region, by increasing the potential costs of confrontation.

Finally such weapons would support Iran's claims to leadership in the Muslim world and offset the prestige Pakistan is likely to enjoy for attaining nuclear status.[6]

Technical and Political Developments

During 1987, Iran continued its efforts to resuscitate its moribund nuclear program. In March, Tehran actively pursued contract negotiations with a consortium of West German, Spanish, and Argentinian firms on restarting construction of the Bushehr reactors, presumably after the Iran-Iraq War winds down. Through the fall of the year, it also took other preliminary steps at the construction site to prepare for renewed work on the plants.[7]

Iran also entered into a $5.5 million agreement with Argentina in May, under which the latter is to modify Iran's U.S.-supplied research reactor in Tehran to permit it to be fueled with 20-percent-enriched uranium, which Argentina is to supply.[8] The material cannot be used for nuclear weapons. Until now, the small reactor has been fueled with weapons-usable 93- percent-enriched uranium, but Iran has been unable to obtain new supplies of the material on the international market. The Argentinian fuel will be covered by IAEA safeguards, because Iran is an NPT party and because Argentina, though not a party, requires IAEA safeguards on all of its nuclear exports.

Given these safeguards, the low enrichment level of the fuel, and the small size of the Tehran research reactor,[9] the transaction will not contribute directly to Iran's ability to manufacture nuclear weapons. By permitting Iran to run the unit—which has been operating only intermittently for lack of fresh fuel—Argentina will, however, be assisting Iran to train nuclear technicians, thereby contributing in a general fashion to Iran's overall nuclear capabilities. The deal, it may be noted, undercuts U.S. efforts to establish a total embargo on nuclear sales to Tehran as a means of constraining the long-term nuclear weapons potential of the Khomeini regime. It is likely to be some time, however, before Argentina is able to produce the fuel for the Tehran reactor, since Argentina's only enrichment plant, at Pilcaniyeu, has to date apparently not been able to enrich uranium above 8 percent.

Iran's nuclear program suffered a serious blow in November 1987, when the Bushehr reactor construction site was attacked in three separate raids by Iraqi warplanes, twice on November 17 and once on November 19. The first two attacks seriously damaged the reactor control building and left 11 civilians dead, including a West German nuclear official. The official was part of a technical team from West Germany's reactor inspectorate (Technischer Ueberwachungsverein) that was examining the facility to determine how much of the equipment that had been delivered in the late-1970s was still serviceable.[10]

The Iraqi attacks were the first since March 4, 1985.[11] In the aftermath of that and prior Iraqi air strikes, Iran sought to have Iraq condemned at the IAEA, but because the reactors were unfinished and contained no nuclear fuel, the Agency did not apply its safeguards at the site and claimed it had no jurisdiction over the matter. Apparently to ensure IAEA involvement in the event of any future attack, in February 1987 Iran moved a small quantity of safeguarded nuclear material to the Bushehr facility. Although the amount involved was apparently too small to trigger formal IAEA safeguards there, after the Iraqi raid, Iran demanded that the Agency conduct an inspection at the site for radiological consequences, publicly comparing the risks to those from the Chernobyl disaster. The Agency initially denied the request, however, after concluding "that the small amount of nuclear materials stored at the site . . . could not create a significant hazard to the public."[12] Nonetheless, it later agreed to visit the site to determine whether the reactors were potentially salvageable.[13]

Iraq's motives for the air raids are unclear. Quite possibly Baghdad perceived the reactor construction site, where Iran has probably invested more than $1 billion, to be an attractive economic target. It is also possible, however, that Iraq was concerned over the long-term strategic threat posed by

Iran's building up its nuclear infrastructure and sought to prevent Tehran from advancing this capability.

Although it would have been at least five years before the first of the Bushehr reactors could conceivably have started operating—assuming West Germany had been prepared to assist in completing the units—from that time forward, the reactor would have produced significant quantities of plutonium in its spent fuel. In theory, Iran might have attempted to extract this plutonium, if it had also built a reprocessing capability. All of these activities would have taken place under IAEA safeguards, because of Iran's status as an NPT party, but Tehran could still have accumulated plutonium under IAEA inspection. It could then have quickly converted this material into weapons, if it had chosen to abrogate its NPT commitments or to withdraw from the treaty, as the pact itself permits on 90 days' notice, if a party determines that its "supreme interests" are jeopardized.

In the late 1970s, it appears that Iraq, itself a party to the NPT, was pursuing this very strategem, using its large Osiraq research reactor as the source of plutonium. (See the section on Iraq in this chapter.) It was this potential that led Israel to destroy the Osiraq plant in June 1981. Now, ironically, Iraq may have made the very same calculation that Israel made and may have taken the very same precaution to prevent an adversary from realizing its nuclear ambitions. In the aftermath of the air strikes, it appeared that completion of the reactors had become even more remote.[14]

A final development of importance is Iran's possible use for the first time of chemical weapons in its war against Iraq. According to a May 1987 United Nations report, Iraq's soldiers suffered wounds from gas attacks in recent clashes with Iran. The U.N. team that prepared the report did not find conclusive evidence as to the source of those injuries, leaving open the possibility that Iraqi soldiers were affected by wind-blown gas from Iraqi shells, rather than by Iranian chemical weapons. If Iran did use such unconventional arms, it would have violated its pledges under the 1925 Geneva Convention, raising questions about its commitment to other arms control measures, such as the NPT.[15] Whether or not Iran has actually used chemical arms, there have been numerous reports that it is acquiring the capability to manufacture them.[16]

Prospects

For now, there is no evidence to indicate that Tehran possesses the capability to manufacture nuclear arms or the necessary nuclear material. The nation, however, has maintained and expanded its costly nuclear research program at a time of considerable economic hardship, stemming from the worldwide slump in crude oil prices and the massive costs of the war with Iraq. In such circumstances, it seems fair to speculate that, as appears to have been true under the Shah, at least a portion of these activities have a military purpose. Given the available evidence, however, there is little reason to believe that Iran is making substantial progress toward nuclear arming.

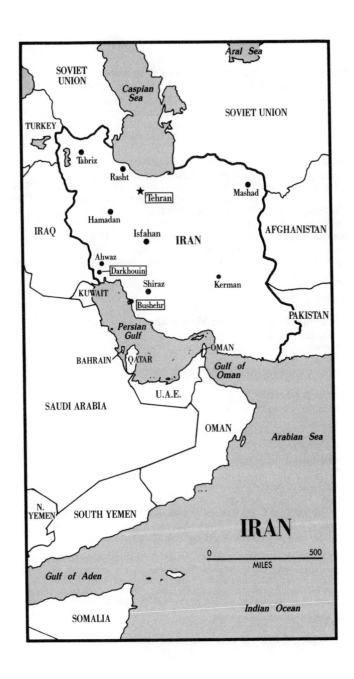

Iran

Power Reactors/Operating or Under Construction

Bushehr I (light-water/low-enriched uranium, 1300 MWe)[a]
- supplier: Kraftwerk Union (West Germany)
- start up: Partially completed; construction suspended in 1979;[b] damaged by Iraqi air strikes in mid-November, 1987.
- fuel source: West Germany (no fuel supplied)
- safeguards: yes

Bushehr II (light-water/low-enriched uranium, 1300 MWe)[a]
- supplier: Kraftwerk Union (West Germany)
- start up: Partially completed; construction suspended in 1979;[b] damaged by Iraqi air strikes in mid-November, 1987.
- fuel source: West Germany (no fuel supplied)
- safeguards: yes

Darkhouin (light-water/low-enriched uranium, 935 MWe)[c]
- supplier: Framatome (France)
- start up: Only minimal site work completed before termination in 1979[b]
- fuel source: France (no fuel supplied)
- safeguards: yes

Uranium Resources/Active Mining Sites/Uranium Mills

- reasonably assured reserves: 5,000 tons discovered in Yazd Province.[d]
- currently active sites: none
- mills in operation: none

Research Reactor

Tehran (light-water/highly-enriched uranium, 5 MWt)[e,g]
- supplier: United States
- start up: 1967[f]
- fuel source: United States (Argentina)[g]
- safeguards: yes

Sources and Notes

a. Office of Technology Assessment, *Technology Transfer to the Middle East*, (Washington, D.C.: U.S. Congress, Office of Technology Assessment, 1984) p. 353.

b. Daniel Poneman, *Nuclear Power in the Developing World*, (London: George Allen & Unwin Ltd., 1982) p. 96. Since 1984, Iran has unsuccessfully sought outside assistance to restart construction.

   Iran's efforts to complete these facilities were seriously set back when Iraqi warplanes bombed the Bushehr site several times in November 1987. See, Mark Hibbs, "Iraqi Attack on Bushehr Kills West German Nuclear Official," *Nucleonics Week*, November 19, 1987, p. 1; Mark Hibbs, "Bushehr Construction Now Remote after Three Air Strikes," *Nucleonics Week*, November 26, 1987, p. 5.

c. James Katz and Onkar Marwah, *Nuclear Power in Developing Countries*, (Lexington, MA: Lexington Books, 1982) p. 206.

d. "Briefly . . . Iran," *Nuclear Fuel*, January 28, 1985, p.11.

e. Office of Technology Assessment, *Technology Transfer to the Middle East*, p. 355.

f. International Atomic Energy Agency, *Nuclear Research Reactors in the Third World*, (Vienna: International Atomic Energy Agency, 1986) p.11.

g. In May 1987 Iran entered into a $5.5 million contract with Argentina under which the latter agreed to modify the Tehran research reactor to permit it to be fueled with 20 percent-enriched uranium, which Argentina would then supply. See, "Iran to Receive Nuclear Technology, Know-How," Noticias Argentinas, 1800 GMT, May 18, 1987, translated in *Foreign Broadcast Information Service/Latin America*, May 19, 1987; "Argentina Confirms Deal for Work on Bushehr," *Nuclear News*, (July: 1987): 54; Richard Kessler, "Argentina to Enforce Curbs on Nuclear Trade with Iran," *Nucleonics Week*, March 19, 1987, p. 12.

Chapter V:
Latin America

The advent of civilian governments in Argentina and Brazil in late 1983 and early 1985, respectively, and a series of subsequent bilateral initiatives aimed at easing the long-simmering nuclear rivalry between the two countries hold the promise of substantially reducing the threat that either will build nuclear weapons. These two are the only nations in the region with programs that might lead to the development of nuclear arms before the end of the century.[1] Both have refused to accept binding non-proliferation commitments under the Non-Proliferation Treaty or the Treaty of Tlatelolco, establishing a nuclear-weapon-free zone in Latin America.

Neither Argentina nor Brazil has faced an external security threat that might arguably call for the development of a nuclear deterrent. Rather, the risk of a nuclear arms race between them has arisen largely because both have viewed nuclear development as a potentially important factor in their enduring competition for regional preeminence and, at a minimum, an area in which neither could afford to fall behind. Over the years, these factors, combined with nationalistic desires for nuclear mastery, have led to a process of action and reaction that gradually propelled the two countries ever closer to nuclear weapon capabilities. In the early 1980s, as military regimes in both states pursued projects that could eventually have given them access to unsafeguarded nuclear weapons material, mutual suspicions intensified, and advocates of nuclear arming in each country appeared to become more outspoken. Today, with both nations under civilian rule, these tendencies appear to be in decline.

During 1987 and early 1988, both countries continued to pursue the development of unsafeguarded sensitive nuclear facilities. In September 1987 Brazil announced that it had for the first time been able to enrich uranium using indigenously developed technology, and in January 1988 it inaugurated a pilot-scale enrichment facility. Thus Brazil took important steps toward matching a capability achieved by Argentina in the early 1980s. At the same time, however, improvements in Argentine-Brazilian nuclear relations led to the implementation of a series of dramatic bilateral initiatives through which the two countries sought to reassure each other that their respective nuclear activities would not lead to the manufacture of nuclear explosives. The high points of these confidence-building efforts were a visit by Brazilian President José Sarney to Argentina's classified uranium enrichment plant at Pilcaniyeu in July 1987, and a reciprocal visit in March 1988 by Argentine President Raúl Alfonsín to Brazil's Aramar nuclear research center, where Brazil's first unsafeguarded uranium enrichment facility was inaugurated. Related efforts to integrate the nuclear power and research programs of the two countries also progressed significantly.

Because of these bilateral nuclear initiatives, the prospects for avoiding the spread of nuclear weapons in Latin America appear to be more favorable than they have been for many years. These promising developments have yet to be institutionalized, however, and it remains to be seen whether they can be sustained as the nuclear capabilities of the two countries continue to advance and as both the political uncertainties of presidential elections in 1989.

Argentina

Since Raúl Alfonsín took office in December 1983 as Argentina's first democratically elected president in over a decade, the threat that Argentina might develop nuclear weapons appears to have steadily declined.[1] During 1987 and early 1988, Alfonsín pursued a series of unprecedented non-proliferation initiatives with Brazilian President José Sarney, that could go far toward ensuring that the long-standing nuclear rivalry between the two nations does not lead to a regional nuclear arms race.

Background

Argentina's nuclear program has long been a symbol of the nation's technological prowess and its aspirations for continental leadership. When Alfonsín took office, that program was the most successful in Latin America and included two operating nuclear power plants,[2] along with uranium-production and nuclear-fuel manufacturing facilities, which gave Argentina increasing independence from outside nuclear supplies.[3]

Two nuclear projects initiated by Argentina's former military leaders, the Ezeiza reprocessing plant and the Pilcaniyeu (pronounced Pil-can-ee-jay-oo) enrichment plant, triggered fears that Argentina might have launched a program to develop a nuclear weapons capability. The decision to build the Ezeiza reprocessing plant, which will provide Buenos Aires with direct access to weapons-usable plutonium, was announced by Argentina's military leaders in 1978. The facility will be under International Atomic Energy Agency safeguards for the foreseeable future, although Argentina has reserved the right to operate it without IAEA oversight whenever it processes fuel from unsafeguarded reactors—which Argentina now lacks.[4] The plant is scheduled for completion in 1990.[5]

The Pilcaniyeu plant, which uses the gaseous diffusion method of enrichment, was also begun in 1978, but the project was kept secret for five years and announced by the military government only weeks before Alfonsín's inauguration. Although Argentine nuclear aides asserted at the time that it had been built to produce only reactor fuel that would not be usable in nuclear weapons, there are strong grounds for believing that the secret project, which is not subject to IAEA safeguards and was begun at a time of growing Argentine militarism, was initiated to provide Argentina with a nuclear weapons option.[6] Indeed, revelation of the plant led several top officials of Brazil's military government to declare in December 1983 that it would acquire a nuclear weapons capability of its own by 1990.[7] The Pilcaniyeu plant had produced a small quantity of very slightly enriched uranium by mid-1986 and is scheduled to begin production of 20 percent-enriched uranium (unusable for nuclear weapons) in mid-1988.[8]

Shortly after taking office, Alfonsín, in a seeming attempt to end the military overtones of the nation's nuclear program, ousted the former head of the Argentine Nuclear Energy Commission (CNEA), an admiral, and replaced him with a civilian, Alberto Costantini. From this point on, however, Alfonsín's efforts to change the direction of the Argentine nuclear program seemed to founder. During 1984 and the first half of 1985, Costantini, backed by nationalistic parliamentarians from the opposition Peronist Party,[9] successfully challenged the president's efforts to cut the nation's nuclear budget and, specifically, to kill funding for the Ezeiza and Pilcaniyeu plants.[10] Similarly, Alfonsín, apparently fearing a divisive fight with these same elements, refrained from pursuing legislation to reorganize the CNEA and make it strictly accountable for materials under its control.[11] The lack of consensus on nuclear policy also appeared to preclude Argentina's ratification of the Treaty of Tlatelolco, a move, said to be favored by Alfonsín, which would bring the country an important step closer to placing all of its nuclear plants under IAEA inspection.[12]

During this period, Alfonsín confronted a series of pressing domestic issues, including Argentina's continuing economic crisis and the prosecution of Argentina's former military leaders for human rights abuses. Undoubtedly, he feared that a pitched political battle over the highly charged question of the country's nuclear future, in which he would be accused of weakening Argentina's long-term strategic potential, would undermine his ability to rally public support to deal with these other urgent challenges.

In mid-March 1985, Argentine sources revealed that, despite this seeming paralysis over nuclear policy, Alfonsín and Brazilian President-elect Tancredo Neves had agreed in principle to open their countries' nuclear installations to mutual inspections.[13] The two leaders were said to have agreed to this at a meeting on February 7, 1985, in Buenos Aires.

Neves's tragic death prior to taking office cast the proposal into limbo, and it appeared unclear whether his successor, José Sarney, whose political mandate was highly uncertain, would have the power or the inclination to make the proposal a reality. Moreover, Brazilian spokesmen at the time seemed to back away from the proposal, claiming that Neves had never committed himself to mutual inspections, but only to further discussions.

During the summer and fall of 1985, however, Alfonsín slowly consolidated his political power, announcing a set of major economic reforms in June that gained wide support, suppressing a wave of bombings by right-wing terrorists, and increasing his party's parliamentary majority in the country's November 1985 elections.[14] Against this background, on November 29 and 30, Alfonsín met with Brazilian President Sarney at Foz de Iguacu, on the Brazil-Argentina border. Among a number of initiatives aimed at improving bilateral economic ties and enhancing the coordination of foreign policies, the leaders signed a joint declaration on nuclear policy, reiterating the commitment of both nations to develop nuclear energy solely for peaceful purposes.

The statement also established a bilateral commission to further nuclear cooperation between them and to "create mechanisms to insure the supreme interests of peace, security and development in the region, without detriment to the technical aspects of nuclear cooperation, which will continue to be governed by the regulations in force [*viz.,* a nuclear cooperation agreement the two countries signed in 1980]."[15] Although this part of the declaration did not refer explicitly to mutual nuclear inspections, apparently because of Sarney's reluctance to embrace this measure publicly, it was understood that inspections would be on the agenda of the commission.[16] Despite Sarney's caution, the declaration, by addressing the nuclear issue openly, was an important step toward reducing nuclear tensions between the countries and seemed to signal that the two leaders were intent on ending the suspicions built up during the years of military rule.[17]

The joint nuclear commission met in late March 1986 and again in mid-July. At their first meeting, the participants appear to have endorsed the mutual inspection concept, but decided that any such system would operate in parallel with the safeguards regime of the IAEA and that data obtained in the course of mutual inspections would not be shared with the Agency.[18] A separate internal Brazilian nuclear-policy review, completed in April, also supported the reciprocal inspection concept, a finding welcomed in Argentina.[19]

The mid-July joint commission meeting, coming in the wake of the April 28 accident at the Chernobyl reactor in the

Soviet Union, focused on nuclear safety issues. When President Sarney visited Buenos Aires on July 29, he and President Alfonsín agreed to create an early warning system to notify each other promptly in the case of a nuclear accident — a step toward further cooperation in the nuclear sector, though not directly relevant to the mutual inspection issue.[20] At the July meeting, the two leaders also signed additional protocols to eliminate customs barriers between the countries and to establish balanced bilateral trade. These steps testified to the historic shift in relations under way between the two states.[21]

During May and June, it may be noted, Alfonsín had confronted a new wave of right-wing violence at home. The terrorism had included an apparent attempt on his life and led to rumors, which proved unfounded, that a military coup might be imminent.[22] Although the military's long-standing distrust of Brazil was a well-known fact of Argentine life, these developments did not deter Alfonsín from pursuing his opening with President Sarney.[23]

On July 30, Argentina quietly took an additional, symbolically important step toward nuclear restraint by ratifying the Partial Test Ban Treaty, prohibiting nuclear tests in the atmosphere, under water, or in outer space. Alfonsín's decision to join the pact and the vote on it in the Argentine congress, however, were not publicly announced, apparently to avoid a possible backlash by nationalist elements. The episode highlighted the continuing political sensitivity of the nuclear issue, even as it demonstrated the increasing control of Argentina's civilian government over the country's nuclear affairs.[24]

Political and Technical Developments

From late 1986 through mid-1988, Alfonsín continued the process of nuclear *détente* with Brazil, an initiative which appeared to gain broad domestic support and to be little affected by a series of political setbacks Alfonsín suffered during this period.

In December 1986, Alfonsín and Sarney, meeting in Brasília, signed some twenty new protocols covering a wide range of bilateral economic issues and entered into several understandings for increased collaboration in the field of civilian nuclear energy, including an agreement to form a nuclear accident early warning system.[25] A report in the Brazilian press several months earlier that a nuclear test site was being built on a Brazilian military reservation in Cachimbo apparently had little impact on the growing trust between the two leaders, and Alfonsín appeared to accept Sarney's assurances that the site was intended only for the testing of conventional munitions.[26] (See the discussion in the Brazil section later in this chapter.)

Although no new initiatives were reported at the Brasília summit concerning the possibility of mutual nuclear inspections, it was disclosed subsequently that in December, Brazil had permitted Argentine nuclear aides to visit key parts of Brazil's classified nuclear research center at the Institute for Nuclear and Energy Research (IPEN), located at the University of São Paulo. The facilities visited included an experimental centrifuge uranium enrichment unit and an as yet unused laboratory-scale plutonium extraction facility, neither of which was subject to IAEA safeguards.[27] Given the sensitivity of these activities, which could eventually permit Brazil to produce nuclear weapons material and which were controlled by the Brazilian Navy, the unprecedented opening of the installations was a powerful demonstration that Brazil did not intend to use the facilities to develop nuclear arms and represented a significant step in building mutual trust on nuclear matters between the two countries.

CNEA influence reduced. Several months later, Alfonsín appeared to increase his flexibility in pursuing these initiatives by consolidating his control over Argentine nuclear affairs. On April 9, 1987, Alberto Costantini resigned in protest as head of the CNEA after Argentina's Economic Ministry severely cut funding for a number of major nuclear projects.[28] The resignation appeared to symbolize the declining political stature of Argentina's nuclear bureaucracy, which, under the nation's previous military government, had been partly protected from austerity measures and, even after Alfonsín had taken office, had been treated deferentially because Argentina's nuclear program was an important symbol of national prestige. Indeed, in a major address in May 1986, Alfonsín—under pressure from Costantini and his nationalistic allies in the opposition Peronist party—had embraced the nuclear plan of his military predecessors, rejecting proposals for a broad retrenchment of the nation's nuclear construction projects.[29]

As Argentina's economic crisis worsened in early 1987, however, the increasing costs and lengthening construction schedules for these projects, together with a preference for non-nuclear energy sources among some senior Argentine planning officials, led to the cuts that, in Costantini's words, "condemn[ed] the CNEA to slow agony and total paralysis," and triggered his resignation.[30] The most direct effects of the budget battle were to delay completion of Argentina's third nuclear power reactor (Atucha II) and the Swiss-supplied heavy-water production plant being built at Arroyito, and, apparently, to cause a suspension of work on a smaller, indigenously designed heavy water plant at Atucha.[31] On a broader plane, Costantini's resignation appeared to signify the decline of the once-powerful CNEA as a political force influencing the overall direction of Argentine nuclear affairs. The fact that Alfonsín continued to give funding priority to the unsafeguarded Pilcaniyeu enrichment plant, however, suggested that he was not insensitive to the aspirations of the nuclear program's traditional supporters.[32]

Limited military interest. Later in April 1987, Alfonsín confronted a resurgence of unrest among Argentina's military, triggered by a mutiny of junior army officers opposed to the on-going prosecutions for atrocities committed under the military regime that had governed the country from 1976 to 1983. Although the uprising ended peacefully after four days, the slow response of the Argentine Army in suppressing the rebellion indicated the depth of sentiment within the military on the issue. In May, stating that the mutiny had

brought the country to "the brink of civil war," Alfonsín suc-
cumbed to pressure from this quarter and introduced legislation to end prosecutions of all but the highest ranking officers involved in the human rights abuses.[33] A subsequent
mutiny in January 1988, led by the same junior officers, was
quickly suppressed by loyal troops, and the mutiny's supporters, apparently confined to the army, were purged, an
indication that Alfonsín had satisfied the military's
concerns.[34]

In contrast to the pervasive behind-the-scenes involvement of Brazil's military in national political affairs, and in
nuclear matters in particular, the concerns of the Argentine
military appeared to be confined to the prosecution question
and to narrow, professional issues, such as military budgets,
modernization of equipment, and pay.[35] Despite the navy's
role in supervising Argentina's nuclear program in the 1970s
and early 1980s, for example, it remained virtually silent on
Alfonsín's slowdown of a number of the nuclear projects it
had initiated as well as on his confidence-building initiatives
with Brazil.

New links with Brazil. Notwithstanding the stir caused by
Costantini's resignation and the military unrest of April
1987, Argentine and Brazilian nuclear aides met again later
that month in Rio de Janeiro and took another small step
toward developing cooperative nuclear relations by agreeing
to launch a joint effort for the production of research reactor
fuel using low-enriched uranium.[36] Both countries had long
relied on imports of highly enriched uranium, principally
from the United States, for this purpose, but Washington
had cut supplies to both states in the late 1970s because they
had refused to place all of their nuclear activities under
IAEA safeguards.[37] In pursuing the joint initiative to develop and produce their own substitute fuel, the two Latin
American states portrayed themselves as making common
cause against continued dependency on outside suppliers
and appeared to legitimize each other's efforts to develop
uranium enrichment capabilities—a sharp contrast to the

competitiveness that had long characterized their nuclear relations.

These cooperative arrangements were extended in July, when Sarney and Alfonsín met in Buenos Aires. The two leaders announced that Argentina intended to purchase slightly enriched uranium (material enriched to 0.85 percent uranium-235) from Brazil's West German-supplied Resende enrichment plant for use in Argentina's nuclear power plants, and that, in turn, Brazil would purchase low-enriched uranium (some enriched to 3 percent and some to 20 percent) from Argentina's Pilcaniyeu enrichment facility for use in Brazil's nuclear power and research reactors, respectively.[38] The initiative to increase mutual nuclear autonomy vis-à-vis outside suppliers again appeared to reflect a growing shift in Brazilian-Argentine relations from rivalry to collaboration.

The development was overshadowed, however, when Alfonsín, in an unprecedented gesture of openness, took Sarney on a forty-minute tour of Argentina's previously classified Pilcaniyeu enrichment plant. The visit, said to have covered all sensitive parts of the plant, was intended by both leaders as a major step toward establishing mutual trust and a non-competitive nuclear relationship between the two countries.[39]

Although the Argentines did not disclose technical details concerning the facility's capabilities and operations and although no arrangements were established for monitoring the output of the unit, the opening of the plant to Brazil's president was an act of great symbolic importance in demonstrating that Argentina had no intent to use Pilcaniyeu for nuclear arms.[40] Indeed, one has only to compare the secrecy surrounding comparably sensitive unsafeguarded installations in India, Israel, and Pakistan to appreciate the historic importance of the gesture.[41] The Pilcaniyeu visit and Brazil's opening of IPEN's research areas to Argentine visitors the previous December, were clear proof that the two civilian leaders had made important progress in overcoming the intense nationalism that had characterized the nuclear policies of their military predecessors—and which, particularly in Brazil, still appeared to have considerable support in military circles. Alfonsín, it may be noted, faced criticism for his gesture from nationalist elements associated with the opposition Peronist party and from some CNEA technocrats, but brushed it aside.[42]

Brazilian nuclear advances. Two months after this extraordinary development, the spirit of nuclear amity between the two Latin American countries was confronted with a new challenge, when President Sarney dramatically announced on September 4, 1987, that Brazil had successfully used centrifuges to enrich uranium at IPEN and was building a pilot-scale uranium enrichment plant at the navy's Aramar Experimental Center in Ipero, some 80 miles west of São Paulo.[43] In principle, the latter facility, which was not to be subject to IAEA safeguards, could eventually permit Brazil to produce weapons-grade uranium free from nonproliferation controls. Despite the nationalistic tone of Sarney's announcement, made on the eve of Brazil's independence day, the Brazilian president apparently sought to avoid straining relations with Argentina by letting it know of his plans ahead of time.[44]

Election loss. At the time, Alfonsín was engaged in a heated election campaign in which a majority of the seats in the Argentine congress and key provincial posts were at stake. Opponents of Alfonsín's Radical Party, in theory, could have sought to exploit the Brazilian advance by arguing that Alfonsín had been naive in allowing Sarney to visit Argentina's most sensitive plant at a time when Brazil was still bent on secretly enlarging its own nuclear capabilities. The issue appears not to have been prominent in the campaign, however, which was dominated by economic issues.

The September 1987 elections resulted in a significant setback for the Argentine president, as the Peronist Party displaced his own as the major grouping in congress and captured a number of key local posts, including the prestigious governorship of Buenos Aires Province. Significantly, however, the Peronist bloc was itself now dominated by moderate reformists, and the grip of ultra-nationalists had been weakened significantly. One apparent result of this shift was that after the elections, a key Peronist spokesman, Guido di Tella, declared that the party intended to support Alfonsín's nuclear opening to Brazil.[45] Although other Peronist sources were quoted as stating that the matter remained open, nuclear confidence-building with Brazil continued to gather momentum in the succeeding months. In December, Alfonsín declared that the two countries were close to formalizing an agreement on "mutual safeguards" covering their respective nuclear programs, and talks on the subject continued at least through April 1988, although few details were disclosed and there has been little to indicate that Brazil is enthusiastic about such formal arrangements.[46]

Nonetheless, by March, Argentine nuclear aides were quoted in the press as stating that Argentina had obtained access to all operating nuclear facilities in Brazil not covered by IAEA safeguards, including a laser enrichment research project run by the Brazilian Air Force, and that IPEN had been visited several times.[47] The capstone to these growing ties came in April, when Alfonsín participated in the dedication of the Aramar centrifuge enrichment plant in Ipero—a visible expression of trust in Brazil's assurances that the plant would not contribute to the manufacture of nuclear arms.[48] As discussed below in the section on prospects, continuation of this trend in the future will depend heavily on political developments within the two Latin American states.

Nuclear exports. If Argentina's domestic nuclear program has lost momentum in recent years, its nuclear export activities have acquired increasing importance. In addition to its nuclear exports to Brazil, as of mid-1986, Argentina had entered into contracts to sell small research reactors to Peru, Colombia, and Algeria.[49] It intends to supply non-weapons-grade, 20 percent-enriched uranium fuel for these units from its Pilcaniyeu enrichment facility. Argentina had also entered into agreements for nuclear cooperation with sixteen nations, including India, Libya—both now dormant—and China,[50] and had sought to participate in a consortium with West Germany and Spain to complete Iran's Bushehr nuclear power reactors, once the Iran-Iraq War ended.[51]

In November 1986, Argentina signed a new nuclear accord with Cuba to assist it in quality assurance and health and safety aspects of nuclear power production; Cuba is building two nuclear power stations at Cienfuegos.[52] In May 1987, Argentina and Uruguay expanded the scope of a 1967 nuclear cooperation accord, and discussions were held on Argentina's supplying a small research reactor in the future.[53] The following month, Argentina and Mexico held talks on Mexico's possible purchase of equipment for the fabrication of nuclear reactor fuel.[54] Later in the year, the CNEA was considering whether to offer a small research reactor to Albania, and in May 1988 Argentina signed a nuclear cooperation pact with Turkey.[55] Although Argentina adopted a policy of requiring IAEA safeguards on all of its nuclear exports in 1986, and although none of the proposed transfers involves equipment or material that could significantly assist recipients in the development of nuclear weapons, Argentina's readiness to contemplate cooperation with Algeria, Cuba, and Albania—three countries that, like itself, have not signed the Non-Proliferation Treaty—raises questions as to how disciplined its nuclear export policies may be in the future.

More controversial in this regard was Argentina's conclusion in May 1987 of an agreement to assist Iran in modifying a five-megawatt U.S.-supplied research reactor in Tehran. The modification is intended to permit the reactor to use 20 percent-enriched uranium fuel, which Argentina would also supply, rather than the weapons-grade 93 percent fuel the unit has used to date and which Iran has been unable to obtain on the international market.[56] Although this is a type of conversion the United States has encouraged for non-proliferation purposes, and although both the reactor and its new non-weapon-grade fuel will be subject to IAEA safeguards, the agreement runs counter to U.S. policy in another respect, since Washington has sought to implement an international embargo on all nuclear sales to Tehran, at least until the end of the Iran-Iraq War.[57] Once again, although Argentina appears to be adhering to the most important supplier norms, it has not embraced the full range of restraints adopted by most Western supplier states. It may be noted that Argentina also contracted to sell Iran $31 million worth of arms in March 1987.[58]

U.S. diplomacy. During the past year, U.S. non-proliferation diplomacy vis-a-vis Argentina has been conducted largely out of public view and has apparently concentrated on quietly encouraging the Argentines to pursue their nuclear rapprochement with Brazil and to adopt a cautious policy on nuclear exports. A U.S. embargo on nuclear fuel and reactor sales to Argentina remains in effect because certain Argentine nuclear installations have not been placed under IAEA safeguards.[59] (See the chart at the end of this section.)

No access to weapons material. A critically important factor improving the climate for non-proliferation restraints in Latin America is that neither Argentina nor Brazil has yet produced significant quantities of weapons-grade nuclear materials—highly enriched uranium or separated plutonium.[60] Thus, for now, neither state has reason to fear that the other may be secretly manufacturing nuclear weapons.

Now that both states are building uranium enrichment plants not subject to IAEA safeguards, however, this situation could change within several years. As of mid-1987, Argentina's Pilcaniyeu facility was reported to be producing uranium enriched to between 1 and 12 percent, according to various estimates.[61] Plans called for the unit to produce "hundreds of kilograms" of 20 percent-enriched uranium by mid-1988 (a kilogram equals 2.2 pounds), but it appears unlikely that this target will be met, despite the priority the project is receiving.[62] Argentine nuclear officials insist that the facility will not enrich material beyond this 20 percent level (which is not usable for nuclear weapons), but as Argentina acquires the capability to produce such material,

Brazilian officials will have no means of verifying that it has not gone beyond this level, creating dangerous ambiguities.[63]

Brazil's unsafeguarded Aramar enrichment plant at Ipero also seems far from producing significant quantities of highly enriched uranium, but, as work at the plant progresses, Argentina will similarly have to worry that Brazil might be producing weapons-grade material there. As noted above, the exchange of visits to nuclear installations did not include disclosure of plant throughput or enrichment levels, nor have monitoring mechanisms been adopted for ensuring that the plants are not modified at some future point to permit the production of weapons-grade uranium. The two countries have reportedly discussed an arrangement under which both would refrain from enriching uranium above 20 percent until the year 2000, but without some means of verifying such pledges, neither could be completely confident that the other was not circumventing them.[64] As noted above, Argentina has sought to gain Brazil's agreement on a bilateral inspection regime, but so far Brazil has apparently been unwilling to take this step.

IAEA safeguards are designed specifically to provide confidence that nuclear materials are not being diverted, but both Argentina and Brazil have chafed at having to accept such controls on nuclear installations they have imported, and so far have rejected IAEA inspections of their indigenous installations as an undue intrusion on national sovereignty. These postures were adopted while both countries were under military rule—when there was evidence that elements of the military hoped to use unsafeguarded facilities to acquire nuclear weapon options. If the trend toward collaborative Argentine-Brazilian nuclear relations continues—and if nationalistic tendencies fostered by the military of both countries fade—IAEA safeguards possibly may appear more attractive. In the meantime, Argentine proposals for bilateral inspections that would be less intrusive than the IAEA system could be a valuable step toward improved verification, though such inspections are not likely to be as technically reliable.

Argentina, it should be noted, will also gain access to significant quantities of weapons-usable plutonium once it begins operating the Ezeiza plutonium extraction plant, now scheduled to come on line in 1990.[65] For the foreseeable future, all plutonium produced at Ezeiza will be subject to IAEA inspection, inasmuch as all sources of plutonium in Argentina—*i.e.*, all spent reactor fuel—are covered by the IAEA regime. This should reassure Brazil that none of the material is being diverted to military uses.

Prospects

The future course of Argentine nuclear affairs will be determined by the interaction of domestic political developments, technological advances in the country's nuclear program, and relations with Brazil. President Alfonsín, who has played a prominent role in international efforts to promote U.S.-Soviet arms control, appears to be genuinely committed to avoiding a nuclear arms race in Latin America.

Alfonsín's term expires in 1989, however, and under the Argentine constitution, he cannot be reelected. Given the momentum he has built for the nuclear opening to Brazil, it is likely that he will be able to sustain the initiative until the end of his term, particularly since he seems to have at least the tacit support of the Peronists, who now largely control the Argentine congress. Whether his successor—and the congress that will then be in power—will continue down this road remains to be seen. Such an outcome would be more likely if the *ad hoc* arrangements that have been established with Brazil to date can be institutionalized in some fashion.

Prospects for continued bilateral confidence-building also could improve if Argentina's uranium enrichment advances continue at the relatively slow pace of the past several years and if all parties thus remain confident that only low levels of enrichment have been achieved. This could permit the adoption of more rigorous verification mechanisms before the possibility arises that Argentina might be producing weapons-grade materials. On the other hand, if Argentina meets its current production target and begins to produce large quantities of 20 percent-enriched material in 1988, it could create the impression that it had the ability to produce weapons-grade uranium at will. Such an assumption could create discomfort in Brazil and possibly impede new confidence-building measures.

Developments in Brazil, where President Sarney will face an election before 1991, will also affect Argentine attitudes. If democratization there falters and the Brazilian military, with its enthusiasm for open-ended nuclear development, takes on a larger political role, or if Brazil's uranium enrichment program rapidly achieves a capability to produce weapons-grade material, support within Argentina for Alfonsín's policy of nuclear rapprochement could erode.

The events of the past eighteen months—the opening of IPEN to Argentine specialists, Sarney's visit to Pilcaniyeu, and Alfonsín's presence at the dedication of the Aramar enrichment unit—are obviously encouraging. Whether their promise of averting a potential nuclear arms race in Latin America can be fulfilled will depend ultimately on the statesmanship of Argentine and Brazilian leaders in the next several years—during a period that will be marked by dramatic political events for both nations.

BOLIVIA

PARAGUAY

● Salta

● Tucuman

Resistencia

Corrientes

BRAZIL

Parana

Los Gigantes

● Córdoba

Santa Fe

Rosario

URUGUAY

Río Tercero
(Embalse)

● Mendoza

Atucha

La Estela

San Rafael

Buenos Aires
(Constituyentes)
(Ezeiza)

Río de
la Plata

Sierra Pintada

Malargüe

ARGENTINA

Mar del Plata

Pacific
Ocean

CHILE

Arroyito

Bahia Blanca

Neuquén

Atlantic
Ocean

Pilcaniyeu

San Carlos
de Bariloche

Rawson

Comodoro
Rivadavia

ARGENTINA

uranium mining area

0   400
MILES

Río Gallegos

Argentina

Power Reactors/Operating or Under Construction

Atucha I (heavy-water/natural-uranium, 320 MWe)
- supplier: Siemens AG (West Germany)
- start up: 1974
- fuel source: Argentina and West Germany (for some process steps); Argentina, principally, after 1984.[a,z]
- heavy water: initial charge, U.S., West Germany.[b]
- safeguards: yes

Embalse (heavy-water/natural-uranium, 600 MWe)
- supplier: Atomic Energy of Canada Ltd. (Canada) and Italimpianti (Italy)
- start up: 1983
- fuel source: Canada and Argentina through 1985; Argentina, principally, after 1985.[a,z]
- heavy water: initial charge, Canada[e]
- safeguards: yes

Atucha II (heavy-water/natural-uranium, 745 MWe)
- supplier: Kraftwerk Union (West Germany)
- start up: 1993[v]
- fuel source: Argentina
- heavy water: Argentina and West Germany[r]
- safeguards: yes

Uranium Resources/Active Mining Sites/Uranium Mills
- reasonably assured reserves: 18,900 metric tons[f]
- currently active sites: Los Gigantes, La Estella, Sierra Pintada[g]
- mills in operation: San Rafael, Los Gigantes, Don Otto, Marlagüe[f]

Uranium Purification (UO$_2$)

Córdoba
- capacity: 150 metric tons per year[c,h]
- supplier: West Germany
- start up: 1982, full capacity 1986[c,h]
- safeguards: yes

Córdoba
- capacity: 150 metric tons per year[c,h,v]
- supplier: Argentina
- start up: planned for 1987, status mid-1988 uncertain[c,h,v]
- safeguards: no

Córdoba
- capacity: 15 metric tons per year[h,s]
- supplier: Argentina
- start up: 1980[h]
- safeguards: no

Uranium Conversion (UF$_6$)

Pilcaniyeu
• Capacity presumed (to serve pilot enrichment plant)(unsafeguarded)

Heavy Water

Arroyito (industrial scale)
• capacity:	250 metric tons per year
• supplier:	Sulzer Brothers (Switzerland)
• start up:	mid-1989[i]
• safeguards:	yes

Atucha (pilot scale)
• capacity:	2-4 metric tons per year[t]
• supplier:	Argentina (with possible foreign aid)[d]
• start up:	status of project uncertain
• safeguards:	no

Enrichment

Pilcaniyeu
• type:	gaseous diffusion
• capacity:	500 kg. per year of 20% enriched uranium planned; actual capacity expected to be lower.[j,bb]
• supplier:	Argentina
• start up:	1983 (experimental unit); 1988 (20% enrichment planned)[bb]
• safeguards:	no

Fuel Fabrication

Ezeiza
• capacity:	Substantial part of requirements for Atucha I and Embalse[z]
• supplier:	Atucha I line, West Germany; Embalse line, Argentina.[j]
• start up:	1982 (Atucha I line)[a]; 1985 (Embalse line)[z]
• safeguards:	Atucha line safeguarded, Embalse line safeguarded only when fabricating safeguarded UO$_2$.[k,z]

Constituyentes
• capacity:	Pilot plant for enriched uranium research reactor fuel
• supplier:	Argentina
• start up:	1976[x]
• safeguards:	only when safeguarded uranium is processed

Reprocessing (Plutonium Extraction)

Ezeiza
• capacity:	15 kg plutonium, 5 metric tons spent fuel per year [e]
• supplier:	Argentina (possible Italian aid)[m,w,y]
• start up:	tests with radioactive material, 1989; initial production, 1990[w]
• safeguards:	only when safeguarded spent fuel is processed[n]

Ezeiza
- capacity: laboratory scale
- supplier: Argentina
- start up: 1969; operated intermittently until dismantled in 1973.[e]
- safeguards: no

Research Reactors [l,o]

RA-0, Córdoba (tank/medium-enriched uranium, 1 Wt)
- supplier: Argentina
- start up: 1965
- safeguards: no

RA-1, Constituyentes (tank/medium-enriched uranium, less than 1 MWt)
- supplier: Argentina
- start up: 1958
- safeguards: yes

RA-2, Constituyentes (tank/highly enriched uranium, less than 1 MWt)
- supplier: Argentina
- start up: 1966
- safeguards: yes

RA-3, Ezeiza (pool/highly enriched uranium, 5 MWt)[u]
- supplier: Argentina
- start up: 1967
- safeguards: yes

RA-4, Rosario (homogeneous, medium-enriched uranium, less that 1 MWt)
- supplier: West Germany
- start up: 1972
- safeguards: yes

RA-6, San Rafael de Bariloche (MTR, highly enriched uranium, 500 KWt)[p, u]
- supplier: Argentina
- start up: 1982
- safeguards: only when safeguarded fuel is present.

RA-7, cancelled (heavy-water/natural-uranium 40-100 MWt)[q]
- supplier: Argentina
- start up: development suspended, 1985 [aa]
- safeguards: no

Sources and Notes

a. "Fuel Fabrication Factory Opened," *Nuclear Engineering International,* May 1982, p. 8; "Nuclear Firms Advance Level of Technology to Meet Objectives," *Energia Nuclear 1983,* translated in *Joint Publication Research Service/Nuclear Development and Proliferation,* hereafter *JPRS/TND,* February 28, 1984, pp. 15-17; "Nuclear Institute's Financial Problems Reported," *Noticias Argentinas,* 1935 GMT February 5, 1985, *JPRS/TND* February 26, 1985, p. 36. Argentina also possesses a significant but not yet completely autonomous zirconium alloy and tube manufacturing capability for sheathing reactor fuels. See ref. x and "Argentina Closer to Fuel Independence," *Nuclear Fuel,* May 20, 1985, p. 5.

b. John Redick, "The Military Potential of Latin American Nuclear Programs," International Studies Series, Sage Publications, 1972, p. 13; personal communication. Between 1980 and 1982, Argentina imported 6 metric tons of heavy water each from the USSR and the People's Republic of China to make up for losses at Atucha I. Richard Kessler, "U.S. Approval for West Germany to Sell 143 Tonnes of Heavy Water to Argentina," *Nucleonics Week*, August 25, 1983, p. 7; Judith Miller, "U.S. Is Holding Up Peking Atom Talks," *New York Times*, September 19, 1982; Richard Kessler, "Argentina to Tender for Heavy Water After June Purchase from China," *Nucleonics Week*, September 25, 1986, p. 5. Additional heavy water was obtained from West Germany (with U.S. permission) in 1983. Kessler, "U.S. Approval."

c. Carlos Castro Madero, "Argentina's Nuclear Energy Program," *Nuclear Europe*, July-August 1983, pp. 31-33.

d. Burt Solomon, "Argentina Bent on Home-Grown Nuclear Program," *Energy Daily*, November 9, 1982, p. 3.

e. Powell A. Moore, Assistant Secretary of State for Congressional Relations, to Senator Gary Hart, August 19, 1982.

f. Reasonably Assured Reserves at less than $130 per kilogram. OECD Nuclear Energy Agency and the International Atomic Energy Agency, *Uranium, Resources Production and Demand* (Paris: OECD, 1986), pp. 84-99.

g. "Uranium Concentrate Plant," *TELAM, Noticias Argentinas* (Buenos Aires), November 16, 1982, translated in Foreign Broadcast Information Service (FBIS)/Latin America, December 9, 1982, p. B4; "CNEA Resumes Uranium Excavation," DYN, 2311 GMT, December 13, 1984, FBIS/Latin America, December 17, 1984, p. B-3.

h. "Argentina to Start Producing U0$_2$ This Year," *Nuclear Fuel*, September 13, 1982, p. 15; "CNEA Steps Up Production of UO$_2$ Plant Not Under IAEA Safeguards," *Nuclear Fuel*, December 29, 1986, p. 9.

i. Richard Kessler, "Production Delayed for a Year at Argentine Heavy Water Plant," *Nuclear Fuel*, July 13, 1987, p. 13.

j. "CNEA Chairman Makes Announcement," *TELAM* (Buenos Aires) 2102 GMT, November 18, 1983, translated in *JPRS/TND*, December 12, 1983, p. 7; Milton R. Benjamin, "Argentina Seen Capable of 4 A-Bombs a Year," *Washington Post*, December 9, 1983; Richard Kessler, "Argentina to Delay Production," *Nucleonics Week*, February 14, 1985. See also reference v (capacity in 1987 will be 20,000 separate work units, to be expanded to 100,000.)

k. Personal communication with informed U.S. official.

l. International Atomic Energy Agency, *Annual Report for 1982*, p. 84.

m. Robert Laufer, "Argentina Looks to Reprocessing to Fill Its Own Needs Plus Plutonium Sales," *Nuclear Fuel*, November 8, 1982, p. 3; Leonard S. Spector, *The New Nuclear Nations* (New York: Vintage Books, 1985) pp. 61-63; Richard Kessler, "Argentina's Alfonsín Pledges Funding for Fuel Projects," *Nucleonics Week*, June 5, 1986, p. 3.

n. Currently only safeguarded spent fuel is available.

o. Pilat and Donnelly, "An Analysis of Argentina's Nuclear Power Program and Its Closeness to Nuclear Weapons," December 2, 1982. Reactors may be operating at reduced levels. See reference x.

p. "Research Reactor Inaugurated," *Nuclear Engineering International*, June 1983, p. 10.

q. Sometimes referred to as *RA-5*.

r. Some of the 143 metric tons of heavy water sold to Argentina by West Germany in 1983 (with U.S. permission) is to be available for Atucha II. Personal communication with U.S. and West German officials.

s. Reportedly this is a second facility in Cordoba; scheduled to be closed after unsafeguarded 150 metric ton/year plant is opened; personal communication with knowledgeable U.S. official.

t. May not be capable of producing reactor-grade heavy water.

u. Currently being converted to 20 percent enriched uranium.

v. Speech by President Raul Alfonsin, Central Atomic Energy Day Ceremony, Embalse Rio Tecero, May 30, 1986; "CNEA Restructuring May Ease Problems," *Nuclear Engineering International* (January 1988): 8.

w. Richard Kessler, "Argentina's CNEA to Begin Testing Pilot Reprocessing Plant at Ezeiza," *Nuclear Fuel*, April 18, 1988, p. 12.

x. Jozef Goldblat, ed., *Non-proliferation, The Why and Wherefore* (Philadelphia: Taylor and Francis, 1985), p. 295.

y. Richard Kessler, "Argentina Denies Receiving West German, Italian Reprocessing Aid," *Nucleonics Week*, May 30, 1985, p. 4.

z. Richard Kessler, "Argentina Moving Ahead with Plans for Fuel Fabrication Independence," *Nuclear Fuel*, July 15, 1985, p. 6; Richard Kessler, "CNEA Ups Production of Fuel Assemblies," *Nuclear Fuel*, March 23, 1987, p.4; fabrication of Atucha II fuel, planned.

aa. Richard Kessler, "Argentina Denies It Plans Large Unsafeguarded Research Reactor," *Nucleonics Week*, August 8, 1985, p. 5.

bb. "CNEA Head Discusses Nuclear Policy Issues," Noticias Argentines, 1305 GMT, November 24, 1987, translated in *FBIS/LAT*, November 30, 1987; Richard Kessler, "Sarney Visit to Pilcaniyeu Was Key to Reciprocal Inspections," *Nucleonics Week*, July 23, 1987, p. 11.

Photo 5.1 shows Argentina's classified Pilcaniyeu uranium enrichment plant in the Andes Mountains. (Photo was taken in late 1983, shortly after the plant's existence was first acknowledged by the Argentine government.)
© *Editoriale Atlantidad.*

Brazil

During 1987 and the first half of 1988, Brazil's civilian president José Sarney took a series of unprecedented steps with his Argentine counterpart to ease the long-standing nuclear rivalry between the two countries. Such initiatives hold the promise of greatly reducing the threat of possible proliferation in the region. Nonetheless, in contrast to the situation in Argentina, Brazil's military remains a major political force and, at the same time, have been staunch supporters of an open-ended nuclear program.[1] As a result, a second more troubling trend in Brazilian nuclear affairs was also apparent during this period, as portions of Brazil's nuclear program supervised by the military made significant progress toward producing weapons-usable, highly enriched uranium free from external non-proliferation controls.

Background

In recent years, Brazil's nuclear affairs have followed two parallel tracks. The first, managed by the state-owned Brazilian Nuclear Corporation (Nuclebras) and subject to strict International Atomic Energy Agency (IAEA) safeguards and other non-proliferation controls, has been aimed at implementing a grandiose nuclear energy program based on imported equipment and technology.[2] Its centerpieces are Brazil's first nuclear power plant (Angra I)—a 626-megawatt reactor supplied by the United States, which entered commercial service in January 1985[3]—and a mammoth nuclear transfer agreement with West Germany signed in 1975. The agreement provided for the sale to Brazil of up to eight 1,300-megawatt nuclear power reactors, a pilot-scale plutonium extraction (reprocessing) plant, and a commercial-scale uranium enrichment facility, using the jet-nozzle technique.

West German deal. Germany's agreement to sell the last two plants was highly controversial because, once completed, the reprocessing facility would provide Brazil with significant quantities of weapons-usable plutonium, and the enrichment plant theoretically could permit Brazil to produce weapons-usable, highly enriched uranium. These fears have proven to be unfounded. After years of major construction delays, massive cost overruns, and severe budget cutbacks mandated in part by the International Monetary Fund, in August 1985, Brazilian President Sarney announced that implementation of the West German deal would be drastically curtailed. Brazil, he stated, would complete only two of the eight West German nuclear power reactors originally envisioned (Angra II and Angra III); the reprocessing plant would be indefinitely postponed; and only the first stage of the jet-nozzle enrichment plant, under construction at Resende, would be completed.[4] The last facility, expected to come on line in 1988, will be able to produce only slightly enriched uranium.[5]

Parallel program. The second track of Brazil's nuclear activities, officially referred to as the "parallel" or "autonomous" program, has been a cause of greater proliferation concern. The program was initiated in 1979 and is directed by various branches of the Brazilian military and the National Nuclear Energy Commission (CNEN), Brazil's agency for nuclear research and development. The program relies on indigenously developed technology, is not covered by IAEA safeguards, and has been conducted largely in secret. Brazil has not joined the Non-Proliferation Treaty, which would require it to place all of its nuclear activities under the IAEA system, and although it has ratified the Treaty of Tlatelolco, which contains a similar requirement, it has not waived certain conditions that must be satisfied before the pact becomes binding on it.[6]

The program was authorized at the end of the military government of Ernesto Geisel in 1979 and was actively supported by Brazil's next military leader, João Figueiredo.[7] Figueiredo ceded power to a civilian government led by José Sarney in March 1985, but Sarney has remained heavily dependent on the military's political support and has not changed the direction of nuclear activities under military control; indeed, in some respects the parallel program has accelerated during Sarney's tenure, as discussed below.[8]

The most troubling aspect of the program from the standpoint of proliferation has been a joint CNEN/Navy effort to develop high-speed centrifuges for enriching uranium at the Institute for Energy and Nuclear Research (IPEN), located at the University of São Paulo.[9] Brazil now produces its own uranium and has unsafeguarded facilities for refining it and converting it into uranium hexafluoride—the form of uranium needed in the enrichment process.[10] Therefore, development of an indigenous centrifuge enrichment unit would mean that Brazil would have a completely autonomous capability to produce weapons-usable highly enriched uranium free from any non-proliferation controls.

Through 1986, it appeared that the IPEN project was progressing rather slowly, but as mentioned previously, in September 1987, a major breakthrough was announced and work has since begun on an unsafeguarded pilot-scale centrifuge enrichment plant at the Navy's Aramar Experimental Center in Ipero, 80 miles west of São Paulo.

Work on uranium enrichment using lasers is also under way at IPEN and at the Brazilian Air Force's Aerospace Technology Center in São José dos Campos, the principal site of Brazil's rocket research and development program.[11] It is highly unlikely, given the difficulties that other nations have experienced in pursuing this technology, that Brazil is close to mastering it.

The navy also oversees a laboratory-scale plutonium extraction unit at IPEN. Despite a flurry of press stories in late 1986 stating that Brazil was using the unit to obtain plutonium, it appears that only simulations of the plutonium-extraction process had been undertaken. Since all of Brazil's plutonium-bearing spent reactor fuel is currently subject to IAEA safeguards, any processing of the material to extract the weapons-usable material would also have to be conducted under IAEA controls, as Brazilian nuclear officials have acknowledged.[12]

Weapons option. Brazil does not now appear to be embarked on a concerted drive to acquire nuclear weapons. Nonetheless, the parallel program is widely perceived to be aimed at providing Brazil with the option of manufacturing them, a position apparently supported by many elements of the Brazilian military.[13] Indeed, in late 1983 and early 1984, following Argentina's surprise disclosure that it had secretly built an unsafeguarded uranium enrichment plant, a number of Brazilian military figures responded by openly pointing to the weapons potential of Brazil's parallel program and declaring that it would provide Brazil with the ability to produce nuclear arms by 1990.[14]

Similarly, after José Sarney took office in early 1985 as the head of the new civilian government, top Brazilian military figures were outspoken in asserting that Brazil should, at a minimum, keep its nuclear weapons option alive by continuing to develop the necessary enrichment and reprocessing capabilities.[15] Some senior military aides, according to press reports, went further to speak in favor of nuclear arming itself.[16]

Alleged test site. In August 1986, what appeared to be new evidence of the military's interest in nuclear arms emerged, when the Brazilian press reported that the Armed Forces General Staff and the Air Force's Institute for Advanced

Studies were building a nuclear weapons test site at a remote military reservation in Cachimbo, deep in the Amazon jungle in the southern part of Para state.[17] The article claimed that shafts, slightly over three feet in diameter and nearly 1,000 feet deep, had been completed in July and implied that they had been built for underground nuclear tests.

The Sarney government quickly issued a denial, stating that "Brazil has no projects for the fabrication of nuclear weapons, neither does it have sufficient technological development for this, nor a testing program to this end."[18] The explanation offered was that the shafts had been sunk at the site during the 1960s and 1970s as part of unsuccessful mineral exploration projects and that the site had subsequently been turned over to the military for rocket testing to take advantage of its partial development.[19]

At the time, some U.S. non-proliferation officials discounted the possibility that the 1,000-foot shafts were intended for nuclear tests, arguing that they appeared too small in diameter for the necessary equipment and that, in any event, Brazil was still a number of years away from possessing the necessary nuclear weapons material for a test device. Other current and former U.S. government experts, however, believe that the shafts would indeed be suitable for testing a device similar in yield to the Hiroshima bomb.[20] The device tested by India in 1974, the first weapon designed by Sweden in the 1950s (but never built), and the original Hiroshima bomb itself were all less than three feet in diameter, it may be noted,[21] and South Africa's Kalahari test site was discovered several years before that nation apparently possessed the material necessary for a nuclear device.[22] Nuclear testing, moreover, seems to be the only obvious use for shafts of such a depth and diameter.

U.S. officials remain unanimous, however, that Brazil has not launched a determined nuclear weapons program, and even those who accept the possibility that Cachimbo was being prepared as a test site see this as an isolated action by one faction of the Brazilian military. They speculate that this faction, in an effort to respond to Argentina's development of an unsafeguarded uranium enrichment plant in 1983, may have been hoping to deceive their Argentine counterparts by suggesting that the Brazilian nuclear program was more advanced than was actually the case.[23]

Countervailing trends. As these diffuse pressures toward the development of a nuclear weapons option continued during 1985 and 1986, an important counter-trend also emerged, as Brazil and Argentina, now both under civilian governments for the first time in decades, took important steps toward integrating their economies and enhancing the coordination of their foreign policies, as described in the first part of this chapter on Argentina. In late November 1985, at Foz de Iguacu, Sarney signed a joint declaration on nuclear policy with the Argentine leader in which both pledged that their countries would develop nuclear energy solely for peaceful purposes and agreed to increase cooperation in the field. The pledge appeared to reflect Sarney's fundamental commitment to non-proliferation, but Sarney did not embrace Alfonsín's call for the development of a system of mutual inspections of the two countries' nuclear installations, agreeing only to establish a bilateral commission to "create mechanisms to insure the supreme interests of peace, security and development in the region, without detriment to the technical aspects of nuclear cooperation."[24]

At the first meeting of the joint Argentine-Brazilian nuclear commission in March 1986, the Brazilian delegation backed the nuclear inspection concept in principle.[25] By this point, support for the idea was growing among non-military elements of the government.[26] Nonetheless, in July of 1986—a month before the alleged nuclear test site at Cachimbo base was disclosed—Sarney was still unprepared to accept an Argentine proposal that a provision establishing such an inspection system be included among a series of major protocols he and Alfonsín signed in Buenos Aires to increase bilateral trade.[27]

The reasons for Sarney's continuing reluctance to accept mutual nuclear inspections were not disclosed, but there can be little doubt that the approach was opposed by his military supporters. Among other factors, opponents of inspections may have been concerned that a rigorous inspection system might unduly constrain the parallel nuclear program at time when Brazil—still far from possessing an unsafeguarded uranium enrichment capability—remained at a disadvantage vis-à-vis Argentina.[28]

Political and Technical Developments

Events from the end of 1986 through mid-1988 continued to reflect the conflicting influences on the Brazilian nuclear program. In an October 1986 presidential decree, the CNEN—a key participant in the parallel program—was brought under the direct control of the National Security Council, composed of the president and the chiefs of the armed services. The nuclear organization had formerly been under the Ministry of Mines and Energy, where its activities were receiving increasingly unsympathetic scrutiny. The shift in oversight responsibility was seen by Brazilian observers as a means for ensuring continued military control over, and support for, the parallel program.[29]

Despite this apparent resurgence of military influence, however, in December 1986, Sarney and Alfonsín, meeting in Brasília, signed some twenty new protocols covering a wide range of bilateral economic issues, established joint nuclear research projects, and agreed to form a nuclear accident early warning system.[30]

Although no new initiatives were reported concerning the possibility of mutual nuclear inspections, it would later be revealed that during December Brazil had permitted Argentine nuclear aides to visit key parts of IPEN, including the experimental centrifuge-enrichment unit and the laboratory-scale reprocessing facility. Given the sensitivity of these military-controlled activities, opening the installation for the visit was an impressive show of good faith, particularly when it is appreciated that even the size of an enrichment centrifuge is often treated as a closely held industrial secret.[31]

Secret accounts. The following month, new evidence of Brazil's commitment to the parallel program emerged, when the Brazilian press revealed that since 1981 the program had been funded through a series of CNEN secret bank accounts, with exotic names like "Delta Three."[32] The secret accounts—which were acknowledged by CNEN head Rex Nazareth—appear to have been a mechanism by which the Figueiredo government helped to ensure steady funding for the autonomous program at a time when the budget for Brazil's commercial nuclear energy program (based on the 1975 West German deal) was being cut drastically under a broad austerity plan imposed by Brazil's creditors. The use of the secret accounts continued for the first year of the Sarney administration, apparently without the knowledge of treasury officials.

Whether the CNEN took advantage of the clandestine funding arrangements to promote nuclear-weapons related activities is not known, but Nazareth himself, at least, has supported a constitutional amendment to restrict Brazil's nuclear program to peaceful purposes—an amendment some senior military figures are known to oppose.[33] The strong commitment to the parallel program indicated by the secret financing operation—along with the shift of the CNEN to military control in October—suggest that Sarney's decision to open the program to outside scrutiny in December 1986 represented an important policy change that undoubtedly faced considerable internal opposition.

The military's keen appreciation of and seeming interest in the strategic potential of the parallel program was again revealed in a series of interviews in March 1987. General Haroldo Erichsen Fonseca, army secretary for science and technology, for example, declared,

To manufacture atomic bombs is not our objective, but if necessary, we will. With the knowledge we are gaining, obviously, we will be in a position to manufacture them. If we have the resources we can do it in 2 years time. [However,] Brazil does not need to build the bomb because currently it does not have any enemies.[34]

Fonseca's words were echoed by General Hermano Lomba Santoro, chief of the Army Technological Center, who stated,

Brazil does not yet have the know-how to build atomic devices . . . [but] with the acquisition of knowledge, the formation of research groups, and the installation of new laboratories to gain mastery over the atom, building the bomb will be possible, but not likely, because that would depend on the government's political decision, which has not yet been made.[35]

Increasing ties. The predilections of the military notwithstanding, in April 1987, Brazil and Argentina took another small step toward developing cooperative nuclear relations by agreeing to launch a joint effort for the production of research reactor fuel using low-enriched uranium.[36]

These cooperative arrangements were extended in July, when Sarney and Alfonsín met in Buenos Aires. During this visit, Alfonsín, in an unprecedented gesture of openness, took Sarney on a forty-minute tour of Argentina's classified Pilcaniyeu enrichment plant.[37] (This historic confidence-building initiative is discussed in detail in the section on Argentina, above.)

New capability. Two months after this new watershed in Argentine-Brazilian nuclear relations, the Latin American nuclear environment experienced an unexpected change of a different sort when President Sarney dramatically announced on September 4, 1987, that Brazil had succeeded in enriching uranium by means of indigenously developed gas centrifuges, and that construction would begin immediately on a pilot-scale uranium enrichment plant at the Navy's Aramar Experimental Center in Ipero, some 80 miles west of São Paulo. The enrichment break-through had been made at the navy-run laboratory-scale centrifuge unit at IPEN (said to house six centrifuges), which had produced a number of pounds of uranium enriched to 1.2 percent uranium-235.[38]

Fifty to one hundred centrifuges were to be built at the Ipero facility, which was projected to produce its first enriched material in early 1988 and, by mid-year, was to be capable of producing 20 percent-enriched uranium to fuel Brazil's research reactors at a rate of "several dozen kilograms" (about 80 pounds) per year.[39] Although even this level of enrichment would be well short of the 93 percent level used for nuclear arms, the IPEN breakthrough indicated that Brazil had acquired the basic know-how to produce weapons-grade material.

As described earlier, at this juncture, Brazil, at a cost of $300 million, was completing the first module of another enrichment plant at Resende, which used the jet-nozzle process. That facility, however, had been supplied by West Germany, which had required that it be placed under IAEA safeguards. The significance of IPEN's achievement was that it provided Brazil with the capability to produce enriched uranium totally free from any non-proliferation controls and thus potentially available for nuclear weapons (if enriched to the necessary level). Moreover, the decision to budget funds to build the Aramar enrichment plant, the first stage of which will cost between $100 and $150 million, indicates Brazil's strong desire to master the IPEN technology on an industrial scale, a step that will bring it closer still to a nuclear weapons capability.[40] Brazil has not placed the plant under the IAEA system, though it could do so if it chose.

A key question is whether the installation will be used to enrich uranium beyond the 20 percent level. One of the principal rationales for the Aramar plant is that it will be used eventually to produce fuel for nuclear-propelled submarines, which Brazil is now developing. The Brazilian Navy is planning to build a prototype, 50-megawatt submarine propulsion reactor at the Aramar center during the next decade, and according to some accounts, the reactor is to be fueled with 70 percent-enriched uranium. To produce the material, the Aramar plant would be gradually expanded by 1992 to contain 3,000 centrifuges, according to these reports.[41] If these plans are pursued, Brazil would in effect acquire a *de facto* nuclear weapons capability, since 70 percent-enriched uranium can be easily upgraded to 93 percent. (Indeed, 70 percent-enriched uranium can itself be used for weapons, but it is not chosen for this purpose since physically smaller and more efficient devices can be made using 93 percent material.) A further complication is that because the facility is not subject to IAEA safeguards or other non-proliferation controls, even if Brazil did not manufacture weapons from enriched uranium produced there, outsiders could not be confident that Brazil had not taken this step, a situation that would create dangerous ambiguities and could intensify nuclear competition with Argentina.

At the time of Sarney's announcement, however, CNEN chief Rex Nazareth stated that the Aramar enrichment plant would not produce more than 20 percent-enriched material, in order to guarantee that the facility would not contribute to a nuclear weapons capability. Brazilian submarine reactors, he continued, would be designed to run on the less enriched material.[42]

Shift to the right. Sarney's decision to announce the IPEN advance himself, on the eve of Brazil's independence day, and to portray the development as a significant national achievement, appeared to be aimed at enhancing the prestige of the military by validating the importance of the parallel program. During 1986, Sarney had gained a considerable popular following after he imposed a comprehensive austerity plan that temporarily curbed Brazil's raging inflation. Sarney's popularity plummeted in mid-1987, however, when inflation returned, and he became increasingly dependent on the support of the military in dealing with Brazil's Congress, which, in addition to its legislative duties, was sitting as a constituent assembly and drafting a bitterly contested new constitution.[43] (Despite the nationalistic tone of his announcement, Sarney apparently sought to avoid straining relations with Argentina by forewarning it of his plans.[44])

For the remainder of 1987, Sarney confronted a worsening political crisis that greatly weakened his ability to govern and cast the country's military in an increasingly prominent political role. Among other setbacks during this period, in October and November, a leftist-dominated committee of the constituent assembly handed Sarney and his military backers a humiliating defeat by adopting draft constitutional provisions limiting Sarney's term to four years, rather than the five he had sought, and establishing a parliamentary form of government.[45] In early 1988, however, Sarney rebuilt his political base by allying himself with a newly formed center-right congressional bloc, and in March, with strong backing from the military, won a key test of strength in the constituent assembly, when the body as a whole voted down the parliamentary government option. (A decision on the length of Sarney's tenure was deferred, although the assembly voted that subsequent presidents would be given a five-year term, an outcome Sarney had strongly supported. In June it ultimately agreed to grant Sarney a full five years in office with elections to be held in 1989.)[46]

Constitutional restriction. In March, the constituent assembly also took action on a constitutional provision governing Brazil's nuclear policy. The provision specifies that "any nuclear activities within the national territory will be permitted only if for peaceful purposes and if approved by the National Congress."[47] The language appears to rule out the development of nuclear weapons and to bring all nuclear activities under civilian control. Moreover, the very inclusion of a provision on nuclear matters in a national constitution is highly unusual and appears to signal a strong commitment to non-proliferation.

In practice, however, the impact of the provision, assuming it survives the remainder of the constitution-drafting process, may be rather limited. First, it does not rule out the accumulation of weapons-grade nuclear materials free from external non-proliferation controls and thus leaves Brazil free to develop a ready nuclear weapons option. Nor does the provision prohibit the development of so-called peaceful nuclear explosives or even the conducting of nuclear tests under this rubric.

Moreover, the provision does not establish mechanisms for day-to-day civilian control of nuclear affairs by, for example, requiring that all nuclear activities be conducted by civilian-led agencies. This would seem to leave the military free to continue its various programs at IPEN, the Aramar Experimental Center, the São José dos Campos Aerospace Technology Center, and the base at Cachimbo. Although the Brazilian congress will, in principle, exercise budgetary control over these activities, U.S. officials, noting the strength of the military as a powerful lobby within Brazil's emerging democratic structures, have questioned whether this oversight mechanism will be effective. It may also be noted that the military lobbied *for* this provision—which, in effect enshrines the country's current declared nuclear policy—in preference to a another proposal, reflecting popular anti-nuclear sentiment, that would have explicitly prohibited the manufacture and storage of nuclear weapons and would have required a national plebescite on the construction of additional nuclear power plants.[48]

A number of important procedural steps remain before the current draft constitution becomes effective. It is thus possible that the nuclear restrictions will be further amended before the charter enters into force.

Confidence-building continues. Throughout the spring of 1987, as these events unfolded and as work proceeded on Brazil's new Aramar enrichment facility, the nuclear dialogue with Argentina continued to gain momentum, seemingly unaffected by the shift to the right in Brazilian politics. By March of 1988, Argentine nuclear aides were quoted in the press as stating that Argentina had access to all operating nuclear facilities in Brazil not covered by IAEA safeguards, including the Air Force's laser enrichment research project as São José dos Campos, and that IPEN had been visited several times.[49]

A new watershed in bilateral nuclear relations came in April, when, as described in the first part of this chapter on Argentina, Alfonsín participated in the dedication of the Aramar centrifuge enrichment plant—visibly expressing his trust in Brazil's assurances that the plant would not contribute to the manufacture of nuclear arms.[50] The number of centrifuges then operating at the Aramar unit was not disclosed, but by this juncture, Brazil claimed to have enriched uranium to 5 percent and possibly to 8 percent, either at the facility or at IPEN's research unit.[51] Overall, it appeared that Sarney's military backers were prepared to support confidence-building measures with Buenos Aires as long as key parts of the parallel program continued to advance.

Confidence-building vs. verification. As important as the Argentine-Brazilian confidence-building initiatives have been, they do not permit either country to monitor the quantities and enrichment level of uranium produced at their respective unsafeguarded nuclear plants or to account for its disposition.[52] Thus, although neither country can today produce highly enriched uranium, as their capabilities grow with the completion of the Aramar and Pilcaniyeu facilities, both states will acquire the option of producing weapons-grade material. Unless additional verification mechanisms are adopted, neither country could then be confident that the other was not taking this step and possibly using the material for nuclear arms.[53] According to one report, Brazil and Argentina may have given each other assurances that they will not enrich uranium above 20 percent, but again, without further verification mechanisms, neither state could be confident that the other was adhering to such a pledge.[54] Both Brazil and Argentina hope to produce twenty-percent enriched uranium during 1988.[55]

Since 1985, as noted above, Argentina has pressed for more rigorous bilateral safeguard arrangements, albeit ones that would be less intrusive than those applied by the IAEA. Brazil, it appears, has resisted these proposals, undoubtedly because of opposition from the armed forces. With the military continuing to play a central role in Brazilian politics—and with President Sarney appearing to be critically dependent on it for his own political future—the prospects for Brazil's accepting a bilateral safeguards regime do not appear to be promising, at least until after the next presidential elections, to take place in 1989, when a leader less dependent on the military might take office. On the other hand, the opening of the unsafeguarded facilities at IPEN, São José dos Campos, and Ipero is a significant step, and the possibility of further progress toward bilateral controls with Argentina should not be ruled out. (Mutual acceptance of IAEA safeguards on all nuclear facilities—a relatively sophisticated and widely adopted non-proliferation verification system—would be a valuable means for providing confidence that neither state was using nuclear materials for weapons. Both have so far rejected the application of the IAEA system to their indigenously developed nuclear facilities, however, as an undue intrusion on national sovereignty.)

U.S. policy. As in the case of Argentina, U.S. non-proliferation efforts vis-à-vis Brazil have been relatively limited, as Washington has quietly sought to encourage the nuclear rapprochement with Argentina. An embargo on the transfer of U.S. nuclear reactors and fuel to Brazil remains in effect because it has not placed all of its nuclear installations under IAEA safeguards.[56]

Prospects

Within a few years, it is probable that Brazil will be able to produce unsafeguarded highly enriched uranium and, if it does so, it could develop a ready nuclear weapons capability—or even nuclear weapons themselves. How far Brazil pursues these technological options is likely to be decided by domestic political factors, particularly by the relative strength of the military, and by the status of relations with Argentina.

From the standpoint of domestic politics, checking the momentum of the parallel nuclear program would become easier if democratization advances rapidly and the military's power wanes, factors that could also speed the strengthening of bilateral nuclear restraints with Buenos Aires. Should Brazil's opening to democracy slow or should events lead to the restoration of a military government, Brazil's nuclear capabilities could surge ahead with few restrictions, creating new pressures on Argentina and re-igniting the region's traditional nuclear rivalry.

President Sarney's initiatives to improve relations with Argentina on a broad front appear to be relatively uncontroversial. Moreover, there has been little public criticism of his decision to open Brazil's classified nuclear installations to Argentine visitors, possibly because of Argentina's willingness to reciprocate by opening the sensitive Pilcaniyeu facility, which is considerably closer to completion than any of Brazil's comparable plants. Moreover, the current level of confidence-building measures has not impeded the rapid development of key parts of the parallel nuclear program. Although Sarney might not be re-elected in 1990, there is no reason to believe that any successor would not continue to pursue these nuclear initiatives with Argentina. The likelihood of such an outcome could be increased, however, if the *ad hoc* arrangements for exchange visits to facilities implemented since late 1986 could be formalized to give them greater permanence. (Whether more far reaching bilateral nuclear restraints might be adopted will probably depend on a reduction in the influence of the military, as noted earlier.)

Developments in Argentina will also affect Brazilian attitudes. A resurgence of nationalism in Argentina, for example, through the ascendancy of traditional Peronist party elements in the country's 1989 elections—a prospect that now appears unlikely given the recent ascendancy of party reformers—could increase bilateral tensions, particularly in the nuclear area. Similarly, if Argentina is perceived to have acquired the ability to produce weapons-grade nuclear materials, this could stimulate calls in Brazil for an acceleration of the parallel program.

The past eighteen months have seen dramatic new initiatives that hold the promise of averting a potential nuclear arms race in Latin America. Whether leaders in Brazil or Argentina will be able to sustain them and build upon them as both countries face political contests in the next several years will be a matter of great importance to the region and to the wider international community.

Caribbean Sea

Atlantic
Ocean

VENEZUELA

GUYANA

SURINAME

FR. GUIANA

COLOMBIA

Macapa

Manaus

Amazon River

Belem

BRAZIL

Fortaleza

Natal

Recife

Cachimbo

Salvador

PERU

Brasilia

BOLIVIA

Poços de Caldas

Belo Horizonte

São Paulo (IPEN)

Resende

Ipero

Rio de Janeiro

PARAGUAY

Santos

Angra dos Reis

Pacific
Ocean

Curitiba

São José dos Campos

Porto Alegre

URUGUAY

ARGENTINA

CHILE

BRAZIL

uranium mining area

0   800

MILES

Atlantic Ocean

Brazil

Power Reactors/Operating or Under Construction

Angra I (light-water/low-enriched uranium, 626 MWe)
- supplier: Westinghouse (U.S.)
- start up: 1982 (commercial operation, 1985)
- fuel source: Initial load, U.S.; current reloads URENCO (W. German, British, Dutch)[a]; Brazilian enriched uranium after 1989. (est.).[b]
- safeguards: yes

Angra II (light-water/low-enriched uranium, 1,300 MWe)
- supplier: Kraftwerk Union (West Germany)
- start up: 1993 (est.)[c]
- fuel source: Initial load, URENCO (W. German, British, Dutch); subsequent loads, Brazilian enriched uranium.[b].
- safeguards: yes

Angra III (light-water/low-enriched uranium, 1,300 MWe)
- supplier: Kraftwerk Union (West Germany)
- start up: 1995 (est.)[c]
- fuel source: Initial load, URENCO (W. German, British, Dutch), subsequent loads, Brazilian enriched uranium.[b]
- safeguards: yes

Uranium Resources/Active Mining Sites/Uranium Mills
- reasonably assured reserves: 163,276 metric tons[d]
- currently active site: Poços de Caldas[d]
- mills in operation: Poços de Caldas[d]

Uranium Purification (UO$_2$)
IPEN, São Paulo
- capacity: more than 10 metric tons per year[e]
- supplier: Brazil, with some W. German equipment.[f]
- start up: 1981 (?)[e]
- safeguards: no

Uranium Conversion (UF$_6$)
Resende
- capacity: planned 500 metric tons per year (eventually 2000 metric tons per year)[g]
- supplier: P.U.K. (France)[h]
- start up: indefinitely postponed[j]
- safeguards: yes (planned)

IPEN, São Paulo (pilot scale)
- capacity: 160 metric tons UF$_6$ per yr.[i]
- supplier: Brazil[i]
- start up: 1984[i]
- safeguards: no

IPEN, São Paulo (laboratory scale)
- capacity: (?) (50 kg. UF_6 produced by 1982).[i]
- supplier: Brazil (with some foreign assistance)[i]
- start up: 1981-1982[l]
- safeguards: no

Enrichment
Resende
- type: jet-nozzle
- capacity: 5 metric tons of 0.85% enriched uranium planned in 1988[k]
- supplier: Kraftwerk Union (West Germany)[l]
- start up: 45 cascades to operate in 1988[k,m]
- safeguards: yes

Belo Horizonte
- type: jet-nozzle
- capacity: laboratory scale
- supplier: Kraftwerk Union (West Germany)
- start up: 1980[n]
- safeguards: yes

Aramar Research Center, Ipero
- type: ultracentrifuge
- capacity: "several dozen kilograms" of 20% enriched uranium by 1989; 50-100 centrifuges[z]
- supplier: Brazil
- start up: 1988[z]

IPEN, São Paulo
- type: ultracentrifuge
- capacity: lab scale ("kilogram quantities" of 1.2% enriched uranium produced; approx. 6 centrifuges)[o]
- supplier: Brazil
- start up: 1986-1987
- safeguards: no

Fuel Fabrication
Resende
- capacity: Planned 100 tons per year for Angra I, II, III[p]
- supplier: West Germany
- start up: 1982 (initial phase)[q]; additional stages, 1990, 1991[m]
- safeguards: yes

IPEN, São Paulo (pilot plant)

Reprocessing (Plutonium Extraction)
Resende
- capacity: pilot scale, 10 kg spent fuel per day[r,s]
- supplier: West Germany
- start up: indefinitely postponed[m]
- safeguards: yes[t]

IPEN, São Paulo (laboratory scale)
- capacity: varying estimates[u]
- supplier: Brazil with some West German equipment[f]
- start up: not operating as of May 1988[u]
- safeguards: only when safeguarded fuel is processed[w]

Principal Research Reactors[x,y]

IEAR-1, São Paulo (Pool/highly-enriched uranium[v] , 5 MWt)
- supplier: United States
- start up: 1957
- safeguards: yes

RIEN-1, Rio de Janeiro (Argonaut/medium-enriched uranium, 10 KWt)
- supplier: Brazil
- start up: 1965
- safeguards: yes

Triga-UMG, Belo Horizonte (Triga I/medium-enriched uranium 100 KWt)
- supplier: United States
- start up: 1960
- safeguards: yes

Sources and Notes

a. "German Uranium for Angra," *Jornal do Brasil,* translated in *Joint Publication Research Service/Nuclear Development and Proliferation,* hereafter *JPRS/NDP,* January 18, 1982, p. 28.

b. Assis Mendonca, "Germany Denies Having Negotiated Another Process," *O Estado de São Paulo,* translated in *JPRS/NPD,* May 13, 1982, p. 21; Charles Thurston, "Brazil Readies Enrichment Plant," *Nuclear Fuel,* December 3, 1984, p. 8. Availability of Brazilian-produced fuel likely to be delayed.

c. "Lack of Payments Delays Construction of Angra II," *O Globo,* July 21, 1987, translated in *JPRS/Nuclear Developments,* September 16, 1987, p. 22; Rik Turner, "Brazilian Financial Crisis Forces Suspension of Angra II Work," *Nucleonics Week,* June 18, 1987, p. 3. Work on both plants was suspended for part of 1987.

d. "Sites of Nuclear Facilities," *O Globo,* September 5, 1987, translated in *JPRS/ TND,* January 28, 1988.

e. Personal communication with informed U.S. official, 1985.

f. Bernardo Kucinski, "Argentine Boast Spurs Brazil into Race for Bomb," *The Guardian,* reprinted in *JPRS/NPD,* February 19, 1982, pp. 6-8.

g. "Researchers Developing Brazil's Know-how on UF-6 Beyond the Plant Now Being Built," *Nuclear Fuel,* September 27, 1982, p. 13.

h. "Uranium Enrichment Plant in Itataia Confirmed," *O Estado de São Paulo,* translated in *JPRS/NPD,* January 25, 1982, p. 22.

i. "Fluorine Technology for Enrichment Developed," *Fôhla de São Paulo,* April 23, 1988, translated in *FBIS/LAT,* April 27, 1988, p. 35.

j. Charles Thurston, "Brazil's First Enrichment Cascade," *Nuclear Fuel,* November 26, 1984, p. 6. "Specifications of IPEN Uranium Enrichment Facility Noted," *Jornal do Brasil,* October 8, 1984. Expansion beyond lab-scale postponed. See reference m.

k. "Nuclebras to Sell Uranium to Argentina," *O Globo*, September 1, 1987, translated in *FBIS/LAT*, September 2, 1987, p. 15. Further expansion indefinitely postponed. See reference m.

l. "KWU Recommends Development of Jet-Nozzle Enrichment Process Here," *O Estado de São Paulo*, translated in *JPRS/NPD*, June 3, 1982, p. 22.

m. Rik Turner, "Brazil's Sarney Defines Emphasis for National Fuel Cycle Development," *Nuclear Fuel*, August 11, 1986, p. 10.

n. Charles Thurston, "Critics See Brazil as Taken For a Ride on Its 'Last Train' to SWU Technology," *Nuclear Fuel*, April 26, 1982, p. 3.

o. Rik Turner, "Brazil's Parallel Program," *Nuclear Fuel*, October 19, 1987, p. 3; "Implications of Mastery of Uranium Enrichment," *Veja*, September 9, 1987, translated in *JPRS/TND*, December 1, 1987, p. 12.

p. "Operation of Fuel Elements Factory in Resende Discussed," *Manchete*, (Rio de Janeiro), translated in *JPRS/NPD*, December 6, 1982, pp. 18-21.

q. Juan de Onis, "Brazil's Crash Program Slows to Realistic Pace," *International Herald Tribune*, October 1982.

r. William W. Lowrance, "Nuclear Futures For Sale: To Brazil From West Germany, 1975," *International Security*, Fall 1976, p. 152.

s. "Resende Site of Uranium Reprocessing Plant Confirmed," *O Estado de São Paulo*, translated in *JPRS/NPD*, May 10, 1983, p. 21. Later start-up date probable; reportedly little construction to date, (personal communication with informed U.S. official.)

t. International storage also required for any plutonium reprocessed from URENCO fuel.

u. "Brazil Says It Now Produces Small Amounts of Plutonium," *Washington Post*, December 18, 1986. Only milligram quantities of plutonium have been produced, if that, according to Brazilian Embassy officials in Washington. See also, Leonard S. Spector, *Nuclear Proliferation Today* (New York: Vintage Books, 1984), pp. 247-252 (possible startup in 1983). Capacity estimates range from minute quantities (scientist Roberto Hukay in "Report on IPEN Reactor," *Jornal do Brasil*, translated in *JPRS/NPD*, February 18, 1983, p. 5) to five kg plutonium per year Kucinski, "Argentine Boast Spurs Brazil into Race for the Bomb.")

v. Currently 90 percent enriched uranium, soon to be converted to 20 percent enriched uranium.

w. Currently, only safeguarded fuel is available.

x. James Katz and Onkar Marwah, *Nuclear Power in Developing Countries* (Lexington: Lexington Books, 1982), p. 100.

y. International Atomic Energy Agency, *The Annual Report for 1981*, p. 70.

z. "IPEN Head Guarantees Nuclear Project Safety," *O Estado de São Paulo*, September 9, 1987, translated in *FBIS/LAT*, September 11, 1987, p. 11; "Funding Needs, Supplies of Parallel Program Discussed," *Exame*, October 14, 1987, translated in *JPRS/JND*, February 24, 1988, p. 21.

Photo 5.2 shows the interior of Brazil's uranium enrichment plant at the Aramar Experimental Center in Ipero. (Photo is thought to show the portion of the plant used to process uranium hexafluoride—the feedstock of the enrichment process—not the centrifuge enrichment units themselves.)
© *Ricardo Chaves – Istoe.*

Chapter VI:
Africa

The only sub-Saharan African nation posing a significant proliferation risk today is South Africa, whose ability to produce nuclear arms and apparent interest in acquiring them may have led it to build a small, slowly expanding nuclear arsenal of perhaps ten to twenty atomic weapons.

South Africa's announcement in September 1987 that it was prepared to begin negotiations on ratifying the Non-Proliferation Treaty (NPT) has opened the theoretical possibility that its existing stocks of nuclear weapons material and all of its nuclear facilities might be placed under international inspection within several years. If implemented, such a step would largely eliminate the threat of proliferation in the region for the foreseeable future. There is considerable doubt, however, as to whether Pretoria will ultimately ratify the pact.

No other country in the region has more than the most rudimentary nuclear program. In recent years, however, Nigerian leaders have repeatedly declared their interest in obtaining nuclear arms, despite the fact that Nigeria is a party to the Non-Proliferation Treaty. In August 1987 for example, former Nigerian Foreign Minister Bolaji Akinyemi, implicitly invoking the nuclear threat from South Africa, called for Nigeria to develop nuclear weapons "to forestall nuclear blackmail" of the black race.[1] Earlier, in April 1986, when asked whether Nigeria should develop nuclear weapons, Akinyemi had declared, "I can't give a direct answer but I'll say that a country the size of Nigeria, with its role and status in the world, cannot rule out any option."[2] Nigerian President Ibrahim Babangida echoed these sentiments in a contemporaneous statement, rejecting the principle of non-proliferation by stating that "the argument about the non-proliferation of nuclear weapons, besides its social overtones, now seems to border on the irresponsibility of [sic] weaker nations."[3]

Notwithstanding these statements, Nigeria does not appear to have taken any steps toward developing nuclear weapons.[4] Indeed, except for South Africa, nuclear programs in sub-Saharan Africa are virtually non-existent. No other state in the region possesses a nuclear power plant, and only Zaire has a research reactor, a one-megawatt, U.S.-supplied unit. Uranium mines and ore-processing mills in Gabon, Niger, and Namibia (under South African control) are the only other significant nuclear installations. While the long-term potential for further proliferation in Africa remains, it is hard to imagine a second nation obtaining a nuclear weapons capability for decades to come.

One additional African nuclear risk must be borne in mind, however: the possibility that nuclear weapons or nuclear weapons material produced by South Africa's current regime might, for example, fall into the hands of a radical faction—black or white—which had gained control of the government and which might then use or threaten to use these nuclear assets to advance extremist objectives.[5] Indeed, should domestic order crumble, governmental authorities could lose control over nuclear weapons or highly enriched uranium, which a non-governmental group might seize to create domestic or international turmoil or possibly sell or take into exile in order to lay the base for a return to power.

While these risks are present in every country possessing nuclear weapons or the potential to produce them, in South Africa the risk is more plausible because of the widespread view that the country's transition to majority rule will be marked by serious civil strife and political instability. In a 1986 television series on Africa the author and narrator, Dr. Ali A. Mazrui, a prominent African intellectual, publicly declared his expectation that the successor regime in Pretoria will take control of South Africa's presumed nuclear arsenal:

In the final racial conflict, nuclear weapons could not be used internally without endangering the whites themselves. When the war does end, blacks will inherit the most advanced infrastructure on the continent. Out of the ashes of apartheid will emerge a black-ruled republic with convincing nuclear credentials.[6]

Such an open anticipation of a nuclear "inheritance" has rarely, if ever, been seen in other settings.

South Africa

For a number of years, South Africa has had the capability to produce enough highly enriched uranium not subject to international non-proliferation controls to manufacture up to several nuclear weapons annually. In view of past South African activities indicating an intent to develop nuclear arms, there is reason for concern that during 1987 and the first half of 1988 Pretoria used this capability either to add to its stocks of nuclear weapons material or, if it has indeed decided to build nuclear arms, to add several weapons to an undeclared nuclear arsenal of perhaps ten to twenty atomic bombs.

South Africa's declaration in September 1987 that it was prepared to begin negotiations on ratifying the Non-Proliferation Treaty (NPT) has raised the possibility that Pretoria may be prepared to give up its ready nuclear weapons potential by placing all of its nuclear activities under International Atomic Energy Agency (IAEA) supervision. As explained below, serious doubts remain as to whether South Africa will ultimately take this step, and, even if it did so, there could still be cause for concern about Pretoria's nuclear program.

286

It is difficult to imagine the government of Prime Minister Pieter W. Botha using its nuclear capability against any external threat that it is likely to confront in the foreseeable future, although some South African leaders may see such weapons as useful deterrents against possible Soviet aggression from nearby Angola.[1] Also, nuclear arms would have little value in dealing with internal strife. South Africa's white minority government has probably maintained its nuclear status despite its lack of obvious military utility to intimidate regional adversaries and lend the minority regime an aura of permanence and inviolability, both domestically and internationally. It has been widely assumed that Prime Minister Botha will not conduct a nuclear test for fear of complicating his relations with the West, but the premises underlying this assumption may need to be reexamined. With South Africa's Western ties already under serious strain because of Botha's unwillingness to share power with the nation's black majority, the added diplomatic costs of a test may not loom as large in Botha's calculations as they once did, particularly since a test would boost white morale and help insulate Botha from his ultra-conservative critics.

Such a step would have serious consequences for global non-proliferation efforts. Another grave danger inherent in Pretoria's nuclear capability, however, as suggested in the introduction to this chapter, is the risk that a radical faction within the country might gain control over nuclear weapons or nuclear weapons material and blackmail other elements in the nation or outside states to advance its political goals.

Background: Maintaining a Nuclear Option Amid Pressures from Abroad

South Africa's strong interest in developing nuclear weapons was unambiguously revealed in early August 1977, when both Soviet and U.S. satellites determined that Pretoria was preparing a nuclear-test site in the Kalahari Desert.[2] Indeed, according to a former Ford Administration non-proliferation official, Washington had intelligence data at least as early as 1976 indicating that South Africa was embarked on a nuclear weapons effort.[3] At the time the Kalahari site was discovered, U.S. officials assumed that South Africa had obtained weapons-usable highly enriched uranium from a pilot-scale uranium enrichment plant at Valindaba, which began operating in 1975.[4] After strong diplomatic intervention by the United States, France, West Germany, and Britain, said to include the threat to break relations with Pretoria, South African Prime Minister John Vorster agreed to dismantle the test site and apparently pledged to the United States that South Africa would not build nuclear arms.[5]

In 1980, as further data on the Valindaba plant emerged, U.S. analysts concluded that Pretoria had not, in fact, been able to produce the highly enriched uranium needed for a test in 1977 and that South African nuclear planners had apparently prepared the test site at that juncture on the basis of over-optimistic projections. In April 1981, however, South Africa announced that it had produced uranium enriched to 45 percent, which it intended to use to fuel the U.S.-supplied SAFARI research reactor.[6] Since it is relatively easy to improve 45 percent enriched uranium to the 93-percent level needed for weapons, U.S. analysts now date South Africa's status as a state capable of producing nuclear weapons from 1980-1981.[7] Nevertheless, the Kalahari test site episode remains important, since it provides compelling evidence of South Africa's interest in nuclear arming.[8] There has also been speculation that a flash observed by a U.S. satellite in September 1979 was that of a South African nuclear test. A panel of experts convened by the Carter White House Office of Science and Technology Policy determined that the event "probably" was not a nuclear detonation, but the panel's conclusions were disputed by the Defence Intelligence Agency and the Naval Research Laboratory. As a result, the event remains shrouded in uncertainty.[9]

Uncertainty about weapons manufacture. Whether South Africa has, in fact, developed nuclear arms, or merely stockpiled nuclear weapons material, remains unclear. Although it has declared that it will not produce nuclear weapons, Pretoria has steadfastly refused to permit verification of this pledge, rejecting repeated demands that it place the Valindaba pilot enrichment plant under IAEA safeguards. As a result, U.S. officials and others remain concerned that highly enriched uranium from the facility is being used for weapons purposes.[10]

Since 1977, the political and military pressures that presumably prompted Pretoria to pursue nuclear explosives in the first place—its isolation in world affairs, the perceived threat from neighboring, black-governed African states, and the need for political symbols of legitimacy and permanence—have not abated. Its March 1984 cease-fire with Angola and a similar agreement a month later with Mozambique seemed to reflect improving regional security for South Africa. But Pretoria's continuing military forays into these and other nearby states makes clear that South Africa's white rulers have continued to see themselves locked in conflict with neighboring states and the anti-South African guerrilla groups these states have supported.[11] Moreover, anti-government agitation within the country has seriously intensified in recent years, triggering repressive measures that in turn have increased South Africa's estrangement from the West.[12]

At the same time, despite South Africa's general record of success on the battlefield, its margin of overall military superiority vis-à-vis some of the front-line states may be declining. According to a number of analysts, the longstanding conventional arms embargo against South Africa, adopted by most Western governments in 1963 and made mandatory by the U.N. Security Council in 1977, has prevented the country from obtaining advanced weaponry, especially aircraft, tanks, and naval equipment. The embargo has been far from airtight, and South Africa has also built up significant domestic conventional-arms production capabilities, as evidenced by the recently unveiled Cheetah jet fighter. Nonetheless some of its adversaries have apparently been able to obtain at least comparable weaponry from the Soviet Union, thereby slowly reducing Pretoria's equipment advantage.[13]

These factors and the evidence of Pretoria's active pursuit of nuclear explosives in the mid-1970s are good reasons to conclude that South Africa has indeed built nuclear arms. Consequently, serious questions can be raised about Pretoria's intention to ratify the NPT, as discussed below.

Diplomatic costs and U.S. nuclear embargo. Pretoria has suffered considerable diplomatic and economic costs to maintain its nuclear option. In June 1977, for example, South Africa was ousted from its permanent position on the IAEA Board of Governors and it has not participated in the IAEA General Conference since 1979 when its credentials were rejected there. Moreover, its nuclear posture has exposed it to repeated attacks by various African and other non-aligned states in the U.N. General Assembly, the IAEA, and related international fora, such as the 1985 Review Conference on the Non-Proliferation Treaty.[14] Although opposition to Pretoria's racial policies underlies many of these assaults, the country's nuclear stance has provided an additional focus for international opprobrium.

Pretoria's refusal to place its entire nuclear program under IAEA safeguards also led to the formal termination in 1980 of U.S. nuclear reactor and fuel exports under the Nuclear Non-Proliferation Act.[15] This not only codified a *de facto* 1975 embargo on U.S. highly enriched uranium fuel for the SAFARI research reactor, but also meant that South Africa was not permitted to take delivery of low-enriched uranium fuel it had contracted to buy from the United States for its two French-supplied nuclear power reactors at Koeberg, which were due to come on line in the early 1980s.

In 1981, the Reagan Administration sought to open a dialogue with the Botha government on nuclear matters by holding out the promise that Washington would authorize nuclear exports to Pretoria that were not expressly prohibited by law. Although the 1980 U.S. fuel embargo, for example, had confronted Pretoria with the problem of finding an alternative source of fuel for the Koeberg reactors the Reagan Administration, despite advance knowledge, turned a blind eye when two U.S. uranium brokering firms arranged for South Africa to purchase a significant portion of the needed fuel from European sellers. Washington also authorized American companies to provide technical services for the Koeberg plants and granted export licenses for a number of dual-use commodities destined for the installations.[16]

This policy—a direct parallel to Washington's "constructive engagement" strategy for dealing with South Africa's racial stance—appeared to have a modest success in early 1984 when the Botha government declared that its own nuclear exports would be made only under strict controls, comparable to those adopted by the Nuclear Suppliers Group, and when it agreed to reopen negotiations with the IAEA on the application of the Agency's safeguards to the semi-industrial-scale enrichment plant it is building at Valindaba. However, the Botha government explicitly rejected placing the smaller Valindaba pilot-scale enrichment plant under comparable controls, thereby retaining its nuclear weapons option. Moreover, Pretoria appeared to betray the Reagan Administration's conciliatory non-proliferation stand in 1983 and 1984 by quietly hiring twenty-five U.S. reactor operators and technicians to work at the Koeberg nuclear power station in disregard of U.S. regulations prohibiting such activities without special authorization.[17] The Americans have since returned to the United States or have been assigned to non-prohibited duties.

Through mid-1985, Western European states also reacted mildly to South Africa's nuclear stance. South Africa bypassed the U.S. nuclear-fuel embargo by obtaining a substantial quantity of bulk low-enriched uranium from Swiss and Belgian sources, for example, and France willingly agreed to fabricate the material into fuel rods so that it could be used in the French-supplied Koeberg plants.

Repression triggers new sanctions. By the summer of 1985, however, a new pattern began to emerge, albeit as a result of growing Western concerns over intensifying cycles of South African racial violence and government repression. On July 24, France imposed a prospective nuclear trade embargo, directly triggered by the Botha government's declaration days earlier of a state of emergency giving South African security forces broad new powers to crack down on black dissidents.[18]

In September 1985, in response to congressional pressure, President Ronald Reagan also implemented a series of anti-South Africa trade sanctions by executive order that included an embargo on all classes of nuclear exports to Pretoria, including those still permitted by the Non-Proliferation Act.[19] Like the French nuclear trade sanctions, the U.S. embargo was imposed exclusively as an expression of American disapproval of apartheid, however.[20]

During late 1985 and early 1986, despite Botha's announcement of a series of carefully limited reforms of apartheid, pressure on the South African government from the British Commonwealth nations, the European Community, and the United States continued to mount as these powers pressed Botha to begin substantive negotiations on a transition to majority rule. Botha's response to these efforts throughout the following spring and summer was one of bitter defiance—and sometimes outright provocation—as he attempted to demonstrate that he would not allow reforms of South Africa's racial policies to be dictated from outside.

In the face of this intransigence, in August 1986 the leaders of six Commonwealth member states voted to impose sanctions on South Africa (despite the opposition of Great Britain, which refused to take this step).[21] The following month, the European Community similarly adopted moderately harsh sanctions against Pretoria, and, in October, the U.S. Congress, overriding President Reagan's veto, enacted legislation strengthening the U.S. sanctions previously implemented by executive order. Among other measures, the new U.S. law prohibited further imports of South African uranium ore and concentrate. It also codified the ban in the Reagan executive order on all classes of U.S. nuclear exports to South Africa. Unlike the executive order, however, the law specified that the export ban (though not the ban on uranium imports) would be lifted if South Africa ratified the NPT or placed all of its nuclear activities under IAEA safeguards, providing an incentive for Pretoria to take this step.[22] As discussed below, the imposition of these various economic penalties could affect South Africa's calculations concerning the future of its nuclear program, but they appear to have had little immediate impact in this regard.

Political and Technical Developments

As noted earlier, South Africa is believed to have had the ability since 1981 to produce approximately 110 pounds (50 kilograms) of highly enriched uranium annually at its pilot-scale uranium enrichment plant at Valindaba.[23] Using the standard assumptions that 33 to 55 pounds (15 to 25 kilograms) of the material is needed to manufacture a 20-kiloton nuclear device (*i.e.*, approximately the size of the Hiroshima bomb), this capability would, in principle, give Pretoria a potential nuclear arsenal of approximately fourteen to twenty-three weapons as of the end of 1987, assuming that 770 pounds (350 kilograms) of highly enriched uranium had been produced in the interim. However, to do that South Africa would have had to operate the Valindaba plant at full capacity throughout the period—an unlikely contingency. Therefore, the South African nuclear stockpile is probably somewhat smaller. Still, this represents continuing growth in South Africa's nuclear potential.

In the early 1980s, when Pretoria was trying to obtain low-enriched uranium (*i.e.* uranium enriched to between three and five percent) as fuel for the Koeberg reactors, it is possible that South Africa was able to purchase a significant amount of this material from the People's Republic of China, without IAEA safeguards. If Pretoria did obtain this material, it could have used some of it as the feed stock for the pilot-scale Valindaba enrichment plant, instead of the unenriched natural uranium that is normally used. In this way the plant's output of weapons-usable, highly enriched uranium could have been more than tripled for a number of years.[24]

China has denied making the sale, and there is still something of a mystery over the source of the Koeberg fuel.[25] Pretoria is known to have obtained 130 tons of low-enriched uranium from Belgian and Swiss sellers in 1981, but each of the two Koeberg plants requires 75 tons to start up and 30 tons for each annual refueling.[26] Inasmuch as Koeberg I has been on-line since 1984 and Koeberg II since 1985, Pretoria has to have obtained additional supplies from some outside source, and American officials remain concerned that China may have been involved.

Pretoria has also built a semi-commercial-scale enrichment plant at Valindaba, which is some thirty times larger than the pilot-scale facility and which is expected to begin operating in 1988. South Africa intends to use the facility, which is not subject to IAEA safeguards, to produce low-enriched uranium to fuel the Koeberg reactors in the future. Like the low-enriched uranium that Pretoria may have received from China, some of this low-enriched uranium could be used at the smaller Valindaba enrichment plant to produce highly enriched uranium. In 1984, as noted above, South Africa began negotiations with the IAEA on an agreement to place the larger facility under IAEA safeguards. Those talks stalled in mid-1986, however, leaving the possibility that the plant may eventually contribute substantially to South Africa's nuclear weapons potential.

Alleged collaboration with Israel. It has been alleged for a number of years that Pretoria has significantly enhanced its nuclear weapons capabilities by extensive cooperation with Israel, another technologically advanced state that, like South Africa, is diplomatically isolated and surrounded by hostile neighbors. According to various reports, which have never been fully substantiated, cooperation between the two countries dates back to the 1950s and has involved sales of South African uranium to Israel to fuel the Dimona reactor and extensive scientific exchanges, including Israeli assistance in developing South Africa's now decommissioned SAFARI II research reactor in the late 1960s.[27]

Most disturbing are the allegations that the flash observed by a U.S. satellite in the South Atlantic in September 1979 was a joint Israeli-South African nuclear test, possibly of a two-kiloton tactical nuclear weapon designed to be fired from a 155mm howitzer or naval gun.[28] The most recent charges are that the two countries are collaborating on the design of a nuclear-powered submarine, that they are building a joint long-range-missile testing facility on Marion Island in the Antarctic, and that South Africa is supplying Israel with enriched uranium for nuclear weapons.[29]

It is difficult to assess the validity of these allegations given the secrecy that surrounds the nuclear programs of both countries. Still, there seems to be little question that Israel and South Africa have close political ties and that they have cooperated extensively in the area of conventional armaments. By one estimate, Israeli sales of conventional weapons to South Africa have amounted to between $400 and $800 million annually.[30] South Africa's most advanced fighter, the Cheetah, is a close copy of the Israeli Kfir and is believed to have been developed with Israeli assistance.[31] The two countries were also said to be collaborating in the development of Israel's advanced Lavi fighter; when Israel cancelled the plane in 1987, there were reports that South Africa was attempting to recruit 600 Israeli technicians who had worked on the project, although Pretoria publicly denied this.[32]

In March 1987, responding to charges that its arms transfers to Pretoria violated the 1977 U.N. arms embargo, Israel agreed not to sign new military contracts with South Africa and to let existing contracts expire. In reporting to Congress on arms trade between the two countries, President Reagan stated that prior to the March decision, "Israel appears to have sold military systems and sub-systems and provided technical assistance on a regular basis."[33] Although the allegations of nuclear links between the two nations remain to be substantiated, they would be consistent with this pattern of bilateral security collaboration and should be taken seriously.

The NPT offer and security anxieties. The recent development with the greatest potential impact on South Africa's nuclear activities, however, was Prime Minister Botha's announcement in Pretoria on September 21, 1987, that South Africa "hopes that it will soon be able to sign the NPT and has decided to open discussions with others to this end."[34] Ratifying the treaty, which would require South Africa to place all of its nuclear installations and all of its nuclear materials (apart from uranium ore) under IAEA oversight, would represent a dramatic reversal of Pretoria's current nuclear policy, which has relied on secrecy and ambiguity to project the impression that it has an undeclared nuclear deterrent.[35]

South Africa made its announcement as the 1987 IAEA General Conference was convening in Vienna. It was expected that at the urging of a group of African states, led by Nigeria, the conference would vote to expel South Africa from the agency. Pretoria's surprising NPT offer thus had the earmarks of a last-minute gambit to avoid this sanction. Nevertheless, its declaration led the Soviet Union—which had backed the African bloc on the issue at a key meeting of the IAEA Board of Governors in June—to withdraw its support for immediate expulsion, and the conference adopted a compromise that postponed a vote on the issue until its September 1988 meeting.[36]

There is good reason to question whether South Africa is serious about joining the NPT. Its new offer, for example, appears to mimic an earlier attempt dating from mid-1984 to put off its IAEA critics with promises—subsequently unfulfilled—that it would accept new nuclear restraints. At that time, Pretoria offered to place its semi-commercial-scale Valindaba uranium enrichment under IAEA safeguards. Negotiations with the IAEA on the details of a safeguards agreement for the facility dragged on for two years and were then broken off because of Pretoria's insistence on conditions that were known to be contrary to long-standing IAEA safeguards practice.[37] The impasse precipitated the 1987 General Conference expulsion crisis, but Pretoria's apparently empty safeguards offer had gained it two years of breathing space in the interim.

The details of Botha's September 1987 announcement on the NPT contained strong indications that he might be attempting to repeat this ploy. Botha hinted that before joining the pact South Africa might insist on resolving how the IAEA would apply its safeguards to South Africa's nuclear program—a highly complex technical issue.[38] He also stated that South Africa intended to hold "negotiations with each of the nuclear-weapon states" on ratifying the accord, even though the treaty itself is non-negotiable. Among other issues, South Africa may insist that, before it signs the pact, the United States and Great Britain (two nuclear-weapon states) rescind the economic sanctions that they have imposed on South Africa in recent years.[39] Both negotiations are likely to be time-consuming, providing Pretoria further grounds for postponing ratification and for extending the one-year deadline imposed by the IAEA General Conference.

Political factors within South Africa provide further grounds for skepticism about Pretoria's readiness to constrain its nuclear options by quickly adhering to the treaty. For example, South Africa's white electorate swung sharply to the right in the May 1987 elections—a race in which national security was a central theme. Although white voters increased Prime Minister Botha's parliamentary majority, the ultra-rightist Conservative Party made gains at the expense of Botha's National Party in many districts and displaced the liberal Progressive Federal Party as the official parliamentary opposition.[40] Following the elections, Botha sought to continue his program of gradual reforms of apartheid, and, in early November—not long after his NPT offer—he made the conciliatory gesture of freeing Govan A. Mbeki, a longtime leader of the outlawed African National Congress, who had been incarcerated for twenty-three years. By early 1988 the right-wing opposition had virtually stalled even these limited reforms, and, in late February, harsh new restrictions on anti-government groups were imposed, demonstrating Pretoria's increasing sensitivity to the threat from extreme conservatives.[41]

By this point, South African troops were also heavily engaged in Angola in support of UNITA (National Union for the Total Independence of Angola) rebel forces. Some clashes, according to South African military spokesmen, pitted South African forces against Cuban troops and Soviet advisers fighting alongside Angolan government forces.[42] During October, South African troops assisted UNITA in a decisive battle to repel an Angolan government offensive supported by Cuban mechanized infantry, tank units, and MiG-23 aircraft. Referring to the episode in November, South African Defense Minister Magnus Malan declared that the defeat of UNITA would have brought South Africa "to the brink of the abyss" eventually leading to communist domination of the region.[43] In a subsequent press conference he stated, "The reality is that if the Cubans and Russians should destroy UNITA, there is no guarantee for us they will stop in the southeast of Angola."[44] In light of such concerns, elements of South Africa's leadership undoubtedly see the country's nuclear capabilities as a valuable deterrent against such possible Soviet and Cuban aggression. South Africa's continuing efforts to destabilize Mozambique and to maintain pressure on Zambia, Botswana, and Zimbabwe through sporadic raids on anti-South Africa guerrilla bases provided further evidence of Pretoria's continuing security anxieties.

Prospects

The growing power of hardliners within the South African leadership and the simultaneous intensification of the country's security concerns make it hard to imagine that Pretoria is now prepared to give up its nuclear "ace-in-the-hole" by ratifying the NPT. Indeed, it is possible, given the situation, that the Botha government might opt, not for the NPT, but for conducting a nuclear test to demonstrate the country's nuclear capabilities. Such a step might be seen as a useful means for intimidating neighbors, rallying white morale, defying international pressures for changes in South Africa's racial policies—and for warning the Soviet Union against further military involvement in the region. It has been assumed that the threat of international sanctions has served so far as a deterrent to a test, but today South African leaders might reason that they are already bearing the brunt of sanctions and have little more to lose.

Nonetheless, the possibility that South Africa will join the NPT should not be completely dismissed, since this step could yield possible benefits if Pretoria were able to trade ratification for concessions from its outside antagonists. At a minimum, South Africa could expect its status as a full member of the IAEA to be reaffirmed. Ratification would also make it legally eligible for nuclear exports from the United States—now barred by provisions of the 1978 Nuclear Non-Proliferation Act and the 1986 Anti-Apartheid Act, prohibiting such exports unless South Africa joins the pact or otherwise places all of its nuclear activities under IAEA safeguards. This has also been the basis for the U.S.-initiated *de facto* embargo on major new nuclear exports from Western Europe, which presumably would be lifted if South Africa joined the treaty.[45]

Obtaining a rollback of other economic sanctions would be less likely because they were enacted on human rights grounds, but ratification might be used as a bargaining chip in negotiations on the withdrawal of Soviet and Cuban forces from Angola. There would also be the more intangible benefit to be gained from embracing an international norm rather than defying it, a step that would reduce, albeit modestly, the country's status as an outcast.

It must also be recognized that by ratifying the NPT, South Africa would not completely give up the option to build nuclear weapons at some future time, inasmuch as the treaty permits a party to withdraw from the pact on ninety days' notice if its "supreme interests" are threatened. Nor would the pact require South Africa to cease the production of weapons-grade uranium, although this material (and all highly enriched uranium it had previously produced) would have to be placed under IAEA safeguards and could not be used for nuclear explosives as long as South Africa remained a party to the accord. This would mean that if Pretoria decided to abrogate the treaty or withdraw from it, it could theoretically remain in a position to manufacture nuclear weapons quite rapidly, perhaps in only a matter of weeks. In effect, by joining the treaty, Pretoria would be accepting significant constraints on its day-to-day nuclear activities, but it would not have to forsake the nuclear option in perpetuity.[46] It is therefore conceivable that under the right circumstances South Africa might, indeed, be persuaded to ratify the pact.

The foregoing factors make it difficult to predict the future course of South Africa's nuclear program. In all likelihood, Pretoria will temporize until the 1988 IAEA General Conference approaches in the fall of 1988. Indeed, as of June 1988, no negotiations on South Africa's joining the NPT had taken place. Whether it ultimtely ratifies the accord, defies its outside critics by conducting a test, or finds an eleventh-hour pretext for maintaining the ambiguous status quo, the months ahead will be ones of high drama in South African nuclear affairs.

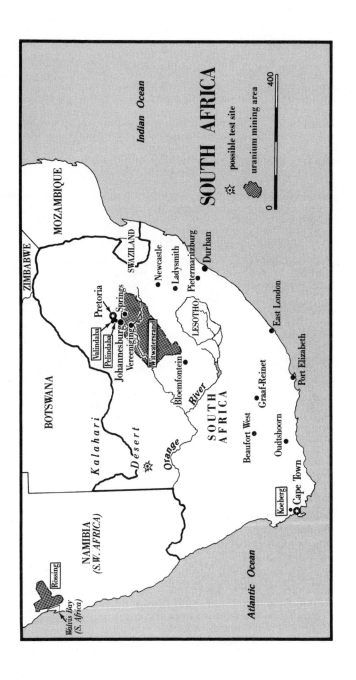

South Africa

Power Reactors/Operating or Under Construction
Koeberg I (light-water/low-enriched uranium, 922 MWe)
- supplier: Framatome (France)
- start up: 1984[a]
- fuel source: Switzerland, France, W. Germany, Belgium, China (?) for initial loads; S. Africa after 1988.[b]
- safeguards: yes

Koeberg II (light-water/low-enriched uranium, 922 MWe)
- supplier: Framatome (France)
- start up: 1985
- fuel source: Switzerland, France, W. Germany, Belgium, China (?) for initial loads; S. Africa after 1987.[b]
- safeguards: yes

Uranium Resources/Active Mining Sites/Uranium Mills
- reasonably assured reserves: South Africa: 385,700 metric tons[c]
  Namibia: 120,000 metric tons[d]
- currently active sites: South Africa: Witwatersrand Basin, Palabora
  Namibia: Rössing
- mills in operation: South Africa: Witwatersrand and Group

                                        Blyvooruitzicht
                                        Buffelsfontein
                                        Chemwes
                                          East Rand Gold and Uranium
                                          Harmony (3 mills)
                                        Hartebeestfontein
                                          Joint Metallurgical Scheme
                                        Randfontein
                                        St. Helena-Beisa
                                        Vaal Reefs (3 mills)
                                        Western Areas
                                        Western Deep Levels
                           Driefontein
                           Palabora
              Namibia: Rössing

Uranium Conversion (UF₆)
Valindaba
- capacity: Sufficient for Valindaba pilot-scale enrichment plant (presumed).
- supplier: Great Britain (?)[e]
- start up: prior to 1975
- safeguards: no

Valindaba
- capacity: commercial scale
- supplier: South Africa (?)
- start-up: 1986[j]
- safeguards: no

Reprocessing (Plutonium Extraction)

Pelindaba[n]
- capacity: hot cell complex; size unknown; able to handle Koeberg, SAFARI fuel[n]
- supplier: South Africa (?)
- start-up: 1987?[o]
- safeguards: only when safeguarded spent fuel present[n]

Enrichment

Valindaba (pilot plant)[g,n]
- type: stationary-wall centrifuge/jet-nozzle[f]
- capacity: 110 lbs. (50 kg.) high-enriched uranium per year[g]
- supplier: South Africa (some equipment reportedly supplied by U.S., West German, French, and Swiss firms)[n]
- start up: 1975; full operation in 1977[i] (sufficient material for nuclear weapon probably not available until 1980-1981).
- safeguards: no

Valindaba (semi-commercial plant)
- type: stationary-wall centrifuge/jet-nozzle[f]
- capacity: 50 metric tons of low-enriched uranium per year[g]
- supplier: South Africa
- start up: 1988[j]
- safeguards: no

Fuel Fabrication

Elprod (Pelindaba)[n]
- capacity: sufficient to fuel SAFARI I reactor (development of line for Koeberg fuel probably under way)
- supplier: South Africa (?)
- start-up: 1981[n]
- safeguards: no

Research Reactors

SAFARI I, Pelindaba (light-water/high-enriched uranium, 20 MWt)
- supplier: Allis Chalmers Corporation (U.S.)
- start up: 1965
- fuel source: United States;[k] after 1981, South Africa.
- safeguards: yes

Pelinduna Zero (SAFARI II) (heavy-water/low-enriched uranium, 0 MWt)
- supplier: South Africa
- start up: 1967[l] (now decommissioned)
- fuel source: United States
- heavy water: United States
- safeguards: yes

Sources and Notes

a. "Koeberg Ups Power," *Rand Daily Mail, Joint Publication Research Service/ Nuclear Development and Proliferation (JPRS/NDP)*, April 17, 1984, p. 36.

b. Ann MacLachlan, "U.S. Firm Plays Role in South Africa Purchase of Uranium," *Energy Daily*, December 10, 1981. George Lardner, Jr., and Don Oberdorfer, "China Was Source of Atomic Fuel for South Africa, U.S. Believes," *Washington Post*, November 18, 1981. The fuel obtained from the Belgian nuclear fuel supply company and the Swiss, French, W. German, Kaiseraugst utility consortium was enriched and fabricated in France; U.S. uranium brokers helped arrange the sale with the knowledge of the U.S. State Department. The United States was to supply fuel for the plant, but U.S. fuel exports to South Africa have been prohibited by law since 1980.

c. Reserves at less than $130 per kg; *Uranium Resources, Production, and Demand*, A Joint Report of the OECD Nuclear Energy Agency and the International Atomic Energy Agency (Paris: OECD, 1986), pp. 299-305.

d. Reserves at less than $130 per kg; *Uranium Resources, Production, and Demand*, A Joint Report of the OECD Nuclear Energy Agency and the International Atomic Energy Agency (OECD: Paris, 1986), pp. 264-268.

e. J. E. Spence, "The Republic of South Africa: Proliferation and the Politics of 'Outward Movement,' " in Lawrence and Larus, eds., *Nuclear Proliferation Phase II*. (Lawrence, KA: University Press of Kansas), p. 217.

f. Possibly based on West German jet-nozzle process, degree of similarity uncertain.

g. Department of Political and Security Council Affairs, United Nations Centre for Disarmament, Report of the Secretary General, *South Africa's Plan and Capability in the Nuclear Field*, Report A/35/402 (New York: United Nations, 1981), p. 22, updated in U.N. documents A/39/470 (September 12, 1984) and A/42/649 (October 16, 1987).

h. C. Raja Mohan, "Atomic Teeth to Apartheid: South Africa and Nuclear Weapons," in K. Subrahmanyam, *Nuclear Myths and Realities* (ABC, New Delhi, 1981), p. 123.

i. David Fishlock, "The South African Nuclear Weapons Scare," prepared for Congressional Research Service, December 1977, p. CRS-5; communications with informed U.S. officials.

j. "Nuclear Self-Sufficiency Expected in 1988," Johannesburg Domestic Service 1600 GMT, May 26, 1987, reprinted in *FBIS/Africa*, May 28, 1987, p. U-11.

k. U.S. exports ceased in 1975.

l. J. E. Spence, "South Africa: the Nuclear Option," *African Affairs*, October 1981, p. 441. The reactor is presently decommissioned; Robert Jaster, "Politics and the Afrikaner Bomb," *Orbis*, Winter 1984, p. 827.

m. "South Africa," *Nucleonics Week*, March 21, 1985, p. 15; "Koeberg Reaches Full Capacity," *The Citizen, JPRS/NDP*, July 16, 1984.

n. Jozef Goldblat, ed., *Non-Proliferation: The Why and the Wherefore*, (Philadelphia: Taylor and Francis, 1985), p. 315; *Report by the Board of Governors and the Director General to the General Conference, South Africa's Nuclear Capabilities*, GC (XXVIII)/724, September 24, 1984, Annex 1, Attachment 2, p. 2. All of South Africa's spent fuel is currently under IAEA safeguards.

o. "Implementation of the Declaration on the Denuclearization of Africa," Report of the Secretary General, U.N. document A/42/649, October 16, 1987 (IAEA safeguards formalized, September 1, 1987).

South Africa's uranium enrichment facilities at Valindaba. Main photo: soon-to-operate semi-commercial enrichment plant. Inset: interior photo of pilot-scale enrichment plant, showing "jet-nozzle" enrichment units.
Courtesy, South African Atomic Energy Corporation.

Chapter VII:
Controls and Safeguards

The nuclear non-proliferation regime—a constellation of international treaties, institutions, codes, and bilateral nuclear trade arrangements—is a major restraint on the spread of nuclear arms. During 1987 and the first half of 1988, the regime was strengthened in a number of important respects, but several troubling events underscored its limitations and indicated the need for better vigilance in enforcing some of its guidelines and standards. Most of the developments mentioned in this section are discussed elsewhere in this volume and will therefore be summarized only briefly.

The Non-Proliferation Treaty (NPT)

Spain's ratification of the NPT on November 5, 1987, closes one of the last gaps in treaty adherence in the West.[1] Although Spain is not known to have ever actively pursued the acquisition of nuclear weapons, the Spanish military was said to have favored keeping this option open and had long resisted joining the accord. Spain's entry into the North Atlantic Treaty Organization (NATO) in 1982, and into the European Economic Community in 1986, however, led to pressures on the Spanish government to conform its policies in this and other areas to those of Spain's security and trading partners. Full participation in the Western defense alliance also undercut any possible rationale for Spain's retaining the option to build an independent nuclear force. These and other factors are said to have led the Spanish military to acquiesce in the bid by the country's civilian leaders to join the pact.[2]

On April 26, 1988, Saudi Arabia announced that it would accede to the NPT. The move followed the revelation in March 1988 that Riyadh had secretly purchased intermediate-range (1,600-1,860 mile) missiles from China of a type that is equipped with nuclear warheads in the Chinese arsenal. Although the purchase initially fueled fears that China might have transferred a nuclear-armed version of the missile, Riyadh's subsequent assurances that the missiles it received carry conventional warheads have been generally accepted. Nonetheless, concerns have remained that Saudi Arabia, while lacking the ability to manufacture nuclear weapons itself, might seek to acquire them in the future, possibly in collaboration with Pakistan. (Riyadh is thought to have provided financing for Pakistan's nuclear weapons development program and might hope to capitalize on this tie.) Saudi Arabia has declared that it will not nuclearize the missiles. The decision to join the NPT will reaffirm and formalize its pledges not to take this step or otherwise to develop or acquire nuclear arms.[3]

On September 21, 1987, South African Prime Minister P.W. Botha finally announced that his country was willing to consider joining the NPT.[4] The announcement, however, came as the 1987 General Conference of the International Atomic Energy Agency (IAEA) was about to take up a measure to expel South Africa from the Agency and has been perceived as little more than an attempt to avert this action.[5] The General Conference postponed a decision on the question until September 1988 to permit the South African initiative to be pursued, but as of June 1988, negotiations on the issue had not begun. Therefore, it appears likely that Pretoria will remain outside the NPT and will soon face a second attempt to oust it from the IAEA. For a discussion of political factors relating to Pretoria's decision-making on the issue, see Chapter VI.

Another issue of importance to the future of the NPT is the progress made during 1987-1988 on U.S.-Soviet arms control through the ratification of the Treaty on Intermediate-range Nuclear Forces (INF) and continuing negotiations on a strategic arms reduction treaty. For many years non-nuclear-weapon state parties to the NPT have complained that the superpowers have not lived up to their obligations under Article VI of the accord to work toward nuclear disarmament, and the issue proved to be one of the most divisive at the 1980 and 1985 NPT review conferences. Although the INF Treaty is recognized as only a first step in the process of U.S.-Soviet nuclear arms reductions, if it is followed by substantial cuts in strategic arms, these developments could strengthen support for the NPT considerably by reducing antagonisms between its weapon-state and non-weapon-state adherents.

The Treaty of Rarotonga
(South Pacific Nuclear Weapon Free Zone).

On December 11, 1986, Australia ratified the Treaty of Rarotonga, bringing it into force and thereby establishing a South Pacific nuclear-weapon-free zone as a valuable new component of the non-proliferation regime. A key issue, however, is whether the nuclear-weapon states will adhere to several protocols to the treaty. Protocol I prohibits the manufacture, stationing, and testing of nuclear explosive devices in territories for which the nuclear-weapon states are responsible; Protocol II bans the use of nuclear weapons against states within the zone; and Protocol III outlaws nuclear testing within its boundaries. The Soviet Union ratified Protocols II and III (the only two applicable to it) on February 3, 1988. The People's Republic of China signed Protocols II and III, (again the only ones applicable) on February

10, 1987, but has yet to ratify them.[6] The United States, Great Britain, and France have refused to sign or ratify any of the provisions, however, and France has continued nuclear testing in the region.[7]

The Limited Test Ban Treaty

While not directly limiting the spread of nuclear arms in South Asia, Pakistan's ratification on March 3, 1988, of the 1963 Limited Test Ban Treaty, prohibiting nuclear weapon tests or other nuclear explosions in the atmosphere, in outer space, or under water, was a valuable gesture.[8] The step signalled Islamabad's willingness to accept at least limited nuclear arms control restrictions in the region. This action brings Pakistan into line with India, which ratified the pact in 1963, and could help counter Indian charges that Pakistan's offer of a comprehensive regional test ban is not serious.[9]

In addition, Argentina ratified the treaty on July 30, 1986, (the action was only made public in the spring of 1987, however). Like Pakistan, Argentina had signed the pact in 1963 but had not ratified it.[10]

The International Atomic Energy Agency Safeguards

According to the Agency's 1986 Annual Report (the most recently published as of mid-1988), during 1986 the Agency "did not detect any anomaly which would indicate the diversion of a significant amount of safeguarded nuclear material—or the misuse of facilities, equipment or non-nuclear material subject to safeguards under certain agreements—for the manufacture of any nuclear weapon, or for any other military purpose, or for the manufacture of any other nuclear explosive device, or for purposes unknown."[11]

During 1986, 9.2 tons (8.4 metric tons) of separated plutonium, enough for more than 950 weapons using the Agency's standard of 8 kilograms per device, were under the Agency's safeguards. Agency safeguards also covered 14.5 tons (13.2 metric tons) of highly enriched uranium (defined by the Agency to be uranium enriched to more than 20 percent), possibly enough for several hundred weapons, depending on the level of enrichment, along with far larger quantities of less sensitive material.[12]

The IAEA conducted 2,050 inspections at 595 installations in fifty-three non-nuclear-weapon states during the year, a slight increase from its activities in 1985. In addition, the Agency operated more than 325 automatic photo and television cameras at nuclear installations around the world; verified that there had been no tampering with some 10,000 seals on nuclear materials and equipment; and analyzed 1,030 uranium and plutonium samples.

The Agency found some 270 discrepancies, most, but not all of which were considered minor, and almost all of which were resolved. Unresolved discrepancies involved the failure of "bundle counters" (used to keep track of the amount of spent fuel produced in Canadian-designed natural uranium/heavy water reactors known as "CANDU" reactors) or surveillance equipment (video and movie cameras used to monitor key points in safeguarded installations between inspections). Although the IAEA report states that "[in] no case is there any indication of a diversion," it also notes that in a number of these unresolved cases the "inventories cannot be reverified," meaning that the Agency's accounting and inspection procedures cannot determine whether plutonium-bearing spent fuel was diverted during the period that its monitoring equipment was malfunctioning.[13] This is the first time the Agency has noted such a problem in its Annual Report. Apparently only CANDU reactors in Canada are involved, not those that are operating in India, Pakistan, and Argentina.

A far more troubling picture of IAEA activities was portrayed by an internal IAEA document, known as the Safeguards Implementation Report (SIR). A copy of the 1986 SIR was obtained and circulated by Green Party members of the European Parliament in May 1988. Among other findings, the 1986 SIR stated that the agency's inspection goals were met at only 37 percent of inspected facilities and that at several of them,

verification activities were incomplete, which means that the inspection goal could not be evaluated as even partially attained in 1986. In such cases, the level of assurance provided by agency safeguards is substantially below the applicable verification standards.[14]

The report also stated that surveillance equipment for monitoring nuclear materials "failed to provide conclusive results" at more than half of the 147 facilities at which it was used.[15] The SIR went on to acknowledge that a shortage of trained inspectors was a problem that "remains one of the most important affecting the efficiency and credibility of safeguards, and it is difficult to forecast when it is going to be solved."

Without further information, it is not possible to determine whether these and other shortcomings noted in the report have created significant opportunities for the diversion of nuclear material. It is not known, for example, whether the deficiencies occurred at facilities that handle materials directly usable for nuclear weapons or that are located in countries thought to harbor an interest in acquiring nuclear arms. On the other hand, it appears that at the least, the Agency is having considerable difficulty in monitoring the materials and facilities under its supervision.

(As this book went to press, the IAEA released data on its 1987 safeguards activities. Overall, the Agency stated, it was "reasonable to conclude that nuclear material under Agency safeguards in 1987 remained in peaceful nuclear activities or was otherwise adequately accounted for." All discrepancies arising during the year, the Agency noted, were satisfactorily resolved.)

The Missile Technology Control Regime

A new component was added to the non-proliferation regime on April 16, 1987, when the United States, Canada, France, Italy, Japan, the United Kingdom, and West Germany announced the formation of a missile technology control regime to restrict the transfers of equipment and technology that might contribute substantially to the development of unmanned nuclear delivery systems. The agreement was the product of four years of negotiations, initiated in 1982 by the United States, and is in the form of a set of parallel export controls adopted by the seven participating states. The seven had been informally enforcing the new rules for about two years prior to the announcement of the new regime.[16] The new controls are discussed in detail in Chapter II, which examines the delivery systems of the emerging nuclear states.

Argentine-Brazil Nuclear Facility Visits

Though intended as an alternative to existing non-proliferation institutions, the unprecedented exchange of visits to sensitive nuclear plants undertaken by Argentina and Brazil in 1987-1988 is a valuable step toward reducing nuclear competition in Latin America. The visits, which have involved the opening of uranium enrichment installations not under the IAEA system, are described in the sections on the two countries in Chapter V. As noted there, the exchanges, while building mutual trust that the facilities at issue are not being used for military purposes, do not permit verification of the amount or the enrichment level of material produced at the plants. As the two nations gain the ability to enrich uranium beyond the very low levels so far achieved, this could lead to serious ambiguities that, in turn, could rekindle their nuclear competition.

Nuclear Supplier Controls

Since the mid-1970s, the industrialized nuclear-supplier countries of the West and the Soviet bloc, operating under the aegis of the Nuclear Suppliers Group and the NPT Nuclear Exporters Committee (see Appendix F), have applied a set of uniform export controls over their nuclear transfers to ensure that they are not used by recipients for military purposes. Central to these controls are periodically updated lists of nuclear commodities whose export is permitted only if the recipient nation agrees to place the article in question under IAEA safeguards. (The lists are known as "trigger lists" because they trigger the application of these safeguards.) Export licensing programs in the supplier countries implement this regime.

Argentina, South Africa, and China, though not formal members of the groups implementing these standards have voluntarily adopted their most important element by requiring IAEA safeguards on their nuclear exports; Brazil has also agreed to require this control on its exports to China under the two countries' 1984 nuclear cooperation agreement. Indeed, the requirement that all officially sanctioned nuclear transfers be made only under IAEA safeguards is gradually becoming an international norm, and no nation has expressly adopted a contrary policy, despite the fact that several non-nuclear-weapon states—in particular, the emerging nuclear states, Argentina, Brazil, India, Israel, Pakistan, and South Africa—have reserved the right to keep indigenously developed facilities and materials outside the IAEA system.

Soviet breach of de facto nuclear embargo. The United States, Australia, Canada, and Sweden have gone beyond the IAEA safeguards requirement by prohibiting major nuclear exports to countries that have not placed *all* of their nuclear activities under IAEA oversight—this rules out significant new nuclear sales to the six just-noted emerging nuclear states. Since the late 1970s, the United States has sought to persuade the other advanced supplier countries to make this requirement for "full-scope" safeguards a condition for major new nuclear supply commitments. Although Belgium, France, Italy, Switzerland, and West Germany have long opposed this tightening of export controls, in recent years they, and all other advanced supplier countries, have adhered to it on a *de facto* basis. (Moreover, in early 1988, West Germany appeared to embrace the standards more definitively when it notified Argentina that future nuclear sales would be contingent on the latter's placing all of its nuclear activities under IAEA oversight.)[17]

The de facto embargo on major nuclear sales to the key emerging nuclear states was dealt a serious setback in April 1988, however, when the Soviet Union agreed to sell two new 1,000-megawatt pressurized water reactors and their fuel to India.[18] The reactors are to be installed on a turnkey basis by 1997 and 1998. The Soviet sale is the first major transfer to a country with a "parallel" unsafeguarded nuclear program since a deal in 1979-1980 in which West Germany and Switzerland respectively agreed to sell Argentina a nuclear power reactor (Atucha II) and a heavy water production plant.[19] Although the Soviet sale to India undermines virtually the only sanction that has been imposed on India for maintaining a nuclear weapons capability, the Soviet reactors will, themselves, be subject to IAEA safeguards, and the Soviet Union will take back the plutonium-bearing spent fuel they produce. Thus, the facilities will not contribute to India's nuclear weapons potential.[20] (The Soviet Union's possible motivations for the sale are discussed in the section of Chapter III of this book dealing with India.)

U.S.-Japan nuclear cooperation agreement. On November 4, 1987, the United States and Japan signed a new agreement on nuclear trade that triggered a controversy over another nuclear supplier control, the right of the United States to restrict the extraction of plutonium produced in enriched uranium fuel it has sold abroad.[21] Until the 1980s, all U.S. agreements for nuclear cooperation (except that with EURATOM, the European Community nuclear agency) gave the United States the right to prohibit the other party to the agreement from extracting plutonium produced in U.S.-origin uranium. The 1987 U.S.-Japan agreement also contained this stipulation, but then effectively waived it by authorizing Japan to extract and use plutonium from U.S. material for the thirty-year life of the pact. Although Washington had included similar advance long-term approvals in several other revised nuclear trade agreements since 1981, the agreement with Japan was the first with a nation that was actually implementing a large-scale program to use plutonium for nuclear energy.

Until the mid-1970s, it was generally assumed within nuclear industry and governmental circles around the world that plutonium would be needed as a nuclear fuel because of an expected shortage of uranium, and many industrialized U.S. nuclear trading partners, including Japan, initiated experimental programs to "recycle" plutonium in their nuclear power reactors and to use it to fuel more advanced "breeder" reactors. (See Glossary.) In the latter half of the 1970s, however, the Ford and Carter Administrations rejected this philosophy, arguing that the unexpected availability of abundant supplies of uranium made the use of plutonium uneconomic and that widescale use of plutonium would unduly increase the risks of proliferation and nuclear terrorism. Given its concerns about plutonium use, the Carter Administration sought to exercise the authority in U.S. nuclear trade agreements to slow plutonium extraction from U.S.-origin uranium—which then comprised the bulk of nuclear fuel around the world—contrary to the expectations of Japan, Switzerland, and other industrialized NPT parties, whose nuclear industrialists and policymakers remained committed to the plutonium option. By the end of the Carter Administration the issue had become a serious irritant in U.S-Japan relations, and Washington was reluctantly acquiescing in Japan's requests to extract plutonium from U.S.-origin material, carefully scrutinizing each request on a case-by-case basis. Although Japan was obtaining the U.S. approvals it sought, it objected to the case-by-case reviews as time-consuming and uncertain.

In 1981, the Reagan Administration—whose officials tended to share the nuclear industry perspective on the value of plutonium as a fuel—partially reversed U.S. policy on the issue, announcing that the United States would not impede the civilian use of plutonium in advanced industrialized countries, such as Japan, that did not pose a significant pro-liferation risk. Washington also began a renegotiation of the U.S.-Japan nuclear cooperation agreement, as mandated by the 1978 Nuclear Non-Proliferation Act. Although one of the objectives of the act had been to *tighten* U.S. controls over plutonium extracted from U.S.-origin uranium, the Reagan Administration, hoping to eliminate a source of fric-tion in U.S.-Japan relations, used the renegotiation to ad-dress Tokyo's concerns over the case-by-case U.S. reviews of Japanese plutonium extraction requests and, as noted above, included a provision approving such requests in ad-vance for the thirty-year life of the agreement.

The tactic triggered a strong protest in Congress when the U.S.-Japan accord was submitted for review. At the heart of Congress's concern was that the generic, or "program-matic," approval of Japanese plutonium extraction requests had the effect of authorizing Japan to accumulate and use tons of nuclear weapons material. Although all this material would be under IAEA safeguards because of Japan's adher-ence to the NPT, opponents of the agreement were con-cerned that the material, only ten to twenty pounds of which would be needed for a nuclear device, would be an attractive target for terrorists, and they feared that Japanese security arrangements might not be sufficient to protect the large quantities of plutonium involved. (Japanese nuclear-plant security personnel, for example, are unarmed.)

Adding to congressional concerns was that the agreement also effectively authorized the shipment to Japan of tons of plutonium from Great Britain and France, where Japan had sent much of its U.S.-origin spent nuclear fuel for plutonium extraction. For security reasons, the material was to be shipped by air, with a refueling stopover in Alaska, a plan that gave rise to vehement opposition to the agreement in that state on environmental grounds, inasmuch as a crash-proof cask for shipping the material had not been developed.[22]

Opposition to the pact within the Reagan Administration contributed to the controversy. The Department of Defense initially opposed the accord because of concerns over the risk of nuclear terrorism, although the Pentagon ended its opposition when Frank Carlucci succeeded Caspar Weinberger as secretary of defense in late November 1987.[23] (Carlucci had approved the accord in mid-1987 when he served as the head of the National Security Council, overruling Weinberger's objections at the time.)

The Nuclear Regulatory Commission also objected to the agreement principally because of concerns that the IAEA's safeguards were not sufficiently advanced to keep track of plutonium flows at large-scale plutonium extraction plants of the type that Japan intended to build. Indeed, the commission raised the possibility that the IAEA might not be able to account for hundreds of pounds of the material once the plant began operating.[24]

As a result of these concerns, by the end of 1987, opposition to the accord appeared to be growing, and on December 17, the Senate Foreign Relations Committee voted to disapprove the pact by a margin of fifteen to three.[25]

The Reagan Administration responded to these developments first by gaining Japanese agreement that plutonium shipments from Western Europe would take a polar route, thus avoiding U.S. and Canadian airspace.[26] Also the administration argued that Tokyo intended to pursue its plans for using plutonium irrespective of the U.S. decision on the new agreement, since Japan also possessed plutonium from non-U.S. uranium; the agreement, the administration stressed, at least ensured that the United States would have a say in the security arrangements Japan adopted as it pursued its plutonium program. On the Nuclear Regulatory Commission's concerns about the future adequacy of safeguards, the administration argued that it expected that significant progress on IAEA accounting techniques would be made by the time that Japan completed its large-scale plutonium plant. Once in place, the improved accounting techniques would greatly reduce the risk of any plutonium diversion.[27] Advocates of the accord also expressed concern that if the agreement were not approved, Japan might cancel its contracts to purchase additional U.S. enriched uranium fuel, significantly worsening the U.S. trade deficit.[28]

Despite the efforts of the Reagan Administration to promote the agreement, the groundswell against it continued in early 1988.[29] On March 21, however, the accord was unexpectedly brought to the Senate floor for a vote, catching its opponents unprepared, and a resolution to disapprove the agreement was defeated by a vote of 53 to 30.[30]

Under the Atomic Energy Act, once a nuclear agreement is submitted to Congress, it becomes effective automatically at the end of ninety days during which both houses of Congress are in session—unless disapproved by a majority of both houses. Thus the Senate's refusal to reject it essentially guaranteed that the accord would go into effect, and it entered into force on April 25.

Clandestine Nuclear Trade

During 1987 and the first half of 1988, an unprecedented number of clandestine nuclear transactions came to light. These episodes involve attempts by emerging nuclear states to circumvent supplier controls in order to obtain, without non-proliferation restrictions, hardware or materials that either would not be exported at all to the country involved or would be exported only under IAEA safeguards. The recently disclosed incidents, in most cases discussed elsewhere in this volume, include:

- The Leybold-Hereaus case, involving the smuggling from West Germany and Switzerland in 1986-1987 of custommade equipment for use in Pakistan's uranium enrichment program;

- The Arshad Pervez case, involving the unsuccessful attempt to smuggle specially hardened steel (for uranium enrichment centrifuges) and beryllium (used in nuclear weapons) from the United States to Pakistan;

- Reports that in 1987 Pakistan obtained key uranium enrichment centrifuge components, known as inverters, from Turkey;

- The diversion of Norwegian and Soviet heavy water in 1983 and 1985, reportedly to India;

- The re-export in 1987 or 1988 of Norwegian heavy water by Romania, reportedly to Israel, without Norway's prior consent;[31] and

- Israel's apparent use of Norwegian heavy water in the Dimona reactor to produce plutonium for nuclear weapons in violation of peaceful use pledges Israel gave to Norway in 1959.

The last several episodes indicate that trafficking in heavy water has been a far more serious issue than previously appreciated. Given the commodity's critical role in permitting Israel and India to expand their nuclear weapons capabilities, it would appear that supplier country controls over the material need to be considerably strengthened. Testimony by U.S. officials stating that Pakistani smuggling operations are still continuing—some of them in the United States—is another indication of the need for heightened attention to export control measures.[32]

Nuclear Submarines

During the first half of 1988, the non-proliferation regime faced a new challenge from an unexpected quarter, as the Soviet Union leased a nuclear-powered attack submarine to India—the first-ever transfer of such a vessel—and the United States authorized Great Britain to sell Canada nuclear-powered attack submarines based on U.S. technology, the first such transfer allowed by Washington to any state other than the United Kingdom.

The Indian submarine is said to be a 1960s vintage "Charlié I" class model, which in the Soviet navy is capable of firing conventional or nuclear-armed cruise missiles while submerged.[33] India does not possess such missiles, and it appears highly unlikely that the ship will ever serve as a platform for launching nuclear weapons. (Indeed, Indian spokesmen have asserted that the vessel, christened the *Chakra*, will be used only for training purposes and will not be deployed in combat.) India is to receive three additional Soviet nuclear submarines in the future, according to some reports.[34]

For its part, Canada plans to purchase ten to twelve nuclear-powered attack submarines from either Great Britain or France to patrol its territorial waters, in particular the area beneath the Arctic ice cap. Since British nuclear submarines use American technology, Washington's approval was needed before the United Kingdom could bid on the deal.[35] As a party to the NPT, Canada is prohibited from fitting any vessels it obtains with nuclear weapons.

Although neither the Indian nor the Canadian submarines will thus be nuclear-armed, the spread of these systems will pose a number of new challenges to global non-proliferation efforts. These challenges are enumerated in the following sections.

Erosion of restraints. Ever since nuclear-propelled submarines were introduced in the 1950s, their spread has been limited to the United States, the Soviet Union, Great Britain, France, and China—the five declared nuclear-weapon states and permanent United Nations Security Council members. Thus, while neither the transfer of nuclear-powered submarines by nuclear-weapon states nor their possession by non-nuclear states is prohibited by the NPT, the Nuclear Suppliers Guidelines, or any other formal non-proliferation rules, the Soviet and U.S. decisions to permit the transfer of the craft to additional states deviate from what has been a significant, if unwritten, arms control norm.

This erosion of restraints on transfers of advanced conventional weapons systems—seen also in China's March 1988 transfer of intermediate-range missiles to Saudi Arabia—damages the legitimacy of international efforts to curb the spread of nuclear arms by pushing the threshold of what is considered an acceptable addition to a regional power's military forces ever closer to the level of nuclear weapons themselves. Moreover, the fact that the attack submarines carry nuclear weapons (*e.g.*, nuclear tipped torpedoes and cruise missiles) in the arsenals of the major powers and the fact that all nuclear-propelled submarines are associated by the public with nuclear-armed strategic missiles tends to create confusion as to whether the acquisition of nuclear weapons is being condoned.

New safeguards challenges. The transfers of these nuclear-powered submarines may also weaken the NPT by exploiting for the first time a key gap in its coverage. The treaty requires all parties to ensure that their nuclear exports to non-nuclear-weapon states for peaceful purposes be subject to IAEA safeguards in the recipient country and that all peaceful nuclear activities within a non-nuclear-weapon state party be under IAEA oversight. Language in the treaty, however, provides some exceptions. It allows parties to transfer nuclear material to non-weapon states without IAEA safeguards if the material is to be used by the recipient for "non-proscribed military purposes," *viz.*, for submarine propulsion. The treaty also permits non-nuclear-weapon state parties, such as Canada, to remove material from safeguards for this purpose.[36]

Heretofore, since no party had taken advantage of these exceptions, IAEA safeguards comprehensively covered all exports to non-weapon states and, if the non-weapon state was a party to the treaty, comprehensively covered all of its nuclear activities. The submarine transfers to India and Canada, however, create a separate category of transfers and activities that are not under IAEA supervision. This will greatly complicate IAEA accounting and could open the door to the diversion of nuclear materials that would otherwise be safeguarded—a possibility that is all the more disturbing because to date most, if not all, nuclear submarines have used weapons-grade uranium as fuel. A nuclear-weapon state, for example, could surreptitiously provide a non-nuclear ally with a nuclear weapons capability by supplying it excessive quantities of weapons-usable uranium in the form of submarine fuel. Or a non-weapon state NPT party could attempt to remove from safeguards more material for submarine fuel than it really needed and use the excess for nuclear arms.

As a practical matter, these risks are likely to be minimized in the Indian and Canadian cases, however, since it appears that the enriched uranium fuel that has been transferred to India and that would be transferred to Canada, if it ultimately purchased submarines from Great Britain or France, will remain under relatively tight controls, despite the fact that it will not be under IAEA supervision. The Soviet Union has stated that it will periodically inspect the fuel it has leased to India and will take the material back after it is used. Canada, in turn, would operate under a strict IAEA regimen that would (1) allow it to remove nuclear material from safeguards only by placing it in a submarine reactor and (2) require Canada to account for the fuel after use and to place it once again under IAEA oversight.

Nonetheless, the precedent of the two submarine transfer cases will inevitably encourage other transfers in the future, and in these instances, controls could be far less stringent.

Production of weapons-grade uranium legitimized. Another impact of the Indian and Canadian submarine deals is that the readiness of NPT states to transfer or use enriched uranium outside of safeguards for naval propulsion will legitimize the production of unsafeguarded enriched uranium for this purpose by non-NPT states. Once a non-NPT country produced the material, however, it would be totally free to use it to build nuclear arms. Brazil, for example, inaugurated a small unsafeguarded uranium enrichment plant in April 1988. Brazil also has a program to develop nuclear submarines and has sought to justify its enrichment activities partly on the ground that it will need enriched uranium to fuel these vessels. If it produces weapons-grade uranium for this purpose, it will also acquire a *de facto* nuclear weapons capability. Similarly, if Argentina revived the nuclear submarine program it initiated in the early 1980s, this would provide a convenient rationale for it to increase its production of unsafeguarded enriched uranium—and potentially obtain its own ready nuclear weapons option.

Added pressure for proliferation in South Asia. Finally, India's lease of the Soviet submarine and its reported plans to acquire several additional ones will have a separate impact on global non-proliferation efforts by increasing pressures for nuclear arming in South Asia. One of the basic reasons for Pakistan's pursuit of nuclear weapons has been its desire to compensate for India's conventional military superiority. The new submarines will heighten the naval component of this conventional threat, inevitably increasing Pakistan's perceived need for a nuclear counter. Should this lead to the further nuclearization of the Subcontinent, not only would India and Pakistan be exposed to grave new risks, but the example of a South Asian nuclear arms race could also greatly damage global non-proliferation norms.

*

The events of the past eighteen months are disturbing indeed. They have seen the advent of a fourth *de facto* nuclear-weapon state; unprecedented transfers of nuclear-powered submarines and intermediate-range ballistic missiles; continued nuclear smuggling activities; and, except in Latin America, little progress toward regional accommodations that might ease pressures for further proliferation. The next eighteen months will see elections in India, Israel, Argentina, Brazil, and, it appears, Pakistan that could lead to political changes affecting the nuclear stance of all of these countries. In this uncertain environment, maintaining efforts to curb the spread of nuclear arms—and developing mechanisms to constrain undeclared nuclear arsenals where they exist—will be an increasingly difficult challenge.

Notes

Chapter II:
Delivering the Bomb

1. This term is gaining increasing acceptance for characterizing the nuclear arsenals of the less-industrialized nuclear powers. See, *e.g.*, Rodney W. Jones, ed., *Small Nuclear Forces and U.S. Security Policy* (Lexington, MA: Lexington Books, 1984).
2. The term ballistic missile refers to a missile which is self-propelled and guided, with a range of many miles. Ballistic missiles carry their own fuel and oxidizer propellants, as opposed to aircraft and cruise missiles which must stay in the atmosphere and get their oxidizer—oxygen—from it. Ballistic missiles also do not generally need aerodynamic control surfaces, because they travel in a free-falling trajectory under the influence of gravity. See Arthur F. Manfredi Jr., *et al.* "Ballistic Missile Proliferation of Non-Major Military Powers," (Washington, DC: Congressional Research Service, August 6, 1987), p. 1.
3. See, *e.g.*, "Commentary on U.S. Military Aid to Pakistan," Delhi General Overseas Service, 1010 GMT, January 6, 1988, reprinted in *Foreign Broadcast Information Service (FBIS)/Near East and South Asia (NES)*, January 7, 1988, p. 49.
4. Extensive new information has come to light in recent years suggesting that early-generation nuclear bombs of undeclared nuclear-weapons states will be considerably smaller and lighter than the first weapons developed by the United States, probably weighing no more than 1,000 to 2,000 pounds (roughly 450 to 900 kilograms),

in contrast to the atomic bombs developed during World War II, which weighed roughly 10,000 pounds (about 4,500 kilograms).

Information, disclosed in 1985, on Sweden's largely secret nuclear-weapons development program of the 1950s and 1960s, for example, indicates that Sweden's prototype nuclear bomb, on which design work was completed by 1958, was to have weighed 1,300 pounds (600 kilograms) and was to have been aerodynamically shaped to permit it to be carried on the exterior of an aircraft. It was to have had a yield of 20 kilotons. By 1965, Swedish specialists had repeatedly tested all of the key components of the weapon, except the nuclear core, and had gained high confidence that the design would work. Sweden's nuclear weapons program was terminated in 1968, although some relevant experimental work continued until 1972. See Christer Larsson, "Build a Bomb!" *Ny Teknik*, April 25, 1985.

Similar results probably could be achieved by Israel, which is thought to have been working on nuclear weapons designs since the mid-1960s, though it is not known to have conducted a test; by India, which tested a single nuclear explosive in 1974; by Pakistan, which is said to have obtained nuclear-weapons design assistance from China but has not tested; and by South Africa. Indeed, photographs taken by former Israeli technician Mordechai Vanunu which he claims are of a model of an Israeli atomic weapon core, show it to be about five inches across, indicating a compact weapon, easily within the 1,000- to 2,000-pound range. In early 1988 it was reported that Pakistan, using a Chinese design, had developed a device weighing only 400 pounds, and earlier reports stated that Pakistan had sought to purchase thirteen-inch steel hemispheres in Western Europe to serve as the skeleton for its atomic bomb, again suggestive of a relatively small device. See Hedrick Smith, "A Bomb Ticks in Pakistan," *New York Times Magazine*, March 6, 1988, p. 38. India's 1974 nuclear test device, which used plutonium as its core, is said to have been, roughly half the diameter of the first U.S. plutonium bomb, and further miniaturization in the thirteen years since India's test would be well within New Delhi's capabilities. (Little is known about South Africa's possible nuclear weapons designs.) Concerning Israel's missiles, see note 5 and accompanying text.

5. "Israel Said to Deploy Jericho Missile," *Aerospace Daily,* May 1, 1985; "Nuclear Efforts of Israel, Pakistan Prompt Meeting of U.S. Group," *Aerospace Daily*, May 7, 1985.

6. Thomas L. Friedman, "Soviet Cautions Israel Against a New Missile," *New York Times*, July 29, 1987. The missile was test-fired for a distance of 500 miles in the Mediterranean Sea and is said to have a range of 900 miles. See Thomas W. Netter, "Israel Reported to Test New Longer-Range Missile," *New York Times*, July 22, 1987.

7. Stephen R. Wilson, "Capable of Developing Long-Range Missiles," Associated Press, AM cycle, March 18, 1984; Radhakrishna Rao, "India's Launch Vehicle Program Moves Ahead," *Space World,* December 29, 1983, p. 29; "A Military Option," *Nature* (December 1981): 507.

8. Tyler Marshall, "India Launches Its First Space Satellite," *Los Angeles Times,* July 19, 1980 (950 miles); "India Becomes 6th Country to Put Satellite in Orbit," *Washington Post,* July 18, 1980 (950 miles); "India's Rocket Could Meet Military Ambitions," *New Scientist,* August 26, 1982 (1,550 miles); Noel Robbins, "Experts Say Satellite Could Be Turned into Nuclear Missile," United Press International, PM cycle, April 18, 1983 (1,550 miles).

9. It is assumed that modifying the SLV-3 and ASLV for nuclear delivery would entail using lower trajectories to permit larger payloads and, possibly, replacing the fourth stage and payload with a nuclear warhead and re-entry vehicle, which could weigh up to 8,800 pounds by one estimate. Radhakrishna Rao, "India's Launch Vehicle Program Moves Ahead," *Space World* (December 1983): 29. A second launch of the ASLV has been scheduled for the summer of 1988. ASLV is an abbreviation for Augmented Satellite Launch Vehicle.

10. "India Aims for Self-Sufficiency in Space," *Space Flight,* June 14, 1986; Maurice Eisenstein, "Third World Missiles and Nuclear Proliferation," *Washington Quarterly* (Summer 1982): 113.

11. "Indian Missile Tests," *Jane's Defense Weekly,* May 16, 1987, p. 931; Aaron Karp, "Ballistic Missile Development," *Journal of Defense and Diplomacy* (December 1987): 15; Richard Weintraub, "India Succeeds in Missile Test Launching," *Washington Post,* Feburary 26, 1988. Indian spokesmen claim the missile is highly accurate. It has been flight-tested to 93 miles and is expected eventually to have a substantially longer range. "Shooting Ahead," *India Today,* March 31, 1988, p. 96.

12. "Pak Might Launch Satellite in '88," *News India* (quoting Karachi Radio), September 11, 1987; Press Trust of India, May 12, 1987. U.S. export controls are discussed below.

13. *South Africa Sunday Times,* Johannesburg, July 20, 1986.

14. John Cushman, "Iraqi Missile Attacks on Iran," *New York Times,* March 2, 1988; Charles P. Wallace, "Iraq, in First Such Attack, Fires Missiles at Iranian Holy City of Qom," *Washington Post,* March 3, 1988. Iraq also is said to have Soviet SS-12s, able to carry a 2750-pound (1250 kilogram) warhead more than 350 miles. Patrick Tyler, "Iraq Targets Bigger Missile on Tehran," *Washington Post,* March 28, 1988.

15. "Iraq Severs Relations with Libya," *Financial Times,* June 27, 1985.

16. John Barham, "Brazil Ignores U.S. Protest Over Arms for Libya," *Sunday Times* (London), January 31, 1988; "Tactical Missile Development Reported," *O Globo*, January 3, 1988, translated in *FBIS/Latin America (LAT)*, January 5, 1988, p. 21.

17. Tony Walker, "Argentina, Egypt in Long-Range Missile Project," *Financial Times*, December 21, 1987. North Korea is said to be a conduit for Chinese Scud-Bs. It is not clear whether it can independently produce the missile, although its reported collaboration with Egypt in the manufacture of the rocket suggests that it can. This would make North Korea yet another independent supplier of the missile.

18. *IISS Military Balance 1987-1988*, (London: International Institute of Strategic Studies, 1987), p. 146. The M-9 is said to have a range between 125 and 375 miles. Production is expected to commence in 1989. Interviews with the author, Washington, D.C., June 1988. Concerning the M-11, which was displayed at an arms exhibit in Chile in April 1988, see "China's M-11 Is Revealed," *Jane's Defense Weekly*, April 9, 1988, p. 655.

19. The missile is referred to as the CSS-2 by the U.S. government and as the DF-3A by China. David Ottoway, "U.S. Asks Soviets, Chinese to Cease Ballistic Missile Sales in the Middle East," *Washington Post*, May 26, 1988; Doug Rabnif, "Fallout from Saudi Missiles," *Christian Science Monitor*, March 30, 1988; "Testimony of Richard Murphy, Assistant Secretary of State for Near Eastern and South Asian Affairs," before the Subcommittee on Arms Control, International Security, and Science, and the Subcommittee on Europe and the Middle East of the House Committee on Foreign Affairs, May 10, 1988 (mimeo).

20. Glenn Frankel, "Israeli Economy Depends on No-Questions-Asked Arms Sales," *Washington Post*, December 12, 1986; "South Africa May Reportedly Test Atomic Weapons," United Press International, AM cycle, December 26, 1986.

21. Manfredi *et al.*, "Ballistic Missile Proliferation," pp. 26-28, compiling sources (see note 2); "Tactical Missile Development Reported," *O Globo*, (see note 16); Alan Elsner, "Arms Expert Says Iraq Could Soon Have Ballistic Missiles," Reuters, AM cycle, December 15, 1987. Iraq is said to be financing the Avibras SS-300 project. See Karp, "Ballistic Missile Development" (see note 11). Libya reportedly is financing the Orbita missiles. See Barham, "Brazil Ignores U.S. Protest Over Arms for Libya," (see note 16).

22. See the section on Brazil in Chapter V, below.

23. Argentina is currently developing a multi-purpose (space launch/ tactical) missile, the Alacran. Referred to in some sources as the Condor II, the Alacran is a two-stage rocket that can carry a 2,000-pound warhead 125 miles into space. (See chart at the end of this

chapter.)

24. "600 Km. Surface-to-Surface Missile Test 3 Aug." Baghdad Voice of the Masses, translated in *FBIS/NES*, August 4, 1987, p. K-1. Iran claimed to have found Soviet markings in the debris from some of the Iraqi attacks on Tehran, but the Soviet Union denied that it had modified the Scuds it had transferred to Iraq and stated that it had not granted Baghdad permission to alter the rockets itself. Questions remain as to whether Iraq has obtained outside assistance, possibly from Brazil or East Germany, in modifying its Scuds. See David Remnick, "Iranians Mob Soviet Embassy," *Washington Post*, March 7, 1988; "Gulf War Missile Barrage Upsets Soviet Iran Ties," *Financial Times*, March 8, 1988; "East German/Iraqi Military Aid," *Current News*, March 23, 1988 (U.S. Department of Defense), p. 12.

Concerning the 560-mile flight test, see Bernard E. Trainor, "Iraqi Missile With Extended Range Is Peril to Iran's Cities and Oil," *New York Times*, May 1, 1988. Regarding Iraq's SS-12s, see Patrick Tyler, "Iraq Targets Bigger Missile on Tehran," (see note 14).

25. The exact role that nuclear missiles might play in a nation's nuclear forces would depend on a number of factors, among them the accuracy of the missiles. If an emerging nuclear power could be confident only that its missiles would be able to hit its adversary's cities, it would most likely reserve the system for use as a last-resort deterrent. In contrast, if the missiles were sufficiently accurate to hit military targets, such as airfields, they might be employed to achieve tactical objectives during a conflict.

26. "Nuclear Efforts of Israel, Pakistan Prompt Meeting of U.S. Group," *Aerospace Daily* (see note 5).

27. Gideon Rafael, "Syria and Israel: Too Near the Brink of a New War," *International Herald Tribune*, January 15, 1987.

28. "Nixon Reveals Four Times He Pondered Nuclear Bomb," *New York Times*, July 23, 1985.

29. Trainor, "Iraqi Missile With Extended Range Is Peril To Iran's Cities and Oil," (see note 24); "Sources View Iraqi Missiles as 'Direct' Threat," *Hadashot*, August 5, 1987, translated in *FBIS/NES*, August 5, 1987, p. L-1.

30. "Missile Technology Control Regime," United States Department of Defense Fact Sheet, April 16, 1987. As noted below, the United States has had a long-standing unilateral policy of strictly controlling transfers of missile and launch vehicle technology.

31. Michael Brzoska and Thomas Ohlson, eds., *Arms Production in the Third World*, (London and Philadelphia: Taylor and Francis, 1986), p. 223.

32. Michael Dunn, "Israel: Jericho II and the Nuclear Arsenal," *De-*

fense and Foreign Affairs Daily, May 9, 1985.

33. *Ibid.* The episode is discussed in the section on Israel in Chapter IV, below.

34. "Launch Assistance for Space Satellite Projects" (National Security Decision Memorandum—NSDM-187, 1972), *Weekly Compilation of Presidential Documents*, Vol. 8, No. 42 (October 16, 1972), cited in Aaron Karp, "Ballistic Missiles in the Third World," *International Security* (Winter 1984/85): 178.

35. Interview with former U.S. official. The official noted that the consensus among U.S. policymakers at the time was that, as a liquid-fueled rocket, the Thor-Delta had minimal military utility for Japan. See also Karp, "Ballistic Missiles," (see note 34), which states that launchers themselves were transferred.

36. Letter from Arnold W. Frutkin, Assistant Administrator for International Affairs, National Aeronautics and Space Administration, to Dr. Homi Bhabha, Chairman, Indian Atomic Energy Commission, March 10, 1965 (author's files).

37. See, *e.g.*, Eisenstein, "Third World Missiles and Nuclear Proliferation," (see note 10).

38. Mark Balaschak, *et al.*, "Assessing the Comparability of Dual-Use Technologies for Ballistic Missile Development," Report for U.S. Arms Control and Disarmament Agency, Contract No. AC0WC113 (Cambridge, MA: Center for International Studies, Massachusetts Institute of Technology, June 1981), pp. 56-60. The U.S.-supplied Thor-Delta technology was not available from Japan, however, since the relevant U.S.-Japan agreement prohibited retransfer of the technology without U.S. approval.

39. *Ibid.* p. 53.

40. "Missiles," *Interavia* (February 1984): 154; David Velupillai, "ISRO: India's Ambitious Space Agency," *Flight International*, June 28, 1980, p. 1468.

41. "Liquid Fuel Engine Tested for PSLV," *Hindustan Times,* December 13, 1985.

42. H. P. Mama, "India Joins the Space Club," *Interavia* (April 1976): 376.

43. *Ibid.*

44. H. Ottl, W. Muller, and Y. S. Rajan, "Overview of Indo-German Collaboration in the Area of Space Research and Applications" in DFVLR/ISRO Colloquium about a Decade of Cooperation in the Field of Space Research and Technology, January 27, 1982, in Bangalore, India (DFVLR-Mitt 83-03), pp. 22-25.

45. *Ibid.*

46. Jayme Boscov, Jose Alberto Bernardes, Tokiashi Yoshino, and B. M. Furlan, "Sonda IV Brazilian Rocket: The Major Step for the Future National Satellite Launcher," *Proceedings of the American*

Institute of Aeronautics and Astronautics, 1986, p. 150; courses of instruction were compiled from DFVLR annual reports.

47. Theo Pirard, "Brazil in Space," *Spaceflight*, June 6, 1980, p. 239.
48. 'Problems, Achievements in Programs with Argentina, PRC," *Technologia & Defensa*, 1986, translated in *Joint Publications Research Service/Nuclear Development and Proliferation (JPRS/TND)*, November 17, 1986, p. 18.
49. Interview with knowledgeable U.S. officials; Jayme Boscov *et al.*, "Brazilian Rocket," p. 150 (see note 46).
50. "Avibras, Engesa Missile Projects Described," *Fôhla de São Paulo*, January 11, 1987.
51. Brzoska and Ohlson, *Arms Production in the Third World*, p. 223 (see note 31).
52. Manfredi *et al.*, "Ballistic Missile Proliferation," p. 41 (see note 2).
53. James A. Russell, "U.S. Firms to Aid Indian Jet Effort," *Defense Week*, May 4, 1987, p. 4.
54. "Falklands in Range of New Missile?" *International Combat Arms* (July 1985): 95; Walker, "Argentina, Egypt In Long-Range Missile Project" (see note 18), (Messerschmidt-Boelkow-Blohm assisted in Condor II project through a third-country subsidiary).
55. "O Globo: Nuclear Missiles Possible in Five Years," *O Globo*, January 13, 1986, translated in *FBIS/Latin America*, January 16, l986, p. D-l.
56. "Tactical Missile Development Reported," *O Globo*, (see note 16).
57. Balaschak *et al.*, "Assessing the Comparability of Dual-Use Technologies," pp. 38-42 (see note 38).
58. Interview with specialist in Middle East armaments.
59. Brzoska and Ohlson, *Arms Production in the Third World*, p. 245 (see note 31).
60. Manfredi *et al.*, "Ballistic Missile Proliferation Potential," p. 26 (see note 2).
61. Interview with former Reagan Administration official.
62. Portions of this section are drawn from Leonard S. Spector, "Foreign Supplied Combat Aircraft: Will They Drop the Third World Bomb?" *Journal of International Affairs* (Summer 1986): 142.
63. This assessment appears widely in the literature. See International Institute for Strategic Studies, *Strategic Survey* (London: IISS, 1974), pp. 37, 38; Jones, *Small Nuclear Forces* (see note 1); Peter Pry, *Israel's Nuclear Arsenal* (Boulder, CO: Westview Press, 1984), p. 99; Richard Burt, "Nuclear Proliferation and the Spread of New, Conventional Weapons Technology," in Stephanie G. Neuman and Robert E. Harkavy, eds., *Arms Transfers in the Modern World* (New York: Praeger, 1979).
64. This is not to say that the most capable warplane in a country's air force will automatically be selected for the nuclear delivery role.

Among other factors, military planners would have to weigh the costs of withholding such aircraft from conventional combat in order to ensure their availability for strategic nuclear missions.

65. Pry, *Israel's Nuclear Arsenal,* pp. 99-103 (see note 63).

66. ***Nuclear-Capable Aircraft – Israel***

Aircraft	Number on Hand Mid-1987	Combat Radius (Total Round Trip to Target and Return)	Equipped for In-Air Refueling?
F-15	52	660 + mi.	yes
F-16A	68	575 + mi.	yes
F-4E	128	712 mi.	yes
Kfir	135	737 mi.	some
A-4N/J	130	920 mi.	yes

All of these aircraft, with the exception of the A-4s, are capable of speeds in excess of Mach 2, and the F-15s and F-16s have the most advanced avionics in the group. Israel possesses tanker aircraft for aerial refueling.

Israel's aging subsonic U.S. A-4N/Js could, in principle, be used for nuclear missions, but they are far less capable than the more advanced aircraft noted above.

Here and in subsequent notes, "combat radius" is defined as the total distance in air a loaded aircraft can fly from base *and return* without intermediate landing or refueling. These estimates assume that the aircraft described is carrying external fuel tanks and ordnance weighing significantly in excess of 1,100 pounds (500 kilograms), the presumed minimum weight of a nuclear bomb produced by an emerging nuclear state, and that the aircraft engages in a "hi-lo-hi" ground attack mission, in which travel to and from the target vicinity occurs at high altitude in order to conserve fuel and the actual attack is conducted at a low altitude for the purpose of greater bombing precision, reduced risk of radar detection, and evasion of air defenses. Sources (for this and subsequent analyses of aircraft data): Aircraft capabilities are found chiefly in Christopher Chant, *Compendium of Armaments and Military Hardware* (New York: Routledge and Kegan Paul, Inc., 1987); Bill Gunston and Mike Spick, *Modern Air Combat* (New York: Crescent, 1983); *Jane's All the World's Aircraft 1986-1987* (London: Jane's Publishing Co., 1986) and previous volumes; and N. Krivini, *Warplanes of the World,* 1983/1984 (Annapolis. MD: Nautical and Aviation Publishing Company of America, 1983). Numbers of aircraft are from International Institute for Strategic Studies, *The Military Balance,* 1987-1988 (London: IISS, 1987).

67.   *Nuclear-Capable Aircraft – India*

Aircraft	Number on Hand Mid-1987	Combat Radius (Total Round Trip to Target and Return)	Equipped for In-Air Refueling?
Jaguar	79	875 mi.	yes
MiG-29	44	715 mi.	probably
MiG-23BN	95	560-805 mi.	no
Mirage 2000H	40	435-932 mi.	yes
MiG-27 D/J	24	497 mi.	no
MiG-27M (on order)	0	497 mi.	no
MiG-21	60	460 mi.	no
Canberra	35	805 mi.	no
Ajeet	72	107-260 mi.	no

The Jaguars, Mirage 2000Hs, and MiG-29s are among the most advanced fighter/ground-attack aircraft produced today.

Although they are less capable, India's older MiG-21 fighters and British-made Canberra bombers are still potentially usable for nuclear delivery, as is the still less capable subsonic Ajeet. India is not known to possess in-air refueling tankers.

68.   *Nuclear-Capable Aircraft – Pakistan*

Aircraft	Number on Hand Mid-1987	Combat Radius (Total Round Trip to Target and Return)	Equipped for In-Air Refueling?
F-16	39	575+	yes
Mirage 5/PA3	50	808	no? (may have been modified)
Mirage III/EP	16	745	no? (may have been modified)
J-6	170	426	no
Q-5	41	400	no

Pakistan is not known to possess aerial tankers.

Pakistan's Chinese Q-5 and J-6 warplanes are far less capable than the U.S. and French aircraft listed above.

69.

	Nuclear-Capable Aircraft – South Africa		
Aircraft	Number on Hand Mid-1987	Combat Radius (Total Round Trip to Target and Return)	Equipped for In-Air Refueling?
Mirage F-1AZ	46	863 mi.	yes
Cheetah	5-6	–	
Buccaneer	5	1,150 mi.	yes
Canberra	5	805 mi.	no

South Africa possesses in-air refueling tankers.

70. Frankel, "Israeli Economy Depends on No-Questions-Asked Arms Sales," (see note 20); "Israel Offers Re-engined Kfir," *Flight International*, April 25, 1987, p. 10. The Cheetah, however, does not use the more powerful and more fuel-efficient U.S.-built J79 engine used in the Israeli Kfir since Israel is required to obtain U.S. permission to re-export the engine, which has not been granted in this instance.

Under U.S. pressure to adhere to the U.N. embargo, Israel agreed in early 1987 not to enter into new military contracts with South Africa, although it will continue to honor existing commitments. See "Israel Will Curb Arms for Pretoria," *New York Times*, March 19, 1987. In late 1987, however, the possibility of a novel transfer of Israeli aircraft technology to South Africa emerged, as Pretoria reportedly sought to recruit 600 Israeli technicians who had worked on the development of the Lavi fighter. Israel had cancelled the project for the highly advanced fighter several months earlier as too costly. See, Hirsh Goodman, "RSA Seeking to Lure Lavi Engineers, Technicians," *Jerusalem Post*, November 9, 1987, reprinted in *FBIS/NES*, November 10, 1987, p. 44. Pretoria has denied engaging in the recruiting effort.

71. Thomas B. Cochran, William M. Arkin, and Milton M. Hoenig, *U.S. Nuclear Forces and Capabilities* (Cambridge, MA: Ballinger Publishing, 1984), pp. 30-31. The discussion here has been considerably simplified.

72. Communications with U.S. officials and supplier-country embassy officials.

73. See note 4.

74. In toss bombing, the pilot takes the aircraft into a steep climb and releases the weapon, propelling it forward in the aircraft's original direction, toward the target. The pilot continues his climbing, maneuvering into a roll that permits him to fly off in the opposite di-

rection. Toss bombing is also used to deliver conventional weapons when a pilot wishes to avoid flying directly over his target, where air defenses may be the heaviest. Thus, flight tests of this type may be a rather ambiguous indicator of nuclear arming.

75. In 1941, for example, Japan destroyed the U.S. air force in the Philippines while it was on the ground, and in 1967, Israel knocked out much of the Egyptian and Syrian air forces in similar strikes.

76. Regarding the refusal of various suppliers to sell nuclear power reactors to Israel and Pakistan, see Neal Sandler, "Israeli Nuclear Community Covets Elusive French Reactors," *Nucleonics Week*, February 14, 1985, p. 3; and "While the Pakistani Atomic Energy Commission has Postponed the Deadline . . . ," *Nucleonics Week*, November 10, 1983, p. 8.

77. Senate Committee on Foreign Relations, *Hearings on the Israeli Air Strike*, 97th Cong., 1st sess., June 18, 19, and 25, 1981. The bombing was apparently conducted by F-16s, with the F-15s flying as escort.

78. Hedrick Smith, "U.S. Assumes Israelis Have A-bomb or Its Parts," *New York Times*, July 18, 1970.

79. U.S. Nuclear Regulatory Commission, *Inquiry into the Testimony of the Executive Director for Operations*, Vol. III (Interviews), February 7, 1978, p. 178. (Released under the Freedom of Information Act to the Natural Resources Defense Council).

80. Senate Committee on Foreign Relations, *Hearings on Aid and the Proposed Arms Sales of F-16s to Pakistan*, 97th Cong., 1st Sess., November 12 and 17, 1981.

81. Enforcing restrictions on South Africa's use of imported aircraft would be particularly difficult since the advanced suppliers have already embargoed military sales to Pretoria, and thus do not have the leverage they have in other cases, where they would be able to condition future sales on the acceptance of these restraints retroactively.

82. The United States, it may be noted, already imposes restrictions on the use of American-supplied aircraft, for example, prohibiting their use for offensive purposes and their transfer to third parties. (U.S. retransfer controls also apply to the Israeli-built Kfir because it uses the American J79 engine.) Thus, the suggested restrictions against the nuclearization of American aircraft would not constitute a complete departure from current practice.

Past enforcement of the no-offensive-use restriction has been erratic. In 1974, the United States halted military tranfers to Turkey in response to the Turkish invasion of Cyprus the same year. Restrictions on transfers were lifted completely in 1978, despite the continued presence of Turkish forces on the island. Conversely, except for the brief delay in F-16 deliveries, the United States did not penalize Israel's use of U.S. aircraft to destroy the Osiraq reactor outside Baghdad in 1981. Despite this record, these restrictions impose useful political restraints on recipients of U.S. military equipment.

83. The case of Israel would present special difficulties since, presumably, it has already prepared some U.S.-supplied aircraft for nuclear missions. Nonetheless, a prohibition on the use for nuclear missions of U.S. warplanes supplied in the future could be a valuable restraint. This would preclude Israel from using the most up-to-date versions of U.S. warplanes—*i.e.* those with the most advanced avionics and electronic warfare equipment—for this purpose and could gradually limit Israel's delivery capabilities as the aircraft it has already adapted for nuclear use become obsolete or are lost through attrition.

84. President Ronald Reagan to Senate Majority Leader Howard H. Baker, Jr., October 28, 1981, as reprinted in *Congressional Quarterly*, October 31, 1981, p. 2135; communications with U.S. officials.

These restrictions, moreover, would complement and strengthen existing non-proliferation conditions on U.S. aid, while overlapping them only slightly. U.S. law currently requires the cessation of American economic and military assistance to any non-nuclear-weapon state that detonates a nuclear explosive device. This after-the-fact sanction is aimed at deterring both nuclear testing and nuclear use. Since it is widely believed that near-nuclear states would not have to test a nuclear weapon to have high confidence that it would work, however, this restriction does not prevent their development of a ready nuclear arsenal. The additional restriction on aid to Pakistan, specifically, which requires that the president certify that Pakistan does not "possess" a nuclear explosive device, goes further but would still permit Pakistan to reach the point of being only "a screwdriver turn" away from deployable nuclear arms. Under either limitation, if aircraft had been readied in advance for nuclear delivery, the near-nuclear aid recipient could still develop a high-performance, quick-response nuclear force that would greatly raise the stakes of any future conflict. The restrictions proposed here, however, could impede recipients from preparing their most capable potential delivery systems in advance.

Chapter III:
Asia – Introduction

1. According to the report of the House International Relations Committee on its 1978 investigation into Korean-American relations ("Koreagate"),

> There are indications in the early 1970's, some steps were taken which appeared designed to pave the way for an ROK [Republic of Korea] nuclear-weapons program. Specifics on this matter came from a subcommittee staff interview (on February 28, 1978) with a former high-ranking Korean Government official who was a member of the WEC [the secret Weapons Exploitation Committee of senior Korean officials]. He told the subcommittee that the WEC voted unanimously to proceed with the development of nuclear weapons. Subsequently, the Korean Government discussed purchase of a nuclear fuel reprocessing facility from France and a mixed-oxide fuel reprocessing lab from Belgium. The explosion of an Indian nuclear device in April 1974 using fissionable material produced with the assistance of a Canadian NRX research reactor led to greater caution by nuclear technology suppliers, however, and the Belgians and the Canadians withdrew offers for certain technology. Negotiations between the ROK and France continued for some time over a reprocessing facility. Ultimately, it appears that by some time in 1975, any ROK nuclear weapons program had been canceled and the negotiations for purchase of a fuel reprocessing facility also ended.

See U.S. Congress, House Committee on International Relations, Subcommittee on International Organizations, *Investigation of Korean-American Relations*, 95th Cong., 2nd Sess., 1978, p. 80.

A lengthy news report following up the House investigation of these matters suggested that Korea, in addition to negotiating the purchase of the reprocessing plant, had acquired numerous other components needed for nuclear weapons. The report quotes a "government arms-control analyst" as saying that the reprocessing plant was "practically the last thing on the list of things they needed, from special machine tools to the non-nuclear components of weapons. . . . They were running all over the world picking up material and equipment." According to the report:

> Shortly after the Indian test, a small group of intelligence and technical experts, including one from the U.S. Atomic Energy Commission, is said to have begun canvassing U.S. embassies for signs of similar activities on the part of governments considered likely to seek nuclear weapons. The basic approach was to search embassy files for requests by foreign governments to import materials and equipment on a "critical list" of items considered indicative of an interest in atomic weapons. Among these items, sources said, were such things as equipment for machining plutonium metal, bulk orders of beryllium and boron, and exotic, explosive chemicals and shaped-charge technology needed to detonate fission weapons.

"When they got to Korea, everything snapped into place," the analyst said. Simply by rummaging through embassy files for references to material and equipment that the Korean government had sought to import from U.S. industry and through military channels, a "substantial number" of items on the critical list came to light.

See Robert Gillette, "U.S. Squelched Apparent S. Korea A-Bomb Drive," *Los Angeles Times*, November 4, 1978.

2. Peter Hayes, "South Korean Nuclear Trade," in William Potter, ed., *The Emerging Nuclear Suppliers and Non-Proliferation* (forthcoming). Hayes also quotes an unnamed former U.S. ambassador to South Korea as stating that Seoul never dismantled the facilities set up to pursue the weapons option, but merely stopped operating them.

3. *Ibid.*

4. *Ibid.* Hayes cites (i) confidential U.S. sources, (ii) John Taylor, "Ottawa Denies U.S. Killed A-Deal," *Globe and Mail*, October 16, 1984, and (iii) the transcript of a Canadian Broadcasting Company "Sunday Morning" program (the last being the source for the allegation that South Korea was seeking plutonium extraction know-how). See also, David Albright, "World Inventories of Plutonium" (Working Paper), Federation of American Scientists, citing T. Shorrock and O. Gadacz, "U.S. Intervention in Nuclear Fuel Project Still a Mystery," *Business Korea* (April 1985): 47.

5. Shin Ho-Chul, "North Korea Signs NPT and Soviets Agree to Supply Nuclear Plant," *Nucleonics Week*, January 2, 1986.

6. Israel confronted a situation somewhat similar to this in 1981, when Iraq was about to begin operating a 40-megawatt research reactor and a plutonium separation laboratory (albeit it a very small one, but one which it might have expanded subsequently). Israel perceived the threat from this latent capability to be so grave that it launched an air raid on the Iraqi reactor and destroyed it. (See the section on Iraq in Chapter IV.)

7. In March 1986, for example, South Korean President Chun Doo Hwan cautioned that another Korean war might be on the horizon. Defense Minister Lee Ki Baek pointed out that such a conflict might be precipitated by North Korea's military buildup, an augmentation that included Soviet-supplied MiG-23 aircraft and Scud-B ground-to-ground missiles. A September bomb explosion at Seoul's international airport further heightened tensions, as South Korea immediately associated the detonation with North Korean attempts to disrupt the Asian Games to be held in Seoul. See "South Korean President Warns of War Risk," *Washington Times*, March 19, 1986; Steven Butler, "Seoul Warns That North Korea Is Readying for War," *Financial Times*, March 21, 1986; John Burgess, "Games Seen Target of S. Korean Attack," *Washington Post*,

September 15, 1986. On more recent trends, see, *e.g.*, Maggie Ford, "Korean Reunification Back on the Agenda," *Financial Times*, December 10, 1987.

8. The NPT, for example, requires all parties to ensure that their nuclear exports will be placed under IAEA safeguards in the recipient state, and this is also required under the Nuclear Supplier Group Guidelines. China has not adhered to either, but these accords are so widely accepted that they have effectively set the rules of international nuclear trade.

Reportedly, China sold, without requiring IAEA safeguards, 3 percent-enriched uranium to South Africa (possibly through intermediaries); 20 percent-enriched uranium to Argentina; and heavy water to Argentina and possibly to South Africa and India as well. See Jack Anderson, "CIA Says China Has Sent A-Fuel to South Africa," *Washington Post*, July 23, 1981; Judith Miller, "U.S. Is Holding Up Peking Atom Talks," *New York Times*, September 19, 1982; Rob Laufer, "Interview with Malone: Defense of Policy and Assessment of 'Hot Spots,' " *Nucleonics Week*, August 19, 1982, p. 1. China denied making the uranium sales. See Christopher S. Wren, "China Denies Selling Uranium to South Africa," *New York Times*, September 26, 1982. However, it acknowledged exporting "a limited quantity of nuclear materials," for which it required recipients to pledge that they would "never transfer the nuclear materials to a third country, particularly South Africa and Israel, or use the same for non-peaceful purposes." See Warren Donnelly and Carol Eberhard, "U.S. Nuclear Cooperation with the People's Republic of China," Issue Brief IB83149, Congressional Research Service, December 27, 1983, p. CRS-4, citing China News Service. The statement did not mention that China had required IAEA safeguards on these transfers, thus leaving unchallenged at least this part of the press accounts.

Regarding China's prior non-proliferation policies, see Kenneth Adelman, Director, Arms Control and Disarmament Agency, "Non-Proliferation Assessment Statement for the Peaceful Nuclear Cooperation Agreement between the United States and China," July 19, 1985.

See also Gary Milhollin, "Dateline New Delhi: India's Nuclear Cover-up," *Foreign Policy* (Fall 1986):161, surmising that China was the source of unsafeguarded Indian heavy water imports.

9. Milton R. Benjamin, "China Aids Pakistan on A-Weapons," *Washington Post*, February 28, 1983; Leslie H.Gelb, "Pakistan Link Perils U.S.-China Nuclear Pact," *New York Times*, June 22, 1984; Miller, "U.S. Is Holding Up Peking Atom Talks" (see note 8); Simon Henderson, "Why Pakistan May Not Need to Test a Nu-

clear Device," *Financial Times*, August 14, 1984.

See also testimony of Richard T. Kennedy, *Hearings on Review of 1985 U.S. Government Non-proliferation Activities*, U.S. Senate Subcommittee on Energy, Nuclear Proliferation, and Government Processes, Committee on Governmental Affairs, April 10, 1986, (Washington: Government Printing Office, 1986), p.17. (China and Pakistan have engaged in nuclear cooperation for years; only non-military cooperation may be continuing.)

10. Adelman, "Non-Proliferation Assessment Statement," p. I-5, (see note 8). Premier Zhao's statement was endorsed by the Congress, the Chinese government's highest vehicle for the pronouncement of public policy.

11. Gelb, "Pakistan Link Perils U.S.-China Nuclear Pact" (see note 9); communications with U.S. officials.

12. Adelman, "Non-Proliferation Assessment Statement," p. I-5, (see note 8). The details of the U.S.-Chinese understanding on the matter are contained in a classified note submitted by the Reagan Administration to Congress along with the agreement. The document is said to contain a U.S.-prepared summary of oral understandings reached between U.S. and Chinese negotiators. Apparently China has not signed the document but has not objected to its being used by U.S. officials to characterize China's position.

13. Daniel Southerland, "U.S., China Sign Accords," *Washington Post*, August 28, 1985. It appears that some unsafeguarded transfers of Chinese nuclear materials to Argentina and possibly South Africa continued into 1985, although these were supposedly based on pre-existing contracts. China also apparently held talks with Iran on nuclear trade, although these appear to have been limited to providing possible assistance in the construction of two partially completed nuclear power plants in Iran. See Patrick Tyler, "Hill Panels Add Conditions to U.S.-China Nuclear Pact," *Washington Post*, November 14, 1985. In an unusual twist, in November 1985, China acknowledged that it had supplied unsafeguarded heavy water to Argentina, a charge Argentina had denied the previous month. See Richard Kessler, "Premier Zhao Ziyang Appeared to Confirm that China . . . ," *Nucleonics Week*, November 14, 1985; Richard Kessler, "Argentina Officials Deny Any Purchases of Chinese Heavy Water," *Nucleonics Week*, October 31, 1985.

14. Atomic Energy Act of 1954, Sections 123 and 130 (1985).

15. S. J. Res. 238 (99th Cong.,1st Sess.) (1985).

16. An amendment to the fiscal year 1986 continuing appropriations bill introduced by Senator John Glenn was adopted by the U.S. Senate on December 9, 1985, but later dropped from the legislation by the House-Senate conference on the bill. See *Congressional*

Record, 99th Cong., 2nd Sess., December 9, 1985, pp. S17141-17163.

17. "U.S., China Agree on Visitation Rights, Clearing the Way for Nuclear Exports," *Nuclear Fuel*, June 29, 1987, p. 11.

18. James P. Sterba, "China's Great Leap Backward?: China Dashes Sales Hopes of Foreign Nuclear Firms," *Wall Street Journal*, April 25, 1986.

19. "Pakistan and China Signed a Comprehensive Agreement for Cooperation," *Nucleonics Week*, September 25, 1986, p. 3; Simon Henderson, "China May Help Build Pakistan's N. Bomb," *Financial Times*, September 29, 1986 (in interview, Pakistani nuclear aide Dr. A. Q. Khan says the pact covers "all nuclear activities.")

20. Stephen Engleberg and Michael Gordon, "Taipei Halts Work on Secret Plant to Make Nuclear Bomb Ingredient," *New York Times*, March 23, 1988; R. Jeffrey Smith and Don Oberdorfer, "Taiwan to Close Nuclear Reactor," *Washington Post*, March 24, 1988.

Washington is said to have learned of the clandestine installation from the deputy director of Taiwan's Institute for Nuclear Energy Research, Colonel Chang Hsien-Yi, who disappeared from Taiwan in January 1988, reportedly with the help of the U.S. Central Intelligence Agency (CIA). See references above. A U.S. visit to the site where the clandestine plutonium unit was being built is said to have confirmed Chang's information.

U.S. officials dismissed the notion that the construction of the plutonium unit might have been a rogue operation undertaken by Taiwanese nuclear aides without higher authorization. (Interview with author, March 1988.)

Taiwan has one of the largest nuclear power programs in the developing world, with six operating nuclear power reactors, all supplied by the United States, which provide 43 percent of the country's electricity. For an overview, see "Datafile: Taiwan," *Nuclear Engineering International* (December 1987): 18.

21. It is not clear how Taiwan could have bypassed IAEA controls, given the considerable quantity of spent fuel that it would have had to divert in order to obtain a bomb's worth of plutonium. Assuming that the plutonium in each spent fuel rod represented .004 of its total weight, to obtain 11 pounds (5 kilograms) of the material, well over a ton (2,750 pounds or 1,250 kilograms) of spent fuel would have had to have been diverted for reprocessing. Since the IAEA would have periodically inspected the reactor to determine its output and the whereabouts of all spent fuel and would have used surveillance cameras and seals to keep track of activities between inspections, diverting this much material would not have been easy.

22. State Department Regular Briefing, 12:15 EST, March 23, 1988.

Safeguards would be violated if spent fuel were moved from a safeguarded storage area to a unit not covered by the IAEA.

23. Engleberg and Gordon, "Taipei Halts Work on Secret Plant" (see note 20.)

24. In the late 1960s and particularly during the mid-1970s, when the United States was opening friendly relations with mainland China, Taiwan made repeated attempts, some apparently secret, to develop a reprocessing capability. Because of Taiwan's precarious security situation and the lack of any clear need for this capability as part of its nuclear energy program, U.S. officials came to believe that these efforts were aimed at eventually producing plutonium for nuclear weapons.

In 1969, for example, Taiwan sought to buy a reprocessing plant from the United States, but the Nixon Administration denied this request and barred U.S.firms from selling key components for such a plant. See Edward Schumacher, "Taiwan Seen Reprocessing Nuclear Fuel," *Washington Post*, August 29, 1976. Taiwan then turned to other possible suppliers—including Belgium and France, from whom it sought to purchase a large reprocessing facility. When the United States intervened, discussions on the sales were broken off. France, however, apparently supplied a number of components useful for a reprocessing facility. See Steven R. Weisman and Herbert Krosney, *The Islamic Bomb* (New York: Times Books, 1981), pp. 152-153.

From 1974 to 1976, Taiwan tried to negotiate an agreement with Great Britain for the reprocessing of Taiwanese spent fuel in England and the return of the plutonium to Taiwan. Once again, the United States stepped in, this time to insist that any plutonium produced under this arrangement be shipped to the United States instead. See Melinda Liu, "Accounting for the N-Factor," *Far Eastern Economic Review*, December 17, 1976, p. 33.

By 1974, the U.S. CIA had concluded:

Taipei conducts its small nuclear program with a weapon option in mind, and it will be in a position to fabricate a nuclear device after five years or so. Taipei's role in the world is changing radically, and concern over the possibility of complete isolation is mounting. Its decisions will be much influenced by U.S. policies in two key areas—support for the island's security and attitudes about the possibility of a nuclear-armed Taiwan. Taipei's present course probably is leading it toward development of nuclear weapons.

See CIA, "Prospects for Further Proliferation of Nuclear Weapons," DCINIO 1945/74, Sanitized Copy, September 4, 1974, released to the Natural Resources Defense Council under the Freedom of Information Act (author's files).

Despite U.S. interventions, by 1975 Taiwan was constructing a hot cell facility (a laboratory-scale reprocessing unit) on its own. The facility was apparently constructed with components purchased from around the world, including some from France. See Schumacher, "Taiwan Seen Reprocessing Nuclear Fuel." Although the facility was capable of separating only small amounts of plutonium, it would have provided Taiwan with valuable experience in this field. In that year, Taiwan asked the United States for permission to reprocess a small amount of spent fuel from a U.S.-supplied research reactor in Taiwan, but the United States did not reply to the inquiry. See Don Oberdorfer, "Taiwan to Curb A-Role," *Washington Post*, September 23, 1976.

In 1976, reports surfaced that Taiwan may have been secretly extracting plutonium from spent fuel at a clandestine reprocessing facility of some kind. See Schumacher, "Taiwan Seen Reprocessing Nuclear Fuel;" Oberdorfer, "Taiwan to Curb A-Role." Although in congressional hearings U.S. officials stated that no reprocessing had actually taken place and that such a facility had not, in fact, been built, U.S. suspicions over Taiwan's activities in this area became so intense that the Ford Administration insisted Taiwan cease all activities in the reprocessing field, dismantle the hot-cell laboratory, and pledge not to engage in any activities related to reprocessing. See U.S. Congress, Senate Subcommittee on Arms Control, International Organizations, and Security Agreements, *Hearings on Non-Proliferation Issues*, September 22, 1976, (Washington, D.C.: U.S. Government Printing Office, 1976), pp. 346-371.

25. Oberdorfer, "Taiwan to Curb A-Role" (see note 24). See also, Schumacher, "Taiwan Seen Reprocessing Nuclear Fuel" (see note 24).

26. Milton R. Benjamin, "Taiwan's Nuclear Plans Concern U.S. Officials," *Washington Post*, December 20, 1978.

27. Bob Woodward, *Veil: The Secret Wars of the CIA* (New York: Simon and Schuster, 1987), p. 170.

In January 1978, IAEA inspector Pierre Noir was electrocuted while repairing a video camera during an inspection visit in Taiwan. An IAEA investigation concluded that Noir's death was an accident, and it appears to bear no relationship to Taiwan's clandestine nuclear activities. Noir was inspecting a U.S.-supplied nuclear power reactor, not the Lung Tan facility, at the time of his death.

28. By 1978, Taiwan was said to have accumulated enough spent fuel to provide plutonium for a half dozen devices. See Benjamin, "Taiwan's Nuclear Plans Concern U.S. Officials," (see note 26).

29. The United States, rather than Canada, took the lead with respect to this initiative because after Canada recognized the People's Re-

public of China in 1972, its ability to intervene politically concerning the use of the Lung Tan reactor and the disposition of its spent fuel has been limited.

30. While the Reagan Administration has continued to supply Taiwan with defensive arms, it has sharply limited the types of weapons provided and their sophistication, and Beijing has pressed Washington to restrict such sales further. President Reagan's trip to China in April 1984, when he invoked Beijing as a strategic counter to Moscow, demonstrated the growing importance to Washington of Sino-U.S. relations. In 1986, the U.S. agreed to provide China with advanced defense technology for the first time, a further indication of the growing ties between the two countries, which Taiwan can only find alarming. See, *e.g.*, "Chinese Sign Record Arms Deal with U.S." *Washington Times*, November 6, 1986.

31. Among other factors, the research reactor's fuel has been irradiated for a far shorter time than power reactor fuel, so that it is far less contaminated with highly radioactive waste products that greatly complicate the plutonium extraction process; the research reactor's fuel can be completely dissolved in nitric acid in the first stage of the plutonium extraction process, while power reactor fuel, which is "clad" in non-dissolvable zirconium, must first be chopped up, a technically difficult operation; and the research reactor's fuel is smaller in size, making it easier to work with in a small-scale plutonium facility.

India

1. During a 1986 interview with the author, for example, a senior aide to Pakistani President Zia ul-Haq described his Indian counterparts as "devious Hindus."

2. This historical summary of the Indian nuclear program is based on a more detailed review found in Leonard S. Spector. *Nuclear Proliferation Today* (New York: Vintage Books, 1984), pp. 23-48.

3. The shift in India's stance began during Charan Singh's six-month tenure as prime minister, which began in July 1979. In August of that year he stated, "We do not want to join the race to make a bomb, but if Pakistan sticks to its plans to assemble a bomb, we will perhaps have to reconsider the whole question." See Michael T. Kaufman, "India Gives Warning of Atom-Arms Race," *New York Times*, August 16, 1979. Other top officials of his government made similar statements during this period.

4. Steven R. Weisman and Herbert Krosney, *The Islamic Bomb* (New York: Times Books, 1981), pp. 43-46. The authors' information comes from two participants in the key meeting, held in Multan, at which Bhutto announced that Pakistan would develop nuclear weapons.

5. For a detailed discussion of some of these activities, including a review of a number of prosecutions for the smuggling of nuclear goods to Pakistan, see Leonard S. Spector, *The New Nuclear Nations* (New York: Vintage Books, 1985), pp. 22-41.

6. See testimony of Thomas R. Pickering, Assistant Secretary of State for Oceans and International Environmental and Scientific Affairs, *Hearings on Nuclear Proliferation: The Situation in India and Pakistan*, Senate Subcommittee on Energy, Nuclear Proliferation, and Federal Services of the Committee on Governmental Affairs, May 1, 1979 (Washington, D.C.: U.S. Government Printing Office, 1979), p. 10; K.K. Sharma, "Pakistan Nuclear Pledge to India," *Financial Times*, April 9, 1979.

7. For example see testimony of Thomas R. Pickering, "India Not to Make Nuclear Arms," Delhi Domestic Service, 0240 GMT, November 20, 1985, reprinted in *Foreign Broadcast Information Service (FBIS)/South Asia*, December 2, 1985, p. C-5; "Kuwaiti Paper Interviews Prime Minister Gandhi," *Arab Times*, September 2, 1985, pp. 8-9, translated in *FBIS/South Asia*, September 4, 1985, p. E-3.

8. Spector, *The New Nuclear Nations*, pp. 92-98, (see note 5).

9. "Gandhi Says National Interest May Require Nuclear Blasts," *Washington Post*, March 14, 1980; Judith Miller, "Cranston Says India and Pakistan Are Preparing for Nuclear Testing," *New York Times*, April 28, 1981; Roger Gale, "India to Press 'Start Button' on Nuclear Fuel Reprocessing Plant," *Energy Daily*, February 5, 1981; Yogi Aggarwal, "India Makes Another Bomb," *Sunday Observer* (Bombay), August 30, 1981 (government had one atomic bomb ready in April, could prepare another one in weeks); K. Subrahmanyam, "Bomb—The Only Answer," *Times of India*, April 26, 1981, p. 1; Milton R. Benjamin, "U.S. Is Delaying Nuclear Exports to India," *Washington Post,* June 23, 1983.

10. This apparently was the view of the Pakistani Army. See Stephen P. Cohen, *The Pakistani Army* (Berkeley: University of California Press, 1984), p. 153; "Shadow of an Indian H-Bomb," *Foreign Report*, December 13, 1984, p. 1. In a 1985 interview with the author, K. Subrahmanyam, director of the Indian Institute for Defence Studies and Analyses, indicated that he assumed Mrs. Gandhi had pursued such activities because not to have done so would have been "irresponsible."

11. See chart at end of chapter. The Cirus research reactor is also unsafeguarded. India, however, is legally prohibited from using its output for nuclear weapons.

12. See Tables 1 and 2.

13. Rick Atkinson, "3 Pakistanis Indicted on A-Arms Charges," *Washington Post*, July 17, 1984; Leslie Gelb, "Peking Said to Balk at Atom Pledges," *New York Times*, June 23, 1984.

14. The accounts were based on a U.S. intelligence briefing to a congressional committee. The report was originally carried by ABC News; Don Oberdorfer, "U.S. Sees India-Pakistan Rifts Not As Signals of Imminent War," *Washington Post*, September 15, 1984; Don Oberdorfer, "Pakistan Concerned about Attack on Atomic Plants," *Washington Post*, October 12, 1984. India was reportedly considering such a raid as early as 1982. See Milton R. Benjamin, "India Said to Eye Raid on Pakistani A-Plants," *Washington Post*, December 20, 1982.

15. "Paper Assesses Pakistani Umbrella Proposal," *Indian Express*, October 15, 1984, reprinted in *FBIS/South Asia*, October 29, 1984, p. E-3; William K. Stevens, "India Worried by U.S. Links to Pakistan," *New York Times*, October 21, 1984.

16. "People's Expectations Are Scary," *India Today*, February 15, 1985, p. 8; "Gandhi on Nuclear Weapons, Sri Lanka, Punjab," Delhi Domestic Service, 0240 GMT, January 31, 1985, reprinted in *FBIS/South Asia*, January 31, 1985, p. E-1; John Elliott, "We've Got Five Years," *Financial Times*, April 4, 1985; "Defense Ministry Security Report Raps Pakistan," Delhi Domestic Service, 1530 GMT April 16, 1985, reprinted in *FBIS/South Asia*, April 17, 1985, p. G-1; "India to Review Nuclear Policy, Gandhi Says," *Washington Post*, May 5, 1985; "Congress-I Party Meets in New Delhi," *FBIS/South Asia*, May 6, 1985.

17. *"Le Monde* Interview," *Le Monde*, June 4, 1985, translated in *FBIS/South Asia*, June 5, 1985, p. E-1, emphasis added. Gandhi's subsequent statements have not repeated this incautious assertion.

18. John Scali, "Good Morning America," American Broadcasting Company, July 11, 1985.

19. Rone Tempest, "India Starts Up New Reactor That Can Make Arms-Grade Plutonium," *Los Angeles Times*, August 9, 1985; "New Delhi Says It Can Make Plutonium from Indian Fuel," *New York Times*, August 9, 1985; Swaminathan S. Aiyar, "Dhruva Reactor an N-Bomb Spinner," *Indian Express*, August 10, 1985. Earlier official descriptions of the reactor, in contrast, had stressed its use for medical isotope production and engineering research. See "New Reactor Capable of Producing Plutonium," Agence France Presse, 0905 GMT, August 8, 1985, reprinted in *FBIS/South Asia*, August 9, 1985, p. E-1.

20. Mohamed Aftab, "Pakistan Concern Over India's Nuclear Move," *Financial Times*, August 8, 1985; "India Can Make 30 N-Bombs a Year," *Pakistan Times Overseas Weekly*, August 18, 1985; "Karachi Raps India's Nuclear Plans, 'Propaganda,' " Karachi Domestic Service, 1715 GMT, August 11, 1985, reprinted in *FBIS/South Asia*, August 13, 1985, p. F-1; *"The Muslim* on India's Nuclear Capabilities," August 13, 1985, (editorial) reprinted in *FBIS/South Asia*, August 21, 1985, p. F-1.

21. The issue of bilateral treaties to establish a foundation for better relations has a long and tortuous history. A no-war declaration was proposed by Indian Prime Minister Jawaharlal Nehru to Pakistani Prime Minister Liaquat Ali Khan in 1959. Liaquat wanted some tangible action to match the declaration, but Nehru thought a declaration would suffice.

A no-war proposal was again introduced by India in 1965, when Prime Minister Lal Bahadur Shastri sought one with regard to Kashmir. Pakistani President Muhammad Ayub Khan refused.

Pakistan next proposed a no-war pact with India in September 1981. The original offer was dismissed by India as a propaganda ploy by which Pakistan hoped to gain additional aid and support from the United States. India argued that Pakistan offered the pact only after "arming to the teeth."

In August 1982, India made a counter-offer of a treaty of peace and friendship, stating that a more comprehensive agreement was necessary, including provisions regarding trade, travel, tourism, etc. But Pakistan has been leery of such broad proposals, fearing that they will only solidify India's regional pre-eminence.

The principal issues currently in dispute in these negotiations are India's demand that Pakistan agree not to allow any foreign bases on its soil and that it agree to the resolution of outstanding disputes through bilateral negotiations. Pakistan, though stating it has no intention of allowing foreign bases, objects to India's attempt to dictate its foreign policy; Pakistan has also been unwilling to give up recourse to multilateral fora, including the United Nations, for settling the Kashmir dispute.

Another Pakistani proposal, which does not appear to have elicited any Indian interest, was for bilateral talks on a mutually acceptable ratio of conventional forces and armaments. This was informally suggested in 1979 and reiterated by Pakistan at the United Nations in 1981.

22. "Report on Kahuta Denied," Karachi Domestic Service, 1703 GMT, September 30, 1985, reprinted in *Joint Publications Research Service (JPRS)/Nuclear Development and Proliferation (TND)*, October 21, 1985, p. 37; "Minister Talks About India's Alleged Attack Plans," Karachi Domestic Service, 1500 GMT, October 16, 1985, reprinted in *JPRS/TND*, November 4, 1985, p. 42; "Plans to Attack Pakistan Nuclear Complex Denied," Delhi Domestic Service, 1540 GMT, November 6, 1985, reprinted in *FBIS/South Asia*, November 6, 1985, p. E-1. India had immediately denied the charges, but Gandhi apparently initiated the no-attack proposal to lay the issue to rest.

23. This information was provided by a senior Indian official during a June 1986 interview with the author in Bombay. See also Vyvyan Tenorio, "India's Supply of Unsafeguarded Pu Grows As Repro-

cessing of MAPS Fuel Begins," *Nuclear Fuel*, August 11, 1986, p. 3.
24. This material had come from the Rajasthan I and II nuclear power reactors and the Cirus research reactor. The former units are subject to IAEA safeguards, which would cover any plutonium produced in their spent fuel. (This means IAEA inspectors periodically conduct on-site inspections to verify that the material is being used only for non-explosive purposes.)

The use of plutonium from the Canadian-supplied Cirus research reactor for nuclear weapons is also prohibited, although the reactor (and the material) are not under the IAEA system. The 1956 Indo-Canadian agreement under which the reactor was supplied specifies that the facility may be used only for peaceful purposes, but the accord did not provide for inspections (either by Canada or the IAEA) to verify India's adherence to this undertaking. India used plutonium produced in the Cirus reactor for its 1974 test claiming that the detonation was a "peaceful nuclear explosion," akin to those then being investigated by the United States and the Soviet Union for civil excavation and similar projects. Canada rejected this interpretation and suspended further nuclear cooperation with India. India has never asserted the right to use Cirus-origin plutonium for weapons, however, and it appears that much of the plutonium produced in the reactor since 1974 has been manufactured into fuel for India's experimental breeder at Kalpakkam.

The Dhruva research reactor, like the Madras I and Madras II nuclear power plants, is also totally free from non-proliferation controls. As noted above, as of late 1985, however, the facility was experiencing operating difficulties and had not produced substantial quantities of spent fuel from which plutonium could be extracted. See Tables 1 and 2 for additional details.

In a July 1988 interview with the author, Indian Atomic Energy Commission Chairman M. R. Srinivasan declared that India was separating plutonium from Madras I spent fuel as part of an effort to accumulate some two tons of plutonium by the year 2000. The material, he said, would be used in the country's first large-scale breeder reactor, for which design work had already begun. It seems unlikely, however, that India would undertake the considerable cost of transporting Madras I spent fuel more than 1,000 miles and of extracting its plutonium solely for the purpose of starting to accumulate fuel for a project for which ground has not even been broken and which could not conceivably come on-line for more than a decade. (Indian nuclear aides, it may be noted, adopted a similar public rationale in 1966, when they first began extracting plutonium from Cirus reactor spent fuel, claiming that the plutonium was needed for projects that could be realized only in the distant future. In fact, Cirus-origin plutonium formed the core of the nuclear device India tested in 1974. India's experimental breeder reactor, which also uses Cirus-origin plutonium as fuel, did not begin operating until 1985.)

25. In late 1985 and early 1986, it appeared that India was seeking to pursue work on the design of nuclear weapons by attempting to purchase "flash X-ray" machines from Sweden and Great Britain. Both governments denied export licenses for the devices, however. See "Inside Kahuta," *Foreign Report*, May 1, 1986, p. 2. Flash X-ray machines are used to take split-second photos through solid materials of very rapid processes and are used in nuclear-weapon development programs to observe dummy nuclear cores as they undergo compression following the detonation of a nuclear-weapon triggering mechanism. In effect, such machines, which played a key role in the Swedish and French nuclear programs, permit verification that the triggering mechanism is working as designed. They may also play a role in designing hydrogen bombs by simulating X-ray pressure waves of the kind used to trigger such weapons.

26. Thus during this period, India continued to expand its nuclear infrastructure but did not, apparently, deploy nuclear weapons, did not conduct further nuclear tests, and declared that it had not made a decision on whether to develop a nuclear deterrent to meet the challenge from Pakistan.

27. Bob Woodward, "Pakistan Reported Near Atom Arms Production," *Washington Post*, November 4, 1986.

28. "Official: India Has Nuclear Weapon Capability," United Press International, AM cycle, November 4, 1986; Ivan Fera and Kannan Srinivasan, "Keeping the Nuclear Option Open," *Economic and Political Weekly*, December 6, 1986, p. 2119.

29. Fera and Srinivasan, "Keeping the Nuclear Option Open" (see note 28).

30. For allegations that a larger plant is under construction, see Fera and Srinivasan, "Keeping the Nuclear Option Open" (see note 28), which states that the plant is called the "Rare Minerals Plant" and is being built "at Ratanhalli, about 12 miles off Mysore in Karnataka." Responding to the allegation, the chairman of the Indian Atomic Energy Commission, M. R. Srinivasan, stated that the facility others had referred to was not an enrichment plant, but a "special materials" plant being built in Kerala state that was involved in processing rare materials such as gallium. See "DAE Chief Denies Industrial HEU Production at BARC," *Nuclear Fuel*, June 29, 1987, p. 6.

31. Until 1980, the United States supplied fuel for these plants, as part of the arrangements covering the sale of the units under a 1963 agreement for cooperation. The 1978 Nuclear Non-Proliferation Act, however, prohibited sales after a statutory grace period expir-

ing in 1980 of reactors and reactor fuel to non-nuclear-weapon states that refuse to accept IAEA safeguards on all of their nuclear installations. This resulted in a bitter controversy with India, which possesses unsafeguarded installations and which viewed the 1963 agreement as a binding commitment by the United States to supply fuel for the Tarapur plants. In 1980, the Carter Administration, maintaining that the shipment was within the statutory grace period, authorized an additional shipment of fuel for the units. In 1982, after India threatened to declare the 1963 agreement void because of unacceptable delays, the Reagan Administration arranged for France to step in as a substitute fuel supplier. See Spector, *Nuclear Proliferation Today*, pp. 39-40, 46-47, (see note 2).

32. "Shadow of an Indian H-Bomb," *Foreign Report*, June 27, 1987.

33. It should also be noted that although India's announcement of its enrichment breakthrough came as a response to the report of Pakistan's progress in the field, India's work on the technology had obviously been initiated a number of years earlier and, it appears, would have progressed whether or not Pakistan achieved weapons-grade levels of enrichment. In this sense, the new enrichment capability—and many other elements of India's burgeoning nuclear program that were initiated prior to the advent of a serious nuclear challenge from Pakistan—should not be considered simply as a response to Pakistani nuclear advances but also as a manifestation of India's broader ambitions to enhance its technological capabilities and overall strategic potential.

34. Brahma Chellaney, "Indian Scientists Exploring U Enrichment, Advanced Technology," *Nucleonics Week*, March 5, 1987, p. 10.

35. *Ibid.*

36. Sheila Tefft, "Dhruva Reaches Full Power, but High Costs and Delays are Criticized," *Nucleonics Week*, May 12, 1988, p. 13.

37. *Ibid.*

38. Department of Atomic Energy, *Annual Report: 1986-1987* (Government of India, Department of Atomic Energy: 1987), p. 42.

39. Steven R. Weisman, "India's Nuclear Energy Policy Raises New Doubts on Arms," *New York Times*, May 7, 1988.

Srinivasan succeeded Raja Ramanna in these posts in early 1987, after Ramanna reached retirement age. Ramanna had led the team that developed and tested India's nuclear device in 1974. The selection of his successor turned into a major contest between Srinivasan and Ramanna's protege, P. K. Iyengar.

At the time, Srinivasan was the head of India's nuclear power program, while Iyengar, who had played a central role in the 1974 test, was the director of the Bhabha Atomic Research Center. It is generally believed that if India is pursuing research and development on nuclear arms, this work is being conducted at the Bhabha Center. In-fighting between the supporters of the two nuclear aides became so intense that at the last minute Ramanna was asked to remain on the job for an additional month. In the end, Srinivasan was chosen for the post. See "Reports, Comment on AEC Staffing Problems," *Times of India*, February 1 & 2, 1987, reprinted in *JPRS/TND*, April 2, 1987, pp. 36-37.

The significance of the selection remains unclear. Iyengar, however, is probably in charge of any work India has undertaken with respect to nuclear weapons and is thought to favor nuclear arming. Thus, the fact that he was not selected for the post could suggest that Gandhi was not prepared to accede to the preferences of this faction and had the political power to keep it in check. On the other hand, since Srinivasan had responsibility over the parts of India's nuclear program that led to the acquisition in late 1985 of the country's first plutonium totally free from non-proliferation controls, his appointment should not be taken as a signal that Gandhi had lost interest in maintaining a ready nuclear option.

40. India possesses two plutonium extraction or "reprocessing," plants, one at the Bhabha Atomic Research Center, in Trombay, and one at Tarapur; a third is under construction at Kalpakkam. The Trombay reprocessing plant is not subject to IAEA safeguards and is designed to extract plutonium from the metallic uranium fuel used in the Cirus and Dhruva reactors.

The considerably larger Tarapur reprocessing plant has the capability of extracting plutonium from both metallic fuel and from the oxide fuels used in India's nuclear power reactors. Since the early 1980s, it has been reprocessing power-reactor fuel from the Rajasthan reactors and from the Madras I reactor; possibly, fuel from Madras II has also been processed there.

IAEA inspectors are present when fuel from the Rajasthan reactors (which themselves are under safeguards) is processed to ensure that plutonium from them is not diverted to military purposes. However, India has not permitted the IAEA to oversee the reprocessing of the fuel from the Madras I plant (or from the Madras II reactor, if material from this reactor has been processed). India manufactured these reactors domestically and declined to place them under the IAEA system. Thus it was not obligated to permit the IAEA to verify how much plutonium from them was produced and how it was subsequently used, leaving it available for nuclear weapons.

41. "Back From the Brink of War," *Asiaweek*, February 15, 1987, p. 11; "Back from the Edge," *India Today*, February 28, 1987, pp. 24-25; "On India's Border, a Huge Mock War," *New York Times*, March 6, 1987.

42. On events in the Siachen Glacier region, see "Indians and Pakistanis Clash in Kashmir," *New York Times*, October 1, 1987; on presidential rule in Punjab, see "India Direct Rule Imposed in Pun-

jab," *New York Times*, May 12, 1987, and "President's Rule in Punjab," *Statesman Weekly*, May 16, 1987; on alleged Pakistani aid to Sikh extremists, see "The Obstacles Remain," *Far Eastern Economic Review*, March 12, 1987, pp. 35-36; and on Pakistani accusations of Indian terrorism, see "Riot Victims Blame Unseen, Uncontrolled Forces," *New York Times*, December 20, 1986; "Roots of the Rift Run Deep," *Far Eastern Economic Review*, January 1, 1987, pp. 16-18; and "Pakistan's Premier Points at India in Fatal Bombings," *Washington Post*, July 17, 1987.

43. Kuldip Nayar, "We Have the A-Bomb, Says Pakistan's Dr. Strangelove," *Observer*, March 1, 1987.

44. See discussion of the controversy in the following section of this chapter on Pakistan.

45. *India Today*, cover story, March 31, 1987.

46. *Ibid*.

47. "Knocking at the Nuclear Door," *Time*, March 30, 1987, p. 42.

48. Tom Diaz, "Gandhi Warns U.S. Is 'Soft' on 'Islamic Bomb,' Threat," *Washington Times*, April 27, 1987.

49. "India Announces Review of Nuclear Policy," Reuters, April 27, 1987; Amalendu Das Gupta, "Challenge and Response," *Statesman Weekly*, May 16, 1987, p. 12.

   This stance was virtually identical to that New Delhi had taken since the spring of 1985, and, indeed, was little different from that of Indira Gandhi in 1984. See Leonard S. Spector, *Going Nuclear*, (Cambridge, MA: Ballinger Publishing Company, 1987), pp. 77-78, 83.

50. See *e.g.*, "Natwar Singh Discusses 'Nuclear Option,' " Delhi Domestic Service, 1230 GMT, October 18, 1987, reprinted in *FBIS/ Near East and South Asia (NES)*, October 19, 1987, p. 51, (Minister of State for External Affairs Natwar Singh quoted as stating "that India does not want to go nuclear, but this position will be reconsidered if Islamabad gets a bomb"); "India Won't Tolerate Pak Nuclear Bomb: Gandhi," *Indian Observer*, November 3, 1987 ("Prime Minister Rajiv Gandhi has said India cannot tolerate Pakistan making a nuclear bomb, and a 'difficult decision may have to be taken to protect our nation' ").

51. See *e.g.*, Diaz, "Gandhi Warns U.S. is 'Soft' on 'Islamic Bomb,' Threat" (see note 48); Shekhar Gupta, "Pitching for Pakistan," *India Today*, April 30, 1987, p. 46.

52. Spector, *Going Nuclear*, p. 80, (see note 49).

53. In an interview in early August, for example, Gandhi contrasted the nuclear programs of the two countries by stating:

   It is the question of the total program. . . . We have not developed a nuclear weapon. We have demonstrated that we have the capability, but we have the will not to make a nuclear weapon. Pakistan is doing exactly the opposite. Where they do not have the capability, they are trying to make a nuclear weapon by, well, by the worst and most devious means—by smuggling things from outside, by stealing things from other countries— whether it is technology, whether it is materials. And it seems very clear to the whole world that Pakistan does have a nuclear weapon program.

See "Rajiv Gandhi Interview by BBC on Current Events," British Broadcasting Company World Service, 1345 GMT, August 16, 1987, reprinted in *FBIS/NES*, August 21, 1987, p. R-1. See also, "Pakistan's 'Nonpeaceful' Nuclear Program Viewed," Delhi Domestic Service, 0830 GMT, November 11, 1987, reprinted in *FBIS/NES*, November 17, 1987; "Gandhi's Talks with U.S. Leaders Reported," Delhi Domestic Service, 0240 GMT, October 21, 1987, reprinted in *FBIS/NES*, October 21, 1987, p. 57. The Pervez case is discussed in detail below in the section of this chapter on Pakistan.

54. "Pakistan Proposes Nuclear Test Ban," *New York Times*, September 14, 1987.

55. "Address by His Excellency Mr. Mohammad Khan Junejo, Prime Minister of the Islamic Republic of Pakistan at the Forty-Second Session of the United Nations General Assembly," September 24, 1987 (text provided by the Embassy of Pakistan), p. 11.

56. Although India reacted with alarm to China's first nuclear test in 1964, India has not responded by building a nuclear deterrent of its own. This is strong evidence that India does not perceive itself to be immediately threatened by China's nuclear arms. Nonetheless, India has cited the potential nuclear threat from China as a principal reason for its rejection of comprehensive non-proliferation measures that would restrict its freedom to develop nuclear weapons in the future.

The Gandhi government's intense focus in its public utterances on nuclear developments in Pakistan is strong evidence, moreover, that Pakistan's nuclear potential—rather than China's nuclear might—is the principal factor governing Indian nuclear decision-making today. Indeed, Gandhi himself has repeatedly made the point, declaring in December 1987, for example, that "we have lived with the Chinese bomb for 20 years. However, I cannot ascertain if we will be able to live with the Pakistani bomb." See 'Gandhi Interviewed on Foreign, Domestic Issues," *Al-Jumhuriayah*, December 3, 1987, translated in *FBIS/NES*, December 10, 1987, p. 42.

57. For example, mutual inspection regimes of limited duration could ease pressures toward nuclear arming between India and Pakistan in the short term, without permanently foreclosing India's nuclear option vis-à-vis China. Similarly, even if neither side could be sure that the other had not previously hidden away some nuclear weapons material—and Pakistan would have as much reason for con-

cern as India in this regard—prospective limits on the production or use of such material would still be a valuable arms control measure.

58. These sanctions include the termination of U.S. foreign aid and Export-Import Bank credits (Foreign Assistance Act, section 670; Export-Import Bank Act, section 2(b)(4)) and the risk of reduced financing from multilateral lending institutions (International Financial Institutions Act, section 701). In addition, under the Nuclear Suppliers Group Guidelines, the nuclear supplier countries have pledged to consult on a possible embargo of all nuclear transfers to non-nuclear-weapon states that conduct nuclear explosions. (Section 129 of the U.S. Nuclear Non-Proliferation Act also specifies that U.S. nuclear cooperation would be cut off in such an event, but this has already essentially ended in the case of India and Pakistan because of their refusal to accept IAEA safeguards on some of their nuclear facilities. See Nuclear Non-Proliferation Act, section 128.)

59. Hedrick Smith, "A Bomb Ticks in Pakistan," *New York Times Magazine*, March 6, 1988 p. 38. India's concern that a test ban might foreclose its nuclear option against China could possibly be addressed by limiting the duration of the ban, for example, by requiring that it be renewed every three or five years.

60. "Pakistan Proposes Nuclear Test Ban," *New York Times* (see note 54); "India Not in Favor of Regional Disarmament," *News India*, November 14, 1986.

61. Among other setbacks in 1987 were the loss by his Congress-I Party of a key state election in June and a bitter split within the party that erupted in July, triggered in part by accusations that his friends and associates had received kick-backs on military contracts. See Nilova Roy, "Gandhi Loses Critical State Election," *Washington Post*, June 19, 1987; Sanjoy Hazarika, "Gandhi Ousts a Leading Critic, A Rival from the Ruling Party," *New York Times*, July 20, 1987; See also, Sanjoy Hazarika, "Gandhi Faces a Revolt by Party Members in Strategic Indian State," *International Herald Tribune*, July 23, 1987 (describing Gandhi's problems in Uttar Pradesh state). Yet another upsurge of terrorism in Punjab state again gave the impression that Gandhi was not able to govern effectively. See "Gunmen Waylay Bus in Punjab; 36 Hindu Passengers are Killed," *New York Times*, July 7, 1987; Sanjoy Hazarika, "Anti-Sikh Violence in Northern India," *New York Times*, July 9, 1987; Suzanne Goldenberg, "Gandhi Facing Increased Criticism for His Failure to Curb Surge in Terrorism," *Baltimore Sun*, July 12, 1987; Sanjoy Hazarika, "Terrorists Kill 25 in Punjab," *New York Times*, August 8, 1987; Bharat Wariavwalla, "Hindu-Moslem Tension Mounts as Gandhi Zigzags," *International Herald Tribune*, August 10, 1987.

Gandhi's domestic woes were exacerbated by the country's worst drought in decades.

He appeared to enjoy a brief respite from these troubles through a foreign policy success, when on July 30, 1987, he signed a peace plan with Sri Lankan President J. R. Jayewardene aimed at ending four years of ethnic violence in Sri Lanka between native Sinhalese and minority Tamils. The Tamil rebels had been receiving support from the large Tamil population in Southern India. See Seth Mydans, "India Signs Pact with Sri Lanka to End Turmoil," *New York Times*, July 30, 1987. Gandhi agreed to send a 3,000 man peace-keeping force to Sri Lanka to help implement the agreement, but by winter tens of thousands of Indian troops had been deployed there and were engaged in intense fighting with Tamil rebel forces, who, after initially accepting the July accord, subsequently had denounced it. By mid-1988, the situation had stabilized somewhat and Gandhi had begun a partial withdrawal of Indian forces.

62. "Gandhi's Talks with U.S. Leaders Reported" (see note 53); "India-Pakistan Talks Urged," *Washington Post*, October 21, 1987; Neil Lewis, "Better Ties Seen in Visit by Gandhi," *New York Times*, October 21, 1987.

At the time, because of the quirks of the Congressional appropriations process, aid for Pakistan had, in fact, been suspended. In 1981, Congress had waived the Symington Amendment for six years through a special statutory provision. That period expired on September 30, 1987, the end of the fiscal year. Legislation to renew aid to Pakistan—and to waive the Symington Amendment for an additional period— had not yet been enacted, however, because it was to be included in an omnibus, government-wide spending bill, known as a "continuing resolution." That legislation had been delayed because of a number of major disputes between Congress and the Reagan Administration over budgetary priorities.

63. The proposal, known as the "Inouye Amendment," after its sponsor, Senator Daniel K. Inouye, is discussed in the next section of this chapter dealing with Pakistan.

64. P.L. 100-202, section 557, amending Foreign Assistance Act, section 620E(d).

65. Foreign Assistance Act, sections 620E(e) and 670(a).

66. The provision, known as the Solarz Amendment, and the administration's testimony regarding its waiver are discussed in the section on Pakistan in this chapter.

67. Hedrick Smith, "A Bomb Ticks in Pakistan," (see note 59). The article stated that the nuclear weapons India had designed, presumably without outside help, weighed "under a ton."

68. Interviews with author, March-June 1988.

69. " 'Constant Vigil' on Pakistani Nuclear Issues," Delhi Domestic Service, 0830 GMT, March 17, 1988, reprinted in *FBIS/NES*, March 17, 1988, p. 50; "Gandhi Comments on Nuclear Issue, Afghanistan," Delhi Domestic Service, 0240 GMT, April 12, 1988, reprinted in *FBIS/NES*, April 12, 1988.

70. Concerning the regional military balance, see, *e.g.*, Ashley J. Tellis, "The Air Balance in the Indian Subcontinent: Trends, Constants, and Contexts," *Defense Analysis* (December 1986): 263; Brian Cloughley, "And Whose 'Zone of Peace' Is It Going to Be, Anyway?" *Far Eastern Economic Review*, April 7, 1988, p. 25; "A Sea Change" and "Hard Choice," *India Today*, December 31, 1987, p. 72.

71. "Soviet Union Leases Nuclear Submarine to Navy," Delhi Domestic Service, 1530 GMT, January 5, 1988, reprinted in *FBIS/NES*, January 6, 1988; Sanjoy Hazarika, "India Tests Its Own Surface-to-Surface Missile," *New York Times*, February 26, 1988.

72. U.S. Department of Defense, *Soviet Military Power*, (Washington, D.C.: U.S. Government Printing Office, 1988), p. 26; Cloughley, "And Whose 'Zone of Peace' Is It Going to Be, Anyway?" (see note 70). After the initial announcement that India had leased the Soviet vessel, there was some question as to precisely what class submarine was transferred. See, *e.g.*, "India," *Nucleonics Week*, February 11, 1987, p. 16 (submarine may be a Victor I or Alfa class). This controversy appears to have been resolved by the authoritative statement in *Soviet Military Power*, cited above, that the sub is a Charlie I class boat.

73. "India," *Nucleonics Week*, (see note 72).

74. "Spokesman on India's Nuclear Subs, Afghanistan," Islamabad Domestic Service, 1500 GMT, January 14, 1988, translated in *FBIS/NES*, January 15, 1988, p. 54 (submarine and other new Indian weapon systems, "reflect India's desire to project its power beyond its frontiers . . . ").

75. Shahid-ur-Rehman, "Pakistan Slams USSR Decision to Give India Nuclear Submarines," *Nucleonics Week*, January 21, 1988, p. 12.

76. "India," *Nucleonics Week* (see note 72).

77. See, *e.g.*, Neel Patri, "India to Press US to Sell High-Tech Defense Goods," *Journal of Commerce*, January 13, 1988. Indeed, later in 1988, the United States would agree to expanded transfers of this type. See Steven Weisman, "U.S. Clears Vital Gyroscope for Indian Jet Fighter," *New York Times*, April 7, 1988.

78. "U.S. Concerned over Implications," *Pakistan Times Overseas Weekly*, January 24, 1988; "Indian Submarine Lease Worries U.S.," *International Herald Tribune*, February 20-21, 1988.

79. "The Ultimate Dream," *India Today*, May 15, 1988, p. 87.

80. See discussion in Chapter II.
81. Shekhar Gupta, "Shooting Ahead," *India Today*, March 31, 1988, p. 96; "Earthshaker," *The Economist*, March 26, 1988. p. 31.
82. Communications with Indian officials, Washington, D.C., May 1988. But see, Richard Sale, "Exclusive: India Said to Upgrade Nuclear Arsenal," United Press International, March 19, 1988, AM cycle (stating that India has developed a nuclear missile warhead).
83. *Ibid*.
84. See the section on Pakistan, in particular the discussion of the convictions of Albrecht Migule, Nazir Vaid, and Arshad Pervez.
85. See, *e.g.*, Pearl Marshall, "India Wanting No Constraints Loath to Seek Heavy Water from Soviets," *Nucleonics Week*, February 18, 1982, p. 4; Neel Patri, "Indian Nuclear Energy Program Lagging and Costly, Says Report," *Nucleonics Week*, March 10, 1988, p. 13.
86. Gary Milhollin, "Dateline New Delhi: India's Nuclear Cover-Up," *Foreign Policy* (Fall 1986): 161.
87. Michael R. Gordon, "Norway Is Missing Atom Arms Water," *New York Times*, May 4, 1988.
88. Norwegian officials were also investigating whether a series of earlier, smaller shipments to West Germany and Switzerland totaling 6 to 8 metric tons might have been re-exported with the 17.4 tons involved in the 1983 diversion. See Mark Hibbs, "Norway Investigating Reports of Heavy Water Diversions," *Nuclear Fuel*, May 30, 1988, p. 9.
89. Serge Schmemann, "Heavy-Water Transfer Defended," *New York Times*, May 7, 1988.
90. "Wanted: Bombs for Business: Nuclear Aid for Pakistan and India," ARD [West German Television], 2115, November 3, 1986.
91. *Ibid*. Transcript (translation) p. 19 (author's files). Transcript and translation provided by Egmont Koch.
92. "Remarks of Ambassador Roland Timerbaev," Friedmann Conference, Columbia University Law School, March 20, 1987, (transcript provided to author by *Columbia Journal of Transnational Law*). Timerbaev stated that the 6.8 ton shipment was composed of a number of smaller shipments, each of which was less than 1 metric ton (1.1 short tons) in size and therefore exempt from IAEA controls. See also, John J. Fialka, "Soviets Say They May Have Been Misled About Destination of a Heavy Water Sale," *Wall Street Journal*, June 21, 1988.

IAEA safeguards are not applied to heavy water in NPT states, since the treaty requires that all nuclear installations in these countries be placed under IAEA oversight; thus any facility where the material might be used would already be under safeguards. Safeguards are to be applied to shipments of more than 1 metric ton to non-NPT countries, which—like India—may possess unsafeguarded heavy-water using installations. To ensure compliance with this rule, exports of more than 1 metric ton are usually subject to strict export licensing controls, but apparently the Soviet Union handled exports of less than 1 metric ton more routinely, permitting Rohstoff Einfuhr to aggregate the 6.8 metric ton shipment and allowing the ultimate purchaser to circumvent the safeguards requirement. (Whether the same ploy was used in the Norwegian case has not been disclosed.)

U.S. regulations, it may be noted, require a "validated" license—which triggers a complicated review process—for exports of heavy water in excess of 50 kilograms, one twentieth of a metric ton. This makes it far more difficult to aggregate large quantities of the material without close governmental scrutiny.

Both Norwegian and Soviet heavy water export controls have been tightened since the 1983 and 1985 episodes.

93. According to Norwegian and West German news accounts, Rohstoff Einfuhr is run by a West German businessman, Alfred Hempel, a figure who has been involved in a number of heavy water transactions, according to U.S. officials. See Gordon, "Norway Is Missing Atom Arms Water," (see note 87).

94. "Testimony of Deputy Assistant Secretary of State Robert A. Peck," *Hearings on the Export of Nuclear Materials*, before the Subcommittee on Asian and Pacific Affairs of the Committee on Foreign Affairs, U.S. House of Representatives, February 18, 1988 (mimeo). Communications with author, April-May 1988.

95. Richard Sale, "India Said to Be Building 20 Nuclear Weapons a Year," United Press International, April 25, 1988, PM cycle. Late 1986 would have been about a year after India first began extracting plutonium from Madras I spent fuel and about the time of the first Western press reports that Pakistan was producing weapons grade uranium; presumably the information had been available to U.S.— and possibly to Indian—intelligence sources a number of months earlier.

In an account published one month earlier, Sale quoted U.S. intelligence sources as stating that India had assembled a "handful of highly sophisticated low-yield atomic bombs" and that there is strong evidence that it had developed a "nuclear warhead for use on a surface-to-surface missile with a 200-mile range." See Sale, "Exclusive: India Said to Upgrade Nuclear Arsenal" (see note 82).

See also, "Shadow of an Indian H-bomb," *Foreign Report* (see note 32). This report states, "India's claim that it could make nuclear weapons but has not yet decided to do so is a myth, American officials have told *Foreign Report*. The bombs exist and need only to be tested to become operational they say."

96. For a detailed analysis of the costs and benefits of nuclear arming for India and Pakistan in the context of regional security factors, see Carnegie Task Force on Non-Proliferation and South Asian Security, *Nuclear Weapons and South Asian Security*, (Washington, D.C.: Carnegie Endowment for International Peace, 1988). The report proposes a step-by-step process of bilateral confidence-building and negotiation to freeze the nuclear status quo in South Asia, coupled with concerted diplomatic efforts by outside powers to encourage this process.

97. Richard M. Weintraub, "India Embraces Najibullah in Bid for Role in Afghanistan," *Washington Post*, May 7, 1988. For an update on the status of the issues plaguing bilateral relations, as they have for years, see Salamat Ali, "The Obstacles Remain," *Far Eastern Economic Review*, March 12, 1988, p. 35.

Pakistan

1. Steven R. Weisman and Herbert Krosney, *The Islamic Bomb*, (New York: Times Books, 1981), pp. 43-46.

    A detailed history, published in 1987, of the early stages of Pakistan's nuclear development, from 1953 through 1971, makes a persuasive case that during this period the program was devoted exclusively to energy production and peaceful research and that Pakistan's leadership did not take steps to exploit its military potential. See Ashok Kapur, *Pakistan's Nuclear Development* (London: Croom Helm, 1987), chapters 3 and 4. The study also makes a convincing case that Zulfikar Ali Bhutto, Pakistan's energy minister during the mid-1960s, made only a nominal contribution in building the program, contrary to Bhutto's subsequent assertions (on which this author relied in *Nuclear Proliferation Today* (New York: Vintage Books, 1984)) that he played a leading role in Pakistani nuclear affairs during this period. Bhutto would later become prime minister and launch the country's nuclear weapons program.

2. For a detailed history of Pakistani nuclear policy under Bhutto from 1971-1977, see Kapur, *Pakistan's Nuclear Development*, chapter 6, (see note 1).

3. Spector, *Nuclear Proliferation Today*, pp.74-81 (see note 1). Negotiations on the plutonium plant began in 1973, prior to the Indian test, and a contract for it was signed in October 1974, some six months afterward.

4. *Ibid*. Pakistan's continuing interest in plutonium extraction is discussed below.

5. Zulfikar Ali Bhutto, *If I Am Assassinated* . . . (New Delhi: Vikas, 1979), p.138.

6. Since all plutonium-bearing spent fuel in Pakistan is subject to IAEA safeguards, if the facility began operating, *i.e.* extracting plutonium from spent fuel, it would be presumed that Pakistan had moved safeguarded material there. And, since Pakistan has not permitted the IAEA to apply safeguards at the unit (which would cover any plutonium separated in it), running the plant would amount, in effect, to removing material from safeguards, violating the IAEA system.

   In late 1981, Pakistan began fabricating its own fuel for its only nuclear power reactor, the Karachi Nuclear Power Plant (KANUPP); previously, all fuel for the plant had been imported from Canada, simplifying the IAEA's task of monitoring the amount of spent fuel the reactor was producing. The new development led the IAEA to declare that because of inadequacies in its monitoring systems, it could no longer guarantee that spent fuel was not being diverted from the reactor. It remains possible that during the interim, Pakistan secretly produced undeclared spent fuel at the facility and surreptitiously removed it in order to extract its plutonium at the New Labs. IAEA controls were subsequently improved, and, by March 1983, the agency was again able to state that it could verify the whereabouts of all spent fuel being produced at the reactor. If a diversion like this took place, however, it is unlikely that the quantities involved could have been sufficient to produce plutonium for a single nuclear device. See Spector, *Nuclear Proliferation Today*, pp. 93-95, (see note 1).

7. "Report of the Inter-Ministerial Working Party Responsible for Investigating the 'Khan Affair,' " Foreign Ministry of the Netherlands, October 1979 (mimeo, English version).

8. *Ibid.* Dr.Khan has repeatedly denied that he has engaged in any illegal conduct, pointing out that no criminal charges were ever brought against him for the activities alleged in the Dutch government report. See *e.g.*, A.Q.Khan, "Letter to the Editor," *International Herald Tribune*, July 1, 1986. Dutch officials state Khan was not prosecuted for his activities in 1974-1975 because it was impossible to prove what information he may have taken. A Dutch prosecution for Khan's attempt to solicit allegedly classified information from two former colleagues was dropped after Khan won an appeal on the procedural ground that he had not been properly served with relevant court documents. Interviews with the author, Amsterdam and The Hague, May 1985.

9. Hafiz R. Khan, "The Kahuta Story," *Defence Journal*, (August 1986): 11-13. Small portions of this article appear to have been taken verbatim from an article by A. Q. Khan that appeared in a Karachi paper on August 1, 1986. See, "Khan Narrates Uranium Enrichment Experience," *Dawn*, August 1, 1986, reprinted in *Joint*

Publications Research Service (JPRS)/Nuclear Development and Proliferation (TND), September 2, 1986, p. 76.

10. Leonard S. Spector, *The New Nuclear Nations* (New York: Vintage Books, 1985), pp. 22-41; Leonard S. Spector, *Going Nuclear*, (Cambridge, MA: Ballinger Publishing Company, 1987), pp. 22-41. Pakistan also used its clandestine purchasing network to acquire plutonium extraction equipment for the New Labs reprocessing plant. See, *e.g.*, Kapur, *Pakistan's Nuclear Development*, pp. 168-171 (see note 1).

11. Spector, *The New Nuclear Nations*, p.31, (see note 10). Migule was given a $10,000 fine and a six-month suspended sentence for his smuggling activities.

12. Testimony of Assistant Secretary of State Thomas R. Pickering, *Hearings on Nuclear Proliferation: The Situation in India and Pakistan*, Subcommittee on Energy, Nuclear Proliferation, and Federal Services of the Committee on Governmental Affairs, U.S. Senate, May 1, 1979, (Washington, D.C.: U.S. Government Printing Office, 1979) p.10.

13. Spector, *Nuclear Proliferation Today*, pp.91-93, (see note 1); Foreign Assistance Act of 1961, Section 670(b)(2) (1981).

14. Interviews with Indian officials, academics, and journalists, New Delhi and Bombay, June 1986. Concerning India's subsequent efforts to press the United States to slow Pakistan's nuclear program, see discussion in the first part of this chapter on India.

15. "Scientist Affirms Pakistan Capable of Uranium Enrichment, Weapons Production," *Nawa-I-Waqt*, February 10, 1984, translated in *JPRS/TND*, March 5, 1984, p.32.

16. "Zia Chastises Western Media for Accounts of Khan's Remarks on Weapons Capability," *Nuclear Fuel*, February 27, 1984, p. 11.

17. Senator Alan Cranston, "Nuclear Proliferation and U.S. National Security Interests," *Congressional Record*, June 21, 1984, p.S 7901. Indeed, in early April 1984, the Reagan Administration publicly opposed legislation that would have cut off U.S.aid unless the President certified that such activities had ceased. Reagan aides claimed that they could not make the necessary certification and that the aid cutoff, which the legislation would set in motion, was unacceptable, given the continuing Soviet presence in Afghanistan. See "United States Security Interests in South Asia: A Staff Report," prepared for the U.S. Senate Foreign Relations Committee (Washington, D.C.: Government Printing Office, April 1984).

18. Seymour M.Hersh, "Pakistani in U.S.Sought to Ship A-Bomb Trigger," *New York Times*, February 25, 1985.

19. *Ibid.*

20. Leslie H.Gelb, "Pakistan Links Peril U.S.-China Nuclear Pact," *New York Times*, June 22, 1984; Leslie H.Gelb, "Peking Said to

Balk at Nuclear Pledges," *New York Times*, June 23, 1984. The design was said to be that of the device China detonated in its fourth nuclear test. Apparently, the United States had evidence as early as 1981 that Pakistan was working on nuclear-weapon triggering mechanisms. See Barry Schweid, "Turks Ship U.S. A-Tools to Pakistan," *Washington Post*, June 28, 1981.

21. Gelb, "Pakistan Links Peril U.S.-China Nuclear Pact;" (see note 20); Gelb, "Peking Said to Balk at Nuclear Pledges" (see note 20). Chinese assistance apparently ended during late 1984, and the administration submitted the pact for congressional review in July 1985. The agreement entered into force in December of that year. See "U.S.and China Exchange Notes," *Nuclear Engineering International* (February 1986): 4.

22. Hedrick Smith, "A Bomb Ticks in Pakistan," *New York Times Magazine*, March 6, 1988, p. 38; David Ignatius, "U.S.Pressuring Pakistan to Abandon Controversial Nuclear-Arms Program," *Wall Street Journal*, October 25, 1984; "Shadow of an Indian H-Bomb," *Foreign Report*, December 13, 1984; Don Oberdorfer, "Pakistani Spurns Soviets' Afghan Pullout Plan," *Washington Post*, July 18, 1986. According to Smith, the Reagan Administration considered explicitly threatening in the letter that the United States would cut off aid if the 5-percent enrichment level were exceeded but rejected this option in favor of the more ambiguous "grave consequences" formulation.

23. See Appendix G. It is generally believed that reliable first-generation nuclear weapons can be built without testing. If Pakistan, as reported, had obtained a previously tested nuclear weapon design from China, it would have added reason to be confident in any untested devices it might build. See discussion of this issue in Chapter II.

24. Smith, "A Bomb Ticks in Pakistan," (see note 22); Oberdorfer, "Pakistani Spurns Soviet's Afghan Plan," (see note 22). In off-the-record interviews with the author in 1988, Reagan Administration sources confirmed that Pakistan gave explicit assurances on the 5 percent enrichment cap. According to one report, the orignial pledges were made during a mid-November 1984 visit to Washington by Pakistani Foreign Minister Yaqub Ali Khan. See "Shadow of an Indian H-Bomb," *Foreign Report* (see note 22).

25. Smith, "A Bomb Ticks in Pakistan" (see note 22). In early 1985, it may be noted, President Zia appeared to allude to the 5 percent enrichment cap when he announced that the Kahuta plant had been able to produce a small amount of enriched uranium but stressed that "it is less than five percent . . . ." See Mary Ann Weaver, "Pakistan 'Over the Hump'—Zia Interview," *Christian Science Monitor*, March 1, 1985; "A Step Nearer the Bomb . . . ," *Observer*

(London), February 24, 1985. In the past, Pakistani officials have asserted that Pakistan developed its uranium-enrichment capability in order to produce fuel for the low-enriched-uranium/light-water reactors that it is planning to build, although few observers find the justification credible. Pakistan has yet to order its first power reactor and could not have one on line for at least a decade. Even with several reactors, moreover, domestic production of enriched uranium would be highly uneconomical. In addition, the nuclear-supplier nations have imposed a *de facto* embargo on nuclear-power-plant sales to Pakistan until it agrees to place all of its nuclear installations, including the Kahuta plant, under IAEA safeguards, making Pakistan's attempt to justify Kahuta on nuclear energy grounds even less persuasive.

26. "Pakistan to Get U.S. Air-to-Air Missiles," *Financial Times*, March 14, 1985; Dusko Doder, "Gorbachev Warns on Afghan War," *Washington Post*, March 16, 1985; Joanne Omang, "Lawmakers Exercise Foreign Aid Initiative", *Washington Post*, March 21, 1985.

27. John Scali, "Good Morning America," American Broadcasting Company, July 11, 1985. In nuclear weapons of the kind Pakistan is believed to be making, a hollow sphere of highly enriched uranium is surrounded by conventional high explosives, that have been specially shaped so that when the conventional explosive is detonated, it crashes inward (or "implodes") symetrically, instantaneously compressing the highly enriched uranium core to form a solid, explosive "critical mass" of the material. Additional hollow spheres of metal, such as natural uranium and beryllium, are typically placed between the core and the high explosives. These smash into the core during the implosion and reflect neutrons back into it to improve the efficiency of the nuclear reaction. The parts of the weapon that surround the core are known as the "triggering package." Any nation developing nuclear arms would want to master the implosion technique before building or testing a nuclear device in order to gain confidence that it would work as planned. India detonated similar dummy nuclear weapons in preparing for its 1974 test. "Reports, Comment on Pakistan Nuclear Development," *Times of India*, July 14, 1986, reprinted in *JPRS/TND*, September 23, 1985, p. 63.

28. Foreign Assistance Act of 1961, section 620E(e).

29. See Foreign Assistance Act of 1961, section 670(a) (1985). (For details, see Appendix G.)

30. Smith, "A Bomb Ticks in Pakistan," (see note 22).

31. "Pakistan Persists," *Foreign Report*, March 27, 1986; U.S. Department of State, Press Guidance, "Pakistan: Post FY 1987 Assistance," March 24, 1986.

32. During 1985, Pakistan also continued to engage in clandestine ef-

forts to acquire equipment for its program. Washington chose to disregard these transgressions, as well as Pakistan's advances at Kahuta and the testing of the triggering package.

In August, for example, it was reported that Pakistan had been trying unsuccessfully to obtain flash X-ray machines. See Simon Henderson, "U.S.Halts High-Tech Camera Sale to Pakistan," *Financial Times*, August 17, 1985.

According to U.S. officials cited in the report, the Pakistani Army had been attempting to purchase small U.S.-made flash X-ray machines from the Hewlett-Packard company. Flash X-ray machines are used to take split-second photos through solid materials of very rapid processes and are used in nuclear-weapons development programs to observe dummy nuclear cores as they undergo compression following the detonation of a nuclear-weapon triggering package.

The machine being sought by Pakistan was too small to be used for this purpose and was intended to calibrate artillery pieces. Nevertheless U.S. officials became concerned because the training to be provided for the small machine was the same as that needed to operate a larger flash X-ray apparatus, such as that Pakistan had obtained from Sweden in 1982. Washington had intervened in that instance and persuaded Sweden not to supply the operating manuals and spare parts needed to run the larger machine, which was apparently sitting idle. U.S. officials became suspicious of Pakistan's purpose when they learned that two individuals who were scheduled to come to the United States for instruction were employees of the Pakistan Atomic Energy Commission.

It may be noted that there are alternatives to using a flash X-ray machine for verifying the effectiveness of nuclear-weapon triggering packages. Thus Pakistan's lack of this equipment does not mean that it could not have conducted the triggering package test revealed in July and judged it a success. See David Albright, "Pakistan's Bomb-Making Capability," *Bulletin of the Atomic Scientists* (June 1987): 30.

Ultimately, in December 1985, Pakistan was apparently able to obtain six additional flash X-ray machines from the Swedish firm, Scandiflash, by using shell companies. See Christer Larssen and Jan Melin, "Third World Countries Buy Swedish Nuclear Weapons Technology," *Ny Teknik*, May 2, 1986, p. 1, translated in *JPRS/TND*, July 30, 1986, p.1.

An additional smuggling operation during 1985 was based in West Germany, where Pakistan is reported to have obtained about 1,900 pounds (880 kilograms) of specially hardened maraging steel. The steel was fabricated into round bars whose diameter exactly matched that of a German-designed uranium enrichment centrifuge of a type that A. Q. Khan is believed to have been building at Kahuta. See Egmont Koch and Simon Henderson, "Auf dunken Wegen zur Atommacht" ("Secret Routes to the Bomb"), *Der Stern*, April 30, 1986, p. 52. Khan is thought to have obtained classified information on this design in the course of his work in 1975 for the Dutch enrichment program at Almelo, where the German design was being vetted. See "Report of the Inter-Ministerial Working Party Responsible for Investigating the 'Khan Affair,' " Foreign Ministry of the Netherlands (see note 7). For a summary of the story, see Spector, *Going Nuclear*, pp. 114-115 (see note 10). In July 1987, Arshad Pervez, a Pakistani-born Canadian, was arrested while trying to export maraging steel illegally from the United States, a case discussed in the text, below.

Also during 1985, Pakistan unsuccessfully attempted to obtain several hundred tons of reactor-grade graphite in the United States, Great Britain, France, and West Germany. In theory, this material could be used to build a natural-uranium fueled reactor to produce weapons-usable plutonium. As described above (see note 6 and accompanying text), Pakistan is believed to have a pilot-scale plutonium extraction facility, known as the "New Labs." Pakistan might want an indigenously built graphite reactor because, at present, both of its reactors (a research reactor and a relatively small nuclear power plant) are subject to IAEA safeguards. This would mean that any plutonium extracted from the reactors' spent fuel would also have to be placed under IAEA oversight and thus would be unavailable for nuclear weapons. See "Pakistan Persists," *Foreign Report* (see note 31).

33. Bob Woodward and Don Oberdorfer, "Pakistan A-Project Upsets Superpowers," *Washington Post*, July 15, 1986; Gerald M. Boyd, "Pakistan Denies Developing Bomb," *New York Times*, July 17, 1986; Don Oberdorfer, "Nuclear Issue Clouds Junejo Visit," *Washington Post*, July 17, 1986; communications with knowledgeable U.S.officials. See also "Pakistan Persists," *Foreign Report* (see note 31).

34. Smith, "A Bomb Ticks in Pakistan," (see note 22); Bob Woodward, "Pakistan Reported Near Atom Arms Production," *Washington Post*, November 4, 1986.

35. Woodward, "Pakistan Reported Near Atom Arms Production," (see note 34).

36. See note 28 and accompanying text.

37. Other factors probably contribute to Pakistan's desire to acquire nuclear arms. The Soviet occupation of Afghanistan, though expected to end shortly with the withdrawal of Soviet forces, undoubtedly heightened Pakistani security concerns and increased fears of Soviet-Indian collaboration during any future Indo-Paki-

stani war. Pakistan's relatively meager nuclear capability and limited delivery systems would have been unlikely, in themselves, to deter aggression by Soviet or Soviet-backed Afghan forces. Nevertheless, Pakistani strategists may have hoped that the country's possession of nuclear weapons would have made Moscow more cautious about intervening militarily through Afghanistan in a future Indo-Pakistani conflict, perhaps out of fear that the heightened stakes might have led to a confrontation with the United States. The Soviet presence in Afghanistan may also have contributed to Islamabad's interest in nuclear weapons by increasing instability within Pakistan. This could have led Islamabad to seek such arms as symbols of national unity.

In a separate area, Pakistani leaders probably believe that nuclear arming will enhance Pakistan's image as the most technically advanced state in the Muslim world and that nuclear status will cement Islamabad's military ties with the Persian Gulf states. Indeed, Pakistan might anticipate that these states could come to view it as a regional protector, of sorts, against possible Iranian aggression.

Nuclear arms may also be valued for reasons of domestic politics. As a symbol of nationhood, they could help unite a society that is yet to be fully integrated into a modern state—and, given the popular support for the nuclear program, could help consolidate the power of Pakistan's current leaders.

38. For a discussion of Bhutto's push for regional non-proliferation, adopted almost immediately after he took the decision to develop a Pakistani nuclear bomb, see Kapur, *Pakistan's Nuclear Development*, pp. 155, 165-166, (see note 1).

39. Concerning the Dhruva reactor, see discussion in the first part of this chapter on India.

During the fall of 1985 a series of unusually outspoken calls by Pakistani political figures for the development of nuclear weapons further exacerbated tensions on the nuclear front. At a November 1985 round-table conducted by a major Pakistani daily, for example, S. M. Kafar, secretary of Prime Minister Junejo's ruling Pakistan Muslim League Party, declared:

We have learned to purify uranium. Now we should, with the help of God, produce an explosion. It will stop all danger of War in this region just as the nuclear strength of the two superpowers has eliminated the danger of war between them since World War II.

See "Panel Supports Pakistan Becoming a Nuclear Power," *Nawa-I-Waqt*, November 15, 1985, translated in *JPRS/TND*, February 7, 1986. Several other participants in the seminar made similar comments. In December, the chief of the Muslim fundamentalist Jamaat-i-Islami Party, Tufail Mohammad, also demanded that the government use its capabilities to produce nuclear arms. See "Leader Urges 'Full Use of Nuclear Capabilities,' " *Muslim*, December 2, 1985, reprinted in *JPRS/TND*, January 9, 1986, p. 70.

The August revelation of Pakistan's attempted purchase of flash X-ray machines, used in testing nuclear-weapon triggering packages, was a further irritant. See note 32.

40. The domestic political scene was made more complicated in Pakistan by President Zia's termination of martial law on December 30, 1985, a step which significantly increased the power of Prime Minister Junejo and the nation's parliament, elected in non-party balloting eleven months earlier.

41. "Pakistan Persists," *Foreign Report* (see note 31).

42. Kuldip Nayar, "India Forcing Us to Go Nuclear: A. Q. Khan," *Muslim* (Islamabad), March 1, 1987; Kuldip Nayar, "We Have the A-Bomb, Says Pakistan's 'Dr. Strangelove,' " *Observer* (London), March 1, 1987. The piece also appeared in a New Delhi weekly. See Steven R. Weisman, "Report of Pakistani A-Bomb Causes Stir in the Region," *New York Times*, March 2, 1987.

43. Embassy of Pakistan, Press Release, "Dr. A. Q. Khan Denies Allegation in London Observer Article," February 28, 1987 (sic).

44. "Abdul Qadir Khan Sets 'Record Straight' on Interview," *Muslim*, March 2, 1987, reprinted in *JPRS/TND*, April 8, 1987, p. 35.

45. The editorial declared:

The contents of the interview are not surprising and probably tend to confirm what people in Pakistan have generally felt and what others in the outside world have suspected . . .

Shorn of all vestiges, the message given by Dr. A. Q. Khan through his interview to Nayyar [sic] is directed at all those detractors of the Islamic bomb. To the Indians, it is a "hands off" message at a time when New Delhi has been carrying out massive warlike exercises all along our eastern border. Concurrently, it is a signal to the Americans not to link the nuclear issue with the aid package since the former is now a fait accompli . . .

For too long the government here had been denying what is obvious to most. On the nuclear issue, as also on other issues affecting the security of Pakistan, the government needs to take the people into confidence about positions that are credible and consistent with the national interest.

We feel the national interest has been served by the message emitted from A. Q. Khan's interview. The government need not feel defensive or peevish on this issue.

See "Bomb Controversy," *Muslim*, March 3, 1987.

46. See discussion in the preceding section of this chapter on India.

Some observers speculated that Khan's comments had been approved by higher authorities, possibly as a warning to New Delhi. The interview had taken place on January 28 at a time when a conflict with India loomed as a serious possibility, but by March, this threat had receded, which, according to this hypothesis, would explain the government's subsequent disclaimer. Other analysts suggested that Khan had been indiscreet and caused considerable embarrassment to the Zia government, which has consistently maintained that Pakistan's nuclear activities are entirely peaceful. This view assumed that a split had developed within Pakistan's nuclear establishment be tween hardliners, who wanted to declare Pakistan's nuclear capabilities and present India and the United States with a *fait accompli*, and more cautious elements, who preferred a policy of ambiguity.

For a detailed discussion of the controversy, see Nayan Chanda, "Yes, We Have No Bomb," *Far Eastern Economic Review*, March 12, 1987; John Elliot, "Net Closes In on Pakistan's Nuclear Capabilities," *Financial Times*, March 7, 1987.

47. At least six substantial segments of the Kuldip Nayar interview appear to be near verbatim repetitions of passages from Khan's *Dawn* article, which appeared on August 1, 1986. In the following excerpts from the Nayar interview as it appeared in the London *Observer* on March 1, 1987, the underlined language is identical to that which appeared in *Dawn*; wording that appears in brackets shows the *Dawn* version when there were slight variations.

"Khan made clear that Pakistan would be prepared to beg, borrow, or steal whatever was required for its nuclear program.

" 'Having said that, I can tell you that *the Western world never talks about its* [their] *own hectic and persistent efforts to sell everything to us. When we bought inverters from Emerson, England, we found them to be less efficient than we wanted them to be. We asked Emerson to improve upon the* [some] *parameters and suggested the method.*

" '*At that period* [time] *we received many letters and telexes and people chased us with figures and details of equipment they had sold to Almelo, Capenhurst, etc. They literally begged us to buy their equipment.*' "

* * *

"Khan spoke with obvious pride of the Kahuta plant, almost as if it were his third child, and described it as a *mechanical miracle.* [It is a herculean task and an ultra centrifuge is undoubtedly a mechanical miracle.] It took three years to complete, he said, and became fully operational at the beginning of 1979. *The procedure involved a sequence of ideas* [usually in setting up a plant the sequence is idea], *decision-making, feasibility report, basic research, construction of a table model,* [construction of] *a pilot plant,* [engineering for the real plant] *and then construction of the facility.*

"The technology at Kahuta has been mastered only by highly industrialized countries and Khan said Pakistan deserved credit for accomplishing a *herculean task* that required expertise in metallurgy, engineering, electronics and nuclear physics.

" '*We took a very bold step and started with all the steps simultaneously. While preliminary work was being done at Rawalpindi and procurement was being done for the most essential and sophisticated equipment and materials,* we were manufacturing the first prototypes [we were setting up a pilot plant at Sihala . . .]' "

* * *

"The Dutch Minister of Justice told the country's Parliament last year that fresh charges would not be filed against Khan . . . *'I never received any answer to my letters, but was prosecuted without my knowledge* [and in my absence]. *The information I had asked for* (from former colleagues) *was ordinary technical information* [available in published literature for many decades]. *I submitted certificates from six world-renowned professors from Holland, Belgium, England* [Britain] *and Germany. The information requested by me* [was public knowledge and] *was not classified.' "*

* * *

" *'Once you know how to run* [make] *reactors, how to produce plutonium, and to re-process it*—all of which Pakistan has mastered as well—*it becomes a rather easy task to produce nuclear weapons.' "*

A slightly different version of the Nayar interview appeared in *Muslim*, also on March 1. It contains the following excerpt, which is a virtual verbatim repetition from the *Dawn* interview:

"Was Kahuta the right site to chose for putting up the nuclear plant? Mr. Khan got rather excited on the subject, *'While outsiders would always think in terms of their convenience, I had two prime factors in mind. The site should be out of normal traffic for security reasons and it should be near the capital* [for full support and quick decisions].

" *'Another factor was* [more important than all these factors was] *consideration for the provision of facilities for my* [our] *scientists and engineers. We never repented our decision and it is solely due to the selection of this site and my presence in the capital that we managed to rush through our program for more than three years before the Western countries came to know of it* [got wind of it] *and embarked upon concerted and coordinated but unsuccessful efforts to kill our infant program.' "*

See Kuldip Nayar, "India Forcing Us to Go Nuclear: A. Q. Khan," *Muslim*, March 1, 1987.

The comparison of the Nayar interview and Khan's article in *Dawn* was first brought to the author's attention by Nazir Zaidi, a Washington-based journalist.

Nayar defended the authenticity of the interview in a column published in December 1987, noting that the Press Council of Britain had issued an opinion on the matter. The opinion, he stated, had concluded, "It is agreed by the parties that a meeting and a conversation took place between the complainant, Dr. A. Q. Khan, and the writer of the article, Kuldip Nayar. Dr. Khan strongly denies quotations attributed to him and the interview reported in the article. On the evidence before it, however, the Press Council has not been satisfied that the interview did not take place or that the quotations were untrue . . . ." See "A. Q. Khan Interview: Journalist Reiterates Position," *Sunday*, December 20-26, 1987, reprinted in *JPRS/TND*, February 25, 1988, p. 23.

48. "Knocking at the Nuclear Door," *Time*, March 30, 1987, p. 42.

49. Arnaud de Borchgrave, "Pakistan's Zia Insists Solarz Is Voice of India in Congress," *Washington Times*, November 16, 1987.

50. John H. Cushman, "Pakistan's Nuclear Effort Worries U.S., " *New York Times*, March 6, 1987.

51. David B. Ottaway, "Pakistani A-Bomb Seen Likely," *Washington Post*, March 8, 1987.

52. David B. Ottaway, "Pakistan's Nuclear Intentions Called into Doubt," *Washington Post*, March 6, 1987.

53. Don Oberdorfer, "Panel Rejects Cut in Aid to Pakistan," *Washington Post*, April 24, 1987.

54. Egmont R. Koch and Simon Henderson, "Nennen wir ihn einfach Kotari, [Let's Just Call Him 'Kotari']" *Stern*, April 29, 1987, pp. 198-201.

55. Mark Hibbs, "German Firm Implicated in Trying to Aid Pakistan Enrichment Effort," *Nucleonics Week*, May 4, 1987, p. 1.

56. Uranium hexafluoride under correct temperature and pressure behaves like dry ice, changing directly from a solid into a gas, a process known as "subliming."

57. Mark Hibbs, "Attempt Revealed to Export to Pakistan HEU-Capable Components," *Nucleonics Week*, May 7, 1987, p. 5.

58. Simon Henderson, "Cologne Company Raided Over Supply of Nuclear Equipment Plans to Pakistan," *Financial Times*, April 30, 1987.

59. James M. Markham, "Bonn Checks Report of Smuggling of Atomic Technology to Pakistan," *New York Times*, May 5, 1987.

60. "Pakistan's Illegal Nuclear Exports," Statement by Congressman Stephen J. Solarz, Chairman Asia and Pacific Affairs Subcommittee, July 14, 1987; Don Oberdorfer, "Lawmakers Say Aid to Pakistan Is in Jeopardy," *Washington Post*, July 22, 1987; Neil A. Lewis, "Suspension Is Asked on Military Aid to Pakistan," *New York Times*, July 23, 1987.

Within a week of Pervez's arrest, two California residents and a Hong Kong business man were also indicted in Sacramento, California, on charges of illegally exporting sophisticated U.S. electronic equipment to Pakistan in 1983 and 1984. Among the items were oscilloscopes used to analyze the non-nuclear high-explosive portion of nuclear devices. See Michael R. Gordon, "U.S. Indicts 3 in the Export of Equipment to Pakistan," *New York Times*, July 18, 1987. Pakistan had attempted to acquire such oscilloscopes previously through the Netherlands. See, Spector, *The New Nuclear Nations*, pp. 25-26, 36, (see note 10).

61. Don Oberdorfer, "U.S. Says Pakistan Must Act to Avoid Aid Cut-off over Nuclear-Export Case," *Washington Post*, July 17, 1987; Don Oberdorfer, "U.S. Asks Pakistan to Stop Producing Bomb-Grade Uranium," *Washington Post*, July 23, 1987.

62. Pat Towell, "House Panel Makes Major Cuts in Foreign Aid Appropriations," *Congressional Quarterly*, August 1, 1987, p. 1726.

63. "Pakistan Spurns Nuclear Inspection," *Washington Post*, August 4, 1987; Michael R. Gordon, "Pakistan Rejects Atomic Inspection," *New York Times*, August 6, 1987.

64. Steven R. Weisman, "Pakistani Parties Denounce the U.S.," *New York Times*, September 3, 1987.

65. These sanctions include the termination of U.S. foreign aid and Export-Import Bank credits (Foreign Assistance Act, section 670; Export-Import Bank Act, section 2(b)(4)), and the risk of reduced financing from multilateral lending institutions (International Financial Institutions Act, section 701). In addition, under the Nuclear Suppliers Group Guidelines, the nuclear supplier countries have pledged to consult on a possible embargo of all nuclear transfers to non-nuclear-weapon states that conduct nuclear explosions. (Section 129 of the U.S. Nuclear Non-Proliferation Act also specifies that U.S. nuclear cooperation would be cut off in such an event, but this has already essentially ended in the case of India and Pakistan because of their refusal to accept IAEA safeguards on some of their nuclear facilities. See Nuclear Non-Proliferation Act, section 128.)

66. Smith, "A Bomb Ticks in Pakistan," (see note 22). India's concern that a test ban might foreclose its nuclear option against China could possibly be addressed by limiting the duration of the ban, for example, by requiring that it be renewed every three or five years.

67. "Pakistan Proposes Nuclear Test Ban," *New York Times*, September 14, 1987; "India Not in Favor of Regional Disarmament," *News India*, November 14, 1986.

68. Michael R. Gordon, "Congress Delays New Pakistan Aid Amid Nuclear Rift," *New York Times*, September 30, 1987.

69. "President on U.S. Aid Cutoff, Nuclear Arms," *Cumhuriyet* (Istanbul), October 4, 1987, translated in *Foreign Broadcast Information Service (FBIS)/Near East South Asia (NES)*, October 6, 1987, p. 42; Michael Getler and Richard Weintraub, "Pakistani Strikes Defiant Tone on Nation's Nuclear Program," *Washington Post*, October 13, 1987.

70. Michael R. Gordon, "U.S. Official Urges New Aid to Pakistan," *New York Times*, October 23, 1987; Robin Pauley, "Pakistan 'Producing High Grade Uranium,' " *Financial Times*, October 26, 1987.

71. "Gandhi's Talks with U.S. Leaders Reported," Delhi Domestic

Service, reprinted in *FBIS/NES*, October 21, 1987, p. 57; "India-Pakistan Talks Urged," *Washington Post*, October 21, 1987; Neil Lewis, "Better Ties Seen in Visit by Gandhi," *New York Times*, October 21, 1987. On October 30, Gandhi, commenting on his visit, declared, "Perhaps for the first time they [the United States] are realizing the gravity of the situation and are worried . . . . If the U.S. really exerts pressure, I have no doubt Pakistan will change its nuclear weapons program." See "Rajiv Gandhi Hails Pact on New Defense Equipment," *News India*, October 30, 1987.

72. Pervez was convicted of illegally attempting to export a 154-pound (70-kilogram) bar of beryllium from the United States to Pakistan. The export of beryllium is controlled because of its use as a neutron reflector to enhance the yield of nuclear weapons. Pervez was also convicted of three counts of giving false statements on export license applications concerning the end use of the twenty-five tons of maraging steel he was seeking; he had claimed the steel was to be used for "high-speed turbines and compressors." He was found not guilty, however, of trying to export the material illegally. On this and on two other counts of the eight-count indictment the jury believed that the government had improperly entrapped him.

Pervez had been the subject of a ten-month undercover investigation involving U.S. and Canadian authorities which began after Carpenter Technology Corporation, a steel-maker based near Reading, Pennsylvania, informed the U.S. government in October 1986 of an inquiry its Toronto agent had received from Pervez for maraging steel. Carpenter had earlier alerted the government after it received an order for the same metal in May of 1985 directly from the Pakistani Embassy in London. See Mark Hosenball and James Adams, "A-Bomb Plot is Linked to Embassy," *Sunday Times* (London), July 26, 1987.

Testimony at Pervez's trial established that the maraging steel—a specialized alloy made from nickel, cobalt and molybdenum with an unusually high tensile strength—is used principally to make uranium enrichment centrifuges of a West German design. The centrifuges are used by the British-Dutch-West German consortium, Urenco; Pakistan is thought to have duplicated them at Kahuta, allegedly by using technology obtained by Dr. A. Q. Khan while he worked at a Urenco plant in the Netherlands. Pervez stipulated that the maraging steel be manufactured as bars 5.9 inches in diameter, a measurement that matches the size of German-designed units, according to scientific witnesses called by the government. These witnesses also stated that 35,000 pounds of the metal would allow Pakistan to build enough centrifuges to produce one nuclear device per year, apparently requiring 55 pounds (25 kilograms) of highly enriched uranium. Pervez had sought 50,000 pounds of the special

steel and had put in a bid for eleven additional 50,000-pound ship-
ments of the metal, to be supplied every four months. See Andy
McCord, "Trial Witnesses Link Pervez to Pakistan Nuclear Plans,"
India Abroad, December 18, 1987; Mike Holderness, "Special
Steel Evidence of Pakistan's Nuclear Plans," *New Scientist,* July 30,
1987; Smith, "A Bomb Ticks in Pakistan" (see note 22).

Testimony by government experts also established that the only
realistic use for beryllium is in the manufacture of nuclear weapons.
See Testimony of John J. Keeney, Deputy Assistant Attorney General, Criminal Division, before the Subcommittee on Asia and Pacific Affairs, Committee on Foreign Affairs, U.S. House of Representatives, February 18, 1988, p. 5, (mimeo).

Among the evidence linking Pervez to the Pakistani government
were entries in his notebooks (that had been seized by Canadian
authorities) identifying his project as "atom" and "military" and
noting that "my expert is procurement manager for nuclear plant."

On February 10, 1988, Pervez was sentenced to five years impris-
onment and an additional term of five years probation—the long-
est prison term yet imposed for attempted nuclear smuggling to an
emerging nuclear state.

73. Simon Henderson, "Pakistan Builds Second Plant to Enrich Uranium," *Financial Times,* December 11, 1987; Neil A. Lewis, "Reports of Pakistan Uranium Plant Weighed," *New York Times,* January 10, 1988. Pakistan denied the allegation that it was building a
second enrichment facility. See "Pakistan Denies New Enrichment
Plant," *Nuclear Engineering International* (February 1988): 7.

The reports of a second enrichment plant would be consistent
with Pakistan's efforts to purchase the autoclaves and other equipment for handling uranium hexafluoride through Leybold-
Hereaus, noted above. They would also help explain why Pervez
was seeking substantial quantities of maraging steel—an initial order of 25 tons, with comparable orders to follow every four months
thereafter.

It is also possible, however, that Pakistan was simply planning to
expand its existing enrichment plant at Kahuta.

74. Don Oberdorfer, "Conferees Won't Penalize Pakistan," *Washington Post,* December 18, 1987.

Contributing to this outcome was an early December legislative
gambit by Pakistan's supporters in the Senate, who gained passage
in a key appropriations subcommittee of a measure that was so un-
palatable that it made an unencumbered extension of aid for Pakistan an attractive option for many fence-sitters.

The proposal known as the "Inouye Amendment," after its sponsor, Senator Daniel K. Inouye, provided that U.S. bilateral aid—
and multilateral bank financing, a funding source of much greater

importance to India than direct U.S. assistance—would be cut off to Pakistan or to India, respectively, if that country were found to be producing unsafeguarded nuclear weapons material, an activity both were believed to be engaged in at the time. However, the provision also permitted the aid cut to be waived if the country subject to the cut was deemed to be producing such material as a response to similar activity by the other. See Neil A. Lewis, "Bill on Atom Arms Would Punish India," *New York Times*, December 5, 1987.

In effect, this meant that the law would have left aid to both countries unaffected, but India bitterly denounced the measure for improperly equating it with Pakistan as a nuclear offender whose conduct had to be forgiven to make it eligible for U.S. support. See "The Pakistan Equation," *India Today*, December 31, 1987.

From Pakistan's standpoint, however, the bill represented an acknowledgement by the United States of its right to pursue an undeclared nuclear deterrent in response to India, a position that was a complete reversal of traditional U.S. non-proliferation policy.

The proposal was ultimately dropped in favor of the legislation discussed in the text.

75. P.L. 100-202, section 557, amending Foreign Assistance Act, section 620E(d).
76. Foreign Assistance Act, sections 620E(e) and 670(a).
77. Under this provision, aid is prohibited for any country that the president determines has illegally exported, or attempted to export illegally from the United States, equipment, materials, or technology to be "used in the manufacture of a nuclear explosive device." (The law then provides that the prohibition may be waived if the president determines that an aid cut-off would be seriously prejudicial to U.S. non-proliferation interests or would otherwise jeopardize the common defense and security.) In mid-January 1988, President Reagan determined that Pakistan had violated this stipulation, known as the Solarz Amendment, but then went on to waive the aid ban.

In testifying on the president's decisions, Deputy Assistant Secretary of State Robert Peck made clear that the provision had been triggered by the activities of Arshad Pervez, who was determined to be working on behalf of the government of Pakistan, contrary to the repeated denials by senior Pakistani officials during the summer and fall of 1987. See, *e.g.*, Richard Weintraub, "Pakistan Denies Connection to Any Nuclear-Export Plot," *Washington Post*, July 22, 1987. In addition, he stated that the maraging steel Pervez was seeking to acquire "would have been used in Pakistan's uranium enrichment plant, and *therefore* would have been 'used in the manufacture of a nuclear explosive device.' " See "Testimony of Deputy Assistant Secretary of State Robert A. Peck," *Hearings on the*

Export of Nuclear Materials, before the Subcommittee on Asian and Pacific Affairs of the Committee on Foreign Affairs, U.S. House of Representatives, February 18, 1988, (mimeo) (emphasis added).

78. On this matter, the key administration witness stated, "We have seen clear indications that procurement of some U.S.-origin goods has been halted, although we are aware of some activities which give us cause for continuing concern." See "Testimony of Deputy Assistant Secretary of State Robert A. Peck" (see note 77).

79. "Sales to Pakistan Affect U.S. Relations," *Cumhiriyet*, September 22, 1987, translated in *FBIS/Western Europe*, September 24, 1987, p. 22; "Pak Snag to U.S.-Turkish Ties," *Defense and Foreign Affairs Weekly*, February 29, 1988. These items, used for controlling the speed of enrichment centrifuges have been on Pakistan's shopping list since the late 1970s, when Pakistan sought to purchase them from Emerson Electric Company in Great Britain, an operation that first brought Pakistan's enrichment activities to public attention. Thereafter, Pakistan attempted to purchase them through Canada by acquiring subcomponents that were not on the Canadian export control list, a ploy it was also said to be using in Turkey. See Weissman and Krosney, *The Islamic Bomb*, pp. 186-188 (see note 1); Spector, *The New Nuclear Nations*, pp. 26-27, 36-37, (see note 10).

80. Smith, "A Bomb Ticks in Pakistan," (see note 22). The article stated that the nuclear weapons India had designed, presumably without outside help, weighed "under a ton."

81. As a measure of how far the program had progressed toward the actual fabrication of weapons, Smith noted that Pakistan had transformed the highly enriched uranium hexafluoride into uranium metal—the form of the element used in nuclear devices—and that some Reagan Administration sources believed that Pakistan had already machined the metal into nuclear-weapon cores.

82. These sources also validated the article's description of the timing of U.S.-Pakistani interactions, especially the failure in October 1985 of President Reagan to challenge President Zia on Pakistan enrichment of uranium to more than 5 percent in violation of pledges given to Washington.

83. Compare Tables 1 and 2 in the preceding section on India, which estimate Indian nuclear capabilities, with Tables 3 and 4 above.

84. There is no question that Pakistani analysts perceive India's stockpiling of unsafeguarded plutonium in strategic terms. See, *e.g.*, "Commentary Alleges Indian Bid for Nuclear Hegemony," *Dawn*, October 6, 1987, reprinted in *JPRS/TND*, December 1, 1987, p. 21.

85. An interesting question in this regard is how large a stockpile Pakistani planners believe is required as a deterrent. A minimal deter-

rent of perhaps fifteen to twenty devices would appear sufficient, but the evidence of Pakistan's expansion plans suggests a large nuclear capability is contemplated.

86. For a discussion of these episodes, involving a coup attempt by right-wing French generals in Algeria in 1961 and resistance by an autonomous Chinese province chief to directives from Beijing during the Cultural Revolution of the mid-1960s, see Spector, *Going Nuclear*, pp. 25-37, (see note 10).

87. Richard M. Weintraub, "India Embraces Najibullah in Bid for Role in Afghanistan," *Washington Post*, May 7, 1988. For an update on the status of the issues plaguing bilateral relations, as they have for years, see, Salamat Ali, "The Obstacles Remain," *Far Eastern Economic Review*, March 12, 1988, p. 35.

88. For a detailed analysis of the costs and benefits of nuclear arming for India and Pakistan in the context of regional security factors, see Carnegie Task Force on Non-Proliferation and South Asian Security, *Nuclear Weapons and South Asian Security*, (Washington, D.C.: Carnegie Endowment for International Peace, 1988). The report proposes a step-by-step process of bilateral confidence-building and negotiation to freeze the nuclear status quo in South Asia, coupled with concerted diplomatic efforts by outside powers to encourage this process.

Chapter IV:
The Middle East—Introduction

1. "War of Liberation," *New York Review of Books*, November 22, 1984, p. 36; Neil Roland, "Soviets Reportedly Offer Nuclear Help to Syria," United Press International, November 28, 1985, citing an interview with Tlas in *Al-Ittihad*, October 4, 1985, translated in *Foreign Broadcast Information Service (FBIS)/Middle East and Africa*, October 7, 1985.
2. Neil Roland, "Soviets Reportedly Offer Nuclear Help,"; Ze'ev Schiff, "Dealing with Syria," *Foreign Policy*, (Summer 1984):94. See also "Defense Minister Interview on Parity with Israel," *Al-Majallah*, December 11-17, 1985, translated in *FBIS/Middle East and Africa*, December 12, 1985, p. H-1 (Tlas states, "We are capable of acquiring a nuclear option in order to achieve strategic balance with the Zionist enemy"); "USSR Reportedly To Train Syrians on Nuclear Weapons," KUNA 1315 GMT, October 12, 1985, translated in *Joint Publication Research Service (JPRS)/Nuclear Development and Proliferation (TND)*, November 25, 1985, p. 66 (citing a Lebanese magazine, *Al-Nahar Al-Arabi Wa Al-Dawli*); "Secret Nuclear Weapons Talks with USSR Reported," Salalah (Syrian) Domestic Service, 1600 GMT, March 21, 1986, translated in *FBIS/Middle East and Africa*, March 25, 1986, p. H-1.
3. "Israel Reported to Test Longer Range Missile," *New York Times*, July 22, 1987.
4. Mohammed El-Sayed Selim, "Egypt," in James E. Katz and Onkar S. Marwah, eds., *Nuclear Power in Developing Countries* (Lexington, MA: Lexington Books, 1982), pp. 138-139.
5. "The Trail to Crazy Island," *Wall Street Journal*, March 16, 1984.
6. "Israel Bids India Join Attack on Pakistan," *Israeli Foreign Affairs*, (April 1987); Shyam Bhatia, "Israelis Plot A-Plant Raid on Pakistan," *Observer*, March 27, 1988.
7. See John M. Goshko, "Saudis To Cut Ties to Iran," *Washington Post*, April 26, 1988. The treaty will not provide mechanisms for verifying the status of the new Saudi missiles, since its provision for comprehensive International Atomic Energy Agency safeguards extend only to declared nuclear materials.

Israel

1. "Revealed: The Secrets of Israel's Nuclear Arsenal," *Sunday Times* (London), October 5, 1986.
2. Concerning "Jericho II," the 400-mile range missile thought to have been deployed in the early 1980s, see "Israel Said to Deploy

Jericho Missile," *Aerospace Daily*, May 1, 1985; "Nuclear Efforts of Israel, Pakistan Prompts Meeting of U.S. Group," *Aerospace Daily*, May 7, 1985; Elaine Sciolino, "Documents Detail Israeli Missile Deal with Shah," *New York Times*, April 1, 1986. The deployment of the missile has been confirmed to the author by several current and former U.S. officials.

"Jericho II" is the name given the missile in Western intelligence circles. Apparently it has a different name in Israel.

The missile is presumed to be deployed with a nuclear warhead, or to be quickly adaptable to take such a warhead. According to Richard Sale, the reporter who authored the *Aerospace Daily* articles cited above, U.S. scientists aided in the development of the warhead. One of these scientists told Sale that he had seen the warhead, which was about two feet long, 20 to 22 inches in diameter, and weighed 226 pounds (about 100 kilograms). See "NBC Nightly News," July 30, 1985. The missile is said to be able to carry a total payload (nuclear explosive, heat shield, etc.) of 1,650 pounds (750 kilograms). See Sciolino, "Documents Detail Israeli Missile Deal with Shah," above.

Concerning the longer-range version of the missile, see Thomas W. Netter, "Israel Reported to Test New Longer-Range Missile," *New York Times*, July 22, 1987. In several radio broadcasts after the test was disclosed, the Soviet Union warned Israel against deploying the system. See Thomas L. Friedman, "Soviet Cautions Israel Against a New Missile," *New York Times*, July 29, 1987. The missile was test-fired to a distance of 500 miles in the Mediterranean Sea and is said to have a range of 900 miles. Reportedly, the May 1987 test was Israel's tenth test of the missile. See "Israel's Jericho Missile," *MidEast Markets*, November 23, 1987, p. 11.

For a discussion of these missiles and Israel's other nuclear-capable delivery systems, see Chapter II.

3. Perhaps the most critical point in Vanunu's revelations was his confirmation of the existence of the plutonium extraction plant itself. Such a facility had long been posited by analysts of Israel's nuclear program, but until Vanunu's detailed description of the complex, its existence had never been conclusively established. In 1982, for example, Israeli analyst Efraim Inbar was still able to write, that "there is no reliable evidence that Israel in fact has a plutonium separation plant. Without such a facility, the plutonium [produced in Dimona] is unusable." See, Efraim Inbar, "The Israeli Basement: With Bombs or Without?" *Crossroads* (Winter/Spring 1982):85.

4. Based on Vanunu's testimony and his photos, Taylor told the *Sunday Times* investigative team:

Assuming that the photographs were taken at Dimona, the models of the interior components of a nuclear weapon are genuine and Vanunu's identification of the nature and purpose of the various facilities and of the materials corresponding to the "models" are generally correct.

The information obtained from Vanunu's statements and photographs as presented to me are entirely consistent with a present Israeli capacity to produce at least five to ten nuclear weapons a year that are significantly smaller, lighter, and more efficient than the first types of nuclear weapons developed by the U.S., U.S.S.R., U.K., France, and China.

See "Revealed: The Secrets of Israel's Nuclear Arsenal" (see note 1).

Barnaby had the opportunity to debrief Vanunu extensively. He told the *Sunday Times* that he found Vanunu's testimony to be "totally convincing." See *ibid.*

5. For a discussion of the differences between fission and fusion weapons, see Appendix B.

Since Israel is not known to have conducted a full-scale nuclear test, its undeclared nuclear arsenal appears to have been developed in part through the testing of non-nuclear components and computer simulations. As discussed below, Israel also collaborated with France during the late 1950s on the development of atomic weapons and may also have obtained data from France's first nuclear test, which took place in February 1960. See "France Admits It Gave Israel A-Bomb," *Sunday Times* (London), October 12, 1986; Steve Weissman and Herbert Krosney, *The Islamic Bomb* (New York: Times Books, 1981), p. 114.

There has also been speculation that a flash observed by a U.S. satellite, which was then over the South Atlantic, in September 1979 was that of an Israeli nuclear test. A panel of experts convened by President Jimmy Carter's Office of Science and Technology Policy determined that the event "probably" was not a nuclear detonation, but the panel's conclusions were disputed by the Defense Intelligence Agency and the Naval Research Laboratory. As a result, the event remains shrouded in uncertainty. See Bernard Gwertzman, "U.S. Monitors Signs of Atom Explosion Off South Africa," *New York Times*, October 25, 1979; "Blowup" *Technology Review* (October 1980); Eliot Marshall, "Navy Lab Concludes the Vela Saw a Bomb," *Science*, February 22, 1980, p. 996; Thomas O'Toole, "New Light Cast on Sky-Flash Mystery," *Washington Post*, January 30, 1980; "Israel Reported Behind A-Blast Off South Africa," *Washington Post*, February 22, 1980. For a review of publicly available data on the subject, including documents which were released under the Freedom of Information Act, see the Washington Office on Africa, "The September 22, 1979, Mystery Flash: Did

South Africa Detonate a Nuclear Bomb?" (May 21, 1985).

Many reports supporting the view that the event was, indeed, a test claim that it was a joint Israeli-South African undertaking. See, e.g.,"CBS Evening News with Walter Cronkite," February 21, 1980 (report by Dan Raviv); Benjamin Beit-Hallahmi, *The Israeli Connection* (New York: Pantheon, 1987), p. 134. But see James Adams, *The Unnatural Alliance*, (New York: Quartet Books, 1984), p. 195 (source states that flash was not an Israeli test, but confirms nuclear collaboration between the two countries).

It has also been alleged that Israel obtained assistance in the design of nuclear warheads for its Jericho II missiles from emigre U.S. scientists. See Jane Hunter, "Israel, South Africa, and the Bomb," *Middle East Report* (November-December 1986): 13 (citing transcript of BBC TWO TV, "Newsnight," 2250 GMT, July 11, 1985); Richard Sale and Geoffrey Aronson, "Exporting Nuclear Triggers: The Strange Case of Richard Smyth," *Middle East Report* (May-June 1987): 40. The latter account states that the warhead for the Jericho II "carries a warhead derived from the US XW-58 warhead."

6. In March 1988, Barnaby, reiterated his view that Israel has produced fusion weapons on "Sixty Minutes," Columbia Broadcasting System, 6:00 p.m. EDT, March 20, 1988.

7. In Israel, Vanunu was not permitted to speak to the press, but as he was being taken to a court appearance in late December 1986, he managed to flash a message to reporters about his abduction. The message, which he had written on his palm, stated, "Vanunu M. was hijacked in Rome Itl 30.9.86 2100 came to Rome by BA fly 504." See Thomas L. Friedman, "Israeli Suspect Flashes a Hint He Was Abducted," *New York Times*, December 23, 1986. Additional information on his abduction was later provided by his brother, who subsequently sought political asylum in Great Britain to avoid prosecution for the disclosure. For details, see "How Israeli Agents Snatched Vanunu," *Sunday Times* (London), August 9, 1987; "Riddle of Vanunu Ship," *Sunday Times* (London), August 16, 1987; "Revealed: The Woman From Mossad," *Sunday Times* (London), February 21, 1988. The Israeli government has never explained how it obtained custody of Vanunu.

8. Glenn Frankel, "Israel Convicts Vanunu of Treason for Divulging A-Secrets to Paper," *Washington Post*, March 25, 1988. Vanunu has appealed his conviction.

9. As to how he could have roamed about the building where he worked taking his 60 photos, Vanunu's stated that perimeter security at the facility was relatively lax, permitting him to smuggle in a camera, and that as a control room technician, he had the run of the building so that he could respond to irregularities that showed up

on his monitors.

There has been speculation that the Israeli government deliberately planted Vanunu to give its nuclear deterrent more credibility, without actually acknowledging that it existed. This scenario appears rather far-fetched in light of Vanunu's detention and conviction—unless it is assumed that these developments, too, are part of an elaborate Israeli ploy.

Vanunu's motives are not clear. Though troubled by Israel's nuclear weapons program, he apparently was not committed to exposing it from the outset. Indeed, he did not bother to develop his photos for many months, until, during a trip around the world, he met a Colombian journalist in Sydney, Australia, who became interested in his story and later tried to help Vanunu sell it to the European press.

10. Pierre Péan, *Les Deux Bombes*, (Paris: Fayard, 1981).

11. For a concise characterization of shared French-Israeli security concerns at the time, see Simha Flapan, "Nuclear Power in the Middle East," *New Outlook* (July 1974): 47-48.

12. Péan, *Les Deux Bombes*, Chapter V, (see note 10).

13. *Ibid.*

14. Péan, *Les Deux Bombes*, Chapters V, VIII (see note 10). The agreement with St. Gobain covering the plutonium plant also included the supply of three less sensitive units: a workshop for fabricating fuel for the reactor, a "hot cell" laboratory for the analysis of irradiated materials, and a storage facility for waste materials coming from the reactor.

15. The precise date when this collaboration began is not clear. One detailed review of the relationship states that the French arms manufacturer Marcel Dassault developed the missile to Israeli specifications, basing it on the French MD-660 and MD-620. Fourteen of the missiles were reportedly delivered to Israel in the mid-1960s, before the subsequent French boycott on further arms sales to Israel. The missile is said to have been a multi-stage, solid-fuel rocket with a payload of about 1,000 pounds and a range of 260 miles. See "Israel: Jericho II and the Nuclear Arsenal," *Defense and Foreign Affairs*, May 9, 1985, pp. 1-2.

In 1974, the missile's existence was confirmed in a CIA analysis of Israel's nuclear capabilities, which was inadvertently released in 1978. See note 63 below.

16. Pierre Péan, *Les Deux Bombes,* Chapter VI, (see note 10).

17. The EL-3 reactor used slightly enriched uranium fuel, moderated by heavy water and cooled by air. The Dimona facility, however, is thought to be both cooled and moderated by heavy water and to use natural uranium fuel. See *ibid.*

18. *Ibid.*, Chapter VI. Péan also states that the cooling ducts were

three times as large as needed for a 24-megawatt reactor.
19. *Ibid.*, Chapter VII. It should be recalled that during the late 1950s and early 1960s, France's government was in considerable turmoil. The Fourth Republic fell in May 1958, under the threat of a coup by right-wing French generals and colonialists based in Algeria, and the Fifth Republic was not formally constutited until September of that year, with De Gaulle ruling by decree in the interim. Even after De Gaulle was invested as president of the Fifth Republic in January 1959, however, France was rocked by further coup attempts—one in January 1960 and a second in April 1961—by these same elements who were bitterly opposed to De Gaulle's decision in September 1959 to grant the French territory independence. (In the latter coup attempt, there is evidence that the rebel forces attempted to take control of a nuclear device being readied for testing at France's Reganne nuclear test site in the Sahara. See Leonard S. Spector, *Going Nuclear* (Cambridge, MA: Ballinger Publishing Company, 1987), pp. 25-32).

De Gaulle had come to power after promising that Algeria would remain French, and many of his rightist supporters—including Soustelle, a powerful figure himself, who as a former governor-general of French Algeria was a bitter foe of independence—felt betrayed by De Gaulle's subsequent reversal on the issue. Indeed, it was De Gaulle's decision to grant Algeria independence that caused Soustelle to resign his post as minister for nuclear research.

De Gaulle's difficulties in consolidating his power during this unsettled period may help explain why he apparently encountered such obstacles in implementing his policies on nuclear cooperation with Israel.
20. Weissman and Krosney, *The Islamic Bomb*, p. 114, (see note 5).
21. "France Admits It Gave Israel A-Bomb," *Sunday Times* (London) (see note 5).

Perrin explained France's reasoning in the *Sunday Times* interview, given one week after the paper had published Vanunu's revelations, stating:

. . . in 1957 we agreed to build a reactor and a chemical plant for the production of plutonium. We wanted to help Israel. We knew the plutonium could be used for a bomb but we considered also that it could be used for peaceful purposes.

It was kept a secret because of the Americans. We had an agreement with them whereby French scientists connected with work on nuclear weapons in Canada (during the second world war) could return to France and use their knowledge, but only on condition the secrets would be kept. We considered we could give the secrets to Israel provided they kept it a secret themselves.

See *ibid.* See also, Hedrick Smith, "U.S. Assumes Israelis Have A-Bomb or Its Parts," *New York Times*, July 18, 1970 (this article quotes unnamed U.S. officials as believing that Israel had close ties to the French nuclear weapons program).

Perrin had been more cautious in interviews he gave in 1980 and 1981, stating only that France had permitted St. Gobain—the firm that had built France's first plutonium plant—to work on a similar project in Israel. See Weissman and Krosney, *The Islamic Bomb*, pp. 113-114 (see note 5); Pringle and Spigelman, *The Nuclear Barons*, (New York: Holt, Rinehart and Winston, 1981) p. 296. Since the firm would have had unique access to some of France's most sensitive nuclear technology, however, this was little different from France's agreeing to supply the plant itself.

Franco-Israeli nuclear cooperation was not a one-way street. In the late 1950s, as France was working on a prototype of its first atomic bomb, Israel reportedly supplied France with a computer needed to make key calculations about its performance. See Péan, *Les Deux Bombes*, Chapter IV, (see note 10). Earlier, in 1953, according to senior French nuclear scientist Bertrand Goldschmidt, France had purchased an Israeli technique for producing heavy water, needed to operate certain types of reactors using natural uranium fuel.

22. De Gaulle is said to have informed Israeli Prime Minister Ben Gurion of his intention to curtail French cooperation on the plutonium plant at a meeting in Paris in June 1960. Referring to the occasion, De Gaulle's memoirs state, "So ended, in particular the cooperation offered by us for the beginning, near Beersheba, of a plant for the transformation of uranium into plutonium from which one fine day there could emerge some atomic bombs." See Charles De Gaulle, *Memoirs of Hope: Renewal and Endeavor* (New York: Simon and Schuster, 1971), p. 266.

In his 1986 interview with the *Sunday Times*, however, Francis Perrin appears to contradict this statement—and Péan's understanding—by stating that "General De Gaulle stopped the collaboration on nuclear weapons with Israel in 1959, although he agreed to supply the plutonium plant because we had a reciprocal agreement and we thought it would be good for France to have this possibility of working with Israel." See "France Admits It Gave Israel A-Bomb," *Sunday Times* (London) (see note 5). It is thus possible that De Gaulle, notwithstanding his official utterances, knowingly permitted work on the unit to continue through the end of 1960. As described below, work on the facility recommenced in 1962, with Israel using French subcontractors.

23. John W. Finney, "U.S. Hears Israel Moves Toward A-Bomb Potential," *New York Times*, December 19, 1960; John W. Finney, "U.S. Misled At First on Israeli Reactor," *New York Times*, December 20, 1960. Péan states that the U.S. Central Intelligence

Agency got wind of the construction at Dimona in 1958, but that the United States did not make a public issue of the matter because Israel insisted that the reactor was intended only for peaceful research and promised to accept inspections by American experts after construction was completed. He states that the affair became public only after it was leaked to the press. As described in note 28 below, however, there is strong evidence that Israel, in fact, deliberately hid the reactor from Washington. In a 1988 communication with the author, a former U.S. nuclear aide familiar with this period of U.S.-Israeli nuclear relations stated he was convinced that Washington did not learn of the Dimona reactor until 1960 and was genuinely surprised by the development.

24. Dana Adams Schmidt, "Israel Assures U.S. on Reactor," *New York Times*, December 22, 1960. On December 21, 1960, Ben Gurion addressed the Israeli Knesset, disclosing the reactor and pledging it would be devoted to peaceful purposes.

25. Finney, "U.S. Misled at First on Israeli Reactor" (see note 23).

26. Alvin Shuster, "Israel Satisfies U.S. on Use of Reactor," *New York Times*, December 23, 1960.

27. Faud Jabber, *Israel and Nuclear Weapons* (London: Chatto and Windus, 1971), p. 35. According to Ben Gurion's biographer, two U.S. scientists visited Dimona in the spring of 1961 and advised President John F. Kennedy that the reactor was not part of a weapons program. Michael Ben-Zohar, *Ben Gurion*, (New York: Adama Books, 1977) p. 273.

28. A good indication of what U.S. officials thought of the reactor can be gleaned from the minutes of a secret session of the Senate Foreign Relations Committee on January 6, 1961, shortly after the story broke. The minutes contain the following exchange between Secretary of State Christian Herter and Senator Bourke Hickenlooper:

Secretary Herter: There has been somewhat of a flurry in connection with the nuclear reactor in Israel . . . It has been a disturbing element in the whole Middle East picture, largely because of the fact that this reactor apparently has been under construction for some time without anything public having been said about it. *Certainly we had never been told about it,* even though we have cooperated with Israel on the building of a small experimental nuclear reactor. *The [deleted] indicate that it is considerably larger than any need for an experimental reactor in Israel*, but the present statements of the Israeli Government are that this is still experimental, leading to a power reactor . . .

Senator Hickenlooper: . . . From whatever information I have had on this, which is some information I will say . . . I think it is very serious, for things that we have done for them to have them perform in this manner *in connection with this very definite production reactor facility* [i.e., a reactor for producing plutonium] which they have been secretly building, *and with a completely straight face denied to us they were building.*

See *Executive Sessions of the Senate Foreign Relations Committee* (Historical Series), Vol. XIII, Pt. 1, 87th Congress, 1st Session, 1961 (1984), pp. 7-8 (emphasis added).

29. See Glossary.
30. Bertrand Goldschmidt, *Le Defi Atomique* (Paris: Fayard, 1980), pp. 205-206.
31. Jabber, *Israel and Nuclear Weapons*, p. 89 (see note 27); "CBS Evening News with Walter Cronkite," (report by Dan Raviv on a book by Israeli journalists Eli Teicher and Ami Dor-On disclosing details of Israel's nuclear weapons program, including an agreement between Israel and South Africa signed in the 1950s for the latter to supply uranium to Israel in return for Israeli nuclear technology; Israeli censors had prohibited publication of the book and the Israeli government revoked Raviv's press credentials after he discolosed its contents.) (see note 5).
32. Communication with former U.S. official, 1986 (Argentina supplied fifteen tons); "Richard Kessler, "Argentine Officials Deny Rumors of [Recent] Nuclear Trade with Israel," *Nucleonics Week*, May 29, 1986, p. 7, (Argentina supplied one ton of uranium to Israel in 1960, triggering U.S. concerns); Jabber, *Israel and Nuclear Weapons*, p. 89, (see note 27) (first load of Dimona reactor reportedly comprised of ten tons from South Africa and four tons from Israeli-produced Dead Sea phosphates).
33. Earlier in 1960, Israel had obtained a small, 5-megawatt research reactor from the United States, but this required enriched uranium, available exclusively from the United States, as fuel.
34. The details of Norway's sale of heavy water to Israel and of the non-proliferation controls that Norway imposed on the transaction were unearthed and brought to public attention by Gary Milhollin, a professor of law at the University of Wisconsin and director of the Wisconsin Arms Control Project. See John H. Cushman, Jr., "U.S. Sent Liquid to Israel for Reactor," *New York Times*, November 10, 1986; Charles R. Babcock, "Norway Eyes Israel's Use of Nuclear Ingredient," *Washington Post*, November 10, 1986; Gary Milhollin, "Heavy Water Cheaters," *Foreign Policy* (Winter 1987-1988): 100.
35. In contrast, the United States supplied heavy water for India's Cirus reactor in 1960 without obtaining the right to inspect the material. In the nuclear device India detonated in 1974, India used plutonium that was produced in the Cirus reactor while U.S. heavy water was present. Comparison suggested by Gary Milhollin.
36. Press Release, Norwegian Department of Foreign Affairs, October 10, 1987. The press release states in part:

. . . The Department of Foreign Affairs can . . . confirm that Norsk Hydro in 1959 was licensed to export 20 tons of heavy water to Israel. A statement to this end was given in 1979.

The license for export to Israel was given on the basis of, and immediately subsequent to, an agreement between the Norwegian and Israeli Governments on the *conditions* for such deliveries . . .

In the agreement, the Israeli Government guarantees that heavy water supplied from Norway to Israel in accordance with the contract the authorities have been informed about, will be used solely for the promotion and development of nuclear energy for peaceful purposes and not for any military purpose. Moreover, the Government of Israel guarantees that none of this material will be transferred to unauthorized persons or sent beyond the jurisdiction of the Israeli Government without having in advance obtained a written consent from the Norwegian Government. The Norwegian Government shall, in accordance with the agreement be given opportunity to assure oneself [sic] that the use of the heavy water is in agreement with these guarantees. As the agreement was signed in advance of the International Atomic Energy Agency having established its security control system, the agreement prescribes that the parties later on shall consult with each other to decide to which [sic] extent it is necessary to modify the agreement with a view to the transfer of the security control functions to the Agency.

(Text courtesy of Gary Milhollin.)

The press release also notes that Norway authorized a 1.1 ton (1.0 metric ton) shipment of heavy water to Israel in July 1970, but refused a contemporaneous Israeli request for 4.4 tons (4.0 metric tons) of the material.

37. Milhollin, "Heavy Water Cheaters," pp. 103-105 (see note 34).
38. Babcock, "Norway Eyes Israel's Use of Nuclear Ingredient" (see note 34); Wolf Blitzer, "Norwegian Heavy Water Said Used for Dimona Plutonium," *Jerusalem Post*, November 19, 1987.
39. See note 28.
40. Milhollin provides some additional details about the Norwegian transfer, but does not settle this issue. He states that the Norwegian heavy water had been initially purchased by Great Britain but that Britain had decided not to use it. He continues,

Influential supporters of Israel in Norway—including the former defense minister—set up a corporation called Noratom to buy it back. Then they quietly pushed an export license through the Norwegian foreign ministry. The license allowed Noratom to ship the unused water directly from Britain to Israel, which it did.

See Milhollin, "Heavy Water Cheaters," p. 107, (see note 34).
41. In a 1987 investigation, Milhollin examined this transfer. He determined that in 1960, all heavy water in France's possession was of either U.S. or Norwegian origin. Under agreements with each of these suppliers France had agreed to obtain the approval of the sup-

plier before transferring any of the material to a third country. Neither supplier country's records, however, indicated that France had ever transferred any of their material; thus, Milhollin concluded, if the transfer to Israel took place, it must have violated the agreement with one or the other supplier country. Milhollin notes that Péan is the only source to describe the French transfer to Israel, but he also argues that the transfer appears to be plausible, since heavy water reactors are usually sold with a supply of this essential material. Milhollin also points out that the Norwegian sale of heavy water to Israel was approved only months before the Norwegian material was shipped to that country in 1959, so that France—in concluding the reactor sale to Israel in 1956-1957—could not have anticipated that a supply of heavy water was going to be available from this alternative source. Milhollin, *Heavy Water Cheaters*, p. 107, (see note 34).

42. *Ibid.*, pp. 105-106. The material is now at the Israeli Nahal Soreq nuclear research center, which houses a small U.S.-supplied research reactor. The Reagan Administration has confirmed the current status of the U.S. material, but has not provided data on why it was originally provided to Israel, or whether it was ever used at Dimona. See J. Edward Fox, Assistant Secretary of State for Legislative Affairs to Lee H. Hamilton, Chairman of the Subcommittee on Europe and the Middle East, House Foreign Affairs Committee, January 21, 1988, *Congressional Record*, 100th Cong., 2d Sess., January 25, 1988, p. E-18. According to Milhollin, no Israeli nuclear installation except the Dimona reactor requires ton quantities of heavy water.

43. By November 1954, Israel already had built a pilot plant for the production of heavy water. See statement of Abba Eban, Israeli Ambassador to the United Nations, November 15, 1954, *Official Records of the General Assembly*, Ninth Session, First Committee, 716th meeting, pp. 335-337.

   It should be noted that the largest proportion of heavy water required to operate a heavy water reactor is needed for the initial inventory of new reactors. Makeup requirements are very small in comparison.

44. St. Gobain, the architect-engineering firm, which, to protect its identity, was operating through a front company, Industrial Company for Chemical Studies and Construction (SIECC), had been in charge of the plutonium plant project and the three less sensitive facilities, while the Société Alsacienne de Constructions Mecaniques (SACM) was responsible for the reactor. St. Gobain remained at the site to work on the three smaller units, but did not, after late 1960, perform work on the plutonium plant. See Péan, *Les Deux Bombes*, Chapter VI, (see note 10).

45. Péan, *Les Deux Bombes*, Chapter VII (see note 10). The subcontractors included Comsip-Automation, specializing in regulation, control, and automation of industrial plants, and Audincourt Ironworks Company, which had put in the complex piping at the Marcoule installation. Péan states that Israel lost about two years as it attempted to put together this new construction team.

46. Most other sources place the start-up of the reactor at late 1963 or early 1964 and have generally given the start-up date of the plutonium extraction plant as 1969 or 1970. See, *e.g.*, "How Israel Got the Bomb," *Time*, April 12, 1976. U.S. intelligence sources speculate that the plutonium unit was going through a shake-down period prior to the 1967 Arab-Israeli War and that significant production did not get under way until at least 1968 or 1969.

47. The visits were initiated in 1964 and conducted annually through 1969. See John W. Finney, "Israel Permits U.S. to Inspect Atomic Reactor, *New York Times*, March 14, 1965 (noting visits in 1964 and 1965); John W. Finney, "U.S. Again Assured on Negev Reactor," *New York Times*, June 28, 1966; John W. Finney, "Israel Could Make Atom Arms in 3 or 4 Years, U.S. Aides Say," *New York Times*, July 6, 1966; Smith, "U.S. Assumes the Israelis Have A-Bomb or its Parts," (noting visits in 1968 and 1969)(see note 21).

48. Smith, "U.S. Assumes the Israelis Have A-Bomb or Its Parts" (see note 21). This article states that American analysts thought Israel had obtained plutonium for nuclear weapons by having it extracted from Dimona-reactor spent fuel in France.

49. Following the 1966 visit, for example, U.S. spokesmen stated that they had reached only the "tentative" conclusion that no weapons-related activities were occurring there. See Finney, "U.S. Again Assured on Negev Reactor" (see note 47).

   Apparently, the Kennedy Administration accepted only sporadic visits in part because it expected to be able to verify how the reactor was being used by monitoring Israeli uranium imports through the Western Suppliers Group, an informal network of Western nuclear exporters, which kept track of uranium sales around the world. This second control, however, apparently did not provide conclusive evidence of Israeli behavior. Pringle and Spigelman, *The Nuclear Barons*, p. 294, (see note 21).

50. Smith, "U.S. Assumes the Israelis Have A-Bomb or its Parts" (see note 21).

51. The Johnson Administration had been concerned that by continuing the limited visits, the United States was giving the impression that nothing untoward was occurring at the site. According to former U.S. officials interviewed by the author, Washington feared that if Israel were in fact pursuing nuclear arms and if this subsequently came out, the United States might be accused of collusion.

The Nixon Administration may have reached a similar conclusion and decided it would be better off halting the annual visits. Other explanations are also possible, however, including the possibility that the United States, which was then seeking to make Israel its strategic partner in the region, did not want to force a highly charged diplomatic issue to a showdown.

It should be noted that at the end of the Johnson Administration and throughout the Nixon Administration, the United States was far less willing to interfere in Israeli nuclear activities than the Eisenhower and Kennedy Administrations had been. Despite the Johnson Administration's commitment to the Non-Proliferation Treaty (NPT), for example, it acquiesced when Israel refused to adhere to the pact after it was opened for signature in 1968, and Washington declined to make ratification a condition for the transfer of U.S. F-4 aircraft that Israel was seeking at the time. At this point, moreover, Johnson was said to have been told of CIA suspicions that Israel had diverted U.S. weapons-grade uranium from a processing plant in Pennsylvania. See text at note 54, below.

The Nixon Administration ended the U.S. visits despite this history and, it appears, after learning in late 1969 that Israel was believed to have diverted 200 tons of uranium concentrate from Europe in 1968 (see text at note 56, below). In 1974, moreover, Nixon offered to sell both Israel and Egypt nuclear power reactors without requiring either state to ratify the NPT (thus leaving the Dimona reactor outside of the IAEA inspection system), even as a CIA report was circulating which concluded that Israel had developed nuclear arms. See note 63. The deal with Israel was stymied by congressional oppostion, however. The 1978 Nuclear Non-Proliferation Act subsequently prohibited nuclear reactor sales to countries that refused to join the NPT or to place all of their nuclear facilities under IAEA safeguards. (Egypt signed the NPT in 1981, which made it eligible for such U.S. nuclear exports.)

52. In 1976, a major review of the Israeli nuclear program in *Time* magazine stated that Israel had stopped work on the plutonium plant in 1964 and that construction was not restarted until early 1968, nearly a year after the Six Day War. (The account states that Moshe Dayan authorized the renewed construction without higher authority.) See "How Israel Got the Bomb," *Time* (see note 46). See also Pringle and Spigelman, *The Nuclear Barons*, p. 296, (see note 21). Under this hypothesis, no improper activities would have been occurring at the site until near the end of the U.S. visits, when in fact the U.S. visitors were starting to become suspicious. Although the author accepted this version of events in *Nuclear Proliferation Today* (New York: Vintage Books, 1984), pp. 123-125, the added evidence of Péan (whose work was translated by the Congressional

Research Service in 1986) and Vanunu, suggests that a stronger—though not conclusive—case can now be made that the plant was completed during the mid-1960s. Significant plutonium production may not have begun until 1968 or 1969, however.

53. In fact, considerably more material was missing from the facility, a total of nearly 600 pounds (about 270 kilograms), but the U.S. Atomic Energy Commission concluded that all but 220 pounds (100 kilograms) of the loss could be explained by process losses, leaving the remainder "unaccounted for." If the larger amount were diverted to Israel, it would have provided enough material for 10 to 18 weapons.

54. "Near Armageddon: The Spread of Nuclear Weapons in the Middle East," American Broadcasting Company, April 27, 1981, transcript pp. 13-14. See also, "C.I.A. Concluded, Ex-Aide Says, That Israel Made Nuclear Arms," *New York Times*, May 2, 1981.

The CIA apparently based its case on a number of circumstantial factors. These included, the fact that the president of NUMEC had extensive ties with the Israeli government, the company's contracts to supply non-military nuclear items to an Israeli firm, and the lax security at the facility. The agency also cited the fact that Israeli A-4 jets were seen practicing bombing runs of a type used only for nuclear arms and that soil samples taken from the Dimona area contained traces of highly enriched uranium, which the CIA assumed came from the NUMEC plant. See Weissman and Krosney, *The Islamic Bomb*, pp. 108-109, (see note 5); Smith, "U.S. Assumes Israelis Have A-Bomb or Its Parts" (see note 21); U.S. Nuclear Regulatory Commission, *Inquiry into the Testimony of the Executive Director for Operations*, Volume III (Interviews), February 1978, p. 178; John J. Fialka, "Report CIA Had Proof in '68 Israel Had A-Bomb Material," *Washington Star*, December 9, 1977.

55. Despite extensive U.S. government investigations, in 1980, the Nuclear Regulatory Commission concluded that there was no "concrete information concerning the final disposition or location of any material which may be missing from this facility." See U.S. Nuclear Regulatory Commission, *Safeguards Summary Event List*, NUREG-0525, rev. 3, December 1980.

Glenn Seaborg, the chairman of the Atomic Energy Commission (whose functions are now exercised by the Nuclear Regulatory Commission and the Department of Energy) at the time the material was determined to be missing, stated in a recently published book, "It is all but certain . . . that the material was lost during complicated chemical procedures that, to save money, were conducted with inadequate care." See Glenn T. Seaborg, with Benjamin S. Loeb, *Stemming the Tide*, (Lexington, MA: Lexington Books, 1987), p. 259.

An interesting new allegation was made by syndicated columnist William Safire, in September 1987. Commenting on the rise of Israeli intelligence aide Rafi Eitan—who ran the Jonathan Jay Pollard spying operation against the United States—Safire states:

> Rafi Eitan and Avraham Bendor [a second Israeli intelligence figure implicated in the Pollard affair] are legendary figures in the world of espionage. Together they led the team that kidnapped Adolf Eichmann in Buenos Aires in 1960 and brought that war criminal before the bar of Israeli justice. Eight years later, the same two Mossad operatives appeared at an Apollo, Pennsylvania nuclear processing plant. After their visit, 587 pounds (266 kilograms) of weapons-grade uranium was reported missing.

See William Safire, "Why Israelis Are Losing in America," *International Herald Tribune*, September 10, 1987.

56. EURATOM, the European Community nuclear agency, has confirmed that the yellowcake was diverted during the transit between Antwerp and Genoa; the only outstanding question is whether Israel was the country responsible, and there appears to be little doubt on this score. When European Community officials first confirmed the loss of the material in 1977, for example, press reports quoted unnamed American and European intelligence sources as being convinced that the material was taken to Israel to fuel the Dimona reactor. See, *e.g.*, William Drozdiak, "Uranium Loss is Admitted," *Washington Post*, May 3, 1977. Various internal U.S. government memoranda on the affair, released under the Freedom of Information Act to the Natural Resources Defense Council and provided to the author, repeatedly cite Israel as the presumed perpetrator. In answers to questions posed by a subcommittee of the House International Relations Committee, for example, U.S. nuclear aides in 1976 went so far as to volunteer how long the material might last if used to fuel the Dimona reactor.

The affair was first brought to public attention by Paul Leventhal, a former staff member of the Senate Governmental Operations Committee and now president of the Nuclear Control Institute, Washington, D.C. The episode is sometimes referred to as the "Scheersberg incident" after the ship involved or as the "plumbat affair," because the drums containing the yellowcake were, reportedly, marked with this label (a Latin reference to lead). For a comprehensive investigation of the incident, see Elaine Davenport, Paul Eddy, and Peter Gillman, *The Plumbat Affair* (London: Deutsch, 1978). Israel has denied that it was responsible.

57. There have been allegations that the West German government of Chancellor Kurt Georg Kiesinger was aware of the ploy and that Israel had received assurances that it would be able to disguise its purchase of the uranium as a private transaction in order to avoid antagonizing the Soviet Union and Israel's Arab neighbors. "Ura-

nium: The Israeli Connection," *Time*, May 30, 1977, p. 32. The most comprehensive analysis of the episode, however, rejects this theory. See Davenport, Eddy, and Gillman, *The Plumbat Affair*, pp. 171-172, just cited.

58. Z. Ketzinel, "Uranium Sources, Production, and Demand in Israel," *Proceedings of the Fourth International Conference on the Peaceful Uses of Atomic Energy*, Geneva, September 6-16, 1971, vol. 8, pp. 113-119, as cited in *Israeli Nuclear Armament*, Report of the Secretary General, A/36/431, September 18, 1981. p. 11.

59. See text at note 36, above.

60. Smith, "U.S. Assumes Israelis Have A-Bomb or Its Parts" (see note 21); "How Israel Got the Bomb," *Time* (see note 46). The Smith article, which states that the United States had been conducting its Middle East policy since 1968 on the assumption that Israel possessed nuclear weapons, indicates that it was based on a CIA briefing to the Senate Foreign Relations Committee. The *Time* article quotes former Israeli Foreign Minister Moshe Dayan extensively, suggesting that he may have been the source for other information in the article.

61. See note 15.

62. Interviews with the author, fall 1987. Egypt was apparently aware of the possibility that Israel might use nuclear arms during the conflict. See, Raymond H. Anderson, "Top Cairo Editor Urges Nuclear Arms for Arabs," *New York Times*, November 24, 1973. Some Israeli scholars believe that Israel's nuclear capabilities played a far more important role in the conflict than has been acknowledged. They believe that it was the threat of an Israeli nuclear response that led to Egypt's cautiousness in exploiting its initial breakthrough in the Sinai and to Syria's decision to halt its advances in the Golan Heights at Israel's 1967 border. See Shlomo Aronson, "The Nuclear Dimension of the Yom Kippur War," *Jerusalem Journal of International Relations* (Vol. 7, Nos. 1 & 2): 107; but see Yair Evron, "The Relevance and Irrelevance of Nuclear Weapons in Conventional War," *ibid.*, p. 143.

The possibility of a superpower nuclear confrontation also developed during the conflict. On the night of October 24-25, the United States placed its nuclear forces on alert. This was a response to a note from Soviet General Secretary Leonid Brezhnev, which threatened to introduce Soviet combat troops into Egypt if Israel, which had surrounded the Egyptian Third Army Corp, did not comply with a U.N. ceasefire. U.S. intelligence had confirmed that Moscow was readying its airborne forces for such a mission. Marvin Kalb and Bernard Kalb, *Kissinger* (Boston: Little Brown and Company, 1974), pp. 489-496. Contributing to American concerns was the possibility that the Soviet Union was also about to deploy tactical nuclear weapons in Egypt. According to a detailed investigation of the incident,

> U.S. intelligence had been tracking a Russian ship carrying radioactive materials since it had entered the Mediterranean via the Bosporus on the 22nd [of October]. Our interviewees confirmed that the U.S. intelligence community was quite positive that there was nuclear material aboard the ship, even though the reason for the radioactivity could not be defined. When the ship docked at Port Said on the 25th, there was some speculation that it was transporting warheads for a brigade of Soviet Scud missiles previously deployed near Cairo. This rumor was never confirmed, and the radioactive emissions could have come from naval weapons with nuclear warheads or from something else. Still, these reports about the movement of nuclear materials on the Soviet ship heightened concern among the members of the WSAG [Washington Special Action Group of top Nixon Administration officials] that a Soviet intervention was imminent and introduced a new dimension to the crisis.

See Barry M. Blechman and Douglas M. Hart, "The Political Utility of Nuclear Weapons," *International Security* (Summer 1982): 137.

From these accounts, it was not Israeli nuclear activity on October 8 that triggered the U.S.-Soviet crisis, as is sometime reported, but the risk that weeks later Israel might decimate Egyptian forces by conventional means. The U.S. alert ended on October 26, after the threat of Soviet intervention eased.

63. In September 1974, for example, a CIA analysis (which was inadvertently released under the Freedom of Information Act to the Natural Resources Defense Council) stated:

> We believe that Israel has already produced nuclear weapons. Our judgment is based on Israeli acquisition of large quantities of uranium, partly by clandestine means; the ambiguous nature of Israeli efforts in the field of uranium enrichment, and Israel's large investment in a costly missile system designed to accommodate nuclear warheads. We do not expect the Israelis to provide confirmation of widespread suspicions of their capability, either by nuclear testing or by threats of use, short of a grave threat to the nation's existence. Future emphasis is likely to be on improving weapon designs, manufacturing missiles more capable in terms of distance and accuracy than the existing 260-mile Jericho, and acquiring or perfecting weapons for aircraft delivery.

See Central Intelligence Agency, "Prospects for Further Proliferation of Nuclear Weapons," DCI NIO 1945/74, September 4, 1974. The mention of Israel's acquisition of uranium appears to be a veiled reference to the plumbat affair. "Ambiguous efforts" in the enrichment field may have been a reference to Israel's work on an experimental process for enriching uranium with lasers (see Robert Gillette, "Uranium Enrichment: Rumors of Israeli Progress with Lasers," *Science* (March 1974): 1172), but more likely is a reference to the NUMEC affair, in which the agency, it is now known, believed Israel played a key role.

In December 1974, Israeli President Ephraim Katzir indirectly confirmed this assessment in an interview with science writers, stating, "It has always been our intention to develop the nuclear potential. We now have that potential." A newspaper account of the interview goes on to state, "The President said that if the need arose, Israel could convert capability into fact in 'a very short time—even in a few days.' " See *The Guardian*, December 3, 1974.

Similarly, in early 1976, Carl Duckett, a senior CIA official, disclosed in a secret briefing to the Nuclear Regulatory Commission that Israel was making nuclear weapons from plutonium produced at Dimona. He went on to say that the amount of plutonium available from the reactor was so substantial that the CIA now regarded the alleged earlier diversion of highly enriched uranium from NUMEC as academic. See U.S. Nuclear Regulatory Commission, *Inquiry into the Testimony of the Executive Director for Operations* (see note 54).

At another supposedly off-the-record briefing to members of the American Institute of Aeronautics and Astronautics in March 1976—the substance of which was reported in the press shortly afterward—Duckett estimated that the Israeli nuclear arsenal contained between 10 and 20 weapons as powerful as that used on Hiroshima. See Arthur Kranish, "CIA: Israel Has 10-20 A-Weapons," *Washington Post*, March 15, 1976.

64. Francis Perrin, for example, when interviewed in 1980, stated, "We are sure the Israelis have nuclear weapons . . . . They have sufficient facilities to produce one or two bombs a year." Weissman and Krosney, *The Islamic Bomb*, p. 110, (see note 5). (At the time, Perrin was still attempting to mask France's direct assistance in supplying the Dimona plutonium plant by stating that French industrial concerns had built it while Paris turned a blind eye; thus it is possible that he was also trying to cloud the fact that the reactor was larger than the 24 megawatts publicly announced.)

Similarly, a comprehensive 1981 review of Israel's nuclear capabilities by a group of experts convened by the secretary general of the United Nations concluded,

Calculating on the basis of its original capacity (which may have been increased) the Dimona reactor is capable of producing annually 8 to 10 kilograms [17.6 to 22 pounds] of plutonium . . . In the period from 1963 to the present, around 100 kilograms [220 pounds] could thus have been produced (assuming 6 to 8 months of operation a year). In light of the various possibilities of plutonium reprocessing [extraction] listed . . . above, it is physically possible that Israel now processes [sic possesses?] enough separated plutonium to manufacture 10 to 15 nuclear warheads.

See *Israeli Nuclear Armament*, p. 12, (see note 58).

(The U.N. review earlier notes a report that the Dimona reactor might have been upgraded to 70 megawatts in 1980, which by 1981, would have increased Israel's potential arsenal only slightly. See "The Middle East's Nuclear Arms Race," *Foreign Report*, August 13, 1980. The U.N. report also assumes that Israel's plutonium extraction capabilities are limited to small hot cells and a reported "pilot"-scale reprocessing plant—the one supplied by France— which, based on published sources at the time, the report estimates to have a very limited capability of 8.8 to 11 pounds (4 to 5 kilograms) of plutonium per year, about a tenth of the capacity described by Vanunu in 1986. See Stockholm International Peace Research Institute, "*SIPRI Yearbook: 1979*, pp. 315-316. The report also mentions the possible contribution of the NUMEC affair and indigenous Israeli enrichment of uranium as making a modest contribution to Israel's potential nuclear stockpile.)

65. "America's Nuclear Pledge to Israel," *Foreign Report*, January 21, 1981, (Israel has 200 weapons, can produce 8 per year); "Israel Said to Deploy Nuclear Missiles," *Aerospace Daily* (see note 2),(Israel might possess as many as 200 weapons); Anthony Cordesman, interview on "NBC Nightly News," National Broadcasting Company, July 30, 1985 (Israel has at least 100 nuclear weapons and perhaps as many as 140).

66. Padriac Sweeney, "Fearing Collapse, IAEA Retreats on Israel," *Baltimore Sun*, October 16, 1983.

67. See generally, Leonard S. Spector, *The New Nuclear Nations* (New York: Vintage Books, 1985), pp. 144-147. Spector, *Going Nuclear*, pp. 295-296 (see note 19).

At the 1985 IAEA session, Israel stated:

Israel holds that all states must refrain from attacking or threatening to attack nuclear facilities devoted to peaceful purposes, and that the safeguards system operated by the IAEA brings evidence of the peaceful operation of a facility. It is within this context that Israel reconfirms that under its stated policy it will not attack or threaten to attack any nuclear facility devoted to peaceful purposes either in the Middle East or anywhere else.

68. "Californian Indicted in Export of Triggers to Israel," *New York Times*, May 17, 1985; John M. Goshko, "L.A. Man Indicted in Export of Potential Nuclear Bomb Component to Israel," *Washington Post*, May 17, 1985. A krytron generates the precisely timed electrical pulse that simultaneously detonates the high explosive "lenses" that surround the weapon's nuclear core.

69. John M. Goshko, "Israel Got U.S.-Made Devices," *Washington Post*, May 14, 1985; John M. Goshko, "U.S. Asks to Inspect Israeli Atom Sites," *Washington Post*, May 15, 1985.

70. *Hearings on Developments in the Middle East, July 1985*, before the

Subcommittee on Europe and the Middle East of the Committee on Foreign Affairs, U.S. House of Representatives, 99th Cong., 1st Sess., July 24, 1985, p. 72. See generally, Spector, *The New Nuclear Nations*, pp. 41-44. (see note 67).

71. Charles R. Babcock, "Computer Expert Used Firm to Feed Israel Technology," *Washington Post*, October 31, 1986; Sale and Aronson, "Exporting Nuclear Triggers: The Strange Case of Richard Smyth" (see note 5). The latter report quotes a former undersecretary of state as saying, "What Smyth did was pass on to Israel virtually hundreds of millions of dollars of advanced U.S. technology."

Israel also appears to have by-passed international controls in obtaining about 52 tons (47 metric tons) of depleted uranium from Luxembourg in April 1984. See Spector, *The New Nuclear Nations*, pp. 141-143, (see note 67). The material—uranium whose fissionable isotope, uranium-235, has been partially culled—is a by-product of the uranium enrichment process. It cannot be used for nuclear weapons, but can be irradiated in a reactor to produce plutonium. Depleted uranium is also used for armor piercing shells, and it appears that this was the use Israel had in mind.

72. "Minister Denies London Report on Nuclear Weapons," Jerusalem Domestic Service, September 28, 1986, reprinted in *Foreign Broadcast Information Service (FBIS)/ Near East and Africa (NEA)*, September 29, 1986, p. I-7; "Herzog Meets Lange, Discusses Nuclear Arms," Jerusalem Domestic Service, reprinted in *FBIS/NEA*, November 12, 1986, p. I-4. See also "Rabin Discusses Nuclear Weapons, Transfer Policy," *Yedi'ot Aharonot*, November 12, 1987, translated in *Joint Publications Research Service (JPRS)/Nuclear Development (TND)*, December 1, 1987, p. 20.

73. "Intelligence Head on Arab Arms" Jerusalem Domestic Service, 0505 GMT, December 24, 1986, translated in *FBIS/Near East and South Asia (NES)*, December 24, 1986.

74. Gideon Raphael, "Syria and Israel: Too Near the Brink," *Washington Post*, January 11, 1987.

75. Mary Curtius, "Israel Needs More US Aid to Spur Economy and Immigration, Economist Says," *Christian Science Monitor*, January 20, 1987.

76. Presumably the U.S. aides are referring to evidence from the U.S. visits of the 1960s and to subsequent satellite photos.

77. "The Middle East's Nuclear Arms Race," *Foreign Report* (see note 64).

78. Having a plutonium extraction plant with a capacity substantially larger than that required for the reactor would be good engineering practice, they note, because the reactor is the more reliable part of the system. In theory, it could be expected to produce

plutonium-bearing spent fuel more or less continuously (including planned shutdowns for refuelling and maintenance), while the plutonium extraction plant could be expected to break down from time to time, necessitating its subsequent operation at higher than normal levels to work off the spent fuel that would have accumulated in the interim.

79. See, *e.g.*, Smith, "U.S. Assumes Israelis Have A-Bomb or Its Parts" (see note 21).
80. See notes 34 and 36.
81. John J. Fialka, "Norway to Seek Study of Israeli Nuclear Materials," *Wall Street Journal*, February 17, 1987.
82. Benny Morris, "Inspection of Norwegian Heavy Water Barred," *Jerusalem Post*, April 16, 1987.
83. *Ibid*; Michael Gordon, "Norway Says Israel Resists a Nuclear Check," *New York Times*, May 26, 1987.
84. "Norway to Renew Heavy Water Inspection Request," *Nucleonics Week*, July 2, 1987, p. 13.
85. "Norway Bid for Heavy Water Supervision Denied," Jerusalem Domestic Service, 2100 GMT, October 3, 1987, translated in *FBIS/NES*, October 6, 1987, p. 20.
86. E. A. Wayne, "Israel Accused Anew of Nuclear Violations," *Christian Science Monitor*, December 2, 1987.
87. "Israel: Norwegian Heavy Water Use to be Probed," *Nucleonics Week*, December 10, 1987, p. 15.
88. "Norway and Israel Resolve Dispute Over Heavy Water," *International Herald Tribune,* June 11-12, 1988; John J. Fialka, "Israel Tentatively Gives Its Approval for Norwegians to Inspect Heavy Water," *Wall Street Journal,* June 13, 1988.
89. See, *e.g.*, "Sources View Iraqi Missiles as 'Direct' Threat," *Hadashot*, August 5, 1987, translated in *FBIS/NES*, August 5, 1987, p. L-1; Elaine Ruth Fletcher, "Iraqi Missile Poses Threat to Israel," *Jerusalem Post*, August 15, 1987.
90. On Israeli concerns about Syrian chemical missile capabilities, see, Raphael, "Syria and Israel, Too Near the Brink," (see note 73); Ian Black, "Israel Tries to Counter Arab Nerve Gas Threat," *Manchester Guardian Weekly*, December 21, 1987.
91. Jack Anderson and Dale Van Atta, "Israel May Hit Syrian Nerve Gas Plant," *Washington Post*, February 24, 1988.
92. "Rabin on Saudi Missiles, Other Issues," *Yedi'ot Aharonot*, April 1, 1988, translated in *FBIS/NES*, April 6, 1988, p. 29.
93. "Shomron Discusses Unrest, Saudi Missiles, Syria," Jerusalem Domestic Service, 0400 GMT, April 9, 1988, translated in *FBIS/NES*, April 11, 1988, p. 31. Shomron went on to note that Israel's response to the growing missile and chemical threat also included efforts to develop anti-tactical ballistic missiles, plans to attack enemy

missiles before they were launched, and civil defense measures that include the issuance of gas masks to the Israeli population.

94. Yohanan Ramati, "Israel and Nuclear Deterrence," *Global Affairs* (Spring 1988, Vol III, No.2).

Libya

1. The story has been reported by Mohamed Heikel, confidant of then Egyptian President Gamal Abdul Nasser, whose assistance Khadafi sought in approaching China. See Mohamed Heikel, *The Road to Ramadan* (New York: Quadrangle/The New York Times Book Co., 1975), pp. 76-77. The story was later confirmed by Mohammed al-Mougariaf, the former Libyan ambassador to India. See American Broadcasting Company, "News Closeup," Monday, April 27, 1981, "Near Armageddon: The Spread of Nuclear Weapons in the Middle East," Transcript, p. 43. The story is widely accepted by U.S. non-proliferation officials.

2. Steve Weissman and Herbert Krosney, *The Islamic Bomb* (New York: Times Books, 1981), p. 60. Among other elements of the arrangement, according to knowledgeable Pakistani and Libyan officials interviewed by Western journalists, Libya specifically requested training in the operation of hot cells, the radiologically shielded units in which plutonium can be extracted from spent reactor fuel.

3. Weissman and Krosney, *The Islamic Bomb,* pp. 211-212 (see note 2); "Niger Says It Sold Uranium to Libya, Use for Nuclear Weaponry Feared," *Washington Star,* April 14, 1981. Niger has since agreed to make future yellowcake sales exclusively to NPT parties with valid safeguards agreements. Niger reportedly believed this standard was satisfied in the case of Libya between 1978 and 1980 because it was a party to the NPT.

4. U.S. Congress, Office of Technology Assessment, *Technology Transfer to the Middle East* (Washington, D.C.: U.S. Government Printing Office, 1985), pp. 385-386. This analysis states that Libya is known to have purchased 788 tons of uranium from Niger and may have purchased about 2,000 tons. See also, "Uranium Exports for First Six Months Given," Agence France Press 0859 GMT, August 27, 1981, translated in *Joint Publications Research Service (JPRS)/Nuclear Development and Proliferation (TND),* September 24, 1981, p. 17, giving slightly lower figures.

5. "Libya Presses India on Nuclear Technology," *Nuclear Engineering International* (November 1979): 7.

6. *Ibid.* See also "Libya Charged with Using Oil to Obtain Nuclear Technology," *Business Times* (Kuala Lumpur), August 30, 1979, (quoting from stories in the *Times of India* and the *Hindu),* trans-

lated in *JPRS/TND,* October 31, 1979, p. 7.

7. "Indo-Libyan Nuclear Accord," *The Telegraph* (Calcutta), August 8, 1984, reprinted in *JPRS/TND,* September 24, 1984, p. 69. India's stance provides further evidence of the caution exhibited by "second tier" nuclear-supplier countries in sharing nuclear technology.

8. Congressional Research Service, *Analysis of Six Issues About Nuclear Capabilities of India, Iraq, Libya and Pakistan,* report prepared for the Subcommittee on Arms Control, Oceans, International Operations, and Environment of the Senate Foreign Relations Committee, 1982, p. 11; Joseph V.R. Micallef, "A Nuclear Bomb for Libya?" *Bulletin of the Atomic Scientists* (August-September 1981): 14.

9. Senate Foreign Relations Committee, *Hearings on the Israeli Air Strike,* June 18, 19, and 25, 1981, 97th Cong., 1st Sess. (Washington, D.C.: U.S. Government Printing Office, 1981) p. 50; Claudia Wright, "Libya's Nuclear Program," *The Middle East* (February 1982): 47.

10. In 1976, Libya also signed a nuclear cooperation agreement with France for the purchase of a 600-megawatt nuclear power plant, but France later barred the deal because of concerns over Libyan-Pakistani cooperation. See "France Is To Build Libyan Atomic Plant," *New York Times,* March 23, 1976; Office of Technology Assessment, *Technology Transfer to the Middle East,* p. 385, (see note 4); Thomas O'Toole, "Libya Said to Buy Soviet A-Power Plant," *Washington Post,* December 12, 1977.

11. "Envoy Says Soviets May Build Nuclear Plant in Egypt," Associated Press, May 10, 1986, AM cycle; "Libya Abandons Plans for First Unit," *Nuclear Engineering International* (April 1986): 6; "On-Again, Off-Again Libyan Nuclear Power Plant Surfaced Once More," *Nucleonics Week,* March 31, 1983, p. 11; Ann MacLachlan, "Libyans Are Seeking Broad International Cooperation in Nuclear Area," *Nucleonics Week,* September 27, 1984, p. 1.

12. "U.S. Bans Libyans from Some Studies," *Washington Post,* March 11, 1983.

13. Guy Duplat, "Possible Breakthrough in Belgian Nuclear Cooperation with Arab Countries," *Le Soir,* August 8, 1981, translated in *JPRS/TND,* September 8, 1981, p. 2; "US Presses Belgians to Cut Libya Ties," *Nuclear Fuel,* April 26, 1982, p.11.

14. Some U.S. officials feared that Libya could use uranium metal as fuel in a crude natural-uranium/graphite reactor to produce plutonium. A crude reprocessing plant for extracting the plutonium might be within the range of Libyan capabilities, especially with assistance from Pakistan or, possibly, Argentina.

Uranium hexafluoride might serve as feedstock if Libya were to build an enrichment plant under its supposed arrangement with Pakistan, or if the material could be sent to Pakistan for enrichment to weapons grade.

The Belgonucléaire facility might not have been subject to IAEA inspections despite Libya's adherence to the NPT, since IAEA rules may exempt such plants. The issue had, apparently, never been decided by the Agency.

15. "Belgium, Libya Reportedly Ready to Sign Nuclear Pact," *Wall Street Journal,* May 18, 1984; Ann MacLachlan, "Belgians Fail To Get Guarantees from Neighbors on Libyan Aid," *Nucleonics Week,* December 6, 1984, p. 7.

16. Fred Hiatt, "Belgium Urged to Reject Pact With Libyans," *Washington Post,* October 9, 1984.

17. MacLachlan, "Belgians Fail to Get Guarantees from Neighbors on Libyan Aid," (see note 15); "Government Stopping Libyan Deal," *Nuclear News* (January 1985); interviews with Western European officials, May 1985.

18. "Libya Aided Argentina in War," *New York Times,* May 14, 1984.

19. "Brazilian Military Concern Over Argentine Talks with Libya," *Correio Braziliense,* May 24, 1983, translated in *JPRS/TND,* June 30, 1983, p. 8; unpublished interview with Carlos Castro Madero, former head of the Argentine Atomic Energy Commission, by John Cooley, ABC News, fall 1984. The events suggest the possibility that Tripoli was seeking a nuclear quid pro quo for its earlier military assistance.

20. "Uranium Mining Aid to Libya," *Correio Braziliense,* November 8, 1984, translated in *JPRS/TND* January 14, 1985, p. 42; "Negotiations Begin on Building Warships for Libya," Agence France Presse 1624 GMT, October 5, 1984, translated in *FBIS/Latin America,* October 9, 1984, p. D-1; "Libya Seeks Military Cooperation," *O Estado de São Paulo,* December 23, 1984, translated in *FBIS/Latin America,* December 26, 1984, p. D-1.

21. Mac Margolis, "Brazil Plans to Resume Weapons Sales to Libya," *Washington Post*, January 28, 1988. Brazil had suspended sales to Libya in 1983 after discovering that four Libyan cargo planes that had landed for refueling in Manaus carried a clandestine East Bloc arms shipment destined for Nicaragua.

22. This episode is described in detail in Joseph C. Goulden, *The Death Merchant* (New York: Bantam Books, 1985), pp. 289-295; see also, Peter Maas, *Manhunt* (New York: Random House, 1986), pp. 176-177, 179-182. Both appear to rely in part on the testimony of John Heath at Wilson's 1983 trial in Houston, Texas, for illegal export of explosives. Heath was an employee of Wilson who was present at the meetings when the nuclear arms were discussed with Libyan officials. Neither Goulden nor Maas had access, however, to the

documents describing the nuclear deal offered the Libyans, which were obtained by the author in 1986 under the Freedom of Information Act and are discussed in detail in Leonard S. Spector, *Going Nuclear* (Cambridge, MA: Ballinger Publishing Company, 1987), pp. 150-159.

According to Heath's testimony at Wilson's 1983 trial, Wilson was motivated by simple greed in pursuing the deal. See Transcript of testimony of John Heath, January 29 and 31 and February 3, 1983, p. 71, *U.S. v. Wilson,* Cr. H-82-139, Federal District Court, Southern District of Texas. In an interview conducted in the fall of 1986, Wilson challenged this version. While confirming that meetings were held with Libyan officials to discuss the nuclear sales, he claimed that Heath "was the one that was really pushing it" because "he wanted to make a commission out of the thing." Indeed, Wilson asserted that he "killed the deal" when interviewed in 1986. See Alan Berlow, *National Public Radio,* "All Things Considered," August 14, 1986, 6:30 PM. The jury in Wilson's trial, however, found Heath a credible witness, and U.S. law enforcement officials reject Wilson's account of his role.

23. See preceding note.
24. See Maas, *Manhunt,* pp. 77, 89-90, 94-96 (see note 21). Wilson was convicted in 1983 for the C-4 deal.
25. Goulden, *The Death Merchant,* p. 290, (see note 21). According to Goulden's account, Donnay claimed that he could obtain the material from a Portuguese associate; the material was said to have come from a nuclear reactor in Germany.
26. Sources differ as to the precise date of Donnay's visit. Goulden states that it took place in the "late spring" of 1981, but Maas places it in February of that year. Heath, in testifying on the matter, stated he was not sure of the date but thought it was "around 1980." The contract, discussed below, which Donnay and Wilson presented to the Libyans is headed "Validity: 15/3/1981" suggesting it was drafted in March of that year. (In European notation, the month appears after the day in such abbreviations.)
27. Heath testimony, pp. 74, 77, (see note 21).
28. Joseph Goulden, *The Death Merchant,* p. 291, (see note 21).
29. Goulden states one additional meeting was held; Wilson's attorney in cross-examining Heath at Wilson's trial, however, referred to Wilson's presence at "several" of them.
30. "Al-Qadhdhafi Lectures University Students," Tripoli Television Service, 1958 GMT, June 21, 1987, translated in *FBIS/NES,* June 26, 1987.
31. "Al-Qadhdhafi Discusses Upcoming Amman Summit," Tripoli Television Service, 2032 GMT, November 2, 1987, translated in *FBIS/NES,* November 3, 1987, p. 19.

32. "Chad Accuses Libyans of Using Napalm, Gas," *Washington Post,* December 23, 1987; E. A. Wayne, "Libya Seeks Chemical Weapons in War Against Chad, US Charges," *Christian Science Monitor,* January 5, 1988.

33. See references in previous note and "The Year in Missiles," *Defense and Foreign Affairs* (March 1988): 22.

34. See references in note 31.

35. John Barham, "Brazil Ignores US Protest Over Arms for Libya," *Sunday Times* (London), January 31, 1988; "Libya Said Financing Missile Construction," Rio De Janeiro Rede Globo Television, 2200 GMT, February 3, 1988, translated in *FBIS/Latin America,* February 4, 1988, p. 32; "Missiles to Libya," *Washington Times,* February 22, 1988.

Iraq

1. Paul Power, "The Baghdad Raid: A Retrospect and Prospect," *Third World Quarterly* (July 1986):860; Michael Dobbs, "France Delays On Iraqi Reactor," *Washington Post,* December 3, 1984; Ann MacLachlan, "France's Prime Minister Denies He Promised to Rebuild Osirak Reactor," *Nucleonics Week,* August 13, 1987, p. 13.

2. Several possible sites for the project were reported to have been identified in 1985-1986, "Iraq Selects Sites," *Nuclear Engineering International* (April 1986):5; "Al-Ittihad: USSR to Select Nuclear Reactor Site," *Al-Ittihad* (Abu Dhabi), March 11, 1985, p. 6, translated in *Foreign Broadcast Information Service (FBIS)/Middle East and Africa,* March 14, 1985, p. E-3.

3. Two U.S. specialists knowledgeable about nuclear weapons design consulted by the author, stated that it would be feasible for Iraq with its limited nuclear skills to make a weapon out of the 27.5 pounds (12.5 kilograms) of highly enriched uranium. A third specialist believed as many as three weapons could be fabricated from the material. Several other non-proliferation experts, probably less familiar with the details of weapons design, were more skeptical, however. Most sources use 33 to 55 pounds (15 to 25 kilograms) as the amount of highly enriched uranium needed for a nuclear explosive, but the amount can apparently be reduced with certain design refinements that are described in unclassified publications. U.S. experts also believe that the fact that Iraq's highly enriched uranium was lightly irradiated in the adjacent Isis reactor in 1980 would not significantly impede the use of the material for a weapon today.

4. Leonard S. Spector, *The New Nuclear Nations* (New York: Vintage Books, 1985), pp. 44-54.

5. See notes 20-22, below and accompanying text.

6. See Power, "The Baghdad Raid" (see note 1); Jed C. Snyder, "The Road to Osiraq: Baghdad's Quest for the Bomb," *The Middle East Journal* (Autumn 1983): 565; U.S. Congress, Office of Technology Assessment, *Technology Transfers to the Middle East* (Washington, DC: Government Printing Office, 1984), p. 388; Lucien Vandenbroucke, "The Israeli Strike Against Osiraq," *Air University Review* (September-October 1984): 35; Leonard S. Spector, *Nuclear Proliferation Today* (New York: Vintage Books, 1984), pp.166-183.

7. Jed C. Snyder, "The Non-Proliferation Regime: Managing the Impending Crisis," *Journal of Strategic Studies* (December 1985):11.

8. See references in note 6 and citations therein. Another controversial aspect of the Osiraq project was the fact that it was to be fueled with highly enriched uranium, material directly usable for nuclear weapons. France originally proposed selling Iraq 158 pounds (72 kilograms) of the material, enough for several weapons. When, under international pressure, France proposed a substitute fuel that could not be used for nuclear arms, Iraq objected, insisting that only the fuel France originally promised would permit a full range of research activities at Osiraq. This insistence, too, has been taken as an indication that Iraq saw the reactor and its fuel as means for advancing toward the bomb. Ultimately, France agreed to provide highly enriched material, but only in smaller quantities so that once Osiraq began operating, Iraq would not have on hand at any time enough readily available weapons-grade uranium for a single weapon, assumed to require 55 pounds (25 kilograms) of the material under IAEA guidelines. (Only 55 pounds (25 kilograms) of fresh fuel would be in Iraq at any time, half of which would be in Osiraq and thus contaminated with radioactivity, and the other half of which was to be lightly irradiated in the adjacent Isis reactor, slightly contaminating it with radioactivity at least temporarily.) This left irradiation of uranium targets in Osiraq (to be subsequently reprocessed in the hot cells or an expanded reprocessing unit) as the major proliferation risk posed by the reactor.

9. Ann MacLachlan, "Iraq Nuclear Export Vetoed," *The Energy Daily,* October 2, 1980, p. 1; Spector, *The New Nuclear Nations,* pp. 165-166 (see note 4). This episode is also highlighted in Snyder, "The Road to Osiraq" (see note 6). Depleted uranium, a leftover of the uranium enrichment process, is uranium from which the uranium-235 isotope has been culled; if the remaining material—uranium-238—is irradiated in a reactor, a portion is transmuted into plutonium. See glossary.

10. It should be noted that under the NPT, Iraq had the obligation to open the Italian hot cells to periodic IAEA inspections only after it had introduced nuclear materials there; until Iraq declared that nu-

clear material had been introduced, IAEA inspectors had the right to check that design information submitted to the Agency was accurate, but no on-going authority to inspect these units or another Italian laboratory capable of fabricating uranium specimens that could have been inserted into Osiraq. Although Iraq had not yet declared the labs to the Agency at the time of the Israeli raid, using the facilities to produce plutonium clandestinely would still have required defeating the tight safeguards on Osiraq itself. See Jed C. Snyder, "The Non-Proliferation Regime" (see note 7) and references in the next note below.

11. H. Gruemm, "Safeguards and Tamuz: Setting the Record Straight," *IAEA Bulletin* (December 1981): p. 1; Christopher Herzog, "Correspondence to the Editor," *International Security* (Spring 1983): 196. Iraq could have pursued the manufacture and testing of non-nuclear atomic weapon components in secret. Regarding the subsequently abandoned Swedish nuclear weapons program of the late 1950s and the 1960s, see Spector, *The New Nuclear Nations,* pp. 65-77, (see note 4).

12. The setbacks to the Iraqi program included an April 1979 explosion that destroyed the Osiraq reactor's core structures while they were awaiting shipment to Iraq in a warehouse in Seine-sur-Mer, France; the June 1980 murder in Paris of Dr. Yahya el-Meshad, an Egyptian nuclear scientist working for the Iraqi Atomic Energy Commission; and a series of bombings and bomb threats against a number of French and Italian companies supplying nuclear equipment for the Iraqi nuclear program. Some observers attribute these acts to Israel. See Spector, *Nuclear Proliferation Today,* pp. 175-178, (see note 6) (also discusses Israeli diplomatic efforts to slow the Iraqi program).

13. Through a series of interim measures at the 1983 and 1984 General Conferences, a final decision on sanctions against Israel had been postponed to succeeding years, enabling the United States to return as a full participant in IAEA activities in mid-1983. See Spector, *The New Nuclear Nations,* pp. 143-146 (see note 4). A motion at the 1986 General Conference for sanctions against Israel—made only days before a major press story indicating that Israel had a more substantial nuclear arsenal than previously assumed—was withdrawn after it became clear it would be defeated. Anti-Israel measures were no more successful at the 1987 session.

14. *Ibid,* pp. 44-54. The discussion of this episode is based on European press accounts, a review of the prosecutor's dossier in the case, an in-person interview with one defendant, and a telephone interview with a second.

15. One defendant stated in an interview that he discussed the price of the plutonium with a "general of the Iraqi Army in charge of mis-

siles," during a May 1982 meeting in Rome. A May 7, 1982, cable to him from a second member of the smuggling ring quotes the price for the material, apparently in preparation for the meeting. (The price was $60,572,000 or $1.78 million per kilo.) The trial of the case was still pending as of early 1988.

16. MacLachlan, "France's Prime Minister Denies He Promised to Rebuild the Osirak Reactor" (see note 1), reporting on a story in the French satirical weekly, *Le Canard Enchaîné*. It appears that nuclear contacts between the two countries have continued, however, with a French nuclear team visiting Baghdad in early 1987.

17. Shlomo Nakdimon, *First Strike* (New York: Summit Books, 1987). The book details Begin's concerns over Iraq's nuclear program, his lack of confidence in IAEA and French controls, and the extensive, but unsuccessful diplomatic efforts he mounted to slow the Iraqi nuclear program. Citing, among other evidence, a December 1980 memo that U.S. ambassador to Israel Samuel Lewis discussed with Begin, the book notes that senior American officials had concluded that the Osiraq reactor would allow Iraq to fabricate nuclear arms by the mid-1980s and that they saw Iraq's large-scale purchases of natural uranium as evidence of its intent to use the facility to produce plutonium. U.S. aides, however, appeared to take greater comfort from French restrictions and IAEA controls than their Israeli counterparts. See pp. 136-137, 144, 177-177.

18. *Ibid.*, pp. 110 (military planning begins December 1979; initial "daring" concept relies on U.S.-supplied F-4s and A-4s, necessitating in-air refueling); p. 124 (first F-16s received July 2, 1980; long-range flight practice begins immediately); p. 168 (plan could not be executed with only the five F-16s then in Israel's possession; air force awaiting arrival of additional warplanes); p. 181 (strike date to be set as soon as second squadron of F-16s is received; exercises confirm F-16s can reach Osiraq and return without in-air refuelling); p. 189 (F-16s formally designated for attack).

19. Bob Woodward, *Veil: The Secret Wars of the CIA 1981-1987,* (New York: Simon and Schuster, 1987), p. 161; Bob Woodward, "Probes of Iran Deals Extend to Roles of CIA, Director," *Washington Post,* November 25, 1987.

20. Elaine Sciolino, "Iraq Cited on Chemical Weapons," *New York Times,* March 15, 1986; Michael Berlin, "U.N. Team Says Chemical Agents Used in Gulf War," *Washington Post,* March 27, 1984.

21. "Iraq Chemical War Cited in U.N.," *New York Times,* May 14, 1987.

22. "Iran Says Iraq Used Nerve Gas," *International Herald Tribune,* March 21, 1988; Patrick Tyler, "Poison Gas Attack Kills Hundreds," *Washington Post,* March 24, 1988.

23. Iraq's continued possession of a 12.5 kilograms of highly enriched

uranium under IAEA inspection—from which a nuclear device might conceivably be fabricated if Iraq chose to violate these safeguards—remains a matter of concern, however.

24. "Iraq Chemical War Cited in U.N.," *New York Times,* (see note 21); Aly Mahmoud, "Saudi Asks Iran to Rejoin Fight Against Israel, *Washington Post,* December 28, 1987; "Dutch, at U.S. Request, Seize Chemical Weapons," *Washington Post,* March 2, 1988.

25. See note 30, below; Michael R. Gordon, "U.S. Thinks Libya May Plan to Make Chemical Weapons," *New York Times,* December 24, 1987.

26. John Cushman, "Iraqi Missile Attacks on Iran: A New Twist to the Old War," *New York Times,* March 2, 1988; Charles P. Wallace, "Iraq, in First Such Attack, Fires Missiles at Iranian Holy City of Qom," *Washington Post,* March 3, 1988. For a detailed discussion of the growing missile capabilities of Iraq and other potential nuclear-weapon states, see Chapter II.

27. Indeed, Iraq has implicitly threatened such an attack. See "Iraq Accuses Iran of Using Poison Gas," *Washington Post,* March 30, 1988.

28. "Sources View Iraqi Missiles as 'Direct' Threat," *Hadashot,* August 5, 1987, translated in *FBIS/Near East & South Asia (NES),* August 5, 1987, p. L-1; Elaine Ruth Fletcher, "Iraqi Missile Poses Threat to Israel," *Jerusalem Post,* August 15, 1987.

29. Jack Anderson and Dale Van Atta, "Israel May Hit Syrian Nerve Gas Plant," *Washington Post,* February 24, 1988.

30. See, *e.g.,* Gideon Rafael, "Syria and Israel: Too Near the Brink," *Washington Post,* January 11, 1987. On Israeli concerns about Syrian chemical missile capabilities, see, Ian Black, "Israel Tries to Counter Arab Nerve Gas Threat," *Manchester Guardian Weekly,* December 21, 1987.

31. Although there have been no reports of Iraqi efforts to design a nuclear device or to perform the necessary preliminary tests, such activities would undoubtedly be carried out in secret and might not be apparent to outside observers in any case.

32. David Ignatius and Gerald Seib, "U.S., Iraq to Restore Full Diplomatic Ties; Baghdad Split with Radical Arabs Is Seen," *Wall Street Journal,* November 8, 1984; Bernard Gwertzman, "U.S. Restores Full Ties with Iraq but Cites Neutrality in Gulf War," *New York Times,* November 27, 1984; "Iraq is Breaking Its Ties with Libya," *New York Times,* June 27, 1985; "Ties with Egypt," Voice of the Masses (Baghdad), translated in *FBIS/NES,* November 16, 1987, p. 1.

Iran

1. Daniel Poneman, *Nuclear Power in the Developing World,* (London: George Allen & Unwin Ltd., 1982), p. 96.

2. Thomas Stauffer, "Ayatollah Rediscovers Nuclear Power, with Kraftwerk Union's Aid," *Energy Daily,* October 2, 1984; "German Team Inspects Stalled Bushehr Plants," *Nuclear News* (June 1984): 95. The West German government has refused to issue export licenses for some 7,000 tons of major nuclear components for the plant. See, Richard Kessler, "CNEA Estimates Bushehr-1 Work Worth $100-million to Argentina," *Nucleonics Week,* August 20, 1987, p. 13.
3. See Akbar Etemad, "Iran" in Harald Mueller, *European Non-Proliferation Policy* (Oxford: Oxford University Press, 1987). Etemad was the chairman of the Atomic Energy Organization of Iran during its period of greatest activity under the Shah.
4. Intelligence data obtained by the United States in the late 1970s indicated that the Shah had set up a secret research group to work on nuclear weapons. According to one knowledgeable specialist, the unit was a "nuclear weapons design team" whose existence so troubled U.S. non-proliferation aides that a then pending agreement for cooperation with Iran in the areas of nuclear research and power was put on hold. Another official recalled that "at one of their research centers we were concerned that paper studies and computer analyses of nuclear weapons were under way;" it appeared, he continued, that "they had gotten a charter from the Shah." A third U.S. insider described the unit as a group doing "advanced research that didn't look too good," but he did not recall clear evidence of work being performed on nuclear arms. It is not clear when these research activities were initiated. (Based on interviews with current and former U.S. officials, spring 1986.) For a detailed review of Iran's nuclear activities under the Shah, see Leonard S. Spector, *Going Nuclear,* (Cambridge, MA: Ballinger Publishing Co., 1987), pp. 45-57.
5. Etemad, "Iran," p. 9, (see note 3); "Iranian Reactor to Go Critical," *Nuclear Engineering International* (December 1984): 13. (The "reactor" referred to is a subcritical training unit, *i.e.,* one that will not sustain a nuclear chain reaction.)
6. See also Etemad, "Iran," pp. 23-28, (see note 3).
7. Tim Coone and Peter Bruce, "Three-Nation Bid for Iran N-Deal," *Financial Times,* March 9, 1987; Richard Kessler, "CNEA Estimates Bushehr-1 Work Worth $100-Million to Argentina," *Nucleonics Week,* August 20, 1987, p. 13.
8. "Iran to Receive Nuclear Technology, Know-How," Noticias Argentinas, 1800 GMT, May 18, 1987, translated in *Foreign Broadcast Information Service (FBIS)/Latin America,* May 19, 1987; "Argentina Confirms Deal for Work on Bushehr," *Nuclear News* (July 1987): 54. See Richard Kessler, "Argentina To Enforce Curbs on Nuclear Trade with Iran," *Nucleonics Week,* March 19, 1987, p. 12.
9. In a larger reactor, it might be possible to irradiate natural uranium

to create plutonium which, after it was separated, would potentially be available for nuclear weapons. In the late 1970s, Israel became concerned that Iraq intended to use its large Osiraq reactor in this way, and in 1981 Israeli warplanes destroyed the facility. The 5-megawatt Iranian reactor, however, is only an eighth of the size of the 40-megawatt Iraqi unit and lacks the power to irradiate significant quantities of uranium in this fashion.

10. Mark Hibbs, "Iraqi Attack on Bushehr Kills West German Nuclear Official," *Nucleonics Week,* November 19, 1987, p. 1; Mark Hibbs, "Bushehr Construction Now Remote after Three Air Strikes," *Nucleonics Week,* November 26, 1987, p. 5. Although Iraq initially denied attacking the installation, it quickly expressed its official regret to Bonn for the death of the West German nuclear engineer at the site.

11. Prior to the March 4, 1985 attack, Iraqi warplanes had bombed the site on March 24, 1984, and February 12, 1985. Iraq's Osiraq research reactor outside Baghdad has also been the target of bombing attacks, one by Iran on September 30, 1980, and the second by Israel on June 7, 1981, which destroyed the facility.

12. Hibbs, "Bushehr Construction Now Remote" (see note 10). Ironically, it was Iraq's delegate who denounced attacks against nuclear installations before a U.N. group in May 1987, declaring that military attacks with conventional weapons against such facilities are "tantamount to the use of radiological weapons because of the release of radioactive material that could result therefrom." See "U.N. Envoy Urges Mid-East Nuclear-Free Zone," Baghdad INA, 1252 GMT, June 4, 1987.

13. Gamini Seneviratne, "IAEA Mission Will Visit Bushehr," *Nucleonics Week,* March 3, 1988, p. 7.

14. Hibbs, "Bushehr Construction Now Remote" (see note 10); "Iraqi Raids Thwart Bushehr Plans," *Nuclear Engineering International* (April 1988):8.

15. Michael J. Berlin, "Iraq Used Poison Gas, U.N. Says," *Washington Post,* May 14, 1987.

16. "Iran Making Toxic Arms, Official Says," *Philadelphia Inquirer,* December 28, 1987; "Iranians Back Off Claims for Weapons," *Washington Times,* December 31, 1987; "Chemical Warfare Planned Against Basra," Kuwait KUNA, 1755 GMT, February 26, 1988, reprinted in *FBIS/Near East South Asia,* February 29, 1988.

Chapter V:
Latin America—Introduction

1. Although Cuba is building two nuclear power reactors with Soviet assistance at Cienfuegos, also called Jugara, these units (and two more that are planned) will be under International Atomic Energy Agency safeguards and are not considered a proliferation concern. In the aftermath of the Chernobyl accident, however, Cuba's construction of the Soviet-supplied reactors evoked fears that they might pose a health and safety threat to the United States, ninety miles away, if they experienced a similarly severe accident. However, the Cuban power reactors are of a substantially different design from the Chernobyl facility. Significantly, the Cienfuegos reactors use water, rather than graphite, as a moderator and will employ an advanced containment system not used at Chernobyl.

Argentina

1. A bloodless military coup on March 24, 1976, ousted Argentina's President María Estela Martinez de Perón, wife of two-time president Juan Domingo Perón, and installed a governing junta composed of the commanders of the three armed forces. The coup, led by army Gen. Jorge Rafael Videla, came after months of rampant inflation, right- and left-wing terrorism, and political indecision. Gen. Videla was sworn in as president and served until March 1981, when he was replaced in rapid succession by Gen. Roberto Viola (March–December 1981), Gen. Leopoldo Galtieri (December 1981–July 1982) and Gen. Reynaldo Bignone (July 1982–December 1983). This period of military rule was marked by political repression, including suppression of opposition parties and wide-scale detention, torture, and killing of suspected left-wing activists, and by continued economic hardship. After Argentina's defeat in the 1982 Falklands War, Gen. Bignone initiated a transition to civilian rule that culminated in the election of Radical Civic Union candidate, Dr. Raúl Alfonsín, to the presidency in October 1983.
2. The plants are the West German-supplied Atucha I and the Canadian-supplied Embalse reactors. Both are natural uranium/heavy water reactors.
3. One key commodity still needed from abroad is heavy water, used in Argentina's power reactors. In a controversial 1980 deal, however, the Swiss firm, Sulzer Brothers, with the approval of the Swiss government, agreed to sell Buenos Aires a safeguarded industrial-scale heavy-water production plant, to be built at Arroyito.

   In 1979, Argentina had solicited bids for both the large heavy water plant and for a third nuclear power plant, Atucha II. Canada and West Germany were asked to submit bids for both plants. Canada stated that it would not sell the plants unless Argentina agreed to maintain all of its nuclear installations—current and future—under IAEA safeguards. Under U.S. urging, West Germany agreed to apply the same conditions, apparently because a heavy water plant, rarely sold in international nuclear commerce, was involved. At the last minute, however, Argentina announced it would split the deal, buying the heavy water plant from Switzerland, which had not made these "full-scope" safeguards a condition for the sale, and purchasing the reactor from Germany, which then declared that it, too, would not require comprehensive safeguards, since it was no longer selling the heavy water plant. Canada considered the German action a betrayal of its previous understanding with Bonn. Switzerland and Germany did require, however, that the reactor, the heavy water plants, any plutonium produced through their use, and any facilities based on their technology be placed under safeguards.

Argentina is also developing an experimental heavy water facility indigenously. (See the chart at the end of this section.)

4. Plans to build a large, indigenous research reactor, RA-7, have apparently been abandoned. See Richard Kessler, "Argentina Denies It Plans Large Unsafeguarded Research Reactor," *Nucleonics Week,* August 8, 1985, p. 5. The facility's spent fuel could have been reprocessed at Ezeiza without IAEA oversight to produce plutonium that could be used for nuclear weapons without violating any international undertakings. Technically, several of Argentina's existing research reactors are subject to IAEA inspection only because of the presence of imported enriched uranium fuel, and, if unsafeguarded fuel (imported from China in the early 1980s or produced indigenously) were used, any plutonium subsequently extracted could be available for weapons. The output of these reactors, however, would be insignificant.

This chapter relies heavily on reporting by Richard Kessler, whose analyses over the years have proven consistently reliable; key details have been verified with U.S. and Latin American embassy officials in Washington, D.C.

5. Richard Kessler, "Argentina's CNEA to Begin Testing Pilot Reprocessing Plant at Ezeiza," *Nucleonics Week,* April 18, 1988, p. 12.

6. Argentina's natural uranium/heavy water reactors do not require enriched uranium fuel. Although there may be some small economic benefit to using slightly enriched uranium in them, no other country does so. Argentina's research reactors do require enriched uranium but the Pilcaniyeu plant's capacity, as announced, was more than sixteen times that necessary to serve these small research

facilities. Moreover, the decision of Argentina's former leaders not to place the plant under IAEA safeguards meant that if it were configured to produce weapons-grade uranium, Argentina would be free to use the material for nuclear arms.

Commencement of the Pilcaniyeu project coincided with the start of construction of the Ezeiza reprocessing plant, and the two appeared to be a direct response to Brazil's 1975 deal with West Germany, under which it was to receive both enrichment and reprocessing capabilities. (Indeed the then head of the Argentine Nuclear Energy Commission acknowledged to one U.S. non-proliferation aide that Argentina could not abandon the Ezeiza plant—then the only one of the two Argentine plants publicly announced—because of the 1975 Brazilian deal.)

These factors and Argentina's increasing militarism in 1978, as evidenced by its provocation of a near-war with Chile over the Beagle Channel Islands and a major build-up of conventional armaments, strongly suggested that the Pilcaniyeu installation was initiated for the purpose of giving Argentina a nuclear weapons option.

The secret decision, in 1978, to build the Pilcaniyeu plant may help to explain why Argentina's military government resisted "full-scope" safeguards so vigorously in 1980, when it was negotiating with Canada and West Germany on the purchase of a nuclear power reactor and a heavy-water production plant, although it should be noted that opposition to such constraints predated the decision to build the enrichment facility.

Argentina produces its own uranium and has unsafeguarded facilities for refining it and for converting it to uranium hexafluoride, the form of uranium needed in the enrichment process. See the chart at the end of the chapter.

7. Leonard S. Spector, *Nuclear Proliferation Today* (New York: Vintage Books, 1984), pp. 257-263. One well-placed Brazilian official, speaking anonymously in 1986 about the sudden disclosure of the facility, echoed these concerns in a more muted tone: "The people here hadn't expected such a development and felt the Argentines hadn't been quite candid. I believe this has created some uneasiness." See Bradley Graham, "Argentine Leader Proposes Moving Capital to Patagonia," *Washington Post,* April 17, 1986.

8. Richard Kessler and Mark Hibbs, "Pilcaniyeu Safeguards Offer Tied to Nuclear Transfer by Argentina," *Nuclear Fuel,* February 11, 1988; Richard Kessler, "Argentina's Alfonsín Pledges Funding for Fuel Cycle Projects," *Nucleonics Week,* June 5, 1986. The plant has a capacity of 20,000 separative work units per year (twice that of South Africa's Valindaba pilot enrichment plant); in principle this capacity is enough to produce up to 220 pounds (100 kilograms) of 90 percent-enriched uranium per year, depending on how the

facility is laid out.

9. Although the Peronists were narrowly defeated by Alfonsín's Radical Civic Union in Argentina's 1983 general elections, they retained a substantial voice in the nation's domestic political debate. Drawing on the coalition put together by Juan Perón, president of Argentina from 1946 to 1955 and again from 1973 until his death the following year, the Peronists achieved political support through a platform of intense nationalism and affiliation with labor. Opposition to Alfonsín's economic policies in 1984, for example, was mounted by the Peronists in conjunction with the General Confederation of Labour (CGT), Argentina's powerful trade union. The November 1985 mid-term congressional elections, however, showed a growing dissatisfaction with the Peronist opposition, especially with the wing of the party most closely associated with union bosses. As discussed below, this part of the party has since been eclipsed by reformist elements, which appear to have supported Alfonsín's nuclear opening to Brazil.

10. Leonard S. Spector, *The New Nuclear Nations* (New York: Vintage Books, 1985), pp. 182-183.

11. See *e.g.* "Alfonsin Proposes CNEA Reforms," *Nuclear Engineering International* (September 1984): 10.

12. Richard Kessler, "Argentina May Be Scaling Down Heavy Water Production Plans," *Nucleonics Week,* May 16, 1985, p. 13. The Treaty of Tlatelolco requires parties to accept IAEA safeguards on all their nuclear installations, but the pact does not become binding on a state that ratifies it until all regional states have taken this step; a ratifying country can voluntarily waive this entry-into-force requirement, however, and accept the treaty as binding. Brazil and Chile have ratified the treaty but have not waived this condition. Argentina has neither ratified the treaty nor waived this condition, and Cuba has not even signed the pact. Except for these countries, virtually all other regional states have both ratified the accord and waived the entry-into-force requirement. See Appendix E.

13. Richard Kessler, "Argentina, Brazil Agree to Mutual Inspection of Nuclear Facilities," *Nucleonics Week,* March 14,1985, p. 14. Unlike ratification of the Treaty of Tlatelolco, which might have the appearance of a unilateral concession made at least partly in response to long-standing pressure from the United States and others, implementation of the mutual inspection proposal would allow Alfonsín to argue that he had gained something in return for relinquishing Argentina's nuclear privacy.

14. Lydia Chavez, "Argentina Plans Stringent Curbs on Economy and New Currency," *New York Times,* June 15, 1985; Lydia Chavez, "Leader Imposes a State of Seige on Argentina," *New York Times,* October 26, 1986; Bradley Graham, "Ruling Party Leads in Vote

by Argentines," *Washington Post,* November 4, 1986. The right-wing bombings were apparently an attempt to compel the government to grant amnesty in the trials of Argentina's former military leaders accused of murder and torture while they were in power during the 1970s. These trials were nearing their conclusion when the bombing campaign took place. In mid-December, Generals Emilio Massera, Roberto Viola, and Jorge Videla were convicted and given stiff prison sentences.

15. "Joint Declaration on Nuclear Policy by the Governments of Brazil and Argentina," November 29, 1985, (copy obtained from the Argentine Embassy, Washington, D.C.).

Some important nuclear cooperation has already taken place under the 1980 Brazil-Argentina nuclear trade pact, including Argentina's lease of 240 metric tons (265 short tons) of uranium concentrate to Brazil, which Brazil "returned" after its own uranium-mining operations were expanded; Argentina's sale to Brazil of 160,000 meters (175,000 yards) of zircalloy tubing for nuclear-power-reactor fuel elements; and Brazil's contract to manufacture a portion of the reactor vessel for Argentina's Atucha II nuclear-power plant, which was delivered in late June 1987. See "Argentina: Atucha-2 Vessel Arrives," *Nucleonics Week, July* 2, 1987.

16. "Alfonsin Wants Nonproliferation," *Jornal do Brasil,* December 1, 1985, translated in *Joint Publications Research Service(JPRS)/Nuclear Developments (TND)* January 9, 1986, p. 16; Richard Kessler and Jeff Ryser, "Argentina-Brazil Committee to Work Out Details of Joint Inspection," *Nucleonics Week,* December 5, 1986, p. 9.

17. To symbolize the new direction in bilateral relations, at the conclusion of the talks, Alfonsín accompanied Sarney to the Itaipu hydroelectric dam, built by Brazil and Paraguay; Argentina had not joined in the project, which its military government had claimed represented a threat to Argentine security. See Richard Kessler, "Argentine-Brazilian Committee to Work Out Details of Joint Inspections," *Nucleonics Week,* December 5, 1985, p. 9.

18. Richard Kessler, "Argentina and Brazil Will Not Provide the IAEA with Information," *Nucleonics Week,* March 2, 1986, p. 9.

19. "Committee Report On Talks with Argentina, Accord with *FRG,"O Estado de São Paulo,* April 18, 1986, translated in *JPRS/ TND,* June 13, 1986, p. 44; Richard Kessler, "Panel Favors Mutual Inspections of Facilities by Argentina, Brazil," *Nucleonics Week,* May 1, 1986, p. 6.

20. Richard Kessler, "Argentine-Brazil Protocol Promotes Nuclear Accident Accord," *Nucleonics Week,* July 31, 1986, p. 1.

21. Tim Coone, "Sarney and Alfonsin to Sign Trade Pact," *Financial Times,* July 29, 1986.

22. Martin Anderson, "Alfonsin Faces New Violence," *Washington*

Post, June 3, 1986; Shirley Christian, "Military Tensions Rise in Argentina," *New York Times,* June 12, 1986; "Dante Caputo Rules Out Coup Possibilities," Telam, 1157 GMT, June 15, 1986,translated in *Foreign Broadcast Information Service (FBIS)/Latin America (LAT),* June 17, 1986, p. B-1.

23. See also note 26 below, and accompanying text.
24. Richard Kessler, "For the First Time, Argentina Has Ratified an International Nuclear Treaty," *Nucleonics Week,* May 7, 1987, p. 6.
25. Ivo Dawnay, "Brazil and Argentina to Set Seal on Collaboration," *Financial Times,* December 10, 1986; Richard Kessler, "Argentina-Brazil Protocols Detail Broad Nuclear Cooperation," *Nucleonics Week,* December 11, 1986, p. 9. For additional details on cooperation between Brazilian and Argentine nuclear firms, see Richard Kessler, "Argentine-Brazilian Firms Pool Nuclear Design Know-How," *Nucleonics Week,* January 15, 1987. The nuclear protocols provided for joint research efforts on advanced fuels for research reactors, the economic feasibility of breeder reactors, and the production of stable isotopes.
26. Richard House, "Brazil Steps Back from Race to Build Nuclear Weapons," *Washington Post,* August 28, 1986; Richard Kessler, "Electronic Monitors Eyed for Argentine-Brazil Mutual Inspections," *Nucleonics Week,* September 11, 1986.
27. Richard Kessler, "Sarney Visit to Pilcaniyeu Was Key to Reciprocal Inspections," *Nucleonics Week,* July 23, 1987, p. 11.
28. Richard Kessler, "Costantini Resigns as CNEA Head in Bitter Funding Dispute," *Nucleonics Week,* April 16, 1987, p. 7.
29. "Speech by President Alfonsin at the Central Atomic Energy Day Ceremony, Embalse, Rio Tercero, May 30, 1986," translated by Congressional Research Service (author's files). Concerning the position of the traditional elements of the Peronist Party, see Richard Kessler, "Argentine Bill Proposes Role for Congress in Nuclear Decisions," *Nucleonics Week,* October 23, 1986, p. 9.
30. "Opposition to Nuclear Plan," *La Nueva Provincia,* June 14, 1987, translated in *JPRS/TND,* August 18, 1987, p. 20. See also, Richard Kessler, "Shakeup Seen for Argentina's CNEA Under New Head Perez Ferreira," *Nucleonics Week,* May 21, 1987, p. 1.
31. As subsequently published estimates revealed, the start-up dates for both Atucha II and the Swiss-supplied heavy water plant would be postponed for one year, to 1993 and mid-1989, respectively, and cost increases for the latter facility had raised serious questions about its economic viability, even among CNEA officials. Richard Kessler, "Production Delayed for a Year at Argentine Heavy Water Plant," *Nuclear Fuel,* July 13, 1987, p. 13; Richard Kessler, "Atucha-2 to Cost $1 Billion More than Originally Estimated," *Nucleonics Week,* November 19, 1987, p. 6. Alfonsin was said to be

seeking to write off the indigenous heavy water plant at Atucha, and subsequent official reviews of the status of Argentina's principal nuclear projects have not mentioned the unit.

32. The nuclear bureaucracy suffered a further blow to its prestige later in 1987, when Alfonsin appointed a special planning committee to oversee implementation of existing nuclear construction plans. See "Atomic Energy Consultative Council Planned," Telam, 1052 GMT, November 19, 1987, translated in *FBIS/LAT*, November 24, 1987, p. 22. In the latter part of the year and in early 1988, moreover, CNEA's technical capabilities were called into question when Argentina's two operating nuclear power plants suffered a series of unplanned outages that ultimately led to rotating blackouts in Buenos Aires. See Tim Coone, "N-Power Shutdown Forces Argentina to Ration Fuel," *Financial Times*, April 19, 1988.

Concerning the priority given the Pilcaniyeu facility, see, Richard Kessler, "Argentina to Begin Enriching 20% U-235 in Mid-1988," *Nuclear Fuel*, May 18, 1987, p. 3; "CNEA Head Discusses Nuclear Policy Issues," Noticias Argentinas, 1305 GMT, November 24, 1987, translated in *FBIS/LAT*, November 30, 1987, p. 26.

33. Martin Anderson, "Alfonsin Presents Bill to Absolve Most Officers," *Washington Post*, May 14, 1987.

34. Robert Graham, "Alfonsin Battles to Keep House in Order," *Financial Times*, January 29, 1988.

35. Daniel Poneman, "Argentina: The Military Threat Remains," *International Herald Tribune*, January 27, 1988.

36. "Nuclear Fuel Pact Signed with Argentina," Agence France Presse, 2333 GMT, April 23, 1987, translated in *FBIS/LAT*, April 24, 1987, p. D-2.

37. See Atomic Energy Act of 1954, section 128 (added by the 1978 Nuclear Non-Proliferation Act).

38. Richard Kessler, "Argentina to Sell Brazil Low- and Medium-Enriched Uranium," *Nucleonics Week*, July 23, 1987, p. 1; Rik Turner, "Brazil Wants to Sell Slightly Enriched Uranium to Argentina," *Nucleonics Week*, July 30, 1987, p. 1. Argentina's nuclear power plants use natural uranium as fuel, but Argentina has hoped to increase their efficiency by substituting slightly enriched material. Brazil's existing and planned nuclear power plants require 3 percent-enriched uranium fuel, but the Resende facility will be able to produce only material enriched to .85 percent—the level needed by Argentina—unless the facility is significantly expanded, which appears unlikely. As of July 1987, it also appeared that Brazil lacked any near-term capability for producing the small amounts of twenty-percent enriched material needed for its research reactors. Argentina's Pilcaniyeu enrichment plant is intended to produce material enriched to these higher levels and thus cross-purchases of

nuclear fuel appeared to make sense.

39. "Joint Argentine-Brazilian Declaration on Nuclear Policy," Viedma, Argentina, July 17, 1987; Michael Gordon, "Brazil and Argentina Start Nuclear Talks," *New York Times*, July 22, 1987; Kessler, "Sarney Visit to Pilcaniyeu Was Key to Reciprocal Visits," (see note 27).

40. "Officials on Navy Nuclear Facilities, Program" *Fôlha de São Paulo*, April 7, 1988, translated in *FBIS/LAT*, April 11, 1988, p. 38.

41. Nonetheless, the important distinction between confidence building and reliable verification must be recognized. See discussion below and in the part of this chapter on Brazil.

42. Kessler, "Sarney Visit to Pilcaniyeu Was Key to Reciprocal Visits" (see note 27).

43. Richard House, "Brazil Says Uranium Enriched," *Washington Post*, September 10, 1987; Rik Turner and Michael Knapik, "Brazil's 'Parallel Program' Publicized by Sarney's Centrifuge Announcement," *Nuclear Fuel*, October 19, 1987, p. 3.

44. *Ibid.*

45. Richard Kessler, "With the Ultra-Nationalist Peronists Again Argentina's Majority Party," *Nucleonics Week*, September 17, 1987, p. 13. On the Peronists shift to the center, see generally, Shirley Christian, "Peronist Leaders Pledge Stability," *New York Times*, September 10, 1987; Tim Coone, "Peronists Hold Key to Power," *Financial Times*, September 15, 1987. For a thoughtful discussion of the elections and their impact on Argentine nuclear policy, see John R. Redick, "Nuclear Restraint in Latin America," Occasional Paper No. 1, Programme for Promoting Non-Proliferation, Center for International Policy Studies, University of Southampton, (June 1988).

46. "Alfonsin Talks with Foreign Correspondents," Argentina Televisora Color Network, 1300 GMT, December 5, 1987, translated in *FBIS/LAT*, December 7, 1987, p. 32; Richard Kessler, "Argentina, Brazil Continue Talks on Nuclear Accord Amid Uncertainty," *Nucleonics Week*, February 25, 1988, p. 6; Richard Kessler, "Sarney and Alfonsin Inaugurate Brazilian Facility," *Nucleonics Week*, April 14, 1988, p.6.

47. Richard Kessler, "Brazil Giving Argentina Access to Operating Nuclear Facilities," *Nucleonics Week*, March 24, 1988, p. 9.

48. "Joint Policy Declaration with Argentina," *Fôlha de São Paulo*, April 8, 1988, translated in *FBIS/LAT*, April 11, 1988, p. 36. The number of centrifuges then operating at the Aramar unit was not disclosed, but by this juncture, Brazil claimed to have enriched uranium to 5 percent, and possibly to 8 percent, either at the facility or at IPEN's research unit. See "Officials on Navy Nuclear Facilities, Program," *Fôlha de São Paulo*, (see note 40); "Sarney, Alfonsin to

Inaugurate Nuclear Plant," *O Globo*, March 2, 1988, translated in *FBIS/LAT*, March 4, 1988, p. 27 (uranium enriched to 8 percent).

49. Spector, *Nuclear Proliferation Today*, pp. 212-213, 228, (see note 7); Spector, *The New Nuclear Nations*, pp. 185-187, (see note 10). Concerning nuclear cooperation with Brazil, see note 15, above.

50. See previous note.

51. "Government to Cooperate on Iranian Nuclear Plant," Noticias Argentinas, 1665 GMT, March 9, 1987, translated in *FBIS/LAT*, March 16, 1987, p. B-1; Richard Kessler, "Argentina Denies Deal with KWU and Iran to Finish Bushehr," *Nucleonics Week*, June 4, 1987, p. 6 (article says negotiations are continuing, but no contract has been signed).

52. "Argentina and Cuba Signed a Cooperative Pact," *Nuclear News* (January 1987): 66; Richard Kessler, "Argentina Plans Deeper Nuclear Ties with Cuba," *Nucleonics Week*, February 11, 1988, p. 3.

53. Richard Kessler, "The Presidents of Argentina and Uruguay Signed a 'Working Agreement,'" *Nucleonics Week*, June 4, 1987, p. 6.

54. Richard Kessler, "Mexico Quietly Seeking Fuel Cycle Technology from Argentina," *Nucleonics Week*, June 25, 1987, p. 2.

55. Richard Kessler, "Argentina is Actively Pursuing Talks on Nuclear Ties with Albania," *Nucleonics Week*, August 27, 1987, p. 6; Richard Kessler, "Argentina is 'Still Undecided' on Nuclear Links with Albania," *Nucleonics Week*, September 10, 1987, p. 6. "Nuclear Cooperation Accord signed with Turkey," Telam, 1801 GMT, May 3, 1988, translated in *FBIS/LAT*, May 5, 1988, p. 12.

56. Tim Coone, "Argentine N-Fuel May Go to Iran," *Financial Times*, March 14, 1987; Richard Kessler, "Argentina's INVAP to Supply Iran Fuel for Research Reactor," *Nucleonics Week*, May 14, 1987, p. 2.

57. One troubling aspect of the Argentine-Iranian nuclear deal have been the repeated rumors that Iran is hoping to obtain uranium enrichment know-how from Argentina, technology that could in principle assist Iran in manufacturing nuclear arms. See Kessler, "Argentina's INVAP to Supply Iran Fuel for Research Reactor" (see note 56).

58. "Government to Cooperate on Iranian Nuclear Plant," Noticias Argentinas, (see note 51).

59. Atomic Energy Act of 1954, as amended, section 128. See also, Richard Kessler "Kennedy Visit Prompts Hopes of U.S.-Argentine Nuclear Thaw," *Nucleonics Week*, March 17, 1988, p. 7. Partly as a result of this embargo, Argentina has turned in recent years to the Soviet Union and the People's Republic of China for heavy water, needed to run Argentina's nuclear power plants, and for highly enriched uranium to fuel the country's research reactors. See Spector,

Nuclear Proliferation Today, pp. 211-212, (see note 7). President Alfonsín held talks on obtaining additional heavy water from China in May 1988. As noted in the text, Argentina is building its own heavy water production facilities (a Swiss-supplied commercial-scale plant and an indigenously developed experimental unit) and hopes to produce enriched uranium for its research reactors at the Pilcaniyeu enrichment plant.

60. Argentina produced gram quantities of the latter material in the late 1960s, but this is not considered significant from the standpoint of proliferation.

61. Richard Kessler, "Argentina to Begin Enriching to 20% U-235 in Mid-1988," *Nuclear Fuel*, May 18, 1987, p. 3 (current target level is 2 percent enrichment); Kessler, "Sarney Visit to Pilcaniyeu Was Key to Reciprocal Inspections," (facility enriching uranium to 8 to 12 percent) (see note 20); Simon Henderson, "Puzzle of Brazil's Enrichment Claims," *Financial Times*, October 7, 1987 (facility producing only 1 percent-enriched material). The Pilcaniyeu enrichment plant thus remains some time away from its design output of 1,100 pounds (500 kilograms) of 20 percent enriched uranium, announced in 1983. A facility with this capability could, in theory, be modified to produce about 220 pounds (100 kilograms) of weapons-grade, 93 percent-enriched uranium annually, enough for four to six weapons, using standard estimates of 33 to 55 pounds (15 to 25 kilograms) of material per device.

62. "CNEA Head Discusses Nuclear Policy Issues," Noticias Argentinas, 1305 GMT, November 24, 1987, translated in *FBIS/LAT*, November 30, 1987, p. 26.

63. *Ibid.*

64. The situation could be greatly complicated if the nuclear submarine programs that Brazil, and possibly Argentina, are pursuing ultimately require highly enriched uranium fuel. In this case—even if additional verification procedures were implemented—it would be extremely difficult to be certain that weapons-grade material produced for propulsion purposes was not being used for nuclear explosives. See "Construction of Nuclear Submarines Revealed," *Fôlha de São Paulo*, September 28, 1986, translated in *JPRS/TND*, October 22, 1986, p. 9 (describing Argentine program); but see "Foreign Secretary on Nuclear Projects, Iran," Noticias Argentinas, 1558 GMT September 16, 1987, translated in *FBIS/LAT*, September 17, 1987, p. 18 (Argentine program suspended in 1983). For a discussion of the Brazilian program, see the section on Brazil, below.

65. Richard Kessler, "Argentina's CNEA to Begin Testing Pilot Reprocessing Plant at Ezeiza," *Nuclear Fuel*, April 18, 1988, p. 12.

Brazil

1. The differing roles of the military in the two countries was starkly contrasted in April 1988, when the Argentine senate enacted a statute prohibiting the participation of the Argentine armed forces in any internal conflict. The same day, Brazil's constituent assembly adopted a provision to be included in Brazil's new constitution specifying that Brazil's armed forces would, in the words of a news account, "continue safeguarding constitutional powers and internal and external order." See "Senate Approves National Defense Law," Buenos Aires Domestic Service, 1600 GMT, April 14, 1988, translated in *Foreign Broadcast Information Service(FBIS)/Latin America (LAT)*, April 15, 1988, p. 20 (broadcast refers to developments on April 13); "Constituent Assembly on Armed Forces Duties," Brasília Radio Nacional da Amazonia, 1000 GMT, April 13, 1988, translated in *FBIS/LAT*, April 14, 1988, p. 22.
2. See Leonard S. Spector, *Nuclear Proliferation Today*, (New York: Vintage Books, 1984) pp. 239-244.
3. "Angra I Inaugurated," *O Estado de São Paulo*, January 18, 1985, translated in *Joint Publications Research Service (JPRS)/Nuclear Proliferation and Development (TND)*, March 12, 1985. The facility first operated in 1982, but underwent an unusually long period of debugging, which delayed commercial operation for three years. The facility has since experienced serious operating problems.
4. Rik Turner, "Brazil's Sarney Defines Emphasis for National Fuel Cycle Development," *Nuclear Fuel*, August 11, 1986, p. 10. Sarney's decision implemented the recommendations of a special commission he had appointed in 1985 shortly after he took office and codified what had been de facto policy for a number of years. See "Brazil Commission Opts to Continue Nuclear Program," Reuters, April 18, 1986; Robert Townley, "Brazil Rekindles Reactor Program and Denies Proliferation Plans," *Nucleonics Week*, August 14, 1986, p. 12.

   The reprocessing plant was intended to extract plutonium from spent nuclear-power-reactor fuel. Brazil planned to recycle the plutonium by using it in fresh reactor fuel instead of low-enriched uranium. At the time, a world-wide uranium shortage was predicted, and it was assumed that such recycling of plutonium would be essential for the economical operation of Brazil's nuclear power reactors. Today, because of the global down-turn in the growth of nuclear energy, there is a glut of inexpensive enriched uranium on world markets. This has undermined the economic rationale for the costly facility.

   Although Brazil cancelled the plant, it had already received extensive plutonium extraction technology from West Germany. Under the terms of the 1975 agreement, however, if Brazil were to build a separate plutonium extraction plant using this technology in the future, it would have to place the unit under IAEA safeguards.

As of mid-1987, the Angra II and Angra III nuclear power reactors were scheduled to be completed in 1993 and 1995, respectively, but further delays are likely.

5. Rik Turner, "Brazil's Nuclebras Wants to Sell Slightly Enriched U [Uranium] to Argentina," *Nucleonics Week*, July 30, 1987. The material will be enriched only to 0.85 percent uranium-235, fractionally above the naturally occurring rate of the isotope, which is 0.7 percent. Brazil's nuclear power reactors require 3 to 5 percent-enriched uranium; nuclear weapons use 93 percent-enriched material.

The German uranium enrichment plant could, in theory, be reconfigured to produce highly enriched material, but this would violate Brazil's understandings with Germany and would be unlikely to escape detection by the IAEA, whose safeguards are being applied to the facility. The Brazil-West German agreement specifies that Brazil must accept IAEA safeguards on any other jet-nozzle enrichment plant it may build in the future.

6. See Appendix E.

7. According to one account, a 1978 "summit" of representatives of the CNEN, Nuclebras, and the National Intelligence Service first determined that Brazil should pursue nuclear activities in parallel with those under the 1975 West German accord. See "Ten Billion Cruzeiros to be Allocated to Nuclear Research," *Jornal do Brasil*, January 16, 1983, translated in *JPRS/TND*, March 21, 1983, p. 28. Geisel is said to have given his approval shortly before he left office in March 1979, and planning activities began later that year. See "Officials on Navy Nuclear Facilities, Program," *Fôlha de São Paulo*, April 7, 1988, translated in *FBIS/LAT*, April 11, 1988, p. 38; "Do It Yourself Reprocessing," *Economist*, January 24, 1987, p. 80.

Activities under the navy's enrichment program commenced in February 1980 and the first enrichment experiment took place in September 1982 at IPEN; two years later nine centrifuges had been linked there in the first experimental "cascade." See "Officials on Navy Nuclear Facilities, Program," just cited.

8. José Sarney took office following indirect elections that were held in January 1985. The winner of the indirect elections, Tancredo Neves—a long-time opponent of military rule—died before he could take office, and Sarney, his running mate, succeeded to the post. Until a few months before the election Sarney had been the leader of the military government's Social Democrat Party—the

party whose candidate, Paulo Maluf, Neves had resoundingly defeated. With his popular mandate thus highly uncertain, Sarney has relied heavily on the political support of the military, which, unlike its counterpart in Argentina, has not been tainted by a recent defeat and has continued to wield considerable influence.

9. The program is under the control of the navy and received funding from the navy, the CNEN, and the National Security Council. See Richard Kessler, "Sarney Visit to Pilcaniyeu Was Key to Reciprocal Inspections," *Nucleonics Week*, July 23, 1987, p. 11; "Officials on Navy Nuclear Facilities, Program," *Fôlha de São Paulo* (see note 7).

10. "IPEN's UF-6 Conversion Technology Said to be Ready for Commercial Use in Brazil," *Nuclear Fuel*, July 28, 1986, p. 5.

11. "Cals on Angra Problems, Laser Beam Enrichment Process," *Jornal do Brasil*, July 7, 1984, translated in *JPRS/TND*, September 24, 1984, p. 48. Additional work on lasers is said to have been conducted at the University of Campinas.

12. "Brazil Says It Now Produces Small Amounts of Plutonium," *Washington Post*, December 18, 1986; Charles Thurston, "Brazil Denies Report of Reprocessing, Plutonium Production at IPEN," *Nuclear Fuel*, December 29, 1986, p. 9. Some confusion appears to have been created when CNEN officials commented that the organization had mastered the technology of plutonium extraction on a laboratory scale, erroneously suggesting that plutonium had been obtained, when, apparently, only the techniques involved had been successfully demonstrated. Concerning allegations that the unit produced plutonium in 1983, see Leonard S. Spector, *Nuclear Proliferation Today*, pp. 247-252, (see note 2).

13. "Production of Atomic Bomb Expected in 1990," *Fôlha de São Paulo*, April 28, 1985, translated in *FBIS/LAT*, May 1, 1985, p. D-1; "Editorial Questions . . .," *Fôlha de São Paulo*, October 14, 1984, translated in *JPRS/TND*, December 19, 1984, p. 36.

14. Spector, *Nuclear Proliferation Today*, pp. 259-262, (see note 2).

15. In June 1985, for example, Admiral José Maria do Amaral Oliveira, chief of the Armed Forces General Staff, publicly opposed a draft amendment to the Brazilian constitution prohibiting the development of nuclear arms, declaring that, "We must not restrict ourselves in the future." See "EMFA [Armed Forces General Staff] Opposes Constitutional Restraint," *Fôlha de São Paulo*, June 22, 1985, translated in *JPRS/TND*, September 23, 1985, p. 51. Two months later, Brigadier General Hugo de Oliveira Piva, director of the Air Force's Aerospace Technology Center, declared that "Brazil will be able to make the atomic bomb within five years" and that a decision on taking this step "is being discussed by the National Security Council." See "Piva Confirms Country Able to Make

Bomb in Five Years," *O Estado de São Paulo*, August 17, 1985, translated in *JPRS/TND*, October 21, 1985, p. 18.

16. In September 1985, Army Minister Leonidas Pires Goncalves, according to a detailed press report, openly urged the development of a Brazilian nuclear bomb during a meeting with senior members of the Brazilian congress and solicited their support for further nuclear technology development. Asserting that Brazilian intelligence services had learned that at the time of the 1982 Falklands crisis Argentina's military regime had intended to invade southern Brazil to recover disputed territory in Rio Grande do Sul province, Pires Goncalves told the parliamentarians, in the words of the news account, "that Brazil should develop its nuclear industry only for deterrence and to prevent the Brazilian Armed Forces from remaining at a disadvantage in case of a military conflict." See "Army Minister Said to Favor Building Atomic Bomb," EFE, 1431 GMT, September 1, 1985, translated in *FBIS/LAT*, September 4, 1985, p. D-2; Richard Kessler, "Argentina Had No Official Comment on News Reports...," *Nucleonics Week*, September 5, 1985, p. 9. The report, acutely embarrassing to the Sarney government, was quickly denied, but Pires Goncalves's views were said to "receive positive reaction" in other military quarters. See "EMFA Chief Denies Interest in Building Atomic Bomb," *O Estado de São Paulo*, September 8, 1985, translated in *JPRS/TND*, December 13, 1985, p. 32; "Setabul Reassures Argentina on Atomic Bomb," *O Globo*, September 5, 1985, translated in *FBIS/LAT*, September 10, 1985, p. D-1. See also, "Army Minister Stresses Need to Complete Nuclear Fuel Cycle," *O Estado de São Paulo*, September 5, 1985, translated in *JPRS/TND*, September 23, 1985, p. 48.

Two weeks later, Navy Minister Enrique Saboya appeared to take a stand nearly as forceful as the one ascribed to Pires Goncalves by urging support, in one Brazilian newspaper's paraphrase, for "mastering the cycle of studies for manufacturing the atomic bomb." See "Navy Minister Said to Support Atomic Bomb Plan," EFE, 0135 GMT, September 14, 1985, translated in *FBIS/LAT*, September 17, 1985.

17. "Further Reportage of Alleged Nuclear Test Site," *Fôlha de São Paulo*, August 8, 1986, translated in *FBIS/LA*, August 12, 1986, p. D-1; Richard House, "Brazil Steps Back from Race to Build Nuclear Weapons," *Washington Post*, August 28, 1986.

18. Richard Townley, "Brazil Rekindles Reactor Program and Denies Proliferation Plans," *Nucleonics Week*, August 14, 1986, p. 12.

19. *Ibid.*

20. According to one specialist, such a test would need only rudimentary instrumentation within the shaft itself; this would be augmented by seismic data from nearby pick-ups and after-the-fact analysis of

radioactive debris in the shaft.

21. Mitchell Reiss, *Without the Bomb* (New York: Columbia University Press, 1988), pp. 228-229, (India's device, including monitoring equipment and safety locks, was three feet in diameter; Indian test shaft was an "L-shaped trench built 107 meters [348 feet] below the surface"); Christer Larsson, "Build A Bomb!" *Ny Teknik*, April 25, 1985, (Swedish weapon was 1.9 feet in diameter).

22. See discussion in section on South Africa.

23. It is also possible that this faction hoped that by building the necessary infrastructure in advance, it could encourage a national decision to build nuclear arms, or perhaps it sought to ensure that it would "get a piece of the action" in the event that a decision to develop nuclear weapons was made at some later time.

24. "Joint Declaration on Nuclear Policy by the Governments of Brazil and Argentina," November 29, 1985. (Author's files.)

25. Richard Kessler, "Argentina and Brazil Will Not Provide the IAEA with Information," *Nucleonics Week*, March 27, 1986, p. 9.

26. This became clear in April, when a special inter-ministerial committee reviewing Brazil's troubled nuclear accord with West Germany released its final report. The committee, established in September 1985 and made up of industrialists and officials from a range of government departments, strongly endorsed the reciprocal inspection idea. See "Committee Reports on Talks with Argentina, Accord with FRG," *O Estado de São Paulo*, April 18, 1986, translated in *JPRS/TND*, June 13, 1986, p. 44; Richard Kessler, "Panel Favors Mutual Inspections by Argentina and Brazil," *Nucleonics Week*, May 1, 1986, p. 6.

27. "Nuclear Inspection Clause with Argentina Rejected," EFE, 1517 GMT, August 19, 1986, translated in *FBIS/LAT*, August 21, 1986, p. D-1. Nuclear cooperation was, however, improved, as both countries agreed to notify the other in the case of nuclear accidents. See Richard Kessler, "Argentina-Brazil Protocol Promotes Nuclear Accident Accord," *Nucleonics Week*, July 31, 1986, p. 1.

28. Whatever the precise reasons for Sarney's reluctance, a statement released by former Navy Minister Admiral Maximiano Fonseca in early September 1986 left no doubt that interest in nuclear arms continued to smoulder among elements of the Brazilian military. In an unusually explicit statement, he declared, "If it were up to me to decide, I would make an atomic bomb and detonate it in front of international observers to demonstrate the extent of national technical know-how . . . One hates to see the big powers developing and detonating atomic, cobalt, and neutron bombs without being able to do the same ourselves." See "Former Navy Minister Advocates Bomb," Agence France Presse, 2136 GMT, September 5, 1986, translated in *FBIS/LAT*, September 8, 1986, p. D-2.

Maximiano Fonseca is said to be notorious for his inflammatory statements, and thus his views might not have been widely shared. Nonetheless, his comments undoubtedly added to the pressures on Sarney to sustain the parallel program.

29. "Former Nuclear Official Protests Military Role," *Fôlha de São Paulo*, November 11, 1986, translated in *JPRS/TND*, December 3, 1986.

30. Ivo Dawnay, "Brazil and Argentina to Set Seal on Collaboration," *Financial Times*, December 10, 1986; Richard Kessler, "Argentina-Brazil Protocols Detail Broad Nuclear Cooperation," *Nucleonics Week*, December 11, 1986, p. 9. For additional details on cooperation between Brazilian and Argentine nuclear firms, see Richard Kessler, "Argentine-Brazilian Firms Pool Nuclear Design Know-How," *Nucleonics Week*, January 15, 1987.

31. Richard Kessler, "Sarney Visit to Pilcaniyeu Was Key to Reciprocal Inspections," *Nucleonics Week*, July 23, 1987, p. 11.

32. "Parallel Program's Achievements, CNEN Secret Accounts Viewed," *Veja*, January 14, 1987, translated in *JPRS/TND*, March 4, 1987, p. 11.

33. "Nazareth on Program Costs, Activities under New Constitution," *Istoe*, September 16 1987, translated in *JPRS/TND*, January 28, 1988, p. 27.

34. "Experts Discuss Development of Nuclear Bomb," *Fôlha de São Paulo*, March 22, 1987, translated in *FBIS/LAT*, March 25, 1987, p. D-1.

35. *Ibid.*

36. "Nuclear Fuel Pact Signed with Argentina," Agence France Presse, 2333 GMT, April 23, 1987, translated in *FBIS/LAT*, April 24, 1987, p. D-2. See discussion in Argentina section, above.

37. The facility, which has produced only low-enriched uranium but which is potentially capable of producing weapons-grade material, was secretly built by Argentina's military government between 1978 and 1983 and is not covered by IAEA inspections.

38. Richard House, "Brazil Says Uranium Enriched," *Washington Post*, September 10, 1987; Rik Turner and Michael Knapik, "Brazil's 'Parallel Program' Publicized by Sarney's Centrifuge Announcement," *Nuclear Fuel*, October 19, 1987, p. 3.

39. "IPEN Head Guarantees Nuclear Project Safety," *O Estado de São Paulo*, September 9, 1987, translated in *FBIS/LAT*, September 11, 1987, p. 11. Each centrifuge is said to be five feet (1.5 meters) in height, with a metal cylinder twenty inches (50 centimeters) in diameter at the middle, that rotates like a "clothes washer" at very high speeds. See "Funding Needs, Suppliers of Parallel Program Discussed," *Exame*, October 14, 1987, translated in *JPRS/TND*, February 14, 1988, p. 21.

40. "Funding Needs, Suppliers of Parallel Program Discussed," *Exame* (see note 39).
41. "Paper discusses Plans for Nuclear Submarine," *O Estado de São Paulo*, April 12, 1987, translated in *FBIS/LAT*, April 22, 1987, p. D-2 (Navy's objective is to enrich uranium to a minimum of 70 percent, using 3,000 centrifuges); "Twenty Percent Enriched Uranium to be Produced by June, *Gazeta Mercantil*, February 5, 1988, translated in *JPRS/TND*, March 23, 1988 (20 percent-enriched uranium to be produced by June 1988, a "higher" level of enrichment to be achieved later.)
42. "CNEN Official Speaks on Nuclear Program," *Fôlha de São Paulo*, September 6, 1987, translated in *FBIS/LAT*, September 10, 1987, p. 19.
43. Sarney has also had to play the role of broker during the country's transition to democracy between a military reluctant to cede power and a populace hungry for a greater say in the country's political affairs. One analysis of Sarney's announcement suggested that by extolling the military he was trying to blunt a controversial proposal by several opposition parties to prohibit the military under Brazil's new constitution from interfering in the country's internal affairs. See House, "Brazil Says Uranium Enriched" (see note 38).
44. *Ibid.*
45. Both steps were taken to accelerate the date of direct elections for the nation's next leader and to replace Sarney, perceived as increasingly ineffectual, with a more powerful figure. Sarney, it will be recalled, had come to office on the death of Tancredo Neves, who had, himself, been selected for the presidency indirectly, by an electoral college. Part of the opposition to Sarney's bid for a five-year term stemmed from the desire for further democratization through direct elections.
46. Alan Riding, "Brazil President Gets 5-Year Term," *Washington Post*, June 3, 1988.
47. "Constituent Assembly Approves Text Governing Nuclear Activities," *O Globo*, March 8, 1988, translated in *JPRS/TND*, April 28, 1988, p. 12.
48. Another factor that weakens the provision is that Brazil's constitution can be amended by majority vote of the Brazilian congress, giving the nuclear restrictions (and the remainder of the charter) little more authority than simple legislation.
49. Richard Kessler, "Brazil Giving Argentina Access to Operating Nuclear Facilities," *Nucleonics Week*, March 24, 1988, p. 9.
50. "Joint Policy Declaration with Argentina," *Fôlha de São Paulo*, April 8, 1988, translated in *FBIS/LAT*, April 11, 1988, p. 36.
51. Officials on Navy Nuclear Facilities, Program," *Fôlha de São Paulo* (see note 9); "Sarney, Alfonsin to Inaugurate Nuclear Plant,"

O Globo, March 2, 1988, translated in *FBIS/LAT*, March 4, 1988, p. 27 (uranium enriched to 8 percent).

52. "Officials on Navy Nuclear Facilities, Program," *Fôlha de São Paulo* (see note 9). The article quotes CNEN President Rex Nazareth as stating that Brazil will keep secret the quantity of enriched uranium and the production capacity of the Aramar Experimental Center, since Argentina had refused to disclose such information about its Pilcaniyeu enrichment facility.

53. The situation could be greatly complicated if the nuclear submarine programs that Brazil, and possibly Argentina, are pursuing ultimately require highly enriched uranium fuel. In this case—even if additional verification procedures were implemented—it would be difficult to be certain that weapons-grade material produced for propulsion purposes was not being used for nuclear explosives.

54. Kessler, "Brazil Giving Argentines Access to Operating Nuclear Facilities" (see note 49).

55. "Officials on Navy Nuclear Facilities, Program," *Fôlha de São Paulo* (see note 9); Richard Kessler and Mark Hibbs, "Pilcaniyeu Safeguards Offer Tied to Nuclear Transfer by Argentina," *Nucleonics Week*, February 11, 1988, p. 4.

56. Atomic Energy Act of 1954, as amended, Section 128.

Chapter VI
Africa—Introduction

1. "Nigerian FM calls for Nuclear Weapons," *Defense and Foreign Affairs Daily,* August 26, 1987, p. 2.

2. "Babangida Remarks on Nuclear Policy," Agence France Presse 1633 GMT, April 14, 1986, reprinted in *Foreign Broadcast Information Service (FBIS)/Near East and Africa,* April 15, 1986, p. T-7.

3. *Ibid.* In 1980, in the midst of Nigeria's oil boom, Chuba Okadigbo, a senior adviser to then Nigerian President Shehu Shagari, stated in an address to the Foreign Policy Association in New York that Nigeria could obtain the technology and materials needed for a nuclear bomb and intended to build one "if it is necessary to bring South Africa to the negotiating table." Okadigbo, who declared that he was speaking for the Nigerian government on the matter, continued, "We won't allow Africa to be subjected to nuclear blackmail," and added that it would be "unreasonable to expect" other African nations not to seek a nuclear weapon to meet South Africa's presumed capability. See Jonathan Kwitny, "Nigeria Considers Nuclear Armament Due to South Africa," *Wall Street Journal,* October 6, 1980. Nigeria's current economic plight makes the possibility of its developing a nuclear weapons program all the more remote.

   On the possibility of black African proliferation more generally, see Tunde Adeniran, "Nuclear Proliferation and Black Africa: The Coming Crisis of Choice," *Third World Quarterly* (October 1981): 673; Robert D'A. Henderson, "Nigeria: Future Nuclear Power?" *Orbis* (Summer 1981): 409; Ladi Adenrele, "Models of Nuclear Weapons Decision Strategy in Africa," *Arms Control* (September 1984): 148; Oye Ogunbadejo, "Africa's Nuclear Future," *Journal of Modern African Studies* (1984): 19.

4. But see, "Nigeria Offers Uranium in Exchange for Enrichment Technology," *O Estado de São Paulo,* September 11, 1987, translated in *FBIS/Nuclear Developments*, January 28, 1988, p.18 (alleging that Nigeria may be seeking to obtain uranium enrichment technology).

5. Discussion of this scenario is not intended to be a prediction that a future South African government will necessarily espouse a radical ideology. Nonetheless, the threat of a radical takeover is one that cannot be ruled out. For a detailed analysis of the risks of nuclear "inheritance," including a review of relevant past examples in France, China, Vietnam, and Iran, see Leonard S. Spector, *Going Nuclear* (Cambridge, MA: Ballinger Publishing Company, 1987), Chapters II and VI.

6. Mary Battiata, "Author Defends 'Africans,' " *Washington Post,* September 6, 1986. Mazrui expressed similar views during a 1985 interview. See David K. Willis, "South African Blacks to Have the Bomb by the Year 2000?," *Christian Science Monitor,* July 1, 1985. See also, Peter Lomas, "Valindaba: Lessons from South Africa's Nuclear Policy," *The World Today* (June 1987): 95, expressing the hope that a future majority South African government might renounce nuclear arms and join the NPT.

South Africa

1. One recent study, while agreeing that South Africa seems to have little military need for nuclear arms, notes that senior South African military officials consider a massive invasion by neighboring black-led states to be a worst-case scenario for military planning purposes. The author of the study notes that tactical nuclear weapons could have utility against such a threat, although he considers this threat to be remote. See Robert S. Jaster, "Pretoria's Nuclear Diplomacy," CSIS [Center for Strategic and International Studies] *Africa Notes,* January 22, 1988.
2. Murray Marder and Don Oberdorfer, "How West, Soviets Moved to Head Off S. Africa A-Test," *Washington Post*, August 28, 1977.
3. Interview with author, spring 1985.
4. David Fishlock, "The South African Nuclear Weapons Scare," paper prepared for the Congressional Research Service, December 1977, p. CRS-5.
5. Marder and Oberdorfer, "How West, Soviets Moved" (see note 2).
6. Caryle Murphy, "South Africa Powers Reactor with Uranium it Enriched," *Washington Post*, April 30, 1981. The Ford Administration had suspended shipments of fuel for the U.S.-supplied SAFARI reactor in 1975. Since 1980, U.S. law has prohibited nuclear fuel exports to South Africa because of South Africa's refusal to place all of its nuclear installations under IAEA safeguards. Nuclear Non-Proliferation Act of 1978, P.L. 95-242, amending Atomic Energy Act of 1954, sections 127, 128 (1978).
7. See note 24, below. A widely cited 1980 U.N. Center for Disarmament study assumed South Africa was capable of producing 50 kilograms of highly enriched uranium annually, beginning in March 1977. See Department of Political and Security Council Affairs, United Nations Centre for Disarmament, Report of the Secretary General, *South Africa's Plan and Capability in the Nuclear Field,* Report A/35/402 (New York: United Nations, 1980). This estimate of the date of the first availability of South African highly enriched uranium, on which the author relied in *Nuclear Proliferation Today* (New York: Vintage Books, 1984), now appears premature.

8. At the time the Kalahari test site was discovered in mid-1977, it may be noted, Washington reacted vigorously, given the clear evidence that a test site was being readied and the uncertainties that then prevailed as to Pretoria's enriched-uranium production capabilities.

9. The Reagan administration has declined to reopen the matter. See also note 28, below.

   One additional piece of circumstantial evidence suggesting that Pretoria is indeed building nuclear weapons is the report that in 1985 it obtained two 600-kilovolt flash X-ray machines from Sweden, through a clandestine purchasing network. The devices are used in nuclear weapon programs to test the non-nuclear "triggering package," a step that can increase confidence in the reliability of untested weapons. See Christer Larsson and Jan Melin, "Third World Countries Buy Swedish Nuclear Weapons Technology," *Ny Teknik*, May 2, 1986, p. 12, translated in *Joint Publications Research Service/Nuclear Developments and Proliferation*, July 30, 1986, p. 1.

10. Interviews with U.S. officials, fall 1987. South Africa claims that placing the pilot-scale enrichment plant under IAEA monitoring would divulge industrial secrets. However, it has never opened talks on the question with the Agency to see if such disclosures could be avoided. Nonetheless, this would necessarily be part of any future discussion of South Africa's joining the NPT, since this step would require that the unit be placed under IAEA safeguards. See generally, summary of IAEA General Conference discussion of South African nuclear program, GC(XXVIII)/724 Annex 2 (Vienna: IAEA, 1984).

11. See, *e.g.*, Bernard Gwertzman and Alan Cowell, "U.S. Recalls Envoy from Pretoria in Response to Raid on Botswana," *New York Times*, June 15, 1985; Anthony Robinson, *et al.*, "S. African Attacks Threaten Bid for Constitutional Talks," *Financial Times,* May 20, 1986.

12. See, *e.g.*, Executive Order 12532 (September 9, 1985) imposing economic sanctions against South Africa; see notes 19 and 20 below and accompanying text.

13. Angola, for example, is said to have MiG-21 and MiG-23 jet fighters in its arsenal. The Cheetah, an up-grade of South Africa's aging Mirage III/As, is said to be able to match the MiG-23. See "General Malan Comments," Johannesburg SAPA, 0025 GMT, July 16, 1986, reprinted in *Foreign Broadcast Information Service (FBIS)/Middle East and Africa,* July 16, 1986, p. U-4. See Glenn Frankel, "U.N. Arms Ban Proves Costly to South Africans," *Washington Post*, February 21, 1985; Christopher Coker, "South Africa: A New Military Role in Southern Africa," *Survival* (March/April

1983): 59; "T.V. Reviews Weapons Buildup in Southern Africa," Johannesburg Television Service, 1800 GMT, November 6, 1985, reprinted in *FBIS/Middle-East and Africa,* November 7, 1985, p. U-13.

For a detailed recent analysis reviewing South Africa's declining advantage in conventional armaments, see Christopher Coker, *South Africa's Security Dilemmas* (Washington, DC: Praeger/Center for Strategic and International Studies, 1987).

14. The Final Declaration of the Third Review Conference on the Treaty on the Non-Proliferation of Nuclear Weapons, for example, specifically criticized South Africa's nuclear posture in two separate provisions, calling on it to place all of its nuclear plants under IAEA safeguards. See also "South Africa's Nuclear Capabilities," Resolution adopted during the IAEA General Conference September 27, 1985, GC(XXIX)/Res/442. In 1987, as discussed below, South Africa was also threatened with expulsion from the IAEA.

15. See note 6.

16. See Leonard S. Spector, *Nuclear Proliferation Today* (New York: Vintage Books, 1984), pp. 295-298; Rick Atkinson, "Reactor Operators Suspected of Working for South Africa," *Washington Post,* January 20, 1985.

17. Leonard S. Spector, *The New Nuclear Nations* (New York: Vintage Books, 1985) pp. 54-59. During 1984, Pretoria also reportedly sought to bypass supplier-country controls in the hopes of eventually obtaining a heavy water plant not subject to IAEA safeguards. Although no supplier nation would sell such a facility without IAEA controls, Pretoria was said to be negotiating with the Swiss firm of Sulzer Brothers to obtain engineering services that would have enabled it to purchase unregulated components for such a plant and assemble them in South Africa. U.S. non-proliferation specialists feared that unsafeguarded heavy water might be used in a clandestine natural-uranium/heavy-water reactor to produce plutonium for nuclear arms. See Spector, *The New Nuclear Nations,* pp. 220-222.

18. Preexisting contracts relating to the operation of the French-supplied Koeberg reactors were not to be affected, however. The July 1985 partial state of emergency was lifted on March 7, 1986, but a nationwide state of emergency was declared on June 12, 1986. See "Nuclear Hardware Not Affected," Umtata Capital Radio, 1100 GMT July 25, 1985, reprinted in *FBIS/Middle-East and Africa,* July 26, 1985, p. U-3.

19. Executive Order 12532, see note 12. Exceptions were allowed to permit nuclear transfers for humanitarian reasons and in support of IAEA safeguards. These sanctions, originally imposed for a year, were extended in September 1986. See Bernard Weinraub, "Rea-

gan Extending Limited Sanctions," *New York Times,* September 5, 1986.

20. The change in the American stance, it should be stressed, was a reflection of public and congressional concerns; the Reagan Administration had consistently opposed sanctions of any kind and implemented them only because of domestic political pressure.

It is also worth noting that the most economically painful nuclear-related sanction—a prohibition on the *importation* of South African uranium—was not imposed at this time, and the United States and Western Europe continued to import significant quantities of the material; Canada, however, banned imports of uranium produced in Namibia, which South Africa continues to occupy despite the expiration of its U.N. mandate to govern the region. See James Branscome, "Canada Bans Future Conversion Contracts for Namibian Uranium at Eldorado Facility," *Nuclear Fuel,* July 29, 1985, p. 10; Dinah Wisenberg, "Antiapartheid Measure Poses Distant Threat to South African Uranium Imports," *Nuclear Fuel,* August 12, 1985, p. 3; James Branscome, "South Africa Will Offer SWU On World Market in 1988," *Nucleonics Week,* February 27, 1986, p.1.

21. The six Commonwealth nations were Australia, the Bahamas, Canada, India, Zambia, and Zimbabwe; together with Britain they formed a seven-nation committee charged by the forty-nine member Commonwealth with developing a policy toward South Africa. Although the Thatcher government rejected the sanctions package subsequently passed by the Commonwealth, in so doing it appeared to accept a milder sanctions program proposed by the EEC. The principal differences were that the Commonwealth package included a ban on extending landing rights to South African airlines and a ban on new investment in South Africa. Mrs. Thatcher would not accept the former ban but did agree to "discourage" further British investment. Britain is one of South Africa's leading trading partners. Karen De Young, "Thatcher's Sanctions Stance Called 'Pathetic,' " *Washington Post,* August 6, 1986.

22. Anti-Apartheid Act of 1986, P.L. 99-440 (1986), section 307 (a). The Anti-Apartheid Act prohibition on the importation of South African uranium into the United States has been the subject of controversy, since it has been interpreted as applying only to uranium ore and concentrate ("yellow cake") but not to more highly processed forms of uranium. Specifically, imports of uranium hexafluoride—a product made from yellow cake—are permitted under Treasury Department and Nuclear Regulatory Commission regulations. Uranium hexafluoride—a gas when slightly heated—is used as the feed stock for the uraniumn enrichment process. Thus the U.S. regulations permit uranium hexafluoride that has been pro-

duced abroad from South African uranium to enter the United States for enrichment in U.S. facilities. Thereafter the enriched uranium can be re-exported as fuel for foreign nuclear power plants or used as fuel in U.S. nuclear power reactors. The U.S. import ban thus affects only a portion of South Africa's uranium trade with the United States and does not affect U.S. uranium enrichment revenues. See Michael Knapick, "Treasury Decides All South African U_3O_8 [yellow cake] is Banned from Import to U.S.," *Nuclear Fuel,* July 13, 1987, p. 12; "NRC Sets South African U. Import Ban," *Nuclear Fuel,* September 21, 1987, p. 13; "Congressmen Ask Court to Reverse NRC Policy on South African U. Import Policy," *Nuclear Fuel,* October 5, 1987, p. 12.

23. See note 7 and accompanying text; "Former IAEA Official on Bomb Production," *Star,* September 14, 1985, reprinted in *FBIS/Middle-East and Africa,* September 17, 1985, p. U-16.

24. Weapons-grade uranium is made up of ninety percent or more uranium-235, a rare isotope that is found in natural uranium in a concentration of less than one percent. South Africa's small Valindaba uranium enrichment facility is capable of increasing the concentration of uranium-235 to weapons-grade, but, using natural uranium as a feed stock, it can produce only enough weapons-grade material for two or possibly three nuclear weapons per year. Because of the peculiarities of the uranium enrichment process, a large proportion of the work (and hence of plant capacity) involved in reaching the highly enriched level needed for weapons is expended in upgrading natural uranium to the low-enriched stage (three percent uranium-235); considerably less effort (and plant capacity) is required to increase the low-enriched material to weapons-grade levels. The Valindaba plant, which uses the jet-nozzle process, is thought to be composed of thousands of nozzle units, each of which incrementally increases the concentration of the material passed through it. After each slight concentration, the improved material is fed into another nozzle for further slight enhancement, a process that is repeated until the desired enrichment level is obtained. To produce highly enriched uranium from natural uranium, a large proportion of the available nozzle units must be devoted to reaching the low-enriched stage. If the enrichment process begins with low-enriched material, however, a larger proportion of the facility can, in principle, be devoted to the task of reaching the higher enrichment level needed for weapons.

25. "China Was Source of Atomic Fuel for South Africa, U.S. Believes," *Washington Post,* November 18, 1981; "China Says Study Shows It Wasn't Uranium Source," *Washington Post,* December 8, 1981. Some U.S. officials believe the Chinese material may have been sold to South Africa through middlemen.

26. Rob Laufer, "Kaiseraugst Purchase Seen As Freeing South Africa from U.S. Contract," *Nucleonics Week,* February 18, 1982, p. 1.

27. See, *e.g.*, James Adams, *The Unnatural Alliance* (New York: Quartet Books, 1984), p. 170.

28. "CBS Evening News with Walter Cronkite," February 21, 1980 (report by Dan Raviv); Benjamin Beit-Hallahmi, *The Israeli Connection* (New York: Pantheon, 1987), p. 134; but see Adams, *The Unnatural Alliance,* p. 195 (source states that flash was not an Israeli test, but confirms nuclear collaboration between the two countries). Two kilotons are the equivalent of 2,000 tons of TNT, about one tenth of the destructive force of the weapon that destroyed Nagasaki.

29. Beit-Hallahmi, *The Israeli Connection,* pp. 123, 129; "South Africa Reportedly May Test Atomic Weapons," United Press International, AM cycle, December 26, 1986.

30. Thomas L. Friedman, "Israel Approves Curbs on Pretoria," *New York Times,* September 17, 1987.

31. "Israel Offers Re-engined Kfir," *Flight International,* April 25, 1987, p. 10; Glenn Frankel, "Israeli Economy Depends on No-Questions-Asked Arms Sales," *Washington Post,* December 12, 1986; "Israel to Curb Arms for Pretoria," *New York Times,* March 19, 1987. The principal difference between the Kfir and the Cheetah is that the former uses the more powerful U.S. GE J79 engine.

32. See Hirsh Goodman, "RSA Seeking to Lure Lavi Engineers, Technicians," *Jerusalem Post,* November 9, 1987, reprinted in *FBIS/Near East-South Asia,* November 10, 1987, p. 44.

33. U.S. Department of State, "Report to Congress Pursuant to Section 508 of the Comprehensive Anti-Apartheid Act of 1986: Compliance with the U.N. Arms Embargo," April 2, 1987.

34. Ann MacLachlan and Gamini Seneviratne, "South Africa Hints NPT Signature, Averts IAEA Suspension Threat," *Nucleonics Week,* September 23, 1987.

35. Technically, only nuclear materials would be safeguarded, but to achieve this it is necessary for the agency to monitor the output of all of a signatory's nuclear plants.

36. MacLachlan and Seneviratne, "South Africa Hints NPT Signature," (see note 34). For a procedural history of the events at the IAEA leading up to the General Conference vote, see "South Africa's Nuclear Capabilities: Report by the Board of Governors," IAEA Document GC(XXXI)/807 (August 24, 1987). The Soviet willingness to postpone sanctions—apparently out of a desire to avoid further politicization of the IAEA—is all the more surprising in view of the fact that the Soviet Union is fighting a proxy war with

South Africa in Angola. Moscow has sent 1000 advisors (and Cuba has sent 35,000 to 40,000 troops) to Angola to assist the Marxist government there contain South African-backed UNITA (National Union for the Total Independence of Angola) rebel forces.

37. Pretoria insisted on two provisos that the agency would not accept. First, it demanded the right to withdraw safeguarded enriched uranium produced in the facility for "non-explosive military purposes," *i.e.*, for nuclear submarine propulsion systems. Second, it insisted on the right to terminate the safeguards agreement in the event it decided that "extraordinary events related to the agreement have jeopardized its supreme interests" or in the event that its rights or privileges of membership in the IAEA were curtailed.

South Africa's demands were derived in part from stipulations found in IAEA safeguards agreements that are drawn up after a country has joined the NPT—and has therefore agreed to place all of its nuclear plants under IAEA inspection. These agreements allow the removal of safeguarded material for non-explosive military purposes, since this is permitted by the treaty itself, and they are subject to a country's right under Article X of the treaty to withdraw from the pact after ninety days if the country's supreme interests are jeopardized by actions relating to the subject of the accord. IAEA policy, however, has been to prohibit these reservations in safeguards agreements that cover only a single plant, agreements which come under safeguards rules that pre-date the NPT.

38. In principle, as explained in the previous note, South Africa's past demands for the right to withdraw safeguarded material for non-explosive military purposes and for the right to terminate safeguards if its supreme interests are threatened could be satisfied under an IAEA safeguards agreement entered into pursuant to the NPT. As a practical matter, however, many technical issues would remain to be resolved, including the question of how to minimize the possibility that once nuclear materials were withdrawn from safeguards for *non-explosive* military purposes they were not subsequently diverted to *explosive* purposes. There is no precedent for such a withdrawal, and if South Africa insisted upon working out the details before it signed the treaty, negotiations could drag on for years. Another technical controversy could arise over the question of how to apply safeguards to South Africa's two enrichment plants without compromising commercially sensitive data on the designs and operation of the plants.

39. In a February 25, 1987, letter to IAEA Director General Hans Blix restating South Africa's position on the then pending negotiations on safeguarding the larger Valindaba enrichment plant, Pretoria's representative in Vienna stated, "The South African Government has also declared that it remains willing to consider accession to the

NPT, provided its basic requirements could be met. Under the present international situation where punitive sanctions and boycotts are being imposed on South Africa by the international community, its basic requirements are certainly threatened." See "South Africa's Nuclear Capabilities," Annex C (full reference in note 36). Pretoria might also try to link its ratification to a pledge by a third nuclear-weapon state—the Soviet Union—by demanding that Moscow withdraw its advisors from Angola.

40. For a detailed analysis of the May elections, see Pauline H. Baker, "South Africa: The Afrikaner Angst," *Foreign Policy* (Winter 1987-1988), p. 61.

41. William Claiborne, "Reforms Seen Slowing in S. Africa," *Washington Post,* February 10, 1988; William Claiborne, "South Africa Cracks Down on Political Opposition," *Washington Post,* February 25, 1988.

42. William Claiborne, "South Africa Acknowledges Fighting Soviets, Cubans in Angola," *Washington Post,* November 12, 1987.

43. William Claiborne, "S. African Military Says Intervention in Angola Staved Off Rebel Defeat," *Washington Post,* November 13, 1987.

44. "South African Leaders Visit Angola War Zone," *New York Times,* November 15, 1987. Heavy fighting continued in Angola into mid-1988.

   A second regional antagonist, Zimbabwe, may also be in the process of significantly strengthening its military capabilities, and one report alleges it may be seeking to purchase the top-of-the-line MiG-29 from the Soviet Union. "Government Buying Arms from PRC, UK, USSR," (Clandestine) Radio Truth (Zimbabwe), 0430 GMT March 9, 1988, reprinted in *FBIS/Near East and South Asia,* March 11, 1988, p. 14.

45. Ratification might also help stave off possible action by two important South African customers, West Germany and Japan, to ban imports of South African uranium.

46. From the standpoint of outside states, concerns would remain that Pretoria had cached some previously produced nuclear arms or highly enriched uranium before accepting IAEA supervision of its entire nuclear program. Moreover, as noted in the text, even after it joined the treaty, Pretoria could retain stocks of weapons-grade uranium under IAEA inspection, raising the possibility that it could rapidly manufacture nuclear arms by abrogating its treaty commitments or withdrawing from the accord.

   It might be possible to address these problems in part through additional measures. For example, the operation of the pilot-scale Valindaba enrichment plant during the time it was unsafeguarded could be reconstructed in detail to determine how much enriched uranium it had produced and thereafter to request South Africa to account for the material and place it under safeguards. To avoid subsequent stockpiling of weapons-grade material, South Africa could be asked to limit the output of its enrichment plants to low-enriched uranium, an operating procedure that could be readily verified. These steps would require additional negotiations, however.

Chapter VII
Controls and Safeguards

1. See the 1988 volume of *Arms Control Reporter*, (Brookline, Mass.: Institute for Defense and Disarmament Studies), p. 602.B.137.
2. Ciro Elliott Zoppo, "Spain as an Emerging Nuclear Supplier" in William C. Potter, editor, *The Emerging Nuclear Suppliers and Nonproliferation* (forthcoming).
3. John M. Goshko, "Saudis to Cut Ties with Iran," *Washington Post*, April 26, 1988.
4. Ann MacLachlan and Gamini Seneviratne, "South Africa Hints NPT Signature, Averts IAEA Suspension Threat," *Nucleonics Week*, September 24, 1987, p. 1.
5. *Ibid.*
6. See the sections on the Pacific Nuclear Weapon Free Zone in the 1986, 1987, and 1988 volumes of *Arms Control Reporter* (Brookline, Mass.: Institute for Defense and Disarmament Studies).
7. Washington's refusal to sign the protocols is said to stem partly from deference to France, a NATO ally. In addition, the Reagan Administration is apparently concerned that support for the nuclear weapon free zone will encourage states within the region to take actions comparable to New Zealand's ban on port calls by nuclear-powered and nuclear-armed vessels, that might interfere with U.S. nuclear deployments in the Pacific. (After New Zealand adopted this ban in August 1986, the United States formally suspended its thirty-five-year old military ties to New Zealand under the ANZUS Treaty.) See Neil A. Lewis, "U.S. Bars Nuclear Free Zone for Group of Pacific Nations," *New York Times*, February 5, 1987; Robert Lindsey, "U.S., in Talks with Australia, Bars Defense of New Zealand," *New York Times*, August 12, 1986.
8. Diplomatic note no. DZG 083/13 from the British Foreign and Commonwealth Office, London, to the Heads of Diplomatic Missions of Governments signatory and acceding at London to the Treaty Banning Nuclear Weapon Tests in the Atmosphere, in Outer Space and Under Water (Limited Test Ban Treaty), March 16, 1988.
9. For further discussion of India's reaction to Pakistani arms control proposals, see the section of Chapter III of this volume on India.
10. Richard Kessler, "For the First Time, Argentina Has Ratified an International Nuclear Treaty," *Nucleonics Week*, May 7, 1988, p. 6.
11. IAEA Annual Report for 1986, p. 43. The IAEA issues its annual report for the preceding year in September.
12. *Ibid.*

13. *Ibid.*
14. See Brooks Tigner, "Europe's Greens Say EURATOM, IAEA Are Lying on Safeguards," *Nucleonics Week*, June 2, 1988, pp. 5-6. Green Party members believed that two of the facilities were in Belgium.
15. *Ibid.*
16. "Missile Technology Control Regime," United States Department of Defense Fact Sheet, April 16, 1987.
17. Richard Kessler and Mark Hibbs, "Pilcaniyeu Safeguards Offer Tied to Nuclear Transfers by Argentina," *Nucleonics Week*, February 11, 1988, p. 4.
18. See "Government to Buy 2 Nuclear Reactors from USSR," Hong Kong, Agence France Presse, 0720 GMT, April 1, 1988, reprinted in *Foreign Broadcast Information Service (FBIS)/Near East and South Asia*, April 1, 1988, p. 42; Amaranath K. Menon, "The Ultimate Dream," *India Today*, May 15, 1988; Ann MacLachlan and Neel Patri, "India, USSR Close to Deal on Two VVER-1000 Reactors," *Nucleonics Week*, May 19, 1988, p. 1.
19. For a discussion of the controversial 1979-1980 reactor and heavy water plant sale, see the section on Argentina in Chapter V of this book, note 3.
20. MacLachlan and Patri, "India, USSR Close Deal on Two VVER-1000 Reactors," (see note 18).
21. United States Congress, House of Representatives, Committee on Foreign Affairs, "Proposed Agreement between the United States and Japan Concerning Peaceful Uses of Nuclear Energy," House document 100-128, 100th Cong., 1st sess., November 9, 1987. Concerning plutonium extraction, see Appendix A.
22. For a summary of the arguments against the pact, see Statement by Senator Glenn on Japan Nuclear Agreement before the Committee on Foreign Relations, United States Senate, December 15, 1987. See also, Paul Leventhal, "U.S.-Japan Accord Invites Proliferation," *Bulletin of the Atomic Scientists*, May 1988, pp. 11-13; Walter C. Patterson, "Japan's Perilous Plutonium Flights," *Bulletin of the Atomic Scientists*, May 1988, pp. 9-11. For a contrary view, see Gerard C. Smith, "A Sound Nuclear Accord with Japan," *Washington Post*, February 19, 1988.
23. On the Pentagon's initial objections to the pact, see Daniel Charles, "DOD Sees Risks in Plutonium Trade," *Science*, November 13, 1987; Andrew Alexander, "Pentagon-State Department Nuclear Feud to Boil in Public View in Senate Hearing," *Atlanta Constitution*, March 5, 1988.
24. Letter of July 27, 1987, from Lando Zech, Jr., Chairman of the Nuclear Regulatory Commission to President Reagan, reprinted in *Nuclear Fuel*, November 16, 1987, p. 3; "NRC Responds to Criti-

cism of Its Comments on U.S.-Japan Pact," *Nuclear Fuel*, January 25, 1988, pp. 3-4.

25. "U.S.-Japan Deal Rejected by Senate," *Nuclear Engineering International* (February 1988): 4.
26. Eduardo Lachica, "U.S. Plans to Fly Plutonium Fuels along Polar Route," *Wall Street Journal*, March 11, 1988.
27. For the Reagan Administration's arguments in support of the U.S.-Japan nuclear agreement, see "Review of Congressional Legal Concerns about Agreement for Peaceful Nuclear Cooperation with Japan," accompanying President Reagan's letter of January 29, 1988, to Senator Claiborne Pell, Chairman, Senate Foreign Relations Committee.
28. "DOE Concedes U.S. Won't Get Business in Japan Unless New Pact Is Approved," *Nuclear Fuel*, February 22, 1988, p. 1.
29. "Congress Reacts Coldly to U.S.-Japan Pact," *Nuclear News* (February 1988): 84; "U.S./Japan Pact Looks Doubtful in Congress," *Nuclear News* (March 1988): 40.
30. "Senate Votes against Cancelling New Nuclear Pact with Japan," *Washington Post*, March 22, 1988.
31. Mark Hibbs, "Norway Investigating Reports of Heavy Water Diversions," *Nuclear Fuel*, May 30, 1988, p. 9.
32. "Testimony of Deputy Assistant Secretary of State Robert A. Peck," *Hearings on the Export of Nuclear Materials*, before the Subcommittee on Asian and Pacific Affairs of the Committee on Foreign Affairs, U.S. House of Representatives, February 18, 1988, (mimeo).

*

Nukem scandal. A troubling development that also damaged the credibility of nuclear regulation—though not directly related to the spread of nuclear weapons—was the revelation in 1987 of a widespread network of corruption and embezzling in Western Europe's nuclear industry. So far, the allegations in this affair include: embezzling by the executives of two related West German companies, NUKEM and Transnuklear Gmbh; their maintenance of a slush fund for bribes and kick-backs in order to obtain contracts for handling nuclear waste from European nuclear installations; and the circumvention of environmental laws covering the transportation of radioactive materials within the European Community. Early rumors that, as part of the scheme, nuclear weapons material had been diverted to Pakistan and Libya have been discredited. See "Suicide of the Atom," *Der Spiegel*, January 18, 1988, pp. 18-30, translated in *FBIS/Western Europe (WEU)*, January 20, 1988, pp. 8-9; and Hans-Dieter Degler, "A City Defends Itself," *Stern*,

January 21, 1988, pp. 11-13 in *Ibid*. On the scandal itself, see Mark Hibbs, "Nukem Director Stephany Resigns in Bid to Restore TN Licenses," *Nucleonics Week*, January 14, 1988, p. 1; Mark Hibbs, Ann MacLachlan, and Laura Pilarski, "Wastes from More Reactors Taken to Belgium by TN," *Nucleonics Week*, January 14, 1988, p. 1; Robert J. McCartney, "West German Probe Widens in Nuclear Shipping Scandal," *Washington Post*, January 15, 1988; Mark Hibbs, Brooks Tigner, and Gamini Seneviratne, "Nukem Suspends Other Directors; More Violations Found in Hanau," *Nucleonics Week*, January 21, 1988, p. 1; Elizabeth Pond, "Major Questions Linger in West German Nuclear Scandal," *Christian Science Monitor*, January 21, 1988; Mark Hibbs, "Bundestag Nuclear Inquiry Could Run Two Years, Spur Policy Debate," *Nucleonics Week*, January 28, 1988, pp. 4-5; and Serge Schmemann, "Nuclear Industry Under Fire in Bonn," *New York Times*, February 7, 1988. On the larger repercussions of the NUKEM affair, see David Marsh, "W. German Nuclear Inquiry Extended Abroad," *Financial Times*, January 16, 1988; David Marsh, "An Industry Threatened by Its Own Fallout," *Financial Times*, January 21, 1988; Ann MacLachlan, Eric Lindeman and Michael Knapik, "TN Affair Causing Repercussions Abroad," *Nuclear Fuel*, January 25, 1988, pp. 5-7; and Mark Hibbs, "West German Nuclear Industry Losing Conservatives' Support," *Nucleonics Week*, February 25, 1988, pp. 3-4. And on the question of the diversion of nuclear material to Pakistan and Libya, see Mark Hibbs, "West Germany Checking Reports of TN Shipments of HEU to Pakistan," *Nucleonics Week*, January 15, 1988, pp. 1-2; Serge Schmemann, "Bonn Can Find No Evidence of Nuclear Treaty Violations," *International Herald Tribune*, January 16-17, 1988; Mark Hibbs, "German NPT Violations in Doubt But Prosecutors Probe New Lead," *Nucleonics Week*, January 21, 1988, p. 1; "Witnesses Testify No Evidence Found of German NPT Violation," *Nucleonics Week*, March 3, 1988, pp. 5-6; and Mark Hibbs, "Nukem Involvement in U Diversion Attempt to be Questioned in Bonn," *Nucleonics Week*, April 28, 1988, pp. 7-8.

33. U.S. Department of Defense, *Soviet Military Power*, (Washington, D.C.: U.S. Government Printing Office, 1988), p. 26; Rita Manchanda, "Nuclear Ambitions," *Far Eastern Economic Review*, December 24, 1987, p. 18; Shekhar Gupta, "A Sea Change," *India Today*, December 31, 1987, pp. 72-74; "India Gets Soviet Nuclear-Powered Sub," *Washington Times*, January 6, 1988; and, Subhash Chakravarti, "India's Nuclear Submarine Lifts Local Arms Race," *London Sunday Times*, January 10, 1988.

34. Shahid-ur-Rehman, "Pakistan Slams USSR Decision to Give India Nuclear Submarines," *Nucleonics Week*, January 21, 1988, p. 12.

35. On President Reagan's decision to allow Canada to purchase U.S. nuclear-submarine reactor technology, see Philip Shabecoff, "Reagan Backs New Nuclear Subs for Canadians with U.S. Design," *New York Times*, April 28, 1988; Herbert H. Denton, "Reagan: Canada Can Buy Sub Reactors," *Washington Post*, April 28, 1988. On the Canadian decision to purchase the submarines see, Department of National Defence, *Challenge and Commitment: A Defence Policy for Canada*, (Ottawa: Canadian Ministry of Supplies and Services, 1987).

36. The loophole was included because of Italian and Dutch interests in reserving the option to build nuclear submarines and because of the British desire to ensure that the treaty did not interfere with its acquisition of nuclear materials from the United States for its nuclear submarines. Concerning the right of non-nuclear-weapon state parties to remove material from safeguards for submarine propulsion systems, see *The Structure and Content of Agreements between the Agency and States Required in Connection with the Treaty on the Non-Proliferation of Nuclear Weapons*, INFCIRC/153, (Vienna: International Atomic Energy Agency, 1972), article 14.

Appendices

It is generally accepted today that designing an atomic bomb—drawing the blueprint—is within the capabilities of most nations. Indeed, a number of American college students have come up with workable designs based on unclassified material.

The major technical barrier to making a nuclear device is obtaining the nuclear material for its core. Twenty-five kilograms (fifty-five pounds) of highly enriched uranium, or eight kilograms (about eighteen pounds) of plutonium are generally considered the necessary minimum, although in both cases more sophisticated designs relying on high compression of the core material, neutron reflecting "tampers," or both, enable a bomb to be built with considerably less material—perhaps fifteen kilograms of highly enriched uranium or five kilograms of plutonium, and even smaller amounts can apparently be used. Neither of these materials occurs in nature, however, and highly complex and expensive facilities must be built and operated in order to make them—an undertaking of considerable difficulty for developing nations without assistance from more advanced nuclear-supplier countries.

Highly enriched uranium. To make a weapon from uranium, the unstable "isotope" of uranium having a total of 235 protons and neutrons in its nucleus (U^{235}) is used. Since natural uranium consists of less than one percent U^{235}, while nuclear weapons use material that is made up of 90 percent or more U^{235}, natural uranium must be upgraded at an *enrichment plant* to achieve this concentration. Uranium enrichment is an extremely complex process and requires considerable investment. For this reason, the uranium enrichment route has been generally considered a less likely path to proliferation than the plutonium option. However, South Africa, Argentina, Brazil, India and (with extensive outside aid obtained mostly by clandestine means) Pakistan have all developed independent uranium enrichment capabilities, and Israel is known to be conducting research in the field.

Enriched uranium can also be used as a fuel in nuclear power or research reactors. The power reactors used in the United States and most other countries (called "light-water reactors") use *low-enriched uranium* fuel, i.e., uranium that has been enriched up to three percent U^{235}. Thus a country can have entirely legitimate, non-weapons-related reasons for developing uranium enrichment technology even though the same technology can be used to upgrade uranium to the high enrichment level useful for nuclear weapons. On the other hand, developing a sizable independent uranium enrichment capability is economically justifiable only for nations with large domestic nuclear power programs or significant potential export markets.

Because highly enriched uranium is sometimes used to fuel research reactors, a nation can have legitimate reasons for obtaining small quantities of this material, despite its usefulness in nuclear explosives. In recent years the United States and France have developed lower-enriched uranium fuels that can be used in lieu of highly enriched material in most of these reactors, however, considerably reducing the proliferation risks these research facilities pose.

Producing highly enriched uranium entails many steps apart from the enrichment process itself, and many other installations and capabilities are necessary. For nations wishing to obtain highly enriched uranium without international restrictions prohibiting its use for nuclear explosives, all of these would have to develop independently, or obtained illegally, since virtually all nuclear exporter states are unwilling to sell nuclear equipment and materials unless recipients pledge not to use them for nuclear explosives purposes and to place them under the inspection system of the International Atomic Energy Agency. (See Appendix C). For illustrative purposes the basic nuclear resources and facilities that would be needed include:

- uranium deposits;
- a uranium mine;
- a uranium mill (for processing uranium ore containing less than one percent uranium into uranium oxide concentrate, or yellowcake);
- a conversion plant (for purifying yellowcake and converting it into uranium hexafluoride, the material processed in the enrichment plant);
- an enrichment plant (for enriching the uranium hexafluoride gas in the isotope U^{235}); and
- a capability for converting the enriched uranium hexafluoride gas into solid uranium oxide or metal (a capability usually associated with a yellowcake-to-hexafluoride conversion plant).

Plutonium. To obtain plutonium a country needs a *nuclear reactor*. This can be one designed specifically to maximize plutonium production (a "production reactor"), a large research reactor, or a power reactor for producing electricity. *Uranium fuel,* usually in the form of uranium-filled tubes (fuel rods) made of zirconium alloy (zircaloy) or aluminium, is placed in the reactor. For most production, power, and for a number of large research reactors, the fuel itself is either natural or low-enriched uranium, which is not usable for nuclear weapons at this point. As the reactor operates, the uranium fuel is partly transformed into plutonium. This is amalgamated in the fuel rods with unused uranium and highly radioactive waste products, however, and must then be extracted. To do this, "spent" fuel rods are taken to a *reprocessing plant* where they are dissolved in nitric acid and the plutonium is separated from the solution in a series of chemical processing steps. Since the spent fuel rods are highly radioactive, heavy lead casks must be used to transport them, and the rooms at the reprocessing plant where the chemical extraction of the plutonium occurs must have thick walls, lead shielding, and special ventilation to prevent radiation hazards.

Although detailed information about reprocessing was declassified by the United States and France in the 1950s and is generally available, it is still a complex procedure from an engineering point of view, and virtually every nation at the nuclear-weapons threshold that has attempted it—Argentina, Brazil, India, Iraq, Israel, and Pakistan—has sought outside help from the advanced nuclear-supplier countries.

Like enrichment facilities, however, reprocessing plants can also be used for legitimate civilian purposes, because plutonium can be used as fuel in nuclear-power reactors. Indeed, through the 1970s it was generally assumed that as the use of nuclear power grew, worldwide uranium resources would be depleted and plutonium extracted from spent fuel would have to be "recycled" as a substitute fuel in conventional power reactors.

In addition, research and development is under way in a number of nations on a new generation of reactors known as breeder reactors. These use plutonium as fuel surrounded with a "blanket" of natural uranium; as the reactor operates, slightly more plutonium is created in the core and the blanket together than is consumed in the core, thereby "breeding" new fuel.

Like plutonium recycling, the economic advantages of breeders depends on natural uranium becoming scarce and expensive. But over the past decade new uranium reserves have been discovered, nuclear power has reached only a fraction of its expected growth levels, and reprocessing spent fuel to extract plutonium (a critical step in both cases) has proven far more expensive and complex than anticipated. Moreover, concern over the proliferation risks of widescale use of plutonium as a fuel has grown. These factors have led one advanced nation, the United States, to abandon its plans to use plutonium fuel, although Japan, France, Britain, and West Germany are continuing to develop this technology actively. Nevertheless, the advanced nuclear-supplier countries are strongly discouraging plutonuim use in nations of proliferation concern.

The longstanding view that plutonium is a legitimate and anticipated part of civilian nuclear programs, however, has allowed Argentina, Brazil, India, and Pakistan to justify their reprocessing programs—even though they currently provide these nations with a nuclear-weapons capability, or may soon do so.

Like the production of enriched uranium, the production of plutonium entails many steps, and many installations and capabilities apart from the reactor and reprocessing plant are needed. For illustrative purposes, the following facilities and resources would be required for an independent plutonium-production capability assuming a heavy-water research or power reactor, employing natural uranium fuel, is used:

- uranium deposits;
- a uranium mine;
- a uranium mill (for processing uranium ore containing less than one percent uranium into uranium oxide concentrate, or yellowcake);
- a uranium purification plant (to further improve the yellowcake into reactor-grade uranium dioxide);

- a fuel fabrication plant (to manufacture the fuel elements placed in the reactor), including a capability to fabricate zircaloy or aluminium tubing;
- a heavy-water research or power reactor;
- a heavy-water production plant; and
- a reprocessing plant.

If the option of building a natural-uranium/graphite reactor is used, the needs would be the same although reactor-grade graphite would have to be produced instead of heavy water. A light-water reactor would necessitate use of low-enriched uranium, implying an enrichment capability was available; if so, highly enriched uranium could, in theory, be produced, obviating the need for plutonium as a weapons material.

Appendix B: Nuclear Weapons—A Primer

A nuclear weapon is a device in which most or all of the explosive energy is derived from either fission, fusion, or a combination of the two nuclear processes. *Nuclear fission* is the splitting of the nucleus of an atom into two (or more) parts. Highly enriched uranium and plutonium, when bombarded by neutrons, will release energy and emit additional neutrons while splitting into lighter atoms. In *nuclear fusion,* light isotopes of hydrogen, usually deuterium and tritium, join at high temperatures and similarly liberate energy and neutrons.

Fission Weapons. Many heavy atomic nuclei are capable of being fissioned; but only a fraction of these are *fissile,* which means fissionable by neutrons with a wide range of velocities. It is this property of fissile material, principally U^{235} and Pu^{239}, that allows a chain reaction to be achieved in weapons employing the fission process. In a *chain reaction,* fissile nuclei that have been bombarded by neutrons split and emit two or more neutrons, which in turn induce proximate nuclei to fission and sustain the process. With each successive fission "generation" additional energy is released, and, if the fission of one nucleus induces an average of more than one fission in the following generation, the energy yield of each generation is multiplied. A fission explosion in the range of 1 to 100 kilotons for example, would occur over a few microseconds and involve over fifty generations, with 99.9 percent of the energy released coming in the last seven. The minimum mass of material necessary to sustain a chain reaction is called the *critical mass.* This value may be lowered by increasing the material's density through compression or by surrounding it with "reflectors" to minimize the escape of neutrons; this makes it difficult to pin down the precise amount of uranium or plutonium required for a bomb.

Two basic nuclear-weapon-design approaches that are used to achieve a supercritical mass (i.e., exceeding the critical level) are the implosion technique and the gun assembly technique. In the *implosion technique,* a peripheral charge of chemical high explosive is uniformly detonated to compress a subcritical mass of plutonium or highly enriched uranium into a supercritical configuration. In the *gun assembly technique,* two (or more) subcritical masses of highly enriched uranium (plutonium cannot be used) are propelled together by a conventional explosion, resulting in a supercritical mass. In both cases, a *tamper* may be used to keep the material from exploding before enough generations of a chain reaction have occurred, and this tamper often doubles as a reflector to reduce the escape of electrons.

Fusion weapons. Fusion of light atomic nuclei requires a high density of fusion material and extraordinary heat, both of which are provided by a fission explosion in a "thermonuclear" or "hydrogen" bomb. Lithium-6 deuteride is the most widely used thermonuclear material, serving as a source of both deuterium and tritium, the atoms whose nuclei merge, in a fusion weapon.

In a *boosted weapon,* fusion material is introduced directly into (or next to) the core of fissile material, improving the efficiency of a fission weapon and thus increasing the yield of a given quantity of highly enriched uranium or plutonium. Although energy is released in the fusion reaction of a boosted weapon, the primary contribution of the fusion material to the explosion is that it provides additional neutrons for the fission process and therefore allows a more rapidly multiplying chain reaction to occur.

Other thermonuclear weapons are designed to capitalize on the energy released in a "secondary" fusion reaction triggered by a "primary" fission explosion. In such devices, fusion material is kept physically separate from a fissile or boosted fissile core that compresses and ignites it. Additional "stages" of fusion or fission material may be included to augment the weapon's yield, with each layer being triggered by ones closer to the core. For example, the *hydrogen bomb* includes a third stage or "blanket" of natural uranium, a widely available fissionable but not fissile material, that is fissioned by fast neutrons from the primary and secondary fission and fusion reactions. Hence, the energy released in the explosion of such a device stems from three sources—a fission chain reaction, the first stage; "burning" of the thermonuclear fuel, the second stage; and the fission of the U-238 blanket, the third stage—with, very roughly, half the total energy stemming from fission and the other half from fusion.

Source: Thomas B. Cochran, William M. Arkin, and Milton M. Hoenig, *U.S. Nuclear Forces and Capabilities* (Cambridge, MA: Ballinger Publishing Company, 1984), Chapter 2.

Appendix C: International Atomic Energy Agency (IAEA) Safeguards

The International Atomic Energy Agency, a Vienna-based U.N.-affiliated organization now having over 110 members, was founded in 1957. By the mid-1960s, it had established a program of on-site inspections, audits, and inventory controls know collectively as "safeguards." Today, the IAEA monitors some seven hundred installations in over fifty nations and the Agency is widely regarded as a principal bulwark against the spread of nuclear arms.

The basic purpose of IAEA safeguards is to deter the diversion of nuclear materials from peaceful uses to military purposes through the risk of timely detection. In simplified terms, the Agency monitors the flow of nuclear materials at nuclear installations by auditing plant records and conducting physical inventories. Seals and cameras are used to ensure materials are not diverted while IAEA inspectors are not present.

To date, the IAEA has never concluded that material under safeguards has been diverted. In September 1981, however, the Agency indicated that it was unable to determine whether material was diverted from Pakistan's KANUPP reactor or from a similarly designed reactor in India because the Agency had not been permitted to apply all of the monitoring apparatus needed at these installations. The Indian deficiency was quickly corrected, but it was nearly a year and a half before the safeguards at the KANUPP reactor were declared adequate. It is possible that during this period plutonium-bearing spent fuel was removed from the reactor without detection.

Apart from these unusual cases, the IAEA safeguards system has some well-recognized limitations. First, and most important, key installations in countries of proliferation concern including enrichment and reprocessing facilities, are not under the IAEA system. Thus, Argentina, Brazil, India, Israel, Pakistan, and South Africa all remain free to use unsafeguarded installations to manufacture material for nuclear weapons. (Even in each of these countries, however, some installations are subject to the IAEA system, and nuclear materials produced in them cannot, therefore, be used for this purpose.) Nations that have ratified the Non-Proliferation Treaty or for which the Treaty of Tlatelolco is in force have accepted safeguards on all their nuclear facilities.

Secondly, certain types of facilities, such as fuel fabrication, reprocessing, and enrichment installations, handle nuclear materials in bulk form, i.e., as powders, liquids, or gasses. Such materials are particularly difficult to safeguard since measurement techniques are not accurate enough to keep track of 100 percent of these substances as they move through the facilities processing them. This makes it theoretically possible to divert a certain small percentage of material for military purposes without detection since this could appear to be a normal operating discrepancy. The problem is especially dangerous at fuel-fabrication plants handling plutonium or highly enriched uranium in powdered form, at reprocessing plants where plutonium is dissolved in various liquids for processing, and at enrichment plants, which use uranium hexafluoride gas as feed.

Low IAEA budgets and manpower have also meant that far fewer inspections are conducted at safeguarded installations than needed to meet the IAEA's safeguards objectives fully. Other problems include the fact that it is almost impossible for Agency inspectors to make unannounced visits to safeguarded installations. Nations subject to IAEA safeguards are also permitted to reject particular IAEA inspectors.

It must be stressed, however, that even if safeguards as applied are imperfect, their deterrent value remains strong since would-be diverters could not have confidence that their misuse of nuclear materials would go undetected.

Finally, even assuming that IAEA safeguards functioned perfectly, their usefulness may be limited when applied to highly enriched uranium and plutonium, materials directly usable for nuclear weapons. Here, even if the IAEA system reacted instantaneously to diversion, it might still be possible for the nation appropriating this material to manufacture nuclear weapons within a matter of weeks if all the non-nuclear components had been prepared in advance, presenting the world community with a *fait accompli*. In such a setting, safeguards cannot provide "timely warning" sufficient to allow the international community to react before the nation diverting the material has achieved its objective. For this reason, the United States has worked actively to curtail commerce with nations of proliferation concern involving plutonium, highly enriched uranium, or enrichment and reprocessing facilities—whether or not safeguards would be applied. Virtually all other nuclear supplier nations have adopted the cautious approach of the United States in transferring such items.

In the event of a safeguards violation, the Agency's Board of Governors has the authority to notify the United Nations Security Council, but not to impose sanctions of any kind.

Appendix D: The Treaty on the Non-Proliferation of Nuclear Weapons (NPT)

The treaty divides the countries of the world into two categories, "nuclear-weapon states" (those which had detonated a nuclear weapon before 1967, i.e., the United States, the Soviet Union, Great Britain, France, and China) and "non-nuclear-weapon states" (those which had not). Under this pact:

• Non-nuclear-weapon states ratifying the treaty pledge not to manufacture or receive nuclear explosives. (Both nuclear weapons and peaceful nuclear explosives are prohibited.)

• To verify that they are living up to this pledge, non-nuclear-weapon states also agree to accept International Atomic Energy Agency safeguards on all their peaceful nuclear activities (an arrangement known as "full-scope" safeguards).

• All countries accepting the treaty agree not to export nuclear equipment or material to non-nuclear-weapon states for peaceful purposes except under IAEA safeguards and nuclear-weapon states agree not to assist non-nuclear-weapon states in obtaining nuclear arms.

• All countries accepting the treaty agree to facilitate the fullest possible sharing of peaceful nuclear technology. (In practice this is a pledge by the advanced nations to help less developed countries build peaceful nuclear programs.)

• All countries accepting the treaty agree to pursue negotiations in good faith to end the nuclear arms race, and achieve nuclear disarmament under international control. (In practice, this applies to the United States and the Soviet Union.)

• A party to the treaty may withdraw on 90-days' notice if "extraordinary events" related to the subject matter of the treaty have "jeopardized" its "supreme interests."

In effect, the treaty is an agreement among countries with differing interests. The less developed countries, for example, give up their right to develop nuclear arms and accept full-scope safeguards. In return, the advanced countries agree to share peaceful nuclear technology, and those with nuclear arsenals agree to pursue arms control.

The treaty does *not* prohibit parties from accumulating nuclear-weapons material (highly enriched uranium or plutonium) as part of their peaceful nuclear energy or research programs as long as the material is subject to IAEA inspection. This means parties to the pact can come dangerously close to possessing nuclear arms without violating the terms of the treaty.

The treaty has also been interpreted to permit parties to make nuclear sales to countries that are not parties, such as India or Argentina, even if these countries have unsafeguarded nuclear facilities. However, the items exported (and nuclear materials produced through their use), must themselves be placed under IAEA safeguards. Thus, for example, U.S. sales of nuclear fuel to South Africa, which has at least one unsafeguarded nuclear installation, are permissible under the treaty as long as the fuel is placed under safeguards in South Africa. (However, U.S. law, the 1978 Nuclear Non-Proliferation Act, prohibited sales to countries with unsafeguarded facilities after March 1980, absent a special presidential waiver. Canada, Sweden, and Australia have also adopted this policy.)

Negotiations devoted specifically to the Non-Proliferation Treaty began in earnest in 1965, when the United States, and later the Soviet Union, submitted draft treaties to the Eighteen-Nation Disarmament Committee. After overcoming a number of potential stumbling-blocks—including disagreement over the form and extent of the proposed safeguards and demands for security assurances by the non-nuclear-weapon states—the treaty was opened for signature on July 1, 1968, and signed on that date by the United States, the United Kingdom, and the Soviet Union, along with fifty-nine non-nuclear-weapon states. The U.S. Senate ratified the treaty in 1970. More than 130 non-weapon states have ratified the treaty, along with the three nuclear-weapon states, mentioned earlier.

France, though not a party, has pledged to behave as though it were. However, China, also not a party, is believed to have taken actions that would be prohibited by the treaty. In the late 1970s and early 1980s, it sold nuclear materials to Argentina and reportedly to India, Pakistan, and South Africa without requiring the application of IAEA safeguards, and it may have directly assisted Pakistan in designing nuclear weapons. In 1984, however, China advised the United States that it would require safeguards on all its future nuclear exports.

Six non-nuclear-weapon states of proliferation concern— Argentina, Brazil, India, Israel, Pakistan, and South Africa—have not ratified the treaty. All have unsafeguarded nuclear activities. Libya, Iraq, and Iran, three additional potential nuclear-weapon states, are parties to the accord.

Three review conferences on the implementation of the treaty have been held in 1975, 1980, and 1985.*

* See, generally *Arms Control and Disarmament Agreements, Text and Histories of Negotiations,* United States Arms Control and Disarmament Agency, 1982 edition, pp. 82-95.

A. Parties to the Non-Proliferation Treaty

Afghanistan	1970	Holy See	1971
Antigua and Barbuda	1985	Honduras	1973
Australia	1973	Hungary	1969
Austria	1969	Iceland	1969
Bahamas, The	1976	Indonesia	1979
Bangladesh	1979	Iran	1970
Barbados	1980	Iraq	1969
Belgium	1975	Ireland	1968
Belize	1985	Italy	1975
Benin	1972	Ivory Coast	1973
Bhutan	1985	Jamaica	1970
Bolivia	1970	Japan	1976
Botswana	1969	Jordan	1970
Brunei	1985	Kampuchea	1972
Bulgaria	1969	Kenya	1970
Burkina Faso	1970	Kiribati	1985
Burundi	1971	Korea (North)	1985
Cameroon	1969	Korea (South)	1975
Canada	1969	Laos	1970
Cape Verde	1979	Lebanon	1970
Central African Rep.	1970	Lesotho	1970
Chad	1971	Liberia	1970
Colombia	1986	Libya	1975
Congo	1978	Liechtenstein	1978
Costa Rica	1970	Luxembourg	1975
Cyprus	1970	Madagascar	1970
Czechoslovakia	1969	Malawi	1986
Denmark	1969	Malaysia	1970
Dominica	1968	Maldives	1970
Dominican Republic	1971	Mali	1970
Ecuador	1969	Malta	1970
Egypt	1981	Mauritius	1969
El Salvador	1972	Mexico	1969
Equatorial Guinea	1984	Mongolia	1969
Ethiopia	1970	Morocco	1970
Fiji	1972	Nauru	1982
Finland	1969	Nepal	1970
Gabon	1974	Netherlands	1975
Gambia, The	1975	New Zealand	1969
Germany (East)	1969	Nicaragua	1973
Germany (West)	1975	Nigeria	1968
Ghana	1970	Norway	1969
Greece	1970	Panama	1977
Grenada	1975	Papua New Guinea	1982
Guatemala	1970	Paraguay	1970
Guinea	1985	Peru	1970
Guinea-Bissau	1976	Philippines	1972
Haiti	1970	Poland	1969

Portugal	1977	Syrian Arab Republic	1969
Romania	1970	Taiwan	1970
Rwanda	1975	Thailand	1972
San Marino	1970	Togo	1970
Sao Tome & Principe	1983	Tonga	1971
St. Lucia	1979	Trinidad & Tobago	1986
St. Kitts & Nevis	1983	Tunisia	1970
St. Vincent &		Turkey	1980
The Grenadines	1984	Tuvalu	1979
Senegal	1970	Uganda	1982
Seychelles	1985	USSR*	1970
Sierra Leone	1975	United Kingdom*	1968
Singapore	1976	United States*	1970
Solomon Islands	1981	Uruguay	1970
Somalia	1970	Venezuela	1975
Spain	1987	Vietnam	1982
Sri Lanka	1979	Western Samoa	1975
Sudan	1973	Yemen, (Aden)	1979
Suriname	1976	Yemen, (Sana)	1986
Swaziland	1969	Yugoslavia	1970
Sweden	1970	Zaire	1970
Switzerland	1977		

B. Countries that have signed but not ratified the Treaty

Kuwait

C. Countries that have neither signed nor ratified the Treaty

Albania	Djibouti	Pakistan
Algeria	France*	Portugal
Angola	Guinea	Qatar
Argentina	Guyana	Saudi Arabia***
Bahrain	India**	South Africa
Brazil	Israel	Spain
Burma	Mauritania	Tanzania
Chile	Monaco	United Arab Emirates
Comoros	Mozambique	Vanuatu
China*	Niger	Zambia
Cuba	Oman	Zimbabwe

* Declared nuclear weapon state
** India has detonated a "peaceful nuclear device."
*** In April 1988, Saudi Arabia announced that it would accede to the treaty.

Appendix E: The Treaty of Tlatelolco

The international non-proliferation regime is strengthened in Latin America by the Treaty on the Prohibition of Nuclear Weapons in Latin America (the Treaty of Tlatelolco), which establishes a nuclear-weapons free zone in the region. Parties to the treaty agree not to manufacture, test, or acquire nuclear weapons or to accept weapons on their territory deployed by others. To verify that these pledges are kept, adherents agree to accept "full-scope" International Atomic Energy Agency (IAEA) safeguards (i.e., IAEA accounting and inspection measures on all of a nation's peaceful nuclear activities). In addition, the treaty establishes the Agency for the Prohibition of Nuclear Weapons in Latin America (OPANAL). OPANAL will undertake special inspections at the request of members who have reason to believe that another party is engaging in prohibited activity, a unique investigatory function not available under the IAEA system.

Under its entry-into-force provisions, the treaty becomes effective once it has been ratified by all eligible countries in the region. However, twenty-two nations have ratified the accord and waived this provision so that the treaty has become effective for these countries. Only four countries have yet to make the treaty operative. Part way there, but avoiding the full-scope safeguards requirements are Brazil and Chile, which have ratified, but not waived the entry-into-force requirement. Further away are Argentina, which has signed but not ratified, and Cuba, which has neither signed nor ratified the accord. Because Cuba has made approval of the treaty contingent upon U.S. withdrawal from the Guantanamo naval base, progress toward full effectiveness has been stymied.

The treaty is supplemented by two protocols that apply to countries outside the region. Protocol I requires that outside nations with territories in Latin America respect the treaty's denuclearization requirements with respect to those territories. Protocol II prohibits nuclear-weapon states from using or threatening to use nuclear arms against treaty parties. All nations with territories in the region, the U.S., U.K., France, and the Netherlands have signed Protocol I, and all but France have ratified it. All nuclear-weapon states have ratified Protocol II.

One highly controversial issue arises from the treaty's definition in Article 5 of a nuclear weapon as a nuclear explosive "which has a group of characteristics that are appropriate for use for warlike purposes." When the United States and the Soviet Union ratified Protocol II they formally stated that in their view this phrase meant that the treaty's prohibitions applied to *all* nuclear explosives, including so-called "peaceful nuclear explosives" since there was no technological difference between them and nuclear weapons. Argentina and Brazil have objected to this interpretation and cited Article 18 of the treaty which states that parties "may carry out explosions for peaceful purposes—including explosions which involve devices similar to those used in nuclear weapons"—under IAEA supervision. Virtually all other treaty parties, however, have accepted the U.S.-Soviet view since they are also parties to the Non-Proliferation Treaty, which expressly prohibits the manufacture of any nuclear explosive.

Treaty for the Prohibition of Nuclear Weapons in Latin America

Country	Year of Signature	Year of Ratification
Argentina	1967	—
Antigua and Barbuda	1983	1983
Bahamas, The	1967	1976
Barbados	1968	1969
Bolivia	1967	1969
Brazil	1967	1968*
Chile	1967	1974*
Colombia	1967	1972
Costa Rica	1967	1969
Dominican Republic	1967	1968
Ecuador	1967	1969
El Salvador	1967	1968
Grenada	1975	1975
Guatemala	1967	1970
Haiti	1967	1969
Honduras	1967	1968
Jamaica	1967	1969
Mexico	1967	1967
Nicaragua	1967	1968
Panama	1967	1971
Paraguay	1967	1969
Peru	1967	1969
Suriname	1976	1977
Trinidad and Tobago	1967	1975
Uruguay	1967	1968
Venezuela	1967	1970

Protocol I to the Treaty

Country	Year of Signature	Year of Ratification
France	1979	—
Netherlands	1968	1971
United Kingdom	1967	1969
United States	1977	1981

Protocol II to the Treaty

Country	Year of Signature	Year of Ratification
China (PRC)	1973	1974
France	1973	1974
U.S.S.R.	1978	1979
United Kingdom	1967	1969
United States	1968	1971

* Not in force because entry-into-force provision not waived.

Source: U.S. Arms Control and Disarmament Agency, *Arms Control and Disarmament Agreements: Texts and Histories of Negotiations* (Washington, D.C.: U.S. Arms Control and Disarmament Agency, 1982), and U.S. Department of State.

Appendix F: Nuclear Suppliers Organizations

Non-Proliferation Treaty Exporters Committee
(Zangger Committee)

Shortly after the treaty came into force in 1970, a number of countries entered into consultations concerning the procedures and standards they would apply to nuclear fuel and equipment exports to non-nuclear-weapon states in order to implement the requirement in the pact that such exports and any enriched uranium or plutonium produced through their use be subject to IAEA safeguards. The countries engaged in those consultations, which were chaired by the Swiss expert, Claude Zangger, were parties to the Non-Proliferation Treaty (or have since become parties) and were also exporters or potential exporters of material and equipment for peaceful uses of nuclear energy.

In August 1974, the governments of Australia, Denmark, Canada, Finland, West Germany, the Netherlands, Norway, the Soviet Union, the United Kingdom, and the United States each informed the Director General of the IAEA, by individual letters, of their intentions to require IAEA safeguards on their nuclear exports in accordance with certain procedures described in memoranda enclosed with their letters. Those memoranda were identical in the case of each letter and included a "Trigger List" of materials and items of equipment which would be exported only under such safeguards. (The individual letters and the identical memoranda were published by the IAEA in September 1974 in document INFCIRC/209).

Subsequently, Austria, Czechoslovakia, East Germany, Ireland, Japan, Luxembourg, Poland, and Sweden sent individual letters to the Director General, referring to and enclosing memoranda identical to those transmitted by the initial groups of governments.

The agreed procedures and Trigger List represented the first major agreement on uniform regulation of nuclear exports by actual and potential nuclear suppliers. It had great significance for several reasons. It was an attempt to strictly and uniformly enforce the obligations of Article III, paragraph 2, of the Non-Proliferation Treaty requiring safeguards on nuclear exports. It was intended to reduce the likelihood that states would be tempted to cut corners on safeguards requirements, because of competition in the sale of nuclear equipment and fuel-cycle services. In addition, and very important in light of subsequent events, it established the principle that nuclear-supplier nations should consult and agree among themselves on procedures to regulate the international market for nuclear materials and equipment in the interest of non-proliferation. Notably absent from the list of actual participants or potential suppliers, as from the list of parties to the Non-Proliferation Treaty, were France, India, and the People's Republic of China.

Nuclear Suppliers Group

In November 1974, within a year of the delivery of these memoranda a second series of supplier negotiations were underway. This round, convened largely at the initiative of the United States, was a response to three developments: 1) the Indian nuclear test of May 1974, 2) mounting evidence that the pricing actions of the Organization of Oil Exporting Countries were stimulating Third World and other non-nuclear states to initiate or accelerate their nuclear power programs, and 3) recent contracts or continuing negotiations on the part of France and West Germany for the supply of enrichment or reprocessing facilities to Third World states.

The initial participants in these discussions, conducted in London were Canada, the Federal Republic of Germany, France, Japan, the Soviet Union, the United Kingdom, and the United States. One of the group's chief accomplishments was to induce France to join in such efforts, since France (which had not joined the Non-Proliferation Treaty or the Zangger Committee) could have undercut reforms of nuclear supply. The French, hesitant about becoming involved and uncertain as to where the effort might lead, insisted that any meetings be kept confidential—which was also the preference of some other participants. So the meetings in London were held in secret. But it soon became known that such meetings were taking place, and this led to suspicion and exaggerated fears of what they were about. The group was inaccurately referred to as a "cartel." Instead, one of its purposes was to foster genuine commercial competition based on quality and prices, untainted by bargaining away proliferation controls.

Two major issues were discussed in the series of meetings which led to a new agreement in late 1975. The first was if, and under what conditions, technology and equipment for enrichment and reprocessing, the most sensitive parts of the nuclear fuel cycle from a weapons proliferation perspective, should be transferred to non-nuclear states. The United States, with support from several other participants, was reported to argue in favor of both a prohibition on such transfer and a commitment to reprocessing in multinational facilities. France had already signed contracts to sell reprocessing plants to Pakistan and South Korea, and West Germany had agreed to sell technology and facilities for the full fuel cycle (including enrichment and reprocessing) to Brazil. They successfully resisted the prohibition proposed by others.

The second issue was whether transfers should be made to states unwilling to submit all non-military nuclear facilities to IAEA safeguards, or whether total industry (full-scope) safeguards should become a condition of sales. The Nuclear Suppliers Group came close to reaching consensus on requiring full-scope safeguards in recipient countries as a condition of future supply commitments, but was unable to persuade the French and the West Germans, though they did not rule out later reconsideration and possible changes by unanimous consent. The group did act to expand safeguards coverage by adopting a "Trigger List" of exports, similar to that of the Zangger Committee, which would be made only if covered by IAEA safeguards in the recipient state.

On January 27, 1976, the seven participants in the negotiations exchanged letters endorsing a uniform code for conducting international nuclear sales. The major provisions of the agreement require that before nuclear materials, equipment, or technology are transferred the recipient state must:

1. pledge not to use the transferred materials, equipment, or technology in the manufacture of nuclear explosives of any kind;

2. accept, with no provision for termination, international safeguards on all transferred materials and facilities employing transferred equipment or technology, including any enrichment, reprocessing, or heavy-water production facility that replicates or otherwise employs transferred technology;

3. provide adequate physical security for transferred nuclear facilities and materials to prevent theft and sabotage;

4. agree not to retransfer the materials, equipment, or technology to third countries unless they too accept the constraints on use, replication, security, and transfer, and unless the original supplier nation concurs in the transactions;

5. employ "restraint" regarding the possible export of "sensitive" items (relating to uranium enrichment, spent fuel reprocessing, and heavy-water production); and

6. encourage the concept of multilateral regional facilities for reprocessing and enrichment.

The guidelines have now been adopted by the United States, Great Britain, France, West Germany, Japan, Canada, the Soviet Union, Belgium, Italy, the Netherlands, Sweden, Switzerland, Czechoslovakia, East Germany, Poland, Australia, and Finland.

The Nuclear Suppliers' Guidelines extended the Zangger Committee's requirements in several respects. First, France (which had not participated in the Zangger group) agreed to key points adopted by that Committee, such as the requirement that nuclear export recipients pledge not to use transferred items for nuclear explosives of any kind and that safeguards on transferred items would continue indefinitely. Secondly, the Suppliers Group went beyond the Non-Proliferation Treaty and the Zangger Committee requirements, by imposing safeguards not only on the export of nuclear materials and equipment, but also on nuclear technology exports. India had demonstrated the existence of this serious loophole by building its own unsafeguarded replica of a safeguarded power reactor imported from Canada. The Suppliers Group was unable to reach agreement on the application of this reform to reactor technology, however, and so confined its recommended application to "sensitive" facilities—i.e., reprocessing, enrichment, and heavy-water production plants built with the use of exported technology. The group's acceptance of this limited reform was facilitated by the fact that such a condition was incorporated by West Germany in its safeguards agreements for sale of enrichment and reprocessing facilities to Brazil, and the French in their safeguards agreements covering their proposed sales of reprocessing plants to the Republic of Korea and Pakistan.

Third, the Suppliers' Guidelines, while not prohibiting the export of these sensitive facilities, do embody the participants' agreement to "exercise restraint" in transferring them, and where enrichment plants are involved, to seek recipient country commitments that such facilities will be designed and operated to produce only low-enriched uranium, not suitable for weapons.

Several supplier countries subsequently announced policies stricter than those in the guidelines. France, West Germany, and the United States all made separate public announcements that they did not, at least for the time being, contemplate any further new commitments to export reprocessing technology. In addition, the United States, Canada, Australia, and Sweden have all made recipient-country acceptance of full-scope safeguards a condition for nuclear transfer.

* * *

Excerpted and adapted from, Charles N. Van Doren, "Nuclear Supply and Non-Proliferation: The IAEA Committee on Assurances of Supply," A Report for the Congressional Research Service (Rep. No. 83-202-8) October 1983, pp. 61-64; U.S. Congress, Office of Technology Assessment, *Nuclear Proliferation and Safeguards* (Washington, D.C.: OTA, 1977), pp. 220-221; U.S. Department of State, "Report to the Congress Pursuant to Section 601 of the Nuclear Non-Proliferation Act of 1978" (January 1979), pp. 25-27.

Appendix G: U.S. Non-Proliferation Restrictions on Aid to Pakistan

Several interrelated U.S. laws seek to influence Pakistani nuclear conduct by the threat to terminate U.S. economic and military assistance. The executive branch has also used this approach, at least implicitly. The key laws and policy initiatives are—

1. *The 1976 Symington Amendment barring aid to non-weapon countries importing uranium enrichment technology: Waived by legislation in 1981 for six years, waiver renewed for two and a half years in 1987.*[1] The Symington Amendment, in essence, prohibits U.S. aid to any non-nuclear-weapon state that imports uranium enrichment technology or equipment but refuses to place all of its nuclear installations under International Atomic Energy Agency (IAEA) safeguards.[2] The provision specifies that the President may waive this ban, however, if he has obtained "reliable assurances that the country in question will not acquire or develop nuclear weapons or assist other nations in doing so" and if he determines that the termination of assistance would have "a serious adverse effect on vital United States interests."[3]

   U.S. aid to Pakistan was cut off in 1979 after it became known that Pakistan was acquiring enrichment technology from Western Europe and building an unsafeguarded enrichment plant at Kahuta.[4] In 1981, following the Soviet invasion of Afghanistan, a special six-year suspension of this provision with respect to Pakistan was enacted, however, to permit the restoration of assistance, amounting to $3.2 billion over the six years.[5] Legislation suspending the law was necessitated by the fact that the President could not take advantage of the waiver provision contained within the Symington Amendment, since he was unable to obtain the necessary "reliable assurances" that Pakistan was not acquiring or developing nuclear weapons.

A two-and-one-half year renewal of the 1981 legislation suspending the Symington Amendment was enacted in December 1987, again necessitated by the lack of reliable assurances concerning Pakistan's nuclear activities.[6]

2. *The 1977 Glenn Amendment barring aid to countries importing reprocessing (plutonium extraction) technology: Waived by Presidential action in 1982.*[7] The Glenn Amendment prohibits U.S. aid for any country that imports reprocessing technology or equipment. Pakistan was importing reprocessing technology from France during the mid-1970s.[8] For this reason, U.S. aid was suspended for approximately a year beginning in August 1977, although the Glenn Amendment provision was not formally invoked.

France ended such transfers in 1978, but clandestine Pakistani purchases of reprocessing equipment apparently continued.[9] The Glenn Amendment was not formally triggered later in the 1970s, however, because this would have been redundant after U.S. aid to Pakistan was suspended in 1979 under the Symington Amendment (prohibiting the importation of uranium enrichment technology).

When the Symington Amendment was waived by legislation in 1981 to permit the restoration of U.S. aid, however, Pakistan was apparently still violating the Glenn Amendment stipulation against importation of reprocessing technology. Thus, a waiver of the Glenn Amendment was also needed.

A proviso in the Glenn Amendment itself permitted the President to waive the aid cutoff if he determined that the termination of assistance would "be seriously prejudicial to the achievement of U.S. non-proliferation objectives or otherwise jeopardize the common defense and security." Such a finding was quietly made in February 1982.[10]

3. *The 1977 ban on aid to non-nuclear-weapon countries that receive, detonate, or transfer nuclear explosives: Currently in force.*[11] Another proviso, enacted as part of the original 1977 Glenn Amendment, prohibits U.S. assistance to any non-nuclear-weapon state that receives or detonates a nuclear explosive device or transfers such a device to any other non-nuclear-weapon state. In 1981, the provision was strengthened by precluding its waiver by the President for more than 30 days unless affirmatively authorized by a joint resolution (passed by a majority of both Houses of Congress and signed into law by the President). This provision remains fully in force and seeks to maintain a critically important non-proliferation firebreak.

4. *The 1984 letter from President Reagan to President Zia warning against high enrichment at Kahuta: Not enforced in 1986.* Between 1981 and 1984, during the period of the first suspension of the Symington Amendment's enrichment technology importation ban, Pakistan completed the Kahuta enrichment plant. In September 1984, President Reagan wrote President Zia seeking assurances that Pakistan would not enrich uranium there to more than five percent—a level not usable for nuclear weapons. The President's letter is said to have warned that enrichment beyond this level would have grave consequences for U.S.–Pakistani relations.[12]

Pakistan agreed to the five-percent limit, but it is now understood to have subsequently surpassed this level in late 1985 or early 1986, producing weapons-grade, highly enriched uranium at the Kahuta installation.[13] This development appears to have had no negative impact on U.S.–Pakistani relations, and in March or April 1986, shortly after it apparently became known to the Reagan Administration, Washington offered Pakistan a second six-year aid package in the amount of $4.02 billion to begin with fiscal year 1988 (October 1, 1987), when the original aid package was set to expire. Thus the threat implicit in President Reagan's letter was not carried out.

5. *The 1985 certification requirement barring aid—and military sales—to Pakistan if it is found to possess a nuclear device: Currently in force, barely satisfied in 1986 and 1987.*[14] As reports of Pakistan's continued progress toward nuclear arms mounted, Congress became concerned that the U.S. laws, in effect, would permit Islamabad to build a nuclear arsenal without penalty, as long as it did not conduct a test or receive or transfer a nuclear explosive device, since only these steps would trigger an aid cut-off.

Accordingly, in 1985 a new provision, applicable only to Pakistan, was enacted stipulating that for each fiscal year, before any aid could be transferred or military equipment sold to Islamabad, the President would have to certify that Pakistan did not "possess a nuclear explosive device" (and that U.S. aid would significantly reduce the risk of its doing so).

The President so certified in late 1985, in late 1986, and again in late 1987—although by the time of the latter two certifications it appeared that Pakistan possessed the essentials for its first nuclear devices, including the necessary highly enriched uranium, in unassembled form.[15]

6. *The 1985 Solarz Amendment barring aid to non-nuclear-weapon countries that illegally export nuclear commodities from the United States for use in nuclear explosives: Invoked and waived in January 1988.*[16] In October 1984, a Pakistani national was convicted of attempting to illegally export to Pakistan 50 high-speed electronic switches, known as krytrons, which

are used in nuclear weapons. The following May, a California businessman was indicted for smuggling over 800 of these devices to Israel. The two episodes led to the enactment of legislation prohibiting U.S. aid to any country that is found by the President to have illegally exported or attempted to illegally export from the United States material, equipment, or technology which could significantly assist it in the manufacture of a nuclear explosive device, if the President also finds that the export was intended to be used for this purpose. (The law permits the President to waive this prohibition, however, if he determines that suspending U.S. assistance to the country involved would be seriously prejudicial to the achievement of U.S. non-proliferation objectives or otherwise jeopardize the common defense and security.)

On December 18, 1987, a Pakistani-born Canadian, Arshad Pervez, was convicted in Philadelphia for attempting to export beryllium, a metal used in nuclear weapons, to Pakistan. The verdict in the case made clear that the jury believed the material was intended to support Pakistan's nuclear weapons program. The government of Pakistan has denied any involvement in the episode. Nevertheless, in mid-January 1988, President Reagan determined that Pakistan had violated the Solarz Amendment. The President simultaneously waived the cut-off in the provision, however, to permit continued assistance to Pakistan.

In sum, on several occasions, the United States has backed away from enforcing the sanction of an aid cut-off against Pakistan, permitting the waiver of the Symington Amendment through legislation in 1981 and again in 1987; waiving the Glenn Amendment by Presidential action in l982; declining to react to the production of highly enriched uranium in 1986, despite the warning in President Reagan's

1984 letter; interpreting the "possession-of-a-nuclear-explosive-device" standard liberally in 1986 and 1987 to avoid a suspension of assistance, even though Pakistan had apparently acquired the wherewithal for its first nuclear devices; and waiving the Solarz Amendment in early 1988, despite the finding that Pakistan had attempted to smuggle material out of the United States to be used in the manufacture of a nuclear explosive device.

Source: Carnegie Task Force on Non-Proliferation and South Asian Security, *Nuclear Weapons and South Asian Security* (Washington, D.C.: Carnegie Endowment for International Peace, 1988).

Notes

1. Foreign Assistance Act of 1961, section 669.
2. To be usable for nuclear arms, uranium must be upgraded, or "enriched," to increase the concentration of desirable uranium atoms from 0.7 percent (the naturally occurring concentration) to 93 percent. This is performed in complex installations known as enrichment plants.
3. Foreign Assistance Act of 1961, section 669(b)(1).
4. During the U.S. cutoff, it may be noted, increased assistance to Pakistan from Western Europe and the Organization of Petroleum Exporting Countries (OPEC) more than offset the loss of U.S. monies, amounting to approximately $60 million annually at the time.
5. Foreign Assistance Act of 1961, section 620E. On October 31, 1981, while this legislation was pending, U.S. customs agents seized at New York's Kennedy Airport a 5000-pound shipment of zirconium metal, marked "mountain climbing equipment," as it was being placed aboard a Pakistani Airlines jet as baggage. The purchaser of the material, which is used in manufacturing nuclear reactor fuel, was reported to be Dr. Sarfraz Mir, a retired Pakistani army colonel. See Leslie Maitland, "U.S. Studying Failed Bid to Export a Key Reactor Metal to Pakistan," *New York Times,* November 21, 1981.

6. P.L. 100–202, section 557, amending Foreign Assistance Act, section 620 E(d). Ironically, the waiver was enacted just after it was reliably reported that Pakistan was building a second uranium enrichment plant at Golra, presumably with imported hardware—the very conduct the Symington Amendment sought to deter. See Simon Henderson, "Pakistan Builds Second Plant to Enrich Uranium," *Financial Times*, December 12, 1987. But see also Neil A. Lewis, "Reports of Pakistan Uranium Plant Weighed," *New York Times*, January 10, 1988.

7. Foreign Assistance Act of 1961, section 670(a)(1)(A).

8. Plutonium is the second nuclear material that can serve as the core of a nuclear weapon (the other being highly enriched uranium). Plutonium is produced in uranium fuel that has been irradiated in a reactor. Plutonium is separated from other constituents of spent reactor fuel at a "reprocessing" plant by chemical processing.

9. Milton R. Benjamin, "Pakistan Building Secret Nuclear Plant," *Washington Post,* September 30, 1980; Senator Alan Cranston, "Nuclear Proliferation and U.S. National Security Interests," *Congressional Record,* June 21, 1984, p. S7901.

10. Presidential Determination 82-7 (February 10, 1982), *Code of Federal Regulations,* Vol. 3, p. 241 (1983). In the case of the Symington Amendment, a suspension had to be implemented through legislation because the "built-in" waiver in that law was, in effect, more rigorous than the one embodied in the Glenn Amendment, and the President was unable to satisfy its requirements.

11. Foreign Assistance Act of 1961, section 670(b), as amended in 1981.

12. Don Oberdorfer, "Pakistan Spurns Soviet's Afghan Pullout Plan," *Washington Post,* July 18, 1986.

13. See, *e.g.*, Bob Woodward, "Pakistan Reported Near Atom Arms Production," *Washington Post,* November 4, 1986; David Ottaway, "Pakistani A-Bomb Seen Likely," *Washington Post,* March 8, 1987; Statement of Department of State Spokesman Charles Redman, Press Briefing, August 10, 1987, transcript prepared by Federal News Service; David Ottaway, "Caution Urged on Aid to Pakistan," *Washington Post,* October 23, 1987; Hedrick Smith, "A Bomb Ticks in Pakistan," *New York Times Magazine,* March 6, 1988, p. 38. See also, testimony of Ambassador Kennedy, *Hearings on U.S. Aid to Pakistan,* before the Subcommittee on Asian and Pacific Affairs of the Committee on Foreign Affairs, U.S. House of Representatives, October 22, 1987.

14. Foreign Assistance Act, section 620E(e).

15. Woodward, "Pakistan Reported Near Atoms Arms Production."

16. Foreign Assistance Act, section 670(a)(1)(B).

Glossary

atomic bomb A bomb whose energy comes from the fission of uranium or plutonium.

blanket A layer of fertile material, such as uranium-238 or thorium-232, placed around the core of a reactor. During operation of the reactor, additional fissionable material is produced in the blanket.

breeder reactor A nuclear reactor that produces somewhat more fissile material than it consumes. The fissile material is produced both in the reactor's core and when neutrons are captured in fertile material placed around the core (blanket). This process is known as breeding. Breeder reactors have not yet reached commercialization, although active research and development programs are being pursued by a number of countries.

CANDU (Canadian deuterium-uranium reactor.) The most widely used type of heavy-water reactor. The CANDU reactor uses natural uranium as a fuel and heavy water as a moderator and a coolant.

centrifuge See ultracentrifuge.

chain reaction The continuing process of nuclear fissioning in which the neutrons released from a fission trigger at least one other nuclear fission. In a nuclear weapon an extremely rapid, multiplying chain reaction causes the explosive release of energy. In a reactor, the pace of the chain reaction is controlled to produce heat (in a power reactor) or large quantities of neutrons (in a research or production reactor).

chemical processing Chemical treatment of materials to separate specific usable constituents.

coolant A substance circulated through a nuclear reactor to remove or transfer heat. The most common coolants are water and heavy water.

core The central portion of a nuclear reactor containing the fuel elements and, usually, the moderator. Also the central portion of a nuclear weapon containing highly enriched uranium or plutonium.

critical mass The minimum amount of fissionable material required to sustain a chain reaction. The exact mass varies with many factors such as the particular fissionable isotope present, its concentration and chemical form, the geometrical arrangement of the material, and its density. When fissionable materials are compressed by high explosives in implosion-type atomic weapons, the critical mass needed for a nuclear explosion is reduced.

depleted uranium Uranium having a smaller percentage of uranium-235 than the 0.7 percent found in natural uranium. It is a by-product of the uranium enrichment process, during which uranium-235 is culled from one batch of uranium, thereby depleting it, and then added to another batch to increase its concentration of uranium-235.

enrichment The process of increasing the concentration of one isotope of a given element (in the case of uranium, increasing the concentration of uranium-235).

feed stock Material introduced into a facility for processing.

fertile Material composed of atoms which readily absorb neutrons to produce fissionable materials. One such element is uranium-238, which becomes plutonium-239 after it absorbs a neutron. Fertile material alone cannot sustain a chain reaction.

fission The process by which a neutron strikes a nucleus and splits it into fragments. During the process of nuclear fission, several neutrons are emitted at high speed, and heat and radiation are released.

fissile material Material composed of atoms which readily fission when struck by a neutron. Uranium-235 and plutonium-239 are examples of fissile materials.

fusion The formation of a heavier nucleus from two lighter ones (such as hydrogen isotopes), with the attendant release of energy (as in a hydrogen bomb).

gas centrifuge process A method of isotope separation in which heavy gaseous atoms or molecules are separated from light ones by centrifugal force. See ultracentrifuge.

gaseous diffusion A method of isotope separation based on the fact that gas atoms or molecules with different masses will diffuse through a porous barrier (or membrane) at different rates. The method is used to separate uranium-235 from uranium-238. It requires large gaseous diffusion plants and significant amounts of electric power.

gas-graphite reactor A nuclear reactor in which a gas is the coolant and graphite is the moderator.

heavy water Water containing significantly more than the natural proportion (1 in 6,500) of heavy hydrogen (deuterium) atoms to ordinary hydrogen atoms. (Hydrogen atoms have one proton, deuterium atoms have one proton and one neutron.) Heavy water is used as a moderator in some reactors because it slows down neutrons effectively and does not absorb them (unlike light, or normal, water) making it possible to fission natural uranium and sustain a chain reaction.

heavy-water reactor A reactor that uses heavy water as its moderator and natural uranium as fuel. See CANDU.

highly enriched uranium Uranium in which the percentage of uranium-235 nuclei has been increased from the natural level of 0.7 percent to some level greater than 20 percent, usually around 90 percent.

hot cells Lead-shielded rooms with remote handling equipment for examining and processing radioactive materials. In particular, hot cells are used for reprocessing spent reactor fuel.

hydrogen bomb A nuclear weapon that derives its energy largely from fusion. Also known as a thermonuclear bomb.

irradiation Exposure to a radioactive source; usually in the case of fuel materials, being placed in an operating nuclear reactor.

isotopes Atoms having the same number of protons, but a different number of neutrons. Two isotopes of the same atom are very similar and difficult to separate by ordinary chemical means. Isotopes can have very different nuclear properties, however. For example, one isotope may fission readily, while another isotope of the same atom may not fission at all. An isotope is specified by its atomic mass number (the number of protons plus neutrons) following the symbol denoting the chemical element (e.g., U^{235} is an isotope of uranium).

jet-nozzle enrichment method A process of uranium enrichment that uses both uranium hexafluoride and a light gas flowing at high speed through a nozzle along curved walls.

kilogram A metric weight equivalent to 2.2 pounds.

kiloton The energy of a nuclear explosion that is equivalent to an explosion of 1,000 tons of TNT.

laser enrichment method A still experimental process of uranium enrichment in which a finely tuned, high-power carbon dioxide laser is used to differentially excite molecules of various atomic weights. This differential excitation makes it possible to separate uranium-235 from uranium-238.

light water Ordinary water (H_2O), as distinguished from heavy water (D_2O).

light-water reactor A reactor that uses ordinary water as moderator and coolant and low-enriched uranium as fuel.

low-enriched uranium Uranium in which the percentage of uranium-235 nuclei has been increased from the natural level of 0.7 percent to less than 20 percent, usually 3 to 6 percent. With the increased level of fissile material, low-enriched uranium can sustain a chain reaction when immersed in light-water and is used as fuel in light-water reactors.

medium-enriched uranium Uranium in which the percentage of uranium-235 nuclei has been increased from the natural level of 0.7 percent to between 20 and 50 percent. (Potentially usable for nuclear weapons, but very large quantities are needed.)

megawatt One million watts; used in reference to a nuclear power plant, one million watts of electricity.

metric ton One thousand kilograms. A metric weight equivalent to 2200 pounds or 1.1 tons.

milling A process in the uranium fuel cycle by which ore containing only a very small percentage of uranium oxide (U_3O_8) is converted into material containing a high percentage (80 percent) of U_3O_8, often referred to as yellowcake.

moderator A component (usually water, heavy water, or graphite) of some nuclear reactors that slows neutrons, thereby increasing their chances of fissioning fertile material.

natural uranium Uranium as found in nature, containing 0.7 percent of uranium-235, 99.3 percent of uranium-238, and a trace of uranium-234.

neutron An uncharged elementary particle, with a mass slightly greater than that of a proton, found in the nucleus of every atom heavier than hydrogen.

nuclear energy The energy liberated by a nuclear reaction (fission or fusion) or by spontaneous radioactivity.

nuclear fuel Basic chain-reacting material, including both fissile and fertile materials. Commonly used nuclear fuels are natural uranium, and low-enriched uranium; high-enriched uranium and plutonium are used in some reactors.

nuclear fuel cycle The set of chemical and physical operations needed to prepare nuclear material for use in reactors and to dispose of or recycle the material after its removal from the reactor. Existing fuel cycles begin with uranium as the natural resource and create plutonium as a by-product. Some future fuel cycles may rely on thorium and produce the fissionable isotope uranium-233.

nuclear fuel element A rod, tube, plate, or other mechanical shape or form into which nuclear fuel is fabricated for use in a reactor.

nuclear fuel fabrication plant A facility where the nuclear material (e.g., enriched or natural uranium) is fabricated into fuel elements to be inserted into a reactor.

nuclear power plant Any device or assembly that converts nuclear energy into useful power. In a nuclear electric power plant, heat produced by a reactor is used to produce steam to drive a turbine that in turn drives an electricity generator.

nuclear reactor A mechanism fueled by fissionable materials that give off neutrons, thereby inducing heat. Reactors are of three general types: power reactors, production reactors, and research reactors.

nuclear waste The radioactive by-products formed by fission and other nuclear processes in a reactor. Most nuclear waste is initially contained spent fuel. If this material is reprocessed, new categories of waste result.

nuclear weapons A collective term for atomic bombs and hydrogen bombs. Weapons based on a nuclear explosion. Generally used throughout the text to mean atomic bombs, only, unless used with reference to nuclear weapon states, (all five of which have both atomic and hydrogen weapons).

plutonium-239 A fissile isotope occurring naturally in only minute quantities, which is manufactured artificially when uranium-238, through irradiation, captures an extra neutron. It is one of the two materials that have been used for the core of nuclear weapons, the other being highly enriched uranium.

plutonium-240 A fissile isotope produced in reactors when a plutonium-239 atom absorbs a neutron instead of fissioning. Its presence complicates the construction of nuclear explosives because of its high rate of spontaneous fission.

power reactor A reactor designed to produce electricity as distinguished from reactors used primarily for research or for producing radiation or fissionable materials.

production reactor A reactor designed primarily for large-scale production of plutonium-239 by neutron irradiation of uranium-238.

radioactivity The spontaneous disintegration of an unstable atomic nucleus resulting in the emission of subatomic particles.

radioisotope A radioactive isotope.

recycle To reuse the remaining uranium and plutonium found in spent fuel after they have been separated at a reprocessing plant from unwanted radioactive waste products also in the spent fuel.

reprocessing Chemical treatment of spent reactor fuel to separate the plutonium and uranium from the unwanted radioactive waste by-products and (under present plans) from each other.

research reactor A reactor primarily designed to supply neutrons for experimental purposes. It may also be used for training, materials testing, and production of radioisotopes.

spent fuel Fuel elements that have been removed from the reactor after use because they contain too little fissile and fertile material and too high a concentration of unwanted radioactive by-products to sustain reactor operation. Spent fuel is both thermally and radioactively hot.

thermonuclear bomb A hydrogen bomb.

thorium-232 A fertile material.

ultracentrifuge A rotating vessel that can be used for enrichment of uranium. The heavier isotopes of uranium hexafluoride gas concentrate at the walls of the rotating centrifuge and are drawn off.

uranium A radioactive element with the atomic number 92 and, as found in natural ores, an average atomic weight of 238. The two principal natural isotopes are uranium-235 (0.7 percent of natural uranium), which is fissionable, and uranium-238 (99.3 percent of natural uranium), which is fertile.

uranium-233 (U^{233}) A fissionable isotope bred in fertile thorium-232. Like plutonium-239 it is theoretically an excellent material for nuclear weapons, but is not known to have been used for this purpose. Can be used as reactor fuel.

uranium-235 (U^{235}) The only naturally occurring fissionable isotope. Natural uranium contains 0.7 percent U^{235}; light-water reactors use about 3 percent and weapons grade, highly enriched uranium normally consists of 93 percent of this isotope.

uranium-238 A fertile material. Natural uranium is composed of approximately 99.3 percent U^{238}.

uranium dioxide (UO_2) Purified uranium. The form of natural uranium used in heavy water reactors. Also the form of uranium that remains after the fluorine is removed from enriched uranium hexafluoride (UF^6). Produced as a powder, uranium dioxide is, in turn, fabricated into fuel elements.

uranium oxide (U_3O_8) The most common oxide of uranium found in typical ores. U_3O_8 is extracted from the ore during the milling process. The ore typically contains only 0.1 percent U_3O_8; yellowcake, the product of the milling process, contains about 80 percent U_3O_8.

uranium hexafluoride (UF$_6$) A volatile compound of uranium and fluorine. UF_6 is a solid at atmospheric pressure and room temperature, but can be transformed into gas by heating. UF_6 gas (alone, or in combination with hydrogen or helium) is the feed stock in all uranium enrichment processes and is sometimes produced as an intermediate product in the process of purifying yellowcake to produce uranium oxide.

vessel The part of a reactor that contains the nuclear fuel.

weapons grade Nuclear material of the type most suitable for nuclear weapons, i.e., uranium enriched to 93 percent U^{235} or plutonium that is primarily Pu^{239}.

weapons-usable Fissionable material that is weapons-grade or, though less than ideal for weapons, can still be used to make a nuclear explosive.

yellowcake A concentrate produced during the milling process that contains about 80 percent uranium oxide (U_3O_8). In preparation for uranium enrichment, the yellowcake is converted to uranium hexafluoride gas (UF_6). In the preparation of natural uranium reactor fuel, yellowcake is processed into purified uranium dioxide. Sometimes uranium hexaflouride is produced as an intermediate step in the purification process.

yield The total energy released in a nuclear explosion. It is usually expressed in equivalent tons of TNT (the quantity of TNT required to produce a corresponding amount of energy).

Sources

1. Congressional Research Service, *Nuclear Proliferation Factbook* (Washington, DC: U.S. Govt. Printing Office, 1977).
2. Energy Research & Development Administration, *U.S. Nuclear Power Export Activities* (Springfield, VA: National Technical Information Service, 1976).
3. Nuclear Energy Policy Study Group, *Nuclear Power: Issues and Choices* (Cambridge, MA: Ballinger Publishing Co., 1977).
4. Office of Technology Assessment, *Nuclear Proliferation and Safeguards* (Washington, DC: Office of Technology Assessment, 1977); Nuclear Power in an Age of Uncertainty (Washington, D.C.: Office of Technology Assessment, 1984).
5. Wohlstetter, Albert, *Swords from Plowshares: The Military Potential of Civilian Nuclear Energy* (Chicago: The University of Chicago Press, 1977).
6. United Nations Association of the USA, *Nuclear Proliferation: A Citizen's Guide to Policy Choices* (N.Y.: UNA-USA, 1983).

Corrections to Prior Volumes in this Series

Going Nuclear

p. 79   The date of Prime Minister Gandhi's statement is incorrectly specified. The correct date is May 1985, as indicated by the footnote.

p. 223   South Africa's credentials were rejected at the 1979 IAEA General Conference, not the 1977 General Conference.

The New Nuclear Nations

p. 157   The visit of the Argentine nuclear trade delegation to Libya took place in mid-1983, not mid-1985.

Nuclear Proliferation Today

p. 51   The name of Dr. P. K. Iyengar is incorrectly spelled.

p. 64   The map incorrectly shows the location of the Thal heavy water plant. It is located 17 miles south of Bombay.

p. 68   The chart should state that the Kalpakkam Fast Breeder Test Reactor will be fuelled with plutonium carbide/natural uranium fuel.

p. 108   The chart should list Canada as one of the suppliers of heavy water for the KANUPP reactor.

p. 147   The capacity of Israel's possible enrichment capacity should be listed as 2-3 kilograms of highly enriched uranium per year.

p. 164   Libya's nuclear power reactor should be listed as "planned" not as "under construction."

p. 309   The map should show Valindaba as adjacent to Pelindaba.

Index

Aeronautical Research and Testing Laboratory (DFVLR), 40, 41

Africa, 21, 283-285. *See also* Libyan nuclear program; South African nuclear program

Afghanistan, 147

Aircraft delivery capability: Argentina, 49; Brazil, 49; India, 48-49, 56, 100, 377n; Israel, 48, 54-56, 178, 336n; Libya, 49; modification for nuclear ordnance, 49-51; Pakistan, 49, 55-56, 125, 337n; potential risk, 51-58; South Africa, 49, 56, 289, 295, 338n; spread of, 25-26; supplier issues, 53-55; types used, 47-49

Akinyemi, Bolanji, 283-284

Alacran missiles, 42

Alfonsín, Raul, 21, 232, 233-243, 247, 262, 269

Algeria, 243, 244

Angola, 298, 299

Aramar enrichment plant, 20, 21, 242, 243, 246, 259, 265, 267, 269

Argentina nuclear program: aircraft delivery capability, 49; background, 233-237; Brazil and, 20-21, 231-232, 235-238, 240-243, 245-248, 262-263, 269-272; developments, 237-247; enrichment, 20-21, 232, 234, 235, 239-241, 245, 247-248; fuel fabrication, 233; heavy water, 239; Iran and, 221-222; Israel and, 171; Libya and, 199; missiles, 16, 30, 34; nuclear facilities map and table, 250-252; plutonium, 247; prospects, 247-248; reactors, 239; reprocessing, 234, 235, 247; safeguards, 234-237, 243, 246-247; status of, 20-21; supplier activities, 171, 199, 221-222, 241, 243-245; United States and, 244-245; uranium, 233; weapons capability, 245, 247; West Germany and, 42

Armacost, Michael H., 138, 139

Asia, 12-15, 17, 19, 35, 69-79. *See also* China; Indian nuclear